The Hand of Compassion

THE
HAND OF
COMPASSION

*Portraits of Moral Choice
during the Holocaust*

Kristen Renwick Monroe

PRINCETON UNIVERSITY PRESS

PRINCETON AND OXFORD

Published by Princeton University Press, 41 William Street, Princeton, New Jersey 08540
In the United Kingdom: Princeton University Press, 3 Market Place, Woodstock,
Oxfordshire OX20 1SY

Library of Congress Cataloging-in-Publication Data

Monroe, Kristen R., 1946–
The hand of compassion : portraits of moral choice during the Holocaust / Kristen
Renwick Monroe.
p. cm.
ISBN 0-691-11863-9 (cl : alk. paper)
1. Righteous Gentiles in the Holocaust.   2. Holocaust, Jewish (1939–1945)—Moral
and ethical aspects.   3. Altruism—Social aspects.   I. Title.

D804 65.M66 2004
172′.1—dc22   2004044251

British Library Cataloging-in-Publication Data is available

This book has been composed in Galliard.

Printed on acid-free paper. ∞

pup.princeton.edu

Printed in the United States of America

1   3   5   7   9   10   8   6   4   2

THE HAND OF COMPASSION WAS FASTER

THAN THE CALCULUS OF REASON.

—Otto Springer

CONTENTS

PREFACE
ix

ACKNOWLEDGMENTS
xv

Stories That Are True
1

CHAPTER ONE
Margot
9

CHAPTER TWO
Otto
55

CHAPTER THREE
John
101

CHAPTER FOUR
Irene
139

CHAPTER FIVE
Knud
165

CHAPTER SIX
The Complexity of the Moral Life and
the Power of Identity to Influence Choice
187

CHAPTER SEVEN
How Identity and Perspective Led to Moral Choice
211

CHAPTER EIGHT
What Makes People Help Others:
Constructing Moral Theory
239

A Different Way of Seeing Things
257

APPENDIX A
Narratives as Windows on the Minds of Others
267

APPENDIX B
Finding the Rescuers
287

NOTES
291

BIBLIOGRAPHY
331

INDEX
355

PREFACE

THIS IS A BOOK ABOUT LOSS. It is a book about love. It is a book about normal, human decency transformed into extraordinary courage by a political regime so evil it confounds human comprehension. It returns us to those secret, frightening places in our own souls, places we seldom enter, touching only elliptically, late at night and alone, when a loved one has died or we are forced to face the eternal, when we cannot escape asking who we are, what we live for, and whether there is any sense in a world in which life and love and all we hold dear are so fragile.

This is a book about moral choice during the Holocaust, and it suggests the tremendous power of identity[1] to shape our most basic political acts.[2] It argues that how we see ourselves in relation to others significantly—even critically—influences our treatment of them by limiting the options we find available, not just morally but cognitively.[3]

This book grew out of my earlier work on altruism. *The Heart of Altruism* asked what caused altruism and then discussed the implications of this analysis for social and political theory.[4] I found the critical impetus for altruism was psychological, a particular cognitive worldview—I called this the altruistic perspective—in which the actor saw himself or herself at one with all humanity. The importance of this worldview as an influence on behavior suggested the value of further research to sharpen understanding of the psychological process by which our sense of ourselves in relation to others both inhibits and shapes political activity.

The present volume addresses this challenge, moving beyond the identification of the altruistic perspective as a general phenomenon and attempting a fuller depiction of this perspective and its role in the moral psychology. It also expands my earlier theoretical analysis by treating altruism as a lens that can shed light onto moral theory.

Traditional moral theory often begins from first principles, making assumptions about the structure of agency and character; theorists then explain what motivates actors and how people's practical moral deliberations occur without asking whether or not people actually do, or even can, measure up to these standards.[5] In this book, I take a different tack. I focus on the moral psychology and ask what an empirical examination of moral exemplars can reveal about the impetus behind moral action. In doing so, I am influenced by recent work on the behavioral consequences of cognitive factors, such as memories, schema, and organizing conceptual frameworks.[6] Research on human cognition remains in the preliminary stages and the challenge for scholars is to find a methodology that links experimental findings from laboratory settings to the more complex political world. I found this link in a freely flowing narrative analysis that permits the listener to decipher how the subject's perceptions influence behavior.[7]

I thus begin with the assumption that the human articulation of moral ideals is constrained by the basic architecture of the mind, the mind's development, our core emotions, social psychology, and the limits on human capacity for rational deliberation. To demonstrate how this works in a world far messier and more complex than a laboratory setting,[8] I analyzed the normative effects of such cognitive factors via in-depth interviews with rescuers of Jews during World War II, individuals whom most of us would find morally commendable—regardless of how we define morality—and whose behavior is not easily explained by the dominant schools of Western philosophy. I then ask what a close examination of rescuers' stories reveals about the moral psychology and teaches us about moral theory.[9] What drove these particular individuals? What caused them to engage in their moral acts? And what insight can this empirical examination shed on broader questions of ethics and morality?[10] In answering these questions, the book addresses one of the most basic questions in moral theory—what causes us to do good—but it does so via a close examination of moral exemplars, not through religious or philosophical analysis.

Existing work on altruism and rescuers has moved beyond the level of correlational analyses to focus attention on an altruistic personality or identity.[11] The present analysis confirms earlier findings suggesting the tremendous power of identity and perspective to shape our most basic behavior. The impetus for rescuer activities originated not in religion, reason, or any conscious, contractarian, or utilitarian calculus but rather in how rescuers thought about themselves and about others around them.[12] It thus was not the most frequently cited forces driving moral choice that led rescuers to risk their lives to save Jews; it was their sense that "we are all human beings." To understand rescuers, we therefore need to ask about their moral psychology, to understand what it was about their identities and, more particularly, their perceptions of themselves in relation to others that worked to constrain and shape the choices they found available, not just morally but empirically. We need to appreciate the ethical consequences of how rescuers classified and categorized people— specific individuals and groups, Jews, bystanders, or Nazis—and where they drew the boundaries of the community of concern.[13]

As I explore what I believe will become one of the new frontiers in social science—our ability to map the human mind and understand the importance of how people think about themselves and about others around them for future behavior—I focus on the manner in which people perceive, comprehend, and interpret the social and political world. Psychologists call these factors cognitive construals.[14] I pay special attention to the construals associated with the actor's self-concept, her categorization of others, the extent to which certain values are integrated into her sense of self, the type and pattern of perspective taking, the actor's sense of efficacy and extensivity, the development of moral salience, and the transformative aspect of altruistic acts for the agent's identity.

This focus on cognitive construals has several advantages. It adds to our knowledge of the moral psychology and reveals something that is missing in the literature on moral choice. It increases our substantive understanding of the psychological foundations of altruism. It furthers knowledge of the critical self-concepts that lead to humane, moral responses to ethnic differences. And, finally, it advances work on the psychological foundations of moral and political activity.

Basic Argument and Organizational Format. Because of the interest in and the importance of the topic, I have tried to craft a work that is scholarly yet accessible to the intelligent lay reader. To do this, material that buttresses my argument, but which is of a more academic interest, is placed in appendices and notes.[15] The basic text of the book itself has been pared down to provide focus to my essential argument.

What is the basic argument in this volume? Essentially, the stories analyzed here suggest ethical acts emerge not from choice so much as through our sense of who we are, through our identities.

The book opens with a prologue that uses an exchange with one rescuer to address issues of memory and the ethics of interviewing.[16] It then presents the rescuers' stories. Because understanding rescuers' moral psychology means interpreting intricate and subtle cognitive differences, I am careful to document these perspectives. I do so through extensive presentation of the "raw data," the narrative transcriptions of minimally edited interviews conducted between 1988 and 1999. The heart of the book thus presents a cognitive view of moral choice through the use of autobiographical sketches, told in the speakers' own words.

Although I interviewed many survivors and rescuers, all certified by Yad Vashem,[17] this book concentrates on the stories of five rescuers. Margot was a wealthy German whose father was head of General Motors for Western Europe. Margot left the Third Reich in protest against Nazi policies, moving to Holland, where she worked to save Jews despite being arrested many times.

Otto was an ethnic German living in Czechoslovakia. Though offered opportunities both to profit from his German status and to sit out the

war in India, Otto stayed in Prague, joined the Austrian Resistance movement, and saved over one hundred Jews before ending up in a concentration camp himself.

John was a Dutchman placed on the Gestapo's Most Wanted List because he organized an escape network to take Jews to safety in Switzerland and Spain. Arrested five times, John was tortured but never revealed
any information. He always managed to escape, even when most of his
network was betrayed, and took important information to Eisenhower
and the Allies in London.

Irene was a Polish nursing student when the war began. After the par-
tition of Poland, Irene was pressed into slave labor. Yet she hid eighteen
Jews in the home of a German major, for whom she was keeping house,
and helped other Jews hidden in the woods.

Finally, Knud is an inventor who took part in the extraordinary rescue
of 85 percent of the Jews in Denmark. Later turned in to the Gestapo for
his acts of treason while in the Danish police force, Knud continued his
rescue activities while living underground and in hiding.

These five are not the only rescuers I interviewed.[18] I focus on just
these few individuals, however, because I found it necessary to construct
detailed and close examinations of individuals in order to convey the rich
complexity of any individual's moral psychology. I chose these five because they reflect the wide variety of background characteristics, such as
religion, education, and national origin, found in rescuers as a group. Yet
each clearly illustrates the critical themes I found in my analysis of all the
rescuers: the tremendous power of identity to constrain choice, the complexity of the moral life, and the importance of our perceptions of self for
moral motivation. These stories thus fill critical gaps in our understanding of the moral psychology. In particular, their stories suggest that if we
can understand how people see the world and themselves in relation to
others, if we can decipher their cognitive frameworks, perceptions, and
categorization schema, we may begin to determine why identity exerts
such a powerful moral influence.

Can a close examination of how these five rescuers thought about moral
issues provide insight into the process itself by which identity worked
to constrain choice for other rescuers? Can we further assume that rescue
behavior during the Holocaust can tell us something of value about how
people think about moral issues in general? Can these narratives shed
light on other forms of moral political action? About the humane response to ethnic violence and genocide in contexts other than the Holocaust? I believe so, and I invite readers to reflect on rescuers' motives as
they think about these stories for themselves and then focus directly on
the puzzle that originally intrigued me: the empirical finding that identity

and perspective trump choice. This finding raises many difficult but fascinating and important questions.

What is the moral psychology, and what is the psychological process through which identity and perspective influence moral action? What part of moral action can we explain through reference to our sense of self in relation to others? Can we develop a theory of moral action that relies not on religion or reason but on identity and how we categorize ourselves in relation to others? If so, what are the contours of such a theory? And finally, can an analysis of rescue behavior help us rethink our most basic theories of human political behavior by focusing attention on the extent to which moral choices result from our fundamental sense of what it means to be a human being and how we categorize ourselves in relation to others?

I fear I have more questions than answers.[19] But the empirical analysis presented here does provide compelling evidence that identity and perspective—especially the cognitive construals that shape how we see ourselves in relation to others—both set and delineate the range of choices we find available cognitively. My findings underline both the complexity of the moral life and the need for moral theory to allow more fully for the extent to which moral action works through a sense of self and the need for human connection. It is the power of identity to shape action, and the importance of perspective in drawing forth particular aspects of the complex psychological phenomenon we call identity or character, that is the missing piece in the literature on moral choice.

ACKNOWLEDGMENTS

IF YOU ARE VERY LUCKY as a scholar you find yourself involved in a research project that takes you places you never knew existed, exposing you to new ideas and helping you understand the world and human relations in different ways. This happened to me in 1988, as I began what I thought would be a short project on altruism.

My early academic work had been in political economy, focusing on econometric models of political support. Analysis of different theories of voting piqued my interest in how the assumptions underlying the models we utilize shape the substantive conclusions we reach, and I turned to a consideration of different approaches to the study of politics. Two edited volumes[1] traced the development of the behavioral movement within the context of twentieth-century American political science, examined the shift toward rational actor theory in the late 1960s, and provided a critical look at both rational choice theory and its contemporary alternatives. My interest in the debate over rational choice theory has been set in a broader context of how—and whether—we can create an empirically rooted, testable science of politics, and how we should best go about this enterprise.

My work on altruism[2] suggested that there are clear limitations to theories grounded in the assumption that human nature is innately self-interested. This work had some small influence in causing rational actor theorists to shift their emphasis from self-interest as the heart of the model to a more general concept of rational action as goal-directed behavior.[3] Participating in this debate, however, led me to think about the forces at work on any innate human nature. Is there a human nature? If so, how much of this nature emanates from self-interested concerns? How is self-interest related to needs for human connection and a sense of community? How do others, through culture and political systems, shape any innate needs? And how do external stimuli call forth different aspects of the self's need to flourish? These interests shifted the focus of my work to a consideration of identity and the power of identity to influence political behavior.

I first noticed the importance of identity as an influence on political and moral choice while writing *The Heart of Altruism*, a narrative analysis of interviews with altruists and entrepreneurs. This analysis suggested that explaining altruism through theoretical frameworks based on self-interest—as economists and evolutionary biologists traditionally do—misses the essence of altruism, which is a particular cognitive worldview in which the altruist feels connected to others through bonds of a common humanity. As part of the research for that book, I interviewed a few people who had rescued Jews during World War II. Like characters in a novel who take on a life of their own, my rescuers stayed with me, inviting me to listen to their stories with a fresh ear, insisting they could teach me not just about altruism but also about broader issues in ethics.

My time with the rescuers forced me to look at a whole range of questions my training as a behavioral social scientist had not encouraged me to think about, questions I came to believe were far more important than many of my initial concerns. It required me to abandon many of the social science concepts and methodologies that had originally charted my own intellectual life. Like a detective following the clues to a mystery, I was forced to inquire about issues far outside my own limited range of expertise and I found myself moving into the domain of the ethicist, the psychologist, even the linguist. In none of these fields was I formally trained and, if I was lucky enough to be constantly learning new things, I fear I also was a great pest to all the people I constantly approached, asking for yet more readings in yet another subject or field. Because of this, my intellectual debts are particularly extensive. Not only must I thank the usual suspects—family, friends, colleagues, and the rescuers themselves—but the myriad scholars who helped me as I scrambled to gain the most rudimentary knowledge in fields that someone far wiser would never have dared to embrace without more extensive formal training.

The rescuers were particularly generous in opening up their lives, and painful memories, to a stranger. Margot Lawson, John Weidner, Otto Springer, and Irene Gut Opdyke are no longer living, but I am most grateful for the time we had together.[4] Otto was able to help me in editing his extensive transcripts and his daughters and sister-in-law also read his chapter.[5] One of Margot's daughters read the final version of the chapter on her mother and one of Margot's grandsons supplied details on aspects of the family left vague by Margot herself. Knud Dyby is—happily—still alive and has seen and approved of the final transcript.[6] Knud and Margot gave permission to publish parts of their own writings, and Irene generously let me relate one story—concerning an anti-Semitic priest—that initially was told to me "off the record." Photographs were provided by the rescuers or their family members. The photograph of Irene speaking to my class came from a tape of her talk. The Weidner Foundation, through Naomi Weidner, gave permission to reprint photographs currently in its possession. To continue this tradition, I will be turning over my edited transcripts to the Holocaust museums in Detroit, Washington, and Los Angeles. I am happy to make the full transcripts available to any other museum, institute, or scholar concerned with them.[7]

I have benefited in incalculable ways from my participation in a wonderfully welcoming professional society, the International Society of Political Psychology (ISPP). My debt to the members of the ISPP, to the members of the American Political Science Association's Organized Section on Political Psychology, to students and faculty in the UCI Program in Political Psychology, and to my colleagues at UCI's Interdisciplinary Center for the Scientific Study of Ethics and Morality cannot be overstated. For their general conversation as well as their generosity in reading all or parts of this manuscript, special thanks must go to Dani Bar-Tal, Augusto Blasi, the late Murray Edelman, Eva Fogelman, Doris Graber, Ken Hoover, Leonie Huddy, Ned Lebow, Gerda Lederer, Robert Keller, Catarina Kinnvall, Milton Lodge, Elizabeth Mitchell, Stanley Renshon, Janusz Reykowski, Shawn Rosenberg, David Sears, Roberta Sigel, Suzanna Smolenska, Ervin Staub, and David Winter. I am grateful to Kathleen McGraw and the other members of the Summer Institute Program in Political Psychology, run jointly by the ISPP and Ohio State University, and to the contributors to *Political Psychology* (Lawrence Erlbaum, 2002), who did much to educate the grateful editor.

Many political theorists and philosophers were kind enough to correct errors and point me in various directions as I tried to learn about ethics. Jean Bethke Elshtain, Joseph Cropsey, Russell Hardin, Jennifer Hochschild, Martha Nussbaum, Laura Scalia, Joanna Scott, and Marion Smiley are chief among them. My time as a Laurence Rockefeller Fellow at Princeton University's Center for Human Values provided critical input at an early stage in my work, and Fred Alford, Jim Glass, and Gaalen Erickson introduced me to work that helped me understand the moral significance of cognitive categorization.

As always, my students taught me far more than I taught them. To Jack Craypo, Connie Epperson, Randy Firestone, Lina Kreidie, Matthew Levy, Kristen Maher, Kay Mathiesen, Saba Oyzurt, Molly Patterson, Ted Wrigley, and Martin Young I owe special debts.

I am exquisitely fortunate in having David Easton, Helen Ingram, Cecelia Lynch, Mark Petracca, and Etel Solingen as colleagues. Each of these dear friends has read my work and commented on innumerable drafts of my manuscripts. Others who provided helpful comments include Barbara Dosher, Wil Lampros, Robert Lane, Frank Lynch, Gertrude Monroe, T.W.G. P'Minter, Fay Robison, and Susanne Rudolph. For their help in preparing the final manuscript, I am indebted to Edna Mejia, Kristin Fyfe, Jenn Backer, and the superb staff at Princeton University Press. I am particularly grateful to Chuck Myers for his patience, editorial judgment, and gentle sense of calm.

While working on this project I have received generous financial support from the National Endowment for the Humanities, the Earhart

Foundation, and the University of California's Institute on Global Peace and Conflict Studies. Parts of this book have appeared in articles in the *American Journal of Political Science*, the *Annual Review of Political Science*, and the *International Political Science Review*.[8] In a few instances, I have quoted passages from rescuers' transcripts that also appeared in *The Heart of Altruism* (1996). I am grateful to Princeton University Press and to the journals cited above for their permission to reprint sections of my work that previously appeared in their volumes. I also am indebted to my coauthors for their permission to draw on our joint work: Kay Mathiesen and Jack Craypo (on moral psychology and virtue ethics), Molly Patterson (on narrative), and James Hankin, Lina Kreidie, Saba Ozyurt, and Renee VanVechten (on identity). Ute Klingemann and Michael Barton worked with me on the original interviews with rescuers. None of these individuals, of course, is responsible for modifications in our joint work or for my errors in interpretation.

Working on the Holocaust imposes special emotional demands on a scholar, and my debt to my husband, children, and mother for their love and understanding is heartfelt and deep. This book is dedicated to my mother, Gertrude Monroe, my first and most enduring moral exemplar.

The Hand of Compassion

Stories That Are True

He was about five-foot tall, sturdy, and he had his little cap in his hand and he was turning it. He kept saying— he must have said it about ten times—"I am ashamed to be a German."

Even the Russian prisoners of war were put in that ditch. And the bodies fell on top of others. They made the Jews, the Gypsies, and the Russian prisoners of war to dig a ditch a kilometer long and they made them take off their clothes, their shoes, and their jewels. And then they shot them and they fell into the ditch.

And he kept saying, "I am ashamed to be a German. I am ashamed!"

When I saw that story in the Holocaust Magazine *it was like reliving it again! I didn't tell them. I don't know where they got it. But I was there when he told Mrs. Fisher, after he came to tell her about her brother dying on the Russian Front. And it was all real.*

THE SPEAKER IS MARGOT, one of the German-born rescuers of Jews in Nazi Europe interviewed as part of the research for this book. Her words come not from one of our formal interviews but from an ordinary telephone conversation, long after our explicit relationship as subject and interviewer had ended, after we had become friends. I must have been working on the computer when Margot called for I later chanced upon Margot's words, typed hastily and stored in an unnamed computer file.

I include this story because it reveals a glimpse of the shock and pain Margot still feels about the war, her conflicting emotions and her sense of disconnect with that time. Because this story, like the others in this book, are stories that are true. Stories that reveal ordinary people caught up in extraordinary events that forced them to be their big selves, events that left a legacy many have still neither made sense of nor fully assimilated. Stories that reveal the speakers' innermost thoughts about themselves and their lives. Stories that are not mine. And therein lies both an ethical dilemma and a remarkable opportunity to gain insight into moral issues that concern us all.

Margot's story is told in full in chapter 1. Like those of the other rescuers in this book, it suggests the striking extent to which action flows from identity, from our most basic sense of who we are. Margot's story reveals how her sense of self constrained the choices she made by limiting the particular options she found available, not just morally but cognitively. By listening carefully to Margot, we not only learn that identity constrains moral choice; we also discover the moral and political significance of how we see the world, and particularly how we see ourselves in relation to others. It is not just our identities that are critical. It is also our own shifting and often idiosyncratic views of ourselves in relation to others that determine how we treat people.

Listening to Margot forced me to confront the most basic questions concerning ethics and normative politics, and much of my analysis contrasts the major theories of moral choice with what I discovered about moral action through listening to Margot and other rescuers of Jews. Does religion or reason drive moral choices? Are certain groups of individuals—women, the better educated, or people in certain occupations—more likely to "do the right thing"? Were Germans more anti-Semitic than other Europeans? What gives one person the moral courage others lack?

Such questions are perhaps obvious ones and I try to address them in this book. But I also encountered other ethical issues that I had not anticipated when I started my research. Is it fair to publish the intimate details of another person's life, even when that person has given her permission? When bonds of trust—and friendship—are established, what particular obligations does that impose on the researcher to protect someone who is, after all, a human being and not just a subject in a research project? Margot's case is instructive in this regard.

Shortly after Hitler came to power, Margot left a promising life in Germany and moved to Amsterdam in protest over Nazi policies. When the war began, Margot thus found herself in the unenviable position of being on the record as a non-supporter of the Nazi regime. Worse, once in Holland she and her husband divorced, and Margot was left with two young, part-Jewish children to raise. Despite her precarious position, Margot showed no hesitation in working to hide Jews and in helping the Resistance, even though she was told that "if caught, we do not know you." Unfortunately, Margot was caught, and arrested six times. She lost contact with her daughters for a while and, through her Resistance activities, had an affair with the Gestapo commander for Amsterdam, a man she later had killed by the Resistance. Margot spoke freely about all of these wrenching wartime events, including her painful divorce and the separation from her daughters; especially hurtful was a continuing emotional ache from the death of her fiancé, Alfred, who was beaten to death by the Gestapo when he tried to get

Margot released from prison, naively believing that Margot was innocent and that the Nazis would listen to reason.

I had sent Margot a copy of the transcribed interviews and asked her to delete anything she felt was too personal before giving permission to have them published. Margot returned the legal form granting permission to publish, but I had the gnawing suspicion that she had not actually read the transcripts.

Was Margot aware of how much of herself she had revealed during our conversations? Had I somehow taken advantage of the friendship we had established? Was I now violating Margot's trust by publishing information that was so personal, even though the friendship had evolved and the interview material was obtained within the clearly defined context of the research project? I agonized about the tension surrounding scholarship, privacy, and friendship, and mentioned my dilemma to one of Margot's daughters. "Does your mother realize some of the things she had told me?" I asked. "Are you sure she's okay with my publishing these interviews?"

Margot's daughter assured me her mother knew what was in the transcripts and that it was all right to publish them. I have taken Margot and her daughter at their word even though I suspect the selfishness peculiar to scholars has swayed my judgment in this instance. I remain conflicted about this and hope the unusual opportunity to share Margot with the reader has justified my decision to publish her personal recollections of this time.

Margot's story raises many other important issues. One of the most significant concerns the reliability of memory, especially the retrieval of traumatic events so long past. How dependable is memory? How self-serving? Is the past reconstructed to make the speaker look good to herself? To others? To help the speaker make sense of what went before?

All the rescuers I interviewed were certified through the rigorous procedures of Yad Vashem, the Israeli agency established after the war to verify and certify genuine rescuers. Hence, I am confident that the rescuers I interviewed actually did perform the extraordinary deeds that originally brought them to my attention.[1] Since I am a political scientist, not a historian, my primary intellectual interest is in understanding the moral psychology, not in documenting the past. The concern to verify specific events is thus lessened somewhat, although it does not entirely disappear. But we are still left to contemplate the particular nature of memories of searing, traumatic events.[2]

In *Holocaust Testimonies* (1991), Lawrence Langer argues that oral testimonies present a far more complex and nuanced aspect of the Holocaust than written work can, precisely because oral testimonies do not contain a central narrative. They amble. They exhibit contradictions and display ambivalence. Oral testimonies, such as Margot's, thus include multiple stories, portraying a range of experiences that happened to the same person. Perhaps, as Langer argues, their very contradictions do more accurately capture the contradictory aspect of complex reality than any written narrative that follows a central and directed plot line.

In another important regard, however, Margot contradicts one of Langer's central claims. Langer makes a credible case that the Holocaust represents a plane apart from life as described in contemporary moral theories. This contention is at odds with the basic premise underlying my book. My approach contrasts traditional scholarly wisdom on ethics with an empirical examination of moral exemplars. I ask how ordinary people—people like Margot—respond in situations that require moral courage. When I find that their actions do not correspond to what the literature on moral choice tells us, I conclude that we need to supplement existing moral theories with a theory that *can* account for the empirical reality of rescue behavior.

For Langer, who analyzed oral testimonies of concentration camp survivors, the Holocaust constitutes an arena in which the normal conceptualizations of the self simply do not hold because victims of the camps were robbed of the agency necessary to make it meaningful to speak of moral choice. They lived in a moral vacuum "[b]ecause the moral systems that we are familiar with are built on the premise of individual choice and responsibility for the consequences of that choice" (Langer 1991: 125). Traditional moral systems, Langer thus contends, cannot explain the Holocaust because the agent had no control over the results of his action. Langer further argues that the Holocaust often broke the connections to and with the self, leaving a prewar, a wartime, and a postwar person, with little to connect these selves. The integration necessary to return someone to the world of ordinary moral discourse was impossible for camp inmates. Langer constructs a compelling case that it is oral testimonies, not written works, that most effectively capture these contradictions in the face of a bewildering series of events.[3]

I found some of this to be true of my conversations with Margot. I had written to Margot asking to interview her and had received an invitation to come to her house one day during the summer of 1988. I arrived around 11:00 in the morning and was welcomed by Margot and her husband, Ted. "Come in. Come in, and have a little lunch," Margot said, leading me to a table piled high with Dutch cheeses, pâtés, and other delicacies. As we followed Ted into the dining room, Margot whispered to me, "Don't say anything about why you're here. He doesn't know what I did during the war."

Totally taken aback by this request, I sat down at the table, noticing that Ted was eyeing me somewhat quizzically, possibly wondering about this strange woman who had just dropped by for lunch.

"Well," I said, "why don't you let me tell you a little bit about myself." I then proceeded to babble on about my children, my husband, my home, anything except my work. Poor Ted hardly had a chance to get a word in, let alone ask why I was visiting his wife.

I realized later that Margot may have been testing me, most likely subconsciously, wondering if I would open up with her as I was asking her to do with me. Certainly, Margot was a master at avoiding painful subjects. She would frequently break off our conversations when we got too close to difficult topics. Her favorite gambit was to exclaim, often quite abruptly, "I got to walk the dog," and exit mid-sentence.

I also slowly realized that Margot told me things once, twice, even many times in a somewhat cavalier manner before she would go back and relate the complete story or tell me the story in a manner that revealed some of the emotional distress the event still invoked for her. Three such events were particularly touching.

Margot had been raised in great affluence and had married a wealthy Jewish banker. (Whether or not the marriage was arranged was never made clear.) When Margot initially spoke of their divorce, she would laugh and say, "Aach! I divorced the bum when I found him coming out of the maid's room one morning, pulling up his pants." Always the same phrase. Always the casual dismissal of the event. Only after we had known each other a long time did I learn that Margot had tried to commit suicide after this happened, an action distinctly at odds with the cavalier retelling of the story. And only from Margot's grandson did I learn that this ex-husband had spent nearly fifty years living very close to Margot in Los Angeles and had only recently died.

Margot twice showed me stories she had written and I soon came to recognize Margot's propensity for touching pain elliptically. (Margot and I shared this tendency, and I wondered if our penchant for cloaking emotions in the literary may have been one reason we became so close.) The first story Margot showed me told of her own incarceration in prison. Margot wrote about the straw that "these poor wretches" had to sleep on, how they were mistreated by the guards, how one girl died, and how Margot herself ran afoul of the authorities, risking her life by sticking out her tongue at one of the guards. The story ended with an account of one of the Jewish women being taken out to be killed. As she was leaving, the woman turned to Margot and asked, "If you get out, find my husband and sons and tell them what happened to me. See that my sons grow into good men," she implored.

When Margot left prison, the first thing she did—after ascertaining that her own daughters were safely hidden in a convent under assumed names—was try to find out what had happened to the woman's family. The husband and sons were still in prison, but Margot was able to get the husband some food and a message about his wife. The husband wrote Margot, thanking her for the food. He and his sons were being shipped out that night to a concentration camp and he was grateful for news of his wife, even though the news was bad. The letter was all mud-stained. It had been sent to Margot by a Dutch railroad worker, who had retrieved it from the sludge in the freight yards after seeing it thrown through the slats in the passing cattle car. "I carried that letter with me for years," Margot wrote, "until the paper it was written on disintegrated."

What was most touching to me was that the story was told in the third person.[4] These "poor wretches" whom Margot describes as sleeping on straw and fighting off the guards were, in truth, Margot and her fellow inmates, not merely some anonymous people. And only at the end of the story, at a point when years have passed, can Margot bear to use the first person. It is only when she tells of carrying the letter until it disintegrated that Margot puts herself into the story as an actual participant.

Margot's use of the literary to touch and handle pain is also evident in a short story she wrote about her beloved Alfred, an excerpt of which is included in the chapter on Margot (chapter 1).

> I tell you something. I wrote about some thing once, when I was not able to write English well. I wanted to write a story, mostly about Alfred. For him. I'll get the book out. I have only one book and I haven't made a copy. I called the girl Isabelle. That's me. But that's not me. Me is . . . I didn't put my name on it. And I thought, "What am I going to do?" Isabelle is my grandmother, who was born in Missouri. When I wrote it, I used a nom de plume. And that's Suzanne de Palma.

Margot brought me her book and placed it in my hands.

> This is in the Library of Congress. Even so, I have not given it to anybody. But you see here? If you want part of it, you're welcome to it. Except I don't know how to make copies of it because it's in a binding. That's the way I think. . . . I'd like you to see it but I can't give it away. Maybe I'll find something and I can have it copied for you. Just wait a little bit, then you can use it. Because it's in the Library of Congress, but if I gave you permission, it's all right. I have to take my dog out for a little walk now. You look at the book.

Alfred's story, which Margot wants to show me but can't bear to part with because "that's me but that's not me," is reflective of the extent to which Margot's story contains multiple voices, even though the speaker is the same person. Any attempt to resolve these different voices would, in Langer's phrase, "betray or falsify" the experience being described (1991: 139).

This is one reason I have published the interviews with minimal editing. Interviews *do* contain contradiction. They *do* reflect confusion. There *is* uncertainty as the rescuers navigate their way around what Langer aptly calls the "moral quicksand of atrocity" (1991: 138). This may simply reflect the reality of the war, but it also may reflect something about identity. By both analyzing and publishing the rescuers' stories in full, I try to walk the fine line between a scholar's responsibility both to detect and identify basic themes and to present the data in a way that accurately captures the complexity of human beings constructing a moral life.

Like Langer, I also found that something was ruptured for the rescuers during the war. Something was broken or lost that was irretrievable. But it was not their sense of self. Nor did I find the moral vacuum that Langer describes. Was this because the rescuers were able to establish what I call human connection? Was it because the rescuers were visitors to the hell that was the Holocaust? True, they were constrained by their own sense of moral duty and character, by a sense of self that left them no choice but to risk their lives for others. Yet many rescuers also described years of postwar nightmares, some of which involved a feeling of being trapped.[5] Since all the rescuers spoke of a lack of choice, I began to wonder about these dreams. Were rescuers' actions a reflection of character, as I have argued previously and will again argue here? Or was it something more sinister, more depressing, as Langer's work on survivors suggests? I cannot be sure.

I understand Langer's anger at attempts to build a "monument of hope in the rubble of decay" (1991: 165), and I am acutely aware that my own moral values make me want to do precisely that, to clench my fist like Sisyphus[6] and scream that we will not be broken by this outrage. It is possible that my own desires for hope have crept into even my minimal editing of the transcripts, or that the questions I posed have injected my own meaning on something that was not there for the rescuers. I do not believe this is the case. But I recognize the limitations of anyone who was not there in grasping the full meaning of life during war and the Holocaust.

If the rescuers themselves experience difficulties retrieving their memories of this time, can the rest of us—we who did not experience it ourselves—hope to understand what the Holocaust was like? At certain points, Margot seems to suggest we cannot. "Oh, honey," she would moan, "nobody who has not been there can ever understand what it was like."

But then she would so desperately try to explain it to me. Margot's story thus forces us to ask if we can ever understand another time, can ever share the reality of another person's life experience, without being there or undergoing the experience ourselves. Certainly there are limitations to this journey, and our successful completion may depend as much on empathy as on intellect. But I believe we can try. It is incumbent on us to try. Perhaps the rescuers, the border crossers[7] between everyday morality and the land so lacking in moral compass, constitute the most qualified guides.

I invite you to let the stories in this book, and my thoughts about their interpretations, lead you to your own judgment about these important questions.

1

Margot

You don't walk away. You don't walk away from somebody who needs real help.

The wealthy only child of the head of General Motors for Western Europe, Margot trained for the German diplomatic corps before moving to Holland in protest against Hitler's policies.

Q. Why don't you just tell me the story of your life, from the beginning.

That's just what I want to tell you. My father was—I can tell you without bragging—a very wealthy man. He was the head of General Motors for Europe. He also handled imports of food. We had bags of candies, almonds from Paris, stuff like that, you know, wholesale.

We had German citizenship. But Hitler took it all away from everybody who didn't like him. Hitler didn't like people who didn't like him. Later the [Dutch] queen had me come and made me an honorable citizen. Now I am American. I was Dutch. But before that I had German citizenship. I was born in Germany in 1909, on April the third. I was raised in Germany actually but I didn't speak German. I spoke only French. I had a French governess. The war broke out in 1914, and my mother said, "Don't speak [French] on the street." But I had to go, like a kid does, and say something to a French girl. Then some German kids came and slapped me half to death.

So, I spent all of World War I in Germany. I was a kid, just a little kid, five years old. Nineteen hundred nine I was born and 1914 it started so I didn't know anything about it. Then I was sent to Geneva to school.

My father was in the import business. He called me in one day. "What do you want to be?" he asked. "Because I have now money, and I can pay for it. But money comes and goes. What you have in your mind and your head will not be taken away from you."

I can hear him like it's yesterday! That's my father. [Margot pointed to a large oil painting hanging over her mantel.] I was sent to England to learn English. And it so happened that every morning I went to Pittman's College. I went down in the ground, on that underground [subway]. I had already a penny in my hand for a paper. Now I liked the rag paper, which was the *Daily Mirror*. It wasn't a fine one. It wasn't the *Times*. And I sit in that underground and I read the paper. Now, this is something you can tell to your children. I found the thing that was for my life in that paper. A story about William of Burleigh.[1] Burleigh had a son. And the son said, "Father, what is diplomacy?" Burleigh took his little boy on his knees—I know it as if I read it today!—and said, "There was a sheik in Arabia who dreamt that he lost all his teeth. So he had a dervish come to interpret the dream. And the dervish said, "It's very simple. All your sons will die before you." *This* dervish he had beheaded. Then the sheik had another dervish come and asked him, "What does it mean? I dreamt I lost all my teeth."

This dervish said, "Go down on your knees, oh high ruler. And thank the almighty Allah that he will give you such long life that you will even so live to see the lives of your sons." To this dervish he gave gold, silver, and jewels. And so Burleigh said, "*This*, my son, is diplomacy."

After World War II, Margot moved to Los Angeles, where she lived until her death. Here she is pictured with her little dog, who—I came to suspect—Margot would suddenly announce needed a walk whenever our conversations became too painful.

When I came home, back to Germany, my father had at home a little room with a lot of books, a library you know, and a couch. And he always called me when he had something serious. So he called me. "Yes, Dad?" I was always scared, because there was always something I was afraid of. But my father never struck me or anything. He was wonderful. He said, "Did you make up your mind what you want to be? I told you I can pay for everything now, but you never know. You can lose your money. It's the same old story."

Anyway, "Yes, Dad," I said. "I want to go into diplomacy." *That* was the thing of my life!

Next thing I know, I was sent to Italy to learn Italian. I was at the University of Florence. I was in Italy when I was about seventeen years old. I was still young. In Italy, at the big exam, there was a big round table. I can see that stuff now like it was yesterday! There was a big round table, and lots of professors around, for the oral exam. When it was through, one of the professors said, "Child, have you ever thought of writing?"

"No, sir."

"You should, you know. And I want to give you advice for your life."

"What?" I was curious.

He said, "Never, never go for your second thought. When you have an idea or a thought or you feel something, stay that way. Never change it. Never."

That advice saved the lives of a lot of people during the war. I didn't know my father knew that. I never told him. But one time when I came during the war to my father in the middle of the night and said, "Oh, my God. The Germans are watching this man. They promised me they wouldn't hurt him. But I got to go to this man and warn him."

"Sit down. Tell me something. When they promised they wouldn't hurt that man, what was your feeling? Did you think they speak the truth? Or did you doubt them?"

"I believed it."

"Then don't do a thing," he told me.

I didn't know that my father knew me so well. I didn't do a thing. And the man was never touched. Can you imagine? Because that professor said, "Stick with your first impression. Don't change it." Isn't that funny? I think it's important. I didn't know how important it would be later on, see. I just thought, "Oh, big deal." You know how it goes.

Can you imagine, how it goes in life sometimes? Little things!

So anyway, then I came home to Germany. I was home a very short time. All my friends go tennis playing. Go swimming. They do everything. Why can't I? My father said, "When you finish learning, you can."

And you know what happened? I had to finish learning. I went to Spain. I was at the University of Madrid. Then, I tell you what happened. In Germany, the League of Nations started a collegium in Heidelberg. I went there. You could study what you wanted. The exam was set for people to go into business consultation, economics, and stuff like that. And politics. Well, I went into politics. Only 302 students made it for politics and I was one of them. You had to know a minimum of four languages. I don't mean knowing just a few words of a language. No, you had to really know them. I was fluent in German, French, English, Italian, and Spanish. Oh, my gosh, this is an awful long study to get into the diplomatic corps. You wouldn't believe how long. You had to know about all the English history. All the Chinese history. You had to know about everybody. It was interesting. But to learn it so thoroughly wasn't so good. I didn't think that was so interesting. But you had to. Then I got married, to a guy I wasn't so happy with.

Q. When did you get married?

I don't know the year. I don't want to remember it, because I got divorced from him. We were married eight years, I think. He had an affair with the maid. It was kind of funny. I caught him coming out in the morning in his underpants from the maid's room. It was something like that. I can't remember. I just don't want to remember.

But with him I had two little girls. We'd already gone away [from Germany] because of Hitler. The war hadn't started. It was in 1935, I think, that I went to Holland. I was still with my husband then. I remember because I divorced in Holland. With him I went to Holland. Because in 1936 my second little girl was born.

Oh, I don't want to talk about him. I think he was a banker. Why should I tell you all what happened? I can't even remember it. Anyway, then he came out with the underpants, and the hell with it! I divorced him. That was in Holland. Then he went with that very maid, he went into hiding. He hid, like a lot of people, who were Jewish.

Q. Your first husband was Jewish?

Yes, my [first] husband was Jewish, and he hid with that girl, the maid. And I was out. So I had separated from my husband by the time the war started. Oh, yes. Separated, but not divorced.

After the Kristallnacht my father came to Holland. When they talk about the Kristallnacht, I tell you what they did. They threw pianos out of the fourth-floor through the window. They threw little babies, in their cribs, through the fourth floor windows. I can't tell you what these Germans did! But I can tell you one thing; the Japanese were worse than the Germans, if there is any such thing that can be worse. I saw things that you wouldn't believe. I can't even talk about it. I have never told him [my second husband]. I never had told him anything about what was going on.

So my father left Germany right after Kristallnacht. He had an apartment near me. In Amsterdam. I was living by myself. Not divorced, but separated, and living with my two children. I had a maid, who watched after the children.

I went to Czechoslovakia around 1939. I was in Prague when the Germans came in. Somebody came to me and said, "Listen, I need somebody I can completely trust. You're the only person I can think of. Would you go for me to Czechoslovakia and do something?"

"Yes, why not?" I went to Czechoslovakia and there was just one hell of a mess. There was an American, in this fabulous hotel where I'm staying. He calls me up in the morning at 6 o'clock and says, "Come on down, quick. The Germans are walking in."

I said, "Yeah, my foot. Let me sleep." I didn't know the Germans are invading in reality. I thought my friends were twisting my leg because we were always doing funny things to each other, practical jokes. Yes, it was in March 1939.[2] God, I can remember that, how they walked in. I tell you what happened. I stood in front of the hotel with a lot of women. They were so mad, these women. One of the women went up to a car that drove by and slapped the German. The German pushed her back and she fell on top of me and I fell back. There was a guy from the hotel, in uniform from the hotel, and he caught me. It was terrible.

Then the Germans wanted the hotel. People came and said, "What are we going to do? They want the hotel?"

"Well, I tell you what. Everybody has a couch. Let's bunk together." Because a lot of people who had fled Germany and were not yet citizens in England had no passport. I went downstairs and told the Germans, "I speak English. I can help you."

"Good. We can use you." So they used me to translate [when they interrogated people]. And I translated wrong. I just lied like you wouldn't believe. I did not tell them the truth.

After the Germans came in, my stuff was at the airport. But I couldn't get out. I don't know how, but I got out by train and I got back home after a while. I was a mess. God, what a mess. An American from New York said, "I came for the mess and a fine mess I'm in."

And I said, "You ain't kidding." It was terrible what a mess we were in. So the Dutch, when they knew what I had done [translating the languages in Czechoslovakia], they asked me if I would help. They said they wouldn't acknowledge me if something happened. But I said, "Fine."

Q. So once you were back in Holland [after the Germans declared war in 1939], did your husband have any contact with your children or with you at this point?

I don't know. Could be. I know that once when I was taken to prison, somebody went to him and that girl he was hidden with and said, "Your wife is in prison. You have to come and help your children."

And he said, "I'm not going to endanger my life for the children." That's the kind of guy he was. But my father took them. My father came in the middle of the night. He had a feeling something was wrong. He put them in a convent with the nuns.

Q. And your children are, of course, part Jewish?

Yes. But God, those Germans took little kids whether they were Jewish, Catholic, or anything else. They couldn't care less. They just killed everybody.

So let's see. It's 1939, and I went back to Holland. The Germans came in May 1940.[3] Boy, that was something! My doctor killed himself. A lot of people killed themselves.

Q. How did you get started helping save people?

I was living in Amsterdam. I helped right away. Well, my father helped more than I. I didn't do so much. My father was in chemical stuff. He had ties to the _____ Works, which were very well-known. They have some in the States, too. He called and told me he had a chemist who is Jewish. "Can you help us?" And we took in the chemist and his wife. We had a lot of people hidden upstairs and so forth.

But, darling, I can't tell you how I got started [helping people]. I can't tell you the whole thing. Because first of all, I think of it all the time. I can't sleep. It's too much for me. I can see things that I can't even talk about, it was so bad. I know that they came in the houses with guns. They didn't bang on the door. They tore the whole door down. They turned the couches over. They cut them open. They broke the sliding glass doors open. You wouldn't believe what happened. I don't believe it and I was there.

But I remember like yesterday! Yesterday! Once I was taken and third-degreed. You know what happened then. The Germans are always so thorough.

I know the German mentality. That was what the Dutch wanted: my knowledge of the German mentality. I know them so well. What had happened one time, the guy comes in and I had a lot of [clandestine] stuff, and my little daughter was in bed already since it was in the night. I stuck this clandestine material under her cot. I thought, "Oh, my God. I hope she doesn't say anything."

The kid didn't open her mouth. I take a book like this and I start to talk, just reading any words. And I read and read and read in Dutch. The German stood behind me and said, "You're reading very well."

"Yes," I told him. "But you don't come so close because the doctor says he doesn't know what the kid has. It could be something that you can catch."

I know that the Germans are deadly afraid of any germs. So he stayed away. The kid wasn't sick! She just was in bed for the night. And all [the material] was in Evelyn's bed. Can you imagine? Everything was in her bed. Evelyn still remembers that.

Q. You were in the Resistance too? You weren't just hiding Jews?

How did I know I was in the Resistance? I came in by mistake! I don't know how I got started! I don't know. I just helped when I could. The Dutch were not like the Norwegians. The Norwegians had that Quisling. The traitor! The Dutch weren't traitors! There was no one traitor there. And the ones that were, were already killed by the Dutch. It was terrible. I tell you. As if we would want to be one of the master race!

One time, we had a man planted into the Gestapo. It was a policeman, a Dutch policeman. One day I had to contact him. So I call him up at Gestapo headquarters [for Amsterdam]. A man answers and I said, "Is Mr. _____ in?" You know, referring to my friend.

"No, he's not in. You got a message?" this voice asks.

I said, "Yes. This is Margot. Would you tell him please dinner is at eight." You know, that was code. That was the end of the conversation. So later when my friend comes to me that evening, he said, "You dolt!"

"What happened?"

"You know who you talked to?" he asks.

"No. What do I care who I talked to? What happened?"

Now there was an expression in Dutch. When you want something you say, "*Rits* for that." For your sweater, for example. *Rits* was money.[4] It was worth about two dollars and fifty cents, or two guilders. It's like saying, "A penny for your thoughts," or "I'd give anything to have that." So my friend says, "The person you spoke with is the Gestapo commander for all of Amsterdam. And he tells me, 'You got a message. "Dinner is at eight." *Rits* for that woman, for that voice.' He wants to meet you."

I said, "Wonderful!"

"No way."

"Oh, yes," I said. "You have a nice lunch tomorrow and you introduce me." And that's what happened. That guy [the Gestapo commander] was my friend. You wouldn't believe what I went through with a friend like that!

Q. So you became friendly with the Gestapo commander for Amsterdam, while you were hiding Jews and helping the Resistance?

[Margot nodded.] You know, a person who has not been there cannot really understand. It's impossible. One time this man [the Gestapo commander for Amsterdam], when he comes into my house, I was standing there, staring, just looking in the street. The Germans took young people away from the street. It doesn't matter whether they were Jewish or not. That had nothing to do with it. They had to work in the German factories in the east. He comes and I look at him and I said, "Isn't that awful?"

Now I tell you something that is true, darling. Honest to goodness. This is something that I never forget. I said, "Isn't that awful, that they're taking away these young people?"

And he said, "So what does one more or less matter?"

I turned on him and I said to him, "I want to tell you something. The Germans will never win the war. Never! There will be a time that you will ask me to help you. And I will say to you what you say to me now: 'So what does one more or less matter?'"

I said those very words to that man, to this Gestapo commander. He got up and came over to me. And he said, "You are a little kid and I love you." And he kissed me on the forehead.

And I said, "I got to go. But you're going to learn a lot." And he laughed.

Now, here the war's over. I got to tell you this. My people—like the

FBI, but in Holland, it's more like the police—they came to me when the war is over and say, "Have you got time tonight?"

"Yes, I always have time. Why?" The war was just over. I said, "Why? What happened?"

"We have to go to the camp, to the German camp," they tell me.

"Okay." I said. "Fine."

So they picked me up at 10 o'clock at night. We got up there. It was up north, west of _____. I didn't know what my people wanted. We got in there and they asked for Mr. such-and-such. I don't even remember the name. They said, "Yes, we'll get him for you."

This German Gestapo commander, the one I was friendly with, was a general. He was always dressed immaculate. His boots were shined. His nails were done. His hair was beautiful. Now, in comes a man. No shoes on. Dirty feet. Dirty nails. Disheveled hair. Horrible looking. It was him. He sees me and gasps. One of the men says, "Do you know that lady? Tell me about it."

I hadn't told anybody about this event. You know, [the story I just told you] when I said the war will be over and you won't win. And he falls on his knees and he says, "You know I only did what I was told to do."

And I despised him like you wouldn't believe. He just clung on to my legs and he says, "You have to help me."

When he was through begging, I said, "So. You're through?"

"Yes, please."

I looked at him and I said, "I know, not too long ago, somebody was standing at my window and said, 'What does it matter a few of these more or less,' when those poor Dutch youngsters were taken away. I said at that time, the tides would be reversed. And since you are ready, I want to ask you people to kill this gentleman, because we don't need one of these 'more or less.' Good night."

I opened the door and I walked out. And the next day the Dutch hanged him. They got the whole story. When or where, I don't know, because I didn't tell them. Isn't that something?

Q. Were you friendly with this man all during the war, this Gestapo head?

Oh, was I! Sure, because I had to.

Q. I'm just struck by how difficult it must have been for you personally. You're a young, attractive woman. There must have been advances made at you?

Oh, yes. We had an affair! I had to. I had to.

Q. How were you able to do that?

I was very young, and I just. . . . [Margot shrugged.] I saved a lot of people, a lot of people.

Once I told my people [in the Resistance], this Gestapo guy says he'll come by with a few friends tonight. He says to me, "But we have to be at 2 o'clock in the *polder*" [the reclaimed land in Holland, which is below water level].

"Well," he says, "we heard that some of the Dutch are going to England and we'll intercept them by 2 o'clock tonight." So I had his men here, over to my house. The Resistance gave me a case of wine. I poured and poured and poured and poured, until they were all a little drunk. Then I heard a small click [the pre-arranged all-clear message]. It was not loud. But I knew it was over. Our people had left. I said [to the Germans], "Well, people, it's time to go home." They wobbled down the stairs. They were drunk like you wouldn't believe! And they yelled at me, "We missed it. We missed it. We're too late."

I just shrugged and said, "Not my fault." It wasn't my fault they missed it. I got them drunk so they couldn't round them up, the people trying to escape.

Things like that happened, you know. You can't tell that to anybody because nobody can understand the gravity of the situation.

Q. Did people around you know what you were doing?

There was a man, a Jewish man, who betrayed others to save his own skin. I knew his daughter was engaged to somebody, and I helped them out of the country. All of a sudden, on my birthday, a year later, somebody came and said, "I have a gift for you." Somebody, I don't even know who it was. The present was a gulden in a diamond-shaped form. I had a charm bracelet, and it said on one side "thanks" and on the other side the date when I got that young couple out. Can you imagine? I often think maybe they were the ones in Jerusalem who told the Yad Vashem people about me. There are lots of people who said that my name was up there [on the Yad Vashem list]. But, of course it wasn't my name now because I married later and changed my name.

Q. Can you tell me what it was like for you during the war?

No. I cannot tell you. You cannot possibly, as a human being, imagine the agony and the fear that people have. Now, for instance, when you wrote that you would like to interview me, my husband said, "What is this all about? What's going on? What happened?"

I said, "Well, she heard that I helped a few people."

"What was going on?" he asked.

"Even if I tell you, you cannot possibly understand." Sixteen years I had been married to him. And I never told him what happened.

Ten years, I woke up every night and heard the poor girls who had a little gold in their mouths cry. No dentist. No nothing. Just a little bit of gold. But you see, all these girls, all these people who had gold, it was taken out. The Germans needed it. I tell you quite frankly, you cannot imagine how it is. The darn thing is, you cannot see the agony and the worry.

So when you said yesterday [that you wanted] a photo of me during this time, well, even afterwards, you did not feel like a photo. Now you come, you're a nice girl, and you say, "Do you have pictures?" Now, here's why you don't. There was this woman who was very religious. A Jewish woman. She was the kind who wears wigs all the time. One weekend we go out to hide her through the forest. And her wig got caught on a tree. Ordinarily, she'd yell, "Ouch!" But she was not even allowed to talk. She can't even tell us to go back for her wig, hanging on the branch of the tree. It's always, "Shhhh, be quiet! So the Germans don't hear and come and kill us all!" Now that's funny, the wig on the tree. You got to laugh a bit. And yet that isn't funny. But you don't take pictures of it. You don't think of pictures. Later, you meet these people [you worked with], you may tell a joke. You may be jovial. But nobody ever thought of taking pictures.

Once we had made in jail with a nail [a] little hole so that we could look out with a half an eye. We saw how the Germans pulled the men on their ears and they screamed. And for ten long years—I swear it's true—I heard every night these people crying. Now, what is the good of saying it all again? Because when you haven't been there, you cannot visualize it. One Jewish woman who heard that I helped a lot of Jewish people, she told me, "You know, my husband was in [a] concentration camp. He lost his wife and his kids. He never wanted to talk about it. He was a lonely man."

I told her, "I can understand it. I never talk to anybody either." I never said anything to anybody. Even my husband had no earthly idea about what I'd done. He was married to me for sixteen years or more when he finally found out. He had no idea. I said, "If I had told you, you wouldn't have understood it. Even if you tried to understand. It was such a terrible thing. It's not life."

You know, my daughter Evelyn, came once from school. And she said, "Mommy, is there a heaven and hell?"

I didn't know. And you know what the kid says to me? "I think hell and heaven is right here on earth." And I think that kid was right.

I have studied in Italy and read Dante's trilogy, *The Inferno, The Pergatario*, and *The Paradise*. It states, when one enters hell, "Leave all hopes behind, you that enter here." That's hell. And I often think that my daughter was right.

These people [during the war] have suffered. Some were better off dead, yet they clung to life. I don't understand how people cling to life when their lives are so bad. Why have some people such a wonderful life and why are some people so terribly suffering? There must be something to it. You cannot understand it. I don't think anybody can understand it if you haven't been in there.

Q. What do you do when you have these dreams or nightmares? When you hear things from that time? You said you would go to bed at night and you would hear the people screaming.

I woke up.

Q. Are you frightened to go to sleep at night?

No. I have never been frightened. But I woke up in the night and I heard the screams. That went on for ten years. Finally, it stopped by itself. You know, time is a big healer they say.

Q. During that period for you, was there something that you clung to that gave you hope?

I'm a religious person. But I don't go to churches. Look what happens with Reverend Swaggart. He goes to bed with somebody. All that holy doings! You don't have to show it that you're so holy. I don't really have any particular faith so to speak. I am baptized but I'm just as well Jewish. I know the Jewish religion very, very well. I know the Catholic religion very, very well. I know everything. I learned it.

Q. What kind of faith do you have?

I believe in God, in one God. But not in falling down on the floor. In Spain, when I studied, I had a teacher. She told me: "Nobody can learn it [faith]." There are lots of things that you can't learn. You can feel things. Some people want other people to talk about it, to tell you what is in them or what they feel. Either I think, "Uh oh, there's something wrong," or "Everything's all right." I *feel* them. You cannot learn certain things. You have either compassion with these people, or you think, "I couldn't care less when they drop dead."

Q. Where does it come from though, these feelings? It must come from someplace.

I think it's born in you. That's what that Spanish teacher said. It is in you. You feel things. I feel an enormous lot of things. Have you ever thought of somebody who just that minute called, or came in, or whatever? Have you ever been in a place where you know you have never been before? But you know it? Suddenly, for a second or just a fraction of a second you think, "I've seen that before"? I stood in the Piazza Michelangelo in Florence. I knew I had never been there before in my life.

It was the first time I came up there. And yet I'd seen it. I knew it. For the longest time.

Q. Are you saying that our soul has a life that moves in and out of the body?

The soul hasn't but your heart. . . . The soul is going on. Now, I was engaged to be married to a man who went to [a] concentration camp. Alfred. I can't show you a picture of us together but from him I have a picture. Just not a picture of me. And one [photograph], from the concentration camp where they took him. There is a big wall that the Dutch made, where the names are. Where people are listed and what happened. To them, the Dutch made that wall with a cross.

Alfred and I weren't arrested together. He didn't know a thing about what I was doing. No, I was already in jail. He just wanted to get me out. He didn't tell me what he tries. I was in prison. He didn't tell them what I was doing and they beat him to death.

Q. Were you in jail then because they suspected you were helping to save Jews?

No. I'm trying to tell you. There's no reason to their arrests. They came in one evening into a house where I shouldn't have been. And they took me in. It's not like here, where you go to an attorney and you say, "Listen, I'm accused of breaking law number 1375" or whatever the law is. No.

I went to jail and Alfred came to my father. My father [said], "Don't go. Don't go to the Gestapo." But Alfred thought he could get me out. So he went there and they took him.

"We'll get it out of you," they said. And so they slapped him until he was gone. There was a gentile man—I think he was Protestant—and later he brought me a cookie jar, which I just gave away this year [1989]—and he said, "I was there and they clobbered him to death."

The day this happened, I thought of him. I said to myself, "Margot, you should worry." When my fiancé died, I knew it that night. I felt he was lying on his back. *Before* the guy came and told me what really happened. I knew. He was beaten to death by the Germans when he was only thirty-eight years old. And I know that night—it was at night—I was sleeping and I felt as if something was detaching from him—I've never talked to anybody about this before—something was detaching from him and he was embracing me and said, "Margot." And then the man comes and said, "You know his last words were 'Margot.'"

"I know."

A rabbi came to me, and a Catholic priest came to me, and they told me the man [Albert] died of a heart attack. And I said, "Bull." I could have said "bullshit" but I didn't. I just told them, "It's not true. He was beaten to death."

Q. Tell me about Alfred.

Oh, Alfred. He was about the most fabulous man. I'll get you his picture in a minute. I have learned so much from him that you wouldn't believe. I said to him, "Don't trust these people."

He just smiled, "If you cannot trust anybody, you may as well not live." He trusted and that was. . . . [Margot shrugged.] Somebody betrayed us because he was too trustful. Now me, I have a little suspicion. I'm a schluz, you know. I always think, "Well, I see how bad people can be." I mean, not bad really but they can do you bad. And you feel it.

Now, I wrote a story. I didn't know how to start it because I'm not a writer. That was my first story. I wanted to write it actually for Alfred. I have also arranged my will that the Holocaust Museum gets—if I have left something—some money. For Alfred. In his memory.

He was a very intelligent man. He loved people and he helped everybody. Now, a lot of people from Germany came over to Holland and they were taken into camps. Not like camps where you'd pay the money to live, like here. No. The Dutch government—which at least didn't send them home, like Roosevelt did here—the Dutch government took them up and put them in camps. Alfred went every week up there and brought food, coal, music, everything to these people.

He had a factory for clothes. I had that factory later. I didn't know anything about clothes. To me, it's like dancing on the moon, what I know about clothes factories. But I did it. I sold to Egypt. To Switzerland. I sold to all the countries. To everywhere. Alfred left it to me. Well, not he himself because he couldn't leave anything. He had no will and he was dead. But the government gave it to me.

So you see I'm trying to tell you that you could be arrested just because they don't like you. You don't have to have done anything. For example, there was a Jewish girl. She went to bed with a guy because he wanted to make whoopee.[5] So what did he care? She had the attributes. She didn't look Jewish or whatever. He didn't think of Jewish. He didn't think of anything. Like hungry, he wanted to eat something. So it has no rhyme or reason. And this is why nobody, nobody who hasn't been there, can ever understand it.

Q. Let me see if I'm understanding what you're saying. Are you saying that you think that people are born, or at least some people are born, with an ingrained sense of compassion, of right or wrong?

I think so.

Q. Is everyone born with it?

No. Well, could be. But some people, already at home they have such a terrible home life that they get angry at everybody. You cannot learn some things in life. But there are lots of people that do you harm and they are disagreeable and they hurt you. Then you just leave them alone and think, "Oh, to hell with them." But on the other hand, you can't help everybody in life.

Q. How do you decide whom to help then?

Well, I didn't decide. There's no decision. It's not like you say, "Oh, well. It's five o'clock. The people come and the judge will come in and so forth." No. There is no decision. You either help or you don't. "Can you do something?" they [the Underground] asked me. They knew that I speak the languages. I spoke German like a German, of course. And I know the [German] mentality.

Q. You were talking about the dreams that you've had at different points.

It is not so much a dream, as it woke you up. You know, you hear it and it wakes you up in the middle of the sleep. Now it's better, of course. But for ten years after this [war] you can still hear them screaming. They had an old woman next door [in jail]. They pulled her by the hair down the stairs. Can you hear her screams? You cannot imagine that sound. Nobody can. No.

But you know, not all Germans did it. I know quite a lot of nice German people. Now, my son-in-law was too young. He died when he was fifty-two, four years ago. He was [a] professional and very good. But his brother-in-law was a Nazi and his brother was not; he was in [a] concentration camp. Same family. Hitler said to people, "You tell me when you don't like your parents. You come and tell us when they say something about you." He wanted people to betray the others.

Q. You were talking about your strong sense of faith. You said you believe in one God. But you don't believe in churches?

I don't believe in these people who tell you what to do and then not do it themselves.

Q. Then you said that you'd been in the Piazza San Marco in Florence and you had a feeling that you'd been there before. Do you believe that the soul lives on beyond people?

It must be. Because I have that [feeling] very often. Sometimes in company, when you know you have never before seen these people in your life, and all of a sudden you hear something which you think you've heard before. It's only a second. Or maybe a part of a second. But that was [what happened] to me in [the] Piazza San Marco. It was up there. I never forget it, if I live to be one thousand years old.

Q. Now, what about Alfred? Do you think that he's lived on in you in some way?

I don't think it's that he is in me, because I was already born and I'm here. But there is not a day in my life that he's not with me. I mean, I married him [Ted], but it's not a childhood love. You know, he's a nice guy and I like him. But we are old. He's eighty-five and I'm eighty so what's the big deal?

There were things from Alfred that I always felt that he takes care of me. Very often, I sit here and I see that dog of mine. When somebody comes, she comes and wants to come close to me. The dog jumps up; she takes care of me. Now, isn't that strange? She's just like Alfred. When I'd say, "This window should be opened," Alfred would say, "Let me do it." Or when I had some worries, "Let me take care of it."

You see? There is something in this life and I would like to know what it is that people hang on so much on life. Is it going to be better or not? My godfather, if he hears that, he'll be furious. He doesn't like me saying that. He doesn't like these things. But there must be something in this life. There must be something. Well, why are we all here? Why are we making ourselves so crazy?

Q. I wonder sometimes about a purpose in life that we don't know about.

My mother always said you come with the empty hand and you go with the empty hand. Well, you were born with empty hands. We have little fingers and you go out with empty hands. What can you take with you? There's that old joke, where that Chinese man said, "I want every son to put some money in my grave." He had seven sons, and after he's buried, each son puts $10 into the grave. Then the last son comes and he puts in a check for $70 bucks and takes the $60 out. Now *he* was smart.

I don't know if we take anything out of life. I don't think so. I don't think you take anything along. I think you start fresh. But start you must. Look, some people love horses. Some are crazy about cats. Some people love birds. And so forth. Have you ever thought about that? Some people look like a dog, like a bulldog. Look at that Jacques Cousteau. He loves fish. He goes down in the ocean. Do you think he was maybe in his former life a fish?

I don't like birds and I don't like fish. But I love dogs. Maybe I was a dog. But I wonder why is it. I don't know if I'd say there's reincarnation. But I wonder if maybe there may be a nirvana. Jesus, when I think what all I studied! And the more I studied, the dumber I was.

Q. I don't know if I should ask you this or not. Forgive me if I'm being too personal. But, as we've spoken during the last few months you've said at several different times that you just turned eighty and that your mother died when she was nearly eighty. I know you've just turned eighty. Your mother's death at the same age seems to have been on your mind at different points.

Yeah, I envy her.

Q. You envy her. You're not afraid of dying?

No, not a bit. I asked my mother once. I said, "Are you afraid of dying?" She was so upset. But I'm not afraid of dying. I never was. But what do you think? It can only get better.

Q. You think it gets better after you die?

Honey, if you have seen what I have seen people do to each other, you wouldn't ask. I sometimes think, "Oh, no. It's not possible." And still I've *seen* it with my own eyes.

Q. That's what I wanted to ask you. You said you have memories. You said you've had dreams. What is there before you die that you would like to get out? To leave behind so that you don't have to deal with it?

[Margot shrugged.] I think you have to fight. Alfred always said life's a constant fight. He was fighting. He was fabulous. I learned so much from this man and come to think of it, I was already older when I met him. I mean, I'd studied and learned. I lived in various countries. I was here and there. I was in Russia. You know, the Russians did a ridiculous thing, because people cannot all be put in one mold. One person wants to get ahead in life and works hard. And one says, "Why should I?" [In Russia] it doesn't make any difference. It all goes to the state anyway. Communism is not for me. You cannot put all people in one thing. You have good ones. You have bad ones. I have German people I like and German people I don't like. But those who were in that skinhead thing, *them* I don't like. They don't like you. Absolutely. I found that out. It doesn't make any difference what you are or what you do. You cannot make it good when they are like that.

My daughter wrote when they had the last election [in Germany] that somebody said to her, "The Nazis are back again."

I wrote back, "They haven't come back again. They never went." They never went, because once it's in you, it's in you.

Q. So you have to fight when you meet people like that?

Well, Alfred always said it's a fight. People all over, they act just the same as here. It didn't make any difference. . . . Like in Moscow, like in the communism, you cannot put them all on one thing. One is like this and one is like that and they never change. They are like that and *they are like that*. You cannot say, "Come on. Change and do this. Do that." They are brought up that way and they feel that way and their parents are that way. You cannot change them.

Q. Margot, you said two things. You said that people are different. And you said that you think some people are born with a sense of compassion. . . . Do you think everyone is born with some kind of a sense of compassion?

No. I don't think that. There are people born from a mother who hates the father because she was made pregnant. She didn't want the baby and when she carries the baby she is already madder than hell for the baby. That you cannot change. The hatred is already in you and that stays in you.

I think people are born with different things in them. Yes. Absolutely. Don't you think so? If I were made pregnant by somebody I didn't like and I had to bear the baby. . . . That's why I am not for these pro-life people. And surrogate mothers, out! I don't like anything that's not natural. That's how it starts out. If you're supposed to get a baby, you get one. If you don't, to hell with that. They play God, these people, and I don't think that's any good. But if a mother or a father is a drunk and hates people, then the kid is born already with hatred in his heart. It doesn't change after you're born. No. I don't think so. It will always be. I think people are born pretty much one way or the other. Yes. They are born the way the mother was.

You know that the Jews, when somebody dies, they don't say "son of Mr. Genendal" or whatever, they say "son of Mrs. so and so." They say your maiden name. Why? Because they don't know whether the guy is the father or not. And you shouldn't lie in the face of death. That's why that is so. Isn't that strange? Now, for instance, there's one thing that Hitler did good. That is, when people have afflictions, any kind of an affliction, they can make whoopee, but they do not get children. And that's a good thing, that they sterilize them. I think that is a good idea. I absolutely agree with that. But I don't agree with making kids artificially and doing all that artificial stuff. I absolutely don't agree. Even the heart transplant, I don't agree. I have subscribed in my driver's license that everything I have that's good, they can use. But personally, I'm not for it. If your time has come and you should die, good-bye my good friend. It's bad but it's only bad for the ones who stay behind.

Q. So you don't think dying is a frightening thing? You're not afraid to die?

No, not at all. Are you afraid to die?

Q. Yes, I think so.

I'm not comparing. I was thirty-two years old when I agreed to work for [the Resistance]. The Dutch had told me, "If you do work for us, we cannot help you if you're arrested. We cannot help you. We don't know you if you get caught. Are you afraid?" I said, "No."

Q. What do you think happens to you when you die?
I think your soul lives on. I don't know how it lives on and I wish to God I did. But it lives on. You live on, in somebody [else] maybe. Listen, I want to tell you something. My first language was French. My parents spoke French to me. Everybody did. I had a French governess. I didn't know a word of German when I was a little kid because nobody spoke German to me. Remember I told you I was scrappled by some kids in the street because I couldn't speak German [during World War I] when I was just a kid. Maybe my parents spoke German to each other. I can't remember. I think so; but they always spoke French to me, always French. So my [early] languages were French or German. Then I got an operation for my appendix. My doctor was a good friend of mine. He said, "Boy, did you blabber."

"What did I say?" And he told me it was all in English. I said, "English! I don't even know English." Oh, I knew a few words, you know. But I only spoke French or German. I told him, "You're nuts. You just can't tell English from French."

"I sure do know English from French. You spoke English."

Now this is the funny part of it. My grandmother was born in Woodville, Missouri. I don't want to say I'm my grandmother but somewhere back there, there was English. I had never studied English. No. I never knew it at the time. I was later sent to England to learn English. But it was much later, after this operation.

This living on after we die, if you want to call it that, it's a nirvana kind of thing. Like what the Hindus have. Now, I don't talk to people about this because nobody asks me. But I often think there must be something. Why did I speak English that time? Only English. He said, "You spoke beautifully."

And I said, "I don't even know English. What are you talking to me about?" But my grandmother was born here [in the United States]. They moved back to Germany to avoid the Civil War. Boy, they'd have saved me a heck of a lot of trouble had they stayed!

Q. Margot, let me ask you about how you view other people in relationship to yourself. How do you see other people?
Some are boring. Some are interesting.

Q. In terms of relating to them, though, do you feel a strong sense of community? Do you believe that there are some people you meet and you just decide you want to be friendly with them or you don't? Or do you believe that there are ties that we all have?

No, I don't think we have ties. I think you meet somebody—like I met you—and I think, "There's a fabulous person. I like her." And that's it. But it's not in a community. I single it out. It's one person I like. And I said, "Oh, I met a guy who's terrible." I don't think anything of it.

Q. Would you help the person that you thought was terrible?

If something happened to that person, certainly. But I would stay away so far that I would probably not be asked to help. But if I can help somebody, I will be happy to do it.

Q. Do you feel you have a choice here? [Margot shook her head, no.] It just happens? That's just the way you are?

Yeah. You don't just stand and think. You have no time to think if something happens. Suppose somebody drowns. If you stop [to] think, "Shall I? Shall I not? Eenie, meenie, miney, mo." You can't do that. You either help or you don't.

Q. Do you think it's just a disposition that some people have toward helping others?

[Margot shook her head, no.] You don't walk away. You don't walk away from somebody who needs real help. But some people who are real nasty. . . . Now, suppose something would happen to Hitler. I often thought, would I help him? Because I never believed that he was dead. Now I believe it more, but at the time I didn't really think he killed himself. But would I help this guy, after what he did? But on the other hand, people didn't have to do it.

Q. You must have taken a tremendous risk, though. You were essentially acting as a double spy.

Yeah, but so what? Listen, I was taken one night and third-degreed, with the lights on me by some guy who looked like a bulldog. I called him bulldog. He was terrible. He said, "If you don't tell us, we'll [he makes a big motion across his neck, like he's cutting his throat]." Then I made a big mistake. You know how you sometimes do? I said something so dumb. I said, "I don't know anything. But if I knew I certainly wouldn't tell you." That was the dumbest thing I ever said. It made him think I knew.

"*That* we got to see!" he said. "If you don't tell us, we will kill you." They put me in big lights. They were standing there. I thought they'd see my heart bust up, here. I could hardly breathe. But I stayed cool, you wouldn't believe. I tell you something. I was cool. And I had the luck! I said, "Now you got a chance that I will blabber it out. But when I'm dead, I can't blabber it."

Q. But weren't you in a situation where you were dating the head of the Gestapo? Didn't that protect you?

This [arrest] was before. After I met that guy, I was able to do something. I tell you one thing I did. The Germans once came into one of the best streets in Holland. Very elegant, like Rodeo Drive in Beverly Hills, only [whereas] in California are fine houses, mostly in Amsterdam are fine apartments because in Holland you don't have so many houses. And this is what happened. A German was killed. My friend [the Gestapo commander], he said, "We're going to make sure a Dutchman gets killed, too." They were going to make sure a Dutchman was taken in because a German was killed.

"How do you know it was a Dutchman who did it?" I asked.

"It can only be a Dutchman," he said. "No possible way that a German killed another German."

I said, "If you give me one of your men, I'll find out who it was." So he gave me one of his men. And I found out that the murdered German man was killed by another German who was jealous because he took his girl! But before I found that out, before I knew anything about it, they went into that elegant street. They took out the men, all the men from the apartments. They took them down, and lined them up like a row of tulips. The women and children had to look out the window. Then they shot them. Can you imagine? That's a minor thing that happened. Isn't that awful?

I asked this [Gestapo] guy, "Could it be a German?"

"No, it can't be a German," he says. "It was a Dutchman."

I showed them. I showed them. What a superior race!

Q. Before you started going out with the man who was head of the Gestapo, you were arrested six times, is that what you said?

Not before. Also during [the time I was seeing him].

Q. So that was not a protection for you?

Oh, no. He didn't know everything.

Q. So he didn't make sure that you weren't picked up or anything like that?

He didn't know that. The Germans, they were all so special. "We are the master race." And all the Dutch—because I was Dutch—all the Dutch were nothing. And everybody else is nobody.

Q. But you still had German citizenship during this period, didn't you?

I didn't have any citizenship. Do you think that Hitler leaves you to be a German?

Q. How did Hitler take your citizenship?

Everybody who was against him [lost their citizenship].

Q. You had to swear a loyalty oath or something?

No, they heard it. They would have killed me. The Germans would have taken me into a German concentration camp in Germany. So I left.

Q. So how did you get into the Resistance?

I don't know how I came. Somebody asked me to help because I knew all these languages and so forth. It's not like you have a particular job with the Resistance. You don't get a job. You just do what you think is right. Somebody comes and says, "Can you hide me?" I know a woman who came and said, "Oh, God. I'm so scared." I said, "Come on the couch." I made a bed for her. Things like that. You help. You don't know, you have no idea. You don't get told, "Go and buy a pound of cucumbers" or something like that. It's not possible.

You can't put that [time] on a normal scale. This is not life. Life is, "At 5 o'clock, I see you."

I remember that I wanted to get a sweater. I went to a store like Bullock's, a very elegant store. I go in there. I knew the girl well. I told her, "I go downtown now but I come back tomorrow morning and I pick it up." Two months later I come back to that store. She said, "Something must have happened to you, because you're so punctual. And you didn't show up, so I knew something happened."

"Yeah, I was in jail."

She said, "I kept it for you." She had kept that sweater for me! Isn't that something? She knew something had to have happened to me because otherwise I would have come back for it.

You don't know these things. You can't know it. It's impossible. You know, they took away everything. Your car, everything. I was on a sled and I said to a young man, "You bicycle, and I'll hang onto that sled. If you see the Gestapo stopping people, then stop and let me off." Well, the guy pedals on. I see a whole bunch of people. I hear, "Papers, please. Papers, please." I climb off. I didn't say anything to the boy, because it was already too close. I climb off. And I slid on the ice with my keister. So here comes a man, bicycling. I said, "Give me your bicycle."

"Sure," he said. I just took the bicycle. I go up and go around the corner. And I fall down and break my leg. Now I have these high boots on. I went into the nearest store, which was a butcher shop. "My God, my leg hurts." I said. The butcher said, "Come on. I take off the shoe." I still feel the pain, you know, with a broken leg, to pull off the boot. Oh, boy. Things like that happened. Now I had to have my leg fixed. But how am I going to get into the hospital? There was no electricity. There was nothing. There was a clandestine cart, a three-wheeler with a place to store meat in and a cover. I was sitting on the cover and they took me to the hospital. A very thin guy—thin because we had no food since the

Germans stole all the food, too—he carried me upstairs. A friend of mine was a surgeon. He said, "I can't do it. I can't take an X-ray picture."

"You can feel it. Break my leg again and set it right." Because it was already a little older, it was already a month or so old. He broke it again and set it right.

Now I tell you another story. We had two people we were hiding in our house upstairs. My friend, who was a Dutchman [working undercover] in the Gestapo, he comes that evening. He takes one look at the woman and says, "Are you crazy?"

"Why?"

"You got that woman up there! She looks like ten Jews, not one. You can't let her out in the street!"

I said, "What you want me to do? What am I going to do?"

And he said, "You are with one foot on the banana peel and the other in the grave."

"What am I going to do?"

"I don't know but do something. Anything. I don't care if you cut her nose off."

So the next day I called my friend, the surgeon. In my house, in my kitchen, the woman was operated on for her nose. And when the war was over, she said, "I have now to give up my name." Because the name we had given her, with the false papers which my father got for her, was a very famous name for chemists. She said, "I have to give up my name; but thank God I can keep my nose!"

Q. When you were arrested, why were you arrested?

There was no reason. What are you talking about? You think there's law? No, you don't know! I can tell you one time what happens but not why I was arrested.

My godfather said, "Take all that stuff [clandestine material] and bring it to the people [in the Resistance]." But I couldn't. I had such a headache, I couldn't even see straight. It was the worst headache I've ever had. So my father had given me an antique table, with wonderful antique legs. You could open that table and put something inside. So I put the stuff in the table and then after I was in bed, I thought I'd better get out. I went out and I take the table and turned the table around so that you can only open it from this side, lift it up so to speak.

That night they came. The Gestapo came. The bell rings in the middle of the night. They took the sliding glass doors off. One guy goes by the table and tries to put it up. But it didn't go. So I think it was meant that I went out of bed—even though it was icy cold, and I froze to death— but I went out to turn the table around and nobody found these papers.

They always said, "Give it to Margot. Nobody finds it with her." My godfather once sent me a book, *Angels Watch over You*. And he is right. Angels do watch over me. When we have big trouble and terrible things, I tell you the truth, I always get out of it. See, when I put everything in retrospect, everything was there.

One time, it was midnight. They came in the night. Oh, when the Gestapo came in the middle of the night it was terrible! I think somebody betrayed us. I went into a house, late at night, after curfew. Somebody saw. It wasn't my house. It was another house. And they took us away.

Another time they were once at my home. I said, "Can my maid make you a cup of coffee? It's so cold sitting up in my nightgown." I wasn't allowed to have a robe on. And it was so cold. They said no. They went out and ate all my sausages and everything. And I was starved. They took me out of bed and they demolished the whole house. I don't know why. You aren't supposed to ask.

Q. So you were living during all this time with your two children?

No. After I was arrested the first time, the children were put into a convent.

Q. Were you able to see them?

I was in jail. And I was guarded. But my kids, I heard them crying at night in my head. There was a German guard. I did the same thing with her that I did with the other guy, the one in the Gestapo. I said, "You know that the Germans won't win. You have an illusion if you believe that."

One of the girls in my cell fainted when I said that. I asked Ingrid [the guard] to find out about my children. The next day she came and said, "The children are okay. Here." And she gives me two apples. Those two apples we shared, it was the biggest gift I've ever had in my life![6] You know, things like that happened. Because all these people were not murderers or crooks. They were just people who didn't belong there. Some were nice college people, or just nice people. You see, I have known the German mentality. When you have a crook who has a gun, they are the big shots. Take the gun away, and they say, "Well, we didn't mean it." You understand? Same thing happened to the Germans.

There was one time in my cell a girl who was terribly sick. I wanted the doctor. To get attention, you pushed something inside the cell and an arm fell out outside. I pushed it and I said, "I want a doctor here." Well, a big fat guy came and called the doctor, who comes with a little guy behind. He never even touched the girl.

"The girl is sick. That poor girl. What has she got?" He gave her a tube to take.

I said, "Wait a minute before you take the tube." I went out and I looked at it. It was something against flies. It wasn't medicine; it was just something to use against flies, like a fly repellant. The kid was dead the next morning. She just died. She was anyway so sick. Then I called again.

I hear them say, "Who is that? Oh, that's the one who's not afraid," I heard them say. They came. I talked, because I was the only one who spoke German. (I spoke German like a German, of course.) He said, "What do you want? Keep still there. Shut up!" And all that crap.

I said, "I won't keep still." Finally he came.

"I want something to disinfect this [cell]," I told him.

He said, "Hah."

Then I got an idea. "Come here. I want to tell you something." When he came closer, I whispered, "The kid had syphilis. Who knows? It could spread." He yelled out immediately, "Disinfectant for cell #17!" You have to know these people. You have to understand how they think.

Q. You said you have things you haven't told anyone about.

I can't tell it. I'll tell you one story if you don't use it. [Deleted.] Can you imagine that? They dug a hollow hole for the Jews and let them do their business—bowel movements. And then they had to eat it! How can you tell that to anybody? Isn't that awful? But I understand. I was in Japan. I saw the dungeons. After the war, we had Dutch people come from Indonesia, which was our country. What they told us about the Japs is the worse thing you have ever seen. The Japs were worse, much worse than the Germans, if there is any such thing. But in Holland everybody was against Germany. The trains went out. They stole all the food. And they sent it out to Germany. The Dutch had nothing to eat. They had to buy it on the black market. You can't imagine. You know, you tell this to somebody, but you cannot possibly imagine those things that happened. There were some good people who tried to kill Hitler. But they couldn't do anything. You know what I always think? Nobody did anything. If the Japs hadn't bombed Pearl Harbor, I wouldn't be alive. It was my luck that the Americans went in. The pope didn't do anything. All the talk was nothing. The French Resistance was good. And you could trust most of the Dutch. I remember how a man came one night. He said he was one of us. But I remembered I'd seen the guy. I have a tremendous memory. I said, "He's a shoemaker. I've seen him talk to a Gestapo man on such-and-such a corner." I knew exactly. We got all these people later, you know.

I wasn't able to see my children during this period. But I knew they were safe. When I heard from that woman that they were safe, I still didn't know where they were. I couldn't ask anything. But when I got out of prison, I learned that my father kept them.[7]

My father was wealthy. I told you. He kept the whole convent. He bought coal on the black market. He bought food on the black market. He bought everything on the black market. My father had all the connections. We had papers forged. We forged things you wouldn't believe: passports, other documents [the Germans wanted]. We had once a guy who was terribly afraid. He came to my father. My father made him a Swiss citizen, and wrote from the American Embassy that the Germans should take care of him because he was a special man. Now, my father knows the German mentality, too. So he sent several unimportant papers, just newspaper clippings, to a family we knew in Switzerland, just casual friends, not people we know very well. Then right after that we sent them a letter, saying that by mistake we sent you some papers. Please send them back. They did. So we got the envelope with the Swiss postmark. When my father showed the Germans the letter, the forged letter making this man a Swiss subject, the German official said, "Yeah, you can show me a letter. But where's the envelope?" And we had the envelope! Our friends had sent it all back. My father did this kind of thing for everybody. You wouldn't believe. There was nobody who came that was not helped. And he was never arrested. He was never caught.

After the war, my kids came home. It was not much of a deal. They were home, and then they went to another school. One of my daughters holds it against me that I did these things. Yes. That I did not use too much time with her, she holds it very much against me. But I couldn't. How can I? It was impossible. She doesn't understand it. She doesn't understand these things. The little one understands it. The little one, born in 1936, will be fifty-three years in May. That's Evelyn. Margaret, the older one, was born in 1933.

Q. Margot, let me ask you. I'm a mother, and I think about the things that you did. One of the things that would be primary in my mind, I think, would be how this would be affecting my children. Forgive me for asking this. When you think about what you did, and you think about some of the costs that you paid. . . .

[Margot interrupted.]

Money?

Q. No. The estrangement with your daughter. The fact that your fiancé was beaten to death. Do you think of that now?

I think of it very often, but I cannot help it. I believe that things are predestined. That's the way it had to come. You can't help it. It wouldn't have helped Margaret. The people she loved died. They were killed. Things happened. A child is impressionable. You haven't seen it. But there's a lot of hatred right now here, too. Somebody once asked me, "Do you think it could happen somewhere else?"

"Anywhere," I said. "Anywhere. Anywhere in the world."

• • •

Q. How do you view human nature?
I like people. Listen. To me it's like this: either you like a person or you don't. If you like him, you do what you can. If you don't, you don't. The hell with them. You don't have to kill them. You can still say, "I don't like them."

Q. But you said on the phone to me that just because you don't like somebody doesn't mean you can't help them.
That's right.

Q. Would you help people you don't like?
Absolutely. But I have very few people I don't like. I don't think there is anybody.

Q. But you also felt that the Gestapo man, the one who begged you, you felt he deserved what he got.
I didn't like him. I hated him. But he was a Gestapo man and did a lot of harm to people. I suffered a lot myself. I was engaged to be married again and they took that man away and they beat him to death. He was supposed to tell what I was doing because I was under suspicion. But he didn't tell and he was beaten to death in a concentration camp. There were all sorts of people in concentration camps. It didn't just go against Jews alone.

Q. Do you think people are basically good or basically bad?
Well, you cannot say. What's good or bad, but thinking makes it so? You think of somebody. As I said, if I like them, that's good. If I don't like them . . . [Margot shrugged.] But I don't know if they're good or bad. That has nothing to do with it. Because I'm not judging anybody.

Q. Do you think people tend to think about other people very often though? Or do they tend to be more self-centered?
I don't think they think much about people, especially if they are very greedy. In the United States people are greedy. Very, very greedy. Money, money, money. What the hell is money? What can you do?

Q. I've heard you say different things about the German character, or the Dutch or the Russian character. Do you think that culture shapes how people are?

Oh, absolutely. The Dutch have something which no other nation has. I know. The Dutch are [the most] bullheaded. You wouldn't believe it! If they don't want to do anything, they don't want to do it and that's it. You cannot persuade a Dutchman to do otherwise. When a Dutchman says no, you can't persuade him. They are the most bullheaded nation in the world.

I'm stubborn, too. You know, when I was young, I was in Russia. During my studies, I had to be everywhere, so to speak. I was in all these countries. I find out that the most sentimental nations, like the Germans and the Russians, are the most ugly ones. The ones that hurt most, they are romantic. Especially the Russians. Look at what Stalin did. He killed all these people. Look at the pogroms in Russia. Now it's a little bit better, but can you trust them? This is the trouble. You don't know.

The Germans are very sentimental, too. Very sentimental, very romantic. And right away, you don't know. Now look, I'll tell you something. I know France very well. When you come to Paris, you feel some sensuality in the air, some erotic, some "Je ne sais quoi." But, wonderful! When you come to Germany, you feel hatred. My daughter said the other day that the Nazis won. She said she called her middle son, the banker, and said, "It seems the Nazis are coming back." They're not coming back; they never left. And that's the truth. They never left.

You know, I was thrown out of a German store, on Lankersheim Boulevard [in Los Angeles]. I came in one day—this was years ago—and there was a typical German there. He was very nasty. I said, "You cotton-picking damn Nazi you!" And he threw me out of the store.

Q. But you yourself are German. You were born German.

Yes, but that has nothing to do with it. You know there are lots of nice Germans who were appalled [by Hitler]. For instance the father of our governess. And my daughter Evelyn's husband was a German doctor. He's dead now, may he rest in peace. He was wonderful. His brother was in concentration camp because he didn't agree [with Hitler]. But the government was telling them what to do.

• • •

Q. I'm trying to understand how you view the world. You say you're an extrovert. Do you see yourself with strong ties to people in the world? Do you believe people are essentially alone? Do you believe we're born into certain groups?

No, I think they herd together. My dog doesn't want to be alone either. I think people like to be together. This guy [my husband] said he was lonely. His wife died and he had nobody. So he was grabbing at me.

Q. But you don't see yourself as alone at all?

No. I was never lonely in my life. I do all sorts of things.

Q. Do you think people have a social responsibility to help other people?

I don't think responsibility, but it's nice to be able to help other people. You know, I wasn't always so poor as I am now. My father was so very wealthy, I am so used to it I couldn't care less about money. I threw it out and helped everybody. I do still help if I can.

Q. Did you give away a lot of money from your father?

Yes. Well, my father lost it all when Hitler took it. He was in Germany and he still had enough to live on but not like he used to. That was a different thing.

Q. How many people did you actually help save?

Oh, you wouldn't count. What am I supposed to say? "You! You're number fifty"? No, it's impossible. I don't know [how many people I saved]. You help whoever you can! When you are asked, you do something. We helped people. Mostly my father helped with all the phony papers. We'd mostly try to get people papers from friendly countries. From Switzerland mostly. So the people we helped were not from Switzerland, we just gave them the papers from Switzerland.

Q. Did you actually physically get people out of the country?

Yes. I told you I got this little charm bracelet sent me from a Jewish man whose family I saved. It has a date on it. They sent it to me from Switzerland. Then later, when I came here [to the United States], everything I had was stolen when I arrived in New York.

Q. You came here in 1951?

December 1951. I stayed with an uncle when I came. He didn't know anything about what I did either. But he came to the boat. He said, "Welcome to the United States. Now forget the past and start a new life."

I didn't forget. I just shoved it away. I started a new life. The next thing I know, I was robbed of everything I had. Isn't that something?

I was in New York, and the police tried to get my stuff back but they couldn't. I got from one of the policemen his car to make a car exam, to have a driver's license from New York. Then I came out here. I have some cousins here who are very wealthy. But they don't want to know me. They never did want to know me. They were afraid I'd want something. I didn't want anything. You may know them. Have you ever heard of L_____ of California? They have young girls' dresses and stuff. These are my cousins. My father's brother's kids. Real cousins. But they wouldn't know me. None of them. They were afraid.

I tell you what happened. Things were so hard, I cried. My youngest daughter said, "Let's go back." My ex-husband has an uncle in San Francisco who was much against the ex because he knew what was going on [with the maid]. He was for me. He was actually the head of the family. He was Jewish. His name was Izzy. We met because we saved him, too. I saved his little girl. Full of lice and fleas, she was, like you wouldn't believe. Well, during the war, Izzy went to his nephew [my ex] to ask him to save Izzy's kids. And the ex didn't save them. So Izzy's boy was killed. Then Izzy came to me for help. He wrote to me.

My father said, "Do you know that handwriting? Is that Uncle Izzy?"

"Yeah, looks like his."

Father said, "He needs money." Immediately, my father gave money. I went there and I helped Izzy. I took Izzy's kids, who were hidden somewhere and were full of lice and fleas. I took the girl home and I saved her. So later when we came to the U.S., we went to San Francisco. When I was so unhappy, we talked to Izzy. I told him, "I go back to Holland. I can't stand it here."

Izzy said, "Why?" I told him. I had brought everything I had. My jewels and everything, all stolen.

Izzy said, "You show them. You stay and you show them." And I stayed. I got a job at the Bank of America as a teller. I didn't even know what a dime was. They made a test. I passed it and I got a job. But you couldn't sit in a bank job at that time. You had to stand up. Oh, my feet hurt me. You wouldn't believe it. It was awful. Then we got an apartment. Of course we had no furniture. We had nothing.

My parents were still living during this time but my parents were in Holland. That's why I wanted to go back. Then I got a job in a Chinese firm and I wanted to let my daughter go back. Because the school called and said, "Your daughter is sitting in school looking out of the window."

I said, "I would [look out the window] too if I don't understand a word and they confuse me," because this is so. I went to the attorney for the exporter I worked for to get a passport for my daughter to come back into the old country. I said, "Evelyn should go back to school in Holland. Besides the schools are much better there."

He said, "Why?"

"She doesn't understand English."

He said, "Leave her here." He convinced me to leave her here, but to take her to a Catholic school. So I took her to a Catholic school. We didn't have the money for the school. I asked my cousin, the oldest one who is dead, this one who wouldn't have given me anything. But I asked him could he loan me a hundred dollars till next week, Friday. I got it back to him right on the dot. It was good she went to the Catholic school here. But it was pretty hard for me. Everything was stolen. I worked like a dog. Well, I haven't actually seen a dog work.

Q. How would you view yourself? How would you describe yourself? You said you were an extrovert. How else would you describe yourself?

I never would describe myself. I have my good sides and my disagreeable sides. I can be a bitch and I can be nice.

Q. When I go home tonight, my husband will ask, "What was this woman like?" What should I say to him?

Well, what would you say? Nothing, nothing special. Just a person. Just an ordinary person.

Q. You don't see yourself as anything special?

No, I'm nothing special.

Q. You don't think you did anything extraordinary?

No. Definitely not.

Q. How can you say that?

Because I *didn't* do anything extraordinary. Lots of people help others. No, I certainly didn't. No, absolutely not. I didn't do that much. If I had had the money my father had I probably would have done more. But he did so much. So whatever I had, I went to my father and he did everything. He helped everybody. He was fabulous. He had good ideas too, as you saw with his handling of the letter we sent to Switzerland.

Q. You seem to be somebody who's willing to take on a lot of responsibilities.

I'm wondering why I'm still alive. That's one thing: I'm not afraid.

Q. You're not afraid?

No, never. I was one time a little bit afraid in prison. They had these coffee mugs out of aluminum. I held it against the hole that the Germans always looked in to spy on us. I said, "If one German comes back I'll stick out my tongue and make an ugly face at him." And by golly, I took that mug down and made that face, and he was standing right there, looking. That set my heart going. But otherwise. . . . I tell you something. I am not afraid because I think if I die, I die. I'm afraid of being hurt, of having pain. I don't like to have pain if I can avoid it, or if that can be avoided for me. I don't want to be sick and linger around. But otherwise, I don't need anything. We live very modestly. We don't go out much. Maybe tonight we go out, because a friend, seventy-five years old, his girlfriend will call and say, "Let's go over to the Sizzler," you know, a family restaurant. Big deal. That's about it.

Q. You seem very self-confident. It seems as if you take the initiative.
I'm very self-confident. I have no inferiority complex whatsoever. I'm very confident.

Q. Would you say you're a leader or a follower?
Leader, yes. I can be a leader easily.

Q. An insider or a loner?
I'm not a loner, not at all. I like to lead and I like to tell people what to do; whether they do it or not is another thing. [Margot shrugged and laughed.] I make a lot of mistakes, a lot of them. But then I say, "That's tough! There's nothing I can do." I'm dumb. I make mistakes. I'm going to be eighty next month; how do you like them apples? Old! I think people live too long. I don't want to live so long. My mother had her seventy-ninth birthday and a few weeks later she died. My father was seventy-nine and he died. I think they were married fifty-three or fifty-four years, just a week short. But I don't want to live so long. I tell him [my husband] I've never been so long with one man.

•   •   •

I have to tell you this. This is something funny. This is not serious. Just something I did when I was young and good smelling. When I was in England, I went to the library and got the names and addresses of famous people. I want some signatures. I didn't think it was valuable or anything. It's just for the fun of it. I told my cousin I'm going to write to them and she said, "I'll tell you one thing. You will never get Bernard Shaw."

I said, "You want to bet? So I wrote to Bernard Shaw. And I got this letter back. It says here,

Dear Miss Scharff, Many thanks for your letter which I greatly appreciate. Those few kind words of yours greatly touched me. Today, I'm an old man and cruel criticisms are so often launched against me. Indeed, I have much to bear. Then it is the innocent words and praise springing spontaneously from the lips of a young girl. (I feel, I *know* that you are young.) It is like balm that soothes the savage beast. My child, it is with the utmost delight that I render you my paltry services of sending you my autograph. Dare I do more? May I perhaps meet the authoress of the charming epistle? There is a restaurant I know, a quiet select spot, the Piccadilly Circus, where we could perhaps have a cozy chat together. Only one

word from you, and my Rolls Royce awaits you. With mingled feelings of hope, fear and despondency, I await your reply. George Bernard Shaw.

Now, when I read that I just roared. I screamed, "That Phyllis! She did
that to me." Right away, I knew that was my cousin Phyllis.

And you know what happened? We *did* write to Bernard Shaw. Everybody said you will never get anything from Bernard Shaw. So I wrote,
"Dear Mr. Shaw, Enclosed please find a schilling. We would like one
word from you." And this letter came, return mail, addressed to me. It
said, "Thanks." Just one word. No signature. Isn't that funny?

I think he wanted to flatter me. I learned later not to be flattered, not
to be taken in by people making you feel important. This Gestapo guy,
he wanted to try this, 'cause he wanted me to tell something and I made
that mistake, you know, when I said, "I don't know but if I knew I
wouldn't tell you." That was my mistake. And I thought of that French
fable. The one where the fox said to the raven, "Give me the cheese."
The fox got the cheese 'cause the fox said to the raven, "You sing so
wonderfully. Why don't you sing a song to me?" The raven opened his
mouth to sing and the cheese fell out! Well, I thought of that, and I said
to myself, "Margot, be careful. Be careful." I talk to myself, see? I didn't
say a word out loud. But I thought of this story which I learned when I
was a kid.

*Q. It's funny isn't it how in times of great stress or crisis, something from
your childhood will come back.*

Oh, yeah, it always comes. Your whole childhood comes back when you
don't behave or do behave and so forth.

*Q. The activities that you did during the war. Did they change you as a
person? Did they affect you?*

No. The only thing is, I suffer still that that man [Alfred] was killed. But
I don't hate anybody for it. That Gestapo commander, you know, if he
had said, "I'm a Nazi. I believe in it." If he had been more manly, it
wouldn't have affected me. But hanging there, hugging onto my legs and
saying, "I only did what I was told to do." The little schlepp! The hell
with him! I said, "Kill him." And they did. They knew that I had something to say and they thought that guy was my friend long enough. No,
no deal. He wasn't worth it.

*Q. You said you believe in fate. In predestination. Do you think man can
control his fate?*

No, you cannot control it because when you control it, that's your fate,
that you should control it. It is your fate that you do it like this. For

instance, if I want to push you, it's my fate that I push you. You know what I mean?

Q. Are you a religious person?

Yes, very. But I don't run to churches, no. I don't run to churches. I don't do it because I think you can pray at home. One religious lady said to me, "I'm not afraid about my son and me because we go to God." I said, "Why? Did you call up and get a special seat up there?" I never forget that! She was mad! The next week she called up and she apologized. I think it's not necessary to go to church. On Sundays these people all say, "I go to church. I want to see what Mrs. Myers wears. Oh, yes, she wears today the lilac one." You know, it's so dumb. I don't go there. Of course, if something happens, I'm very religious. I believe in God. Absolutely.

Q. When you say you believe in God, is that the same God for Jews as for Christians?

[Margot nodded yes.]

Q. It doesn't matter to you?

It doesn't matter to me. There's only one God. Of course, I'm not a Buddhist. I'm not a Zen Buddhist. You know, when I was in Italy I studied religion and all of them I knew about, except the Mormons. I heard about that one only after I came here. During the war, I worked together with a Catholic priest. Every Monday, the priest was supposed to come for dinner. One Monday, he didn't show up. We found out he was in a concentration camp. The Germans spit on him. They said, "You kneel in front of us." And he didn't. Oh, it was a terrible thing. We got him out. Finally.

Q. Do you have any particular ethical credo that has guided your life? Any system of ethical beliefs?

No. You don't steal. You don't hurt anybody. You don't lie. Well, I lie sometimes. When I was in the Resistance I lied a lot. When I was in Prague and I had to translate, you should have heard what I told them! I didn't believe it myself.

Q. How did you develop your ethical beliefs?

[Margot shrugged.] That was me. I don't know. You know, when you travel around you see people from all countries, from all walks of life.

Q. How did your rescue activities make you feel about yourself?

Not at all.

Q. They didn't affect you?

Nothing special, no. No feeling.

Q. Were you surprised that you were able to do the things you did?

No. Because since I have seen so many people, in so many countries, I knew quite a bit of life. I think people are basically the same all over the world.

Q. Was it important to you that you were the one who saved the people?

No. They just had to be saved. I wish I could have done more. I haven't done much.

Q. Let me ask you a question about religion. You mentioned you believe in God. Do you think there's a heaven, an afterlife?

No. My daughter once came home from school. She was a little afraid. She said, "Mommy, I think heaven and hell are right here on earth." And I think she's right. I think that's so. Why are some people in such terrible shape and some have it so good? I think it's right here. But I could be made to believe in that nirvana, what the Buddhists believe in, that you come back maybe as something else. Often I think, why do some people like ducks. And some are so crazy about birds. Maybe they were birds in their former life. Heaven knows.

Q. Do you think it might be?

If we would just know.

Q. So you'd like to think that there may be a reincarnation, but you're not sure.

I'm not sure. I don't know.

Q. Let me ask you what really is the hardest question for me, the hardest to understand. What do you think it was that made you able or willing to risk your life, when so many other people did not?

Well, I think it's just me. I would risk it now. I wouldn't care. I don't care whether I die or not. I never cared, and especially when my man was killed. There's a guy came out, I think he was Protestant. He had a thing for cookies and he brought a cookie jar to me. He told me he saw him [Alfred] die, being beaten. And that night, when that happened—and that is not a lie—I dreamt he was lying on the floor. His soul or something went out of him, and he embraced me with nothing that you could. . . . [Margot stopped and sat quietly, as if thinking.] It was as if he had taken me along. Now there is not a day in my life that he is not with me. It's like the man is with me, because I learned an awful lot through him. I learned a lot of life through this man. He was good to everybody. I said, "Don't trust these people," in the beginning when we were together. And he said, "If you don't trust anybody, you shouldn't live." He trusted everybody and that woman betrayed us. It was a woman who betrayed us. Some people, you have a feeling about. I have a tremendous feeling, my daughter has even a better feeling, that somebody is—I don't want to say good—but somebody is agreeable. Somebody is false. Somebody wants bad with you. Somebody wants good with you. I have a tremendous feeling for some things. It's like intuition. Yes, intuition. I don't know the characters of people but it's just a feeling. But you know, I met so many people. Everybody wants to go to Germany. It's okay with me. I wouldn't go and live in Germany for all the tea in China.

Sure, I've gone back [to visit]. I liked my son-in-law. He was too young to know anything. He was a young guy. The war is over in 1946 and he was a ten-year-old kid. What does he know? But his family were wonderful. The father, too. The father was a very well-known theologian and philosopher named Herman Raschke. He was a very wonderful guy.

Q. Can you tell me something more about your family background? You said your father was very wealthy. What about your mother? What was she like?

My mother. She was like a mother should be, but she wasn't so understanding, like my father. My mother once in a while had a loose hand. My father never touched me. With my father, everything was good. But she was a good woman and I took her along. I showed her this and showed her that. I took her to Palm Springs. I took her to Las Vegas. I showed her everything.

Q. It doesn't sound like you were as close to her as to your father.

I was close to her like a kid is to a mother. But I want to tell you something. My mother once said to me, "I've seen the whole world. But I've never seen San Francisco." I had just taken her to all these other places and I said to myself, "Oh, God." It cost me so much money. I had to take care of the kids. And I was robbed, don't forget. I had to start from nothing. Now my mother wants this? Oh, forget it. And I didn't show her San Francisco. To this day today, I'm sorry that I didn't take her to San Francisco. I should have. I did everything I could for my mother. I did it mostly also for my father. Because I took a trip with my father every year.

Q. Did you have siblings?

I'm an only child. But my father had people he took care of and he had them study and had them learn everything.

Q. When you were growing up, did you move around a lot?

Move? What do you mean, move? In the house?

Q. Live in more than one place?

No, only when I was in school. I was in school in Geneva. I went to school in London and school in Italy and to school in Spain.

Q. Where did you consider home?

I didn't consider anything home. Later I considered Holland home, because I was so well-known. I was kind of celebrated there, you know. You like to be a little celebrated. It gives you a lift.

Q. Was there any particularly traumatic or disabling event when you were young?

No. My uncle died when I was a kid. I liked my uncle very much. But I didn't lose anybody I was particularly close to when I was young. Only the uncle.

Q. When you were growing up, were you conscious of the fact that your father was an important and powerful man?

Yes, I think so. Because wherever I went, they'd say, "Oh, are you related to Hans Scharff?"

"Yes," I said. "That's my father." And people bent over to help you. You don't have to make ovations to people. One is just like the other.

Q. Was that important to you in your later rescue activities?

No. It was not important. My father always gave me money, as much as I wanted. I started a bank account. I said to my friend, "I'll tell you what. I'm going to England now. I'll give you power of attorney so if you want some money or if I want money, go and get it and hand it to me." I didn't know you could write to the bank. Well, I wrote to her that I would like to have a little money. And I didn't get an answer. When I got home, I heard that she took all the money from my account—all of it— and went away with a married man to Italy. That taught me another lesson. See, you learn. And yet I don't ever learn. You make the same mistakes all the time.

Q. Did you consider your rescue activities political?

No. Here I'm quite active in politics because it's interesting. When I was finished studying [diplomacy] I said, that's it for me. No more politics. That's it. Then when I came here I was interested in everything, because people were so interesting. So I did it and I thought, "Well, that's something, to see what's going on."

Q. So even though you were part of the organized political resistance, you were doing it more out of humanitarian reasons?

It wasn't so organized. I was just asked to help. That was it. You help in your own way.

Q. From the pictures on your walls of the Reagans and George Bush, you're obviously a Republican in this country.

Yes. But I'm not a Nazi.

Q. Were you aware of the situation for the Jews during the Hitler period? When did you become aware of what was happening to the Jews?

In Germany, long ago.

Q. Did you read Mein Kampf?

No. But there was a guy sitting behind me in college. He thought I was 100 percent Jewish. He was a Nazi, through and through. He wrote me a letter, a little note. "How come you have blue eyes?"

I wrote back, "Inherited." And that's true.

Q. Did you know about the Nazi program?

Yes. A friend of mine had to go to the Hague because they thought she was Jewish. She made something up. She said, "My mother had an affair with her dentist. So I'm not Jewish, because the dentist was gentile." She had the cleaning woman swear to it. The dentist was dead; he couldn't say otherwise. The mother was dead, too. The Germans didn't quite believe it so they had her come to the Hague. Now, if you have a nose here, longer than your earlobe, you're considered Jewish. That was how they did it. If the nose was longer than the earlobe. And also your legs. I have extremely long legs. But the Jews have shorter legs.

It is so dumb that you have to laugh about it. That was how they decided this girl was not Jewish. And they let her go. Her name was Gretl Heiss. I never forget her. We were scared stiff about her when she went.

Q. Can you remember the first time when you realized what was going on, how you felt?

That was in Germany, when I studied. Oh, there was a wife of the head of a bank, like the Bank of America. We had the kaffee klatsch in the afternoon. One day she said, "Well, people. Why don't we try Hitler? Maybe he can get us out of the mess."

I said, "Do you realize what's going on when Hitler comes? Do you see what's coming?"

"Oh, what can be worse?" they said. The Germans lost the first war and they wanted to be reinstated. This was the whole schmear. What can you do?

Q. Are you a member of any important group?
No. I was once asked to be a member of the Republican Women, but the hell with them.

Q. Do you have any groups that are really special to you?
No. It's not necessary.

Q. How about your role models? People that you emulate. People that you admired a great deal.
I only liked my father because he was smart. He helped everybody. I wish I were as smart as he is.

Q. You said he was very affectionate with you.
Not affectionate, no. He never hugged me or so. But he said if I have anything, I should come to him, and whatever I had, worries or so forth, I came.

Q. How did he treat you personally?
I made every year a trip with him.

Q. Just the two of you? Not with your mother?
Yes. Then one morning he said, "Look at all the people looking here. They think this old geezer has a nice young girl."
    I laughed.
    "Dad, I look exactly like you." I looked just like my father at the time, I was so similar to him. I said, "No such luck."

Q. He gave you a lot of attention though?
Yes. He did. Because when I had something I came to him.

Q. Did you feel you had unconditional love from him? Did you feel he loved you without any conditions or reservations?
Yeah, he loved me. He wanted a boy when I was born. Once I drove away on a motorcycle. When I came back he stood there and said, "Stop."
    "I can't."
    "Let it fall. And he took me in his arms and I let the damn thing fall. Also, I drove away in a car once when I was a little kid. My cousin was in the back showing where we go. The chauffeur said, "Stop," but I couldn't. I could drive but I didn't know how to stop. So he [my father] jumped up [on the running board] and said, "Take your feet away [from the pedals]!"

Q. You were driving the car?

Yes. He slapped on my legs, he was standing outside, at the time you had these things where you had the tire on the outside. Running boards. He slapped on my legs. My God. I still feel it. The sound!

Q. It sounds as if you had a very happy childhood. How old were you when you went off to boarding school?

The first time, I think I was fifteen. I went to Geneva. I was better off in Geneva because I understood the people better.

Q. Did you like the Swiss?

The Swiss? Well, in Geneva they have the French Swiss. They are different than the German Swiss. The Swiss were very much attached to the Germans. The Swiss had a love affair with the Germans and were inclined to the Nazi way. But the French Swiss, the ones in Geneva, no.

Q. Was there anybody else, other than your father, who was particularly important to you when you were growing up? Anyone who influenced you?

Oh, I had lots of friends.

Q. But it was mostly your father. [Margot nodded, yes.] How about the church?

No.

Q. Was there anything in common about the people you helped?

No. They were just people.

Q. You didn't know most of the people that you helped, then.

No. I know a lot of them now, the ones that stayed in my house. I now know a lot of the people whom I helped. When they said that the last German was out, since there was no bell 'cause there was no electricity, I yelled [upstairs to the hiding place], "Come on down, it's over!" I wanted to say it. But I lost my voice.

Q. You couldn't say it?

Now, every time I'm excited I lose my voice. It's psychological. I had broken my leg and had my leg in a cast. I sat there in my room. In Holland you have nothing but flowers. So they gave flowers. Everybody came to thank me, to shake my hand. The house was full of people.

Q. You started out, really before we even started the interview, talking about making conscious choices, and you said you didn't really think you [did that]. Was there really a conscious choice that you made?

I don't make a choice. It comes, and it's there.

Q. It just comes. Where does it come from?

I don't know. I don't think so much because I don't have that much to think with. That was what the professor said: "Take your first feeling and don't think." And I said, "I got nothing to think with."

Q. Do you think it comes from the basic—what I've heard other people say, and I'm asking. I don't want to put words in your mouth here—what I've heard other people say when I've asked them this is that they didn't think they could live with themselves if they'd done something other than that [help Jews]. Is that true for you?

It has nothing to do with it.

Q. It was just totally unconscious?

Yes. You don't think about these things. You can't think about these things. It happened so quickly.

Q. But it isn't really totally quickly. There's a tremendous amount of strategic planning that has to be done.

Well, I was young. I could do it. Today, I don't know. I'd have to try it. But I was thirty-two years old. That was pretty young.

Q. You didn't sit down and weigh the alternatives?

God, no. There was not time for these things. It's impossible.

Q. So it's totally spontaneous. It comes from your emotions.

It's pretty near impossible. You couldn't do that. You wouldn't understand what it means. Suppose somebody falls in the water, as I said before. You want to think, "Should I or should I not?" The guy would drown. You know, that's no way.

Q. Was empathy a part of it at all?

Meaning what?

Q. Feeling that this could be me?

No, never even thought of it.

Q. How about duty?

That could be me, yes. Because I'm often saying to him [my husband], it's a miracle that I'm still alive. I wonder that they didn't kill me.

Q. But you didn't think that at the time? [Margot shook her head.] No. How about feelings of duty? [Margot again shook her head.] No. Did you feel sorry for the people? Pity?

I don't know. I don't feel anything, to be honest.

Q. How about the repercussions of your actions? Did you think about what might happen because you were doing this?

You don't think about it. No way.

Q. You didn't worry about possible consequences for you, for your family?

No. No way.

Q. Did you have any expectations about how you thought people would respond to you? You're shaking your head no. No anticipation about what your father might have thought?

No. My father helped wherever he could. No way. No.

Q. Now, many people would say that what you did was an extraordinarily good deed and that you should be rewarded.

That's what they say now. The hell with it. I don't want any reward.

Q. Were you honored by Yad Vashem? [Margot nodded.]

Yeah. But I didn't even know it until I got a letter from Professor Oliner (a scholar interviewing rescuers), who said that he heard about me and he would like to interview me or would send somebody to come interview me.[8] I didn't even know what he wanted. So I wrote back, "Dear sir, I don't even know you. What is it all about?"

Q. So you didn't even know about the Yad Vashem Medal?

No. I wrote back to Oliner. Because I'm unlisted, I have my phone number on my letter paper. He called immediately. He said he was in Jerusalem and he heard about me. I said, "You did? What a surprise!" I didn't know.

Q. Now, you said you didn't talk about this for a long time.

No. I didn't talk at all except when he [Oliner] came into the picture.

Q. So this has been about three or four years ago [mid-1980s]?

Yes. I never told anybody.

Q. So you went for almost forty years without talking about it [the war]?

Never even gave it a thought to tell anybody.

Q. Did you talk about it with your husband?

No! He [Ted] didn't know anything. He said, "What is that all about?" Then when I was asked to go to Washington, D.C., for the opening of the Holocaust museum, he said he'd come along.[9] But he paid his own way. I was invited.

Q. Forty years without talking about this at all. Why was that?

Never. I didn't think anybody was interested. Besides, I wanted to write something down once. When I started, a lady said, "Oh, that's so long ago. Nobody's interested." So I forgot it again.

Q. Has it been painful for you to talk about it? To drag up memories?

Yes. After a while I was a little bit—I am very much inclined to depression. I'm very often depressed. But that has nothing to do with this. It's my nature. I'm depressed and I thought, "Oh, God, so many friends died." Now many friends die because they're so old. I wrote a Christmas card to that lady whose nose was operated on in my house. Her son wrote back that the mother died. I don't think he even knew who I was, because Lawson wasn't my name then. Scharff was my maiden name. I took it back after I divorced my husband.

Q. That's amazing, that you went for that long without talking about it. But a lot of people I've spoken with said the same thing. They didn't want to think about it.

We don't want to talk about it. There's nothing to say.

Q. If you knew now exactly what was entailed in rescuing Jews, would you do it again?

Yes, at once.

Q. Do you think there was ever any guilt involved?

No, I don't think I did so much anyway. And those lousy krauts, they can fly a kite for all I care.

Q. It sounds as if you really just didn't care what people thought about what you did.

No. The Dutch were helpful. And the krauts, the hell with them! They thought anyway they were the master race. They were the top. They were this and they were that. The hell with them!

Q. Was there ever a critical moment in your life when you were alone, when you felt somebody needed to help you?

No. When I was alone, I was alone. Yeah, I had some tough times here, I must confess. Very tough. And those lovely, lovely cousins I had. . . . [Margot shrugged.] They didn't do a thing for me. They wouldn't do anything.

Q. Do you ever talk to them now?

No. He calls me once in a while; we have a cousin in England, he tells me I should call my cousin in England, and he insists and he is so old.

Q. What would you like to talk about that we haven't already talked about?

I could tell you for days—not hours, but for days—the things that happened. I wrote once a story. I don't want to give it out. I put a third name on it, not mine, though it's about all the things I did. I remember going over the roofs with little kids to save them. We walked across the roofs of houses. I had them on my arm, little babies. Then I had a German passport, a ten-year German passport. I got it from the Dutch government. They stole the passport and they made sure the picture was in it with your thumb and handprints. They made everything you wanted. They stole the original with nothing in it, you know. Of course there was a curfew, and I was always on the street. But I had papers that meant something! A ten-year passport meant that you are a special person. Oh, nobody had such a fabulous passport.

I tell you something. I wrote about some thing once, when I was not able to write English well. I wanted to write a story, mostly about Alfred. For him. I'll get the book out. I have only one book and I haven't made a copy. I called the girl Isabelle. That's me. But that's not me. Me is . . . I didn't put my name on it. And I thought, "What am I going to do?" Isabelle is my grandmother, who was born in Missouri. When I wrote it, I used a nom de plume. And that's Suzanne de Palma.

[Margot brought me her book and placed it in my hands.]

This is in the Library of Congress. Even so, I have not given it to anybody. But you see here? If you want part of it, you're welcome to it. Except I don't know how to make copies of it because it's in a binding. That's the way I think. . . . I'd like you to see it but I can't give it away. Maybe I'll find something and I can have it copied for you. Just wait a little bit, then you can use it. Because it's in the Library of Congress but if I gave you permission, it's all right. I have to take my dog out for a little walk now. You look at the book.

[The introduction to Margot's book reads as follows:]

"It has been said many times that one might be able to relive one's past. I don't believe this. However, if it were at all possible, I hear people say that they would return to Mother Earth as the very same person they are now. But they would change most of the events and occurrences that happened in their lives. They swore that they would not repeat the mistakes they had made but would instead alter the flow of happenings and thus reconstruct the course of history. Impossible. I believe in all the wonderful and tragic moments and would never change one instant in my life, even if I could. The trials, errors, heartaches, delights, and ecstasies are part of life itself. The deep love of two beings melted into one is the ultimate fulfillment. The hardships that teach understanding form the character within one's self. The injustices against the innocent are the experience and knowledge of grim reality. Above all, there is the ability to help and alleviate the pain of fellow human beings. This I believe is the ultimate goal of our short existence on this earth."

[The rest of the book tells of Albert and Isabelle meeting, falling in love, growing closer, and, eventually, of Albert's being beaten to death by the Gestapo when he voluntarily goes to them to try to get Isabelle released from prison. The end of the book reads:]

"All at once, she felt a hand on her shoulder. She looked up but saw no one. Yet she could feel her beloved Alfred beside her saying, as once he did so long ago, 'Do not stand on my grave and weep. I am not there. I do not sleep. I am a thousand winds that blow. I am the diamond in the snow. I am the sunlight on ripened grain. I am the gentle Autumn's rain. When you awaken in the morning's hush, I am the swift uplifting rush of quiet birds in circled flight. I am the soft stars that shine at night. Do not stand at my grave and cry. I am not there. I did not die.'"

[Margot came back from her walk and began casual conversation but quickly realized I had been crying.]

Yes, darling, it was really something.

Q. But you're so sensitive. You're such a sensitive person and you went through all these things. I don't. . . . [At this point, I broke down and Margot hugged me, giving comfort to me when I should have been able to give her comfort.]

You, too. You're my sister. We are related somehow. Who knows? Something must have happened to us. I don't know how other people think and how the others feel. Here, let me read you something. Wait a minute. Here it is. "If I cannot change things. . . ." That's what Alfred always said to me, "If I cannot change things, take them as they are and be satisfied." He used to say it. Somebody else said, "I walked a mile with laughter, she chattered all the way, but I was none the wiser for all she had to say. I walked a mile with sorrow and not a word spoke she. But, oh, the things I learned when sorrow was with me." See? I carried the grief together and the burden that life was. Alfred and Isabelle—that's me. We're part of each other.

I tell you how it was. The world was on fire. Honey, we were sitting there. . . . We heard the fighting going on. We heard the cannons there. We were sitting together, in front of a fireplace. No light on. No nothing. It was in the dark. We had cabbage lights. How I wish I could transmit into mankind the peace that reigned within us then.

So you see, I would do the same thing again. They are the Nazis. We are the Jews. In memory of Alfred. That's why I wrote that book. I felt better after I had written it. For Alfred, whose understanding and thoughtfulness taught me the wisdom and profoundness of life. I was already thirty-two years old and I didn't know a damn thing. And in 1943, the Germans killed him. In January 1943, he was killed. I remember that like yesterday.

Years later, I went to the Hertogenbosch, to the concentration camp in the Netherlands where they killed Alfred.[10] And I showed the camp to him [Ted, my husband]. He is a Swede. He's a little coldish; but I don't think he's cold really. I think he can't show it. I don't think he can show anything. I have given him this book to read. I don't think he really read it, to be honest. I mean, you read sometimes or you hear some things, and some you don't hear.

Q. It's quite hard.

Well, that's true you know, honey. It's absolutely true. This is how it goes in life. And there isn't a day, not a day, that he [Alfred] is not with me. And that's why I think. . . . I'll give you the picture [of him]. That was him. And if you turn it around, that was the Hertogenbosch, in the concentration camp where they killed him. They beat him to death. I have his little picture with me all the time.

Q. What was Alfred's last name?

Slokovsky. He was from Eastern Germany.

Q. Oh. He was German also. How did you meet him?

A friend of mine said, "Come over and we'll play a little cards. We'll play bridge." And he came, very late. It was curfew time.

I said, "Well, let's try to get a vehicle to go home." You know, the Germans took your car. They took everything. So we got a taxi chauffeur. The driver took me home but said, "Sir, I can't go further. I'll be shot."

So I said to Alfred, "If you want to stay on my couch, it's fine with me." So I made the couch up and he stayed until the next morning. At 7:00, he went home. Then he sent me some roses to thank me for the night. That was it. That's how it went.

• • •

Margot died in July 2002.

Otto

The hand of compassion was faster than the calculus of reason.

At the end of the war Otto (pictured on the left) was interned in a camp for refusing to divorce his Jewish wife. Ironically, this arrest may have saved Otto's life since his incarceration for so-called crimes against the race closed other Gestapo investigations into activities that carried the death penalty.

I'M BORN ON THIRTIETH OF DECEMBER 1907, in Prague, Czechoslovakia, as a German. You may know that at that time, nearly four million Germans lived in Czechoslovakia. Our family was not Sudeten German. The Sudeten Germans lived near the border, in the mountainous area of Sudeten, as these mountains are called. They were in Czechoslovakia since seven hundred years. They were not Teutonic. But my family came for the same reasons. We were called into Czechoslovakia with the industrial revolution. Both my grandfathers came as engineers and became entrepreneurs. And so we were second-generation immigrants.

So. My grandfathers came around 1860. My mother's father died as an employer of fifteen hundred. He was a wealthy industrialist in Holubrov.[1]

Q. Did you speak German?

German *is* my native language. At that time, Czech was the language of the servants. The Germans dominated at that time and I learned to speak Czech perfectly only when I was nineteen years old. Before that, I spoke bastardized Czech. But I was German. I had not only a German passport, I had a German education. I was educated in Czechoslovakia in the German-speaking Charles University in Prague. My father was a professor in this German-speaking university.[2] He was a surgeon, an orthopedic surgeon. See, here, just for curiosity's sake, this is a hand-calligraphed business card of my father. My father was a physician so this picture is of medicine challenging death. It's nice. . . . These are all of my father's decorations, Austrian decorations. During the war, he was chief surgeon of the Fifth Army in the Austro-Hungarian Empire. And as such, he operated on two archdukes.

My father taught at the German University of Prague. We are descendants of the third oldest European university, founded in Prague in 1348. The first was Paris. The second Bologna. And the third, also the first in Eastern Europe, was Prague.

My mother was an heiress. Also a very great socialite, and we were mostly brought up by educators. I had a French governess. So my first language was German but I was taught French rather early. I was better at French. My third language was Czech. But I spoke so good Czech that I could pass for a Czech, or a native Czech. And I had to in many instances, later. But I consider my first language German. Absolutely.

I was the oldest in the family. I have two sisters. One is ten years younger than I. The older one is Imme and she is two years younger than I. Her husband died and she went to Germany. She was expelled from Prague but under special conditions. She was expelled as a German. After the war, the Czechs expelled all the Germans. According to the law, they could not expel people who had fought against Nazis and who were hurt by the Nazis. I qualified on both counts. But I had trouble staying

Before his death, Otto (pictured here in the 1980s) lived
in an ecumenical home in Marin County, California.

in Czechoslovakia. By coincidence . . . I had stayed in a concentration
camp with the commander of the later Prague uprising in May 1945.
There were terrible massacres of Germans going on. The Czechs had
learned very well from the Germans [how to kill]. They even killed pregnant women. Through this friend, I got my sister out minutes before the
ultimate happened, before she was killed. She was not harmed physically
but emotionally, it was terrible.

It was very ugly. And [because of this] my younger sister is in a mental
institution permanently. I was able to get her out but it was too much.
She was labile. She was very sensitive. I will see both of them in August
and September. They are both living in Germany now.

My sister Imme, the one who is also one of my rescuees, lives in Ham-

burg now. Her rescue has a funny aspect. The guy who was the commander of this partisan unit, he was a colonel and we had been in the
same concentration camp during the war, so we were good friends. When
the Czechs were killing women, I called him and he pulled her out. And
then I am not sure. At that time, I thought he was just being nice but
now I realize he may have been trying to recruit me to the Communist
Party. It was after the war, you know, and already the communist government had its people in the Ministry of the Interior. I think because of this
man that my old father got a truck which was so large it could pick up
furniture and he used it to leave the country voluntarily. My sisters left
the same way. But I saw two years ago, when I was there, the document
my sister got from the Czechs. Two qualifications were necessary to
leave. You had to prove that you fought the Nazis and that you suffered
by them. My sister could not show any of these qualifications. But in this
space on this paper, where the reason for this extraordinary waiver was
given to my sister, he wrote, "what her brother did during the Resistance." So it was a case of my acts saving her later.

But this jumps ahead.

Oh, my childhood was like a fairy tale! My grandfather had a fantastic
house in the neighborhood of Prague. A fantastic house! It was a large
family and the family was always here, reunited during summer vacations.
It was a very beautiful childhood. I was very close to my parents. Very
close. I was never beaten, although it was pretty common at that time.
My father gave me just one spanking. Then he was so sorry that he
bought a big stuffed brown bear and brought it to me. So, I had a happy
childhood and went to the German-speaking university, where I majored
in mechanical engineering. I graduated with a master's degree in mechanical engineering. There I met a girl named Hannah Adler. She was,
by the way, a second cousin once removed of Alfred Adler, the psychologist. I fell in love with her. Since 1928, I loved her. But we couldn't get
married because at that time a man had to be able to feed his family
before he was allowed to marry. So we had a long, long engagement. She
was my fiancée for a long time. Then the Nazis took over in Germany in
1934, the year we both graduated. I'm in mechanical engineering, and
she is an architect. And we followed [events] from the beginning.

For instance, in Czechoslovakia, it's a German university so the Jews
were subjected to German policies and were beaten up already in 1934.
We, of course, sided with the Jews, because my fiancée was Jewish. At
first, I didn't know. We didn't ask about such things. It was not relevant.
But it became *very* relevant and I married her only in 1938 on the second
of July at a time where the Jewish laws were already in force in Germany,
since September 1935.[3] Czechoslovakia was occupied from the fifteenth

of March 1939, by the Germans and they leapfrogged us. They jumped over us and established now that their laws are retroactive. My marriage should have never taken place. It was illegal somehow. And then there were other stipulations which hurt us very much. For instance, I was considered a criminal against the race. My children, if there were any or if any would be born, they would be recognized as full-blooded Jews. Legally, they were full-blooded Jews and should have been sent right away to Auschwitz.

So, I had a very good job and I had many Jewish friends, of course. We learned something from those who fled from Berlin: that if you want to do something for the Jews or just keep yourself [safe], you better have money. I was lucky that I could improve my position at that time so that I had some money.

At first nothing moved [happened]. But then, you must remember we never heard about atrocities in Poland until 1942. The Polish territories were already hermetically sealed off. We heard rumors. We heard also belatedly rumors from the BBC. But either we didn't believe it or we really thought the Jews were being resettled.

Kristallnacht, we heard about, of course. But Kristallnacht was in Germany. At that time we were still in free Czechoslovakia. We got very much touched [emotionally] by this Kristallnacht.[4] But nothing happened to *us* because it was in a foreign country. So, my wife and I were carrying on the living of our lives reasonably normally, even though I was considered a criminal against the race.

Now, one thing happened. In 1938, as far as I know, we were the only German/Jewish mixed marriage in Prague. Therefore, it was not convenient for them [the Germans] to deal with this. For every category, there were rules and regulations. To make new rules and regulations, for just one couple, well, apparently the civil servant in charge of that thought that's not worthwhile; that's too much bother. And he put our files somewhere. So we were never accosted as criminals against the race. The fact that we were the only ones is really what saved us for four years. There is no other explanation.

There was another so-called mixed-race couple. I knew them, of course. Everybody knew each other in these circumstances. But they had already American visas so that they didn't intend to stay in Prague. That was the difference. We thought of leaving, too. Oh, yes. I had even a very generous offer from the company where I worked as a diesel engine designer. The director of the Skoda Works offered to send me and my wife to Calcutta as a representative. That would have solved the problem. But my wife had an only sister. She was hidden then in Amsterdam, in the same street as Anne Frank, actually. She survived there. So she was al-

ready in Amsterdam and my wife's parents would have had to stay alone
in Prague. My wife didn't want to leave her parents alone in this situation. That was the reason why we stayed.

Eventually Hannah's parents were sent to Lodz, Poland.

• • •

I had already been involved in rescue activities [of Jews] before I was
approached by the Austrian/British Resistance. Oh, yes. I had done
many things. This is interesting. We had two disappointed Sudeten Germans. They both had Czech girlfriends. One was just a high official and
the other one had become a lawyer for the Gestapo and knew every
Gestapo man very well. His girlfriend persuaded him to do something
against the Nazis. Through them, we got connected. We cooperated very
closely. This man had a friend who was still in the Gestapo in a very high
rank. He was commander of the archives, of all the files. He worked with
us so that when somebody was arrested, we had only to ask him to help,
through intermediaries, of course. We had all the details about the particular cases, who might be endangered and so on. He worked for the
Resistance to the end of the war. Everybody recognized that he was a
Resistance fighter so he survived the end of the war without any problem.

I was denounced to the Gestapo for hiding Jewish property. My parents-in-law were shipped out to Lodz in 1941, in October. We were told
that they were just being resettled, and we wanted to believe that. We
had already a bad feeling about it. But nothing more than a feeling.

We had thought about trying to hide my parents-in-law or simply trying to get false papers for them and my wife during this time. Naturally,
this is something one wondered about. But my in-laws were in the second transport and we were unprepared. Then, after it happened, we
thought we were very clever just to be hiding their bits of furniture and
valuables. But our janitor denounced me. So I was summoned to the
Gestapo one morning. The official who questioned me had the accusatory paper held so that I could read the signature. So I told him, "Look.
I know who denounced me and he is a criminal." This was true.

"He is a criminal," I said, "and I would have expected the German
commander here to be more careful in selecting your collaborators."

I didn't know, but I had a feeling, that this criminal commissar hated
the Czechs more than he hated the Germans married to Czech Jews. Yes?

"The denouncer is a Czech?" he asked.

"Yes."

"*Schweinehund!*" he yelled, and he threw the accusatory paper into the
wastepaper basket. I didn't stop there but I told him, "As for me, sir, it is
a matter of honor to prove my innocence. I want you to come. Both of

us [will] go together to my apartment and you show me where I can hide five rooms of furniture in two rooms."

"Oh, no," he said, "That's not necessary."

Then I noticed something. I saw a cartridge, a hunting cartridge, a shotgun cartridge, on his desk and I said, "You are also a hunter?"

"Yes," he replied, "but I can't get any cartridges. This is spent. I can't get them anymore. They are all gone for the war product."

"Of course, you can't get them," I told him. "But I can get them. I know that the people on the black market wouldn't sell them to you, but they would sell them to me." I bought two hundred of them, gave them [to him] as a gift. Since that time, I had a friend. For instance, he let go several people when I asked. That is how it started.

Q. How does this actually happen? Do you just go to him and ask him to let people go?

He would take the file and examine it. If it was not too severe, he'd just say, "Oh, okay." Several people were let go that way.

With these three people I described, we had quite an organization. I knew at least which Gestapo was orthodox and dangerous or who had already some doubts about the Nazi regime and could be contacted and might help, either on his own or after bribery.[5] Sometimes these were people I knew as friends. But only in some cases. Mostly they were strangers. I think that about fifteen of the Jews I saved this way did survive the war.

So this is now in 1942. My wife was already at that time wearing the yellow star. But she was fortunately a blonde and [had] no so-called Jewish features. That helped a lot to survive. There were plenty of regulations about that [star]. It had to be on all sides stitched to the outer garment and Hannah developed a technique where these six corners were fastened with one string. When she broke the string, she could hide the star with one movement. According to necessity, she switched from wearing a star to wearing no star. She was very skilled at these things.

So it went on. I was several times denounced to the Gestapo. The reasons varied. For instance, my friend was a Jew and director of one of the largest coal importing companies in Czechoslovakia. He was there until 1940 as a director, with a very high salary. The Germans already had a law that every company that had Jewish participation above 25 percent had to get a Nazi controller. Now, if a German manager would have come into the company and looked into the books, he would have found that plenty of Jewish shares were taken over by a Czech company. It was very complicated how we hid it. But we made the company look officially 23 percent Jewish owned. Actually, much more was [owned by Jews]. I don't remember how much. Now, we were a company majority-owned by a Berlin company in Germany, and minority-owned by Czechs. Since we were a German company and had not a single German employee, a German manager had to be brought in. The Germans pressured them to get a German manager. So, I was German. My friend came up with an idea. What if I joined our company in the capacity of upper-level manager? I had a German passport, which I obtained quite illegally but it was a valid passport. It was very risky. But I did it because I felt one needed money for these rescue operations. I needed money and I got it.

I took this job as a managing person in the company for the money, which I could then use to bribe people to help get people out of Nazi control. Money was very important in those times. You will hear later that my German boss, the chairman of our board, when I was arrested, he paid my full salary to my Jewish wife. Officially, he could not do this. So he had to take it out of his own pocket. That's what ultimately saved her life, because I was already in a concentration camp. Money was very important for our own survival, because a Jew had rations which were good only for slow starvation. But we had a single full-ration card. Now, we had to buy nearly everything on the black market and you could do so only with plenty of money. Already since early 1943, I had to travel every month between Prague and Vienna on intelligence business. Part of the expenses I charged to the company, but the rest I had to finance myself.

So, this company was my full-time job. It was risky for me because we were a very well-known family in Prague amongst Germans there. Plenty of people must have seen me. I had even a company car, at a time where hardly anyone got permission to drive cars. But even though many people knew that I had married a Jew, nobody of these people denounced me. In the end we were denounced by our competitors.

Q. So it wasn't that you wanted the job to have the money to have a higher standard of living.

No, absolutely not. We were glad simply that we lived. It is important that you know that although I did get money in this way, the money was to be used to help rescue people, that I did not take this job for the money to use for myself. Remember that anything could be done with bribery. For instance, I saved my friend. There was a special category, called "a Jew important for the war economy," something like that. So I made him that. I had already a friendship going with a Nazi who was also disappointed [in the regime], although he was a high-ranking officer of the Sicherheitsdienst (SD) to which the Gestapo was subordinate. The SD was among others in charge of the "final solution" of the Jewish question. The money was needed for a host of illegal operations. He signed my applications for this Jew to stay automatically. I got him [this Jew] out from nine transports. It was nearly monthly that he was called into a transport and I had gotten him out [every time]. It lasted close to a year. But then, due to a completely different reason, he was taken into a transport. It was quite ironic. He wouldn't part with his luxurious apartment. Now, a Jew having this wonderful apartment, of course it caused notice. In such a case, they had a special system called Polizeiweisung. That means "by order of police." It means that when a Nazi came to Prague and knew there was a nice apartment occupied by a Jew, then the Gestapo grabbed the Jew and put him on a transport before anybody could intervene. That's what happened to my friend, Richard Lustig. I should have tried to talk him into leaving the apartment. But I was not thinking that much because I thought it was not that important. The system was new at that time. I should have known better. We're looking at this with hindsight now, of course. Many people to whom I've told this story have said they were struck by this man, who had been pulled off transports about nine times, yet he still didn't feel that he was in jeopardy. It seems strange to you now, I know, that he wasn't concerned that perhaps he was attracting attention by having this elegant apartment. Well, many Jews acted like the proverbial ostrich. Also, it was technically not so easy [to get an apartment] because all these empty apartments for the Germans were held in abeyance. So really, I don't know where he could have gotten an apartment. As Jews, it would have been hard [for him] to get another apartment.

Q. How did you handle the strains of all this?

That was rough. I had been in a concentration camp. It sounds odd, but if truth be told, being arrested by this [particular] department is what saved my life. We found out the complete story after the war. I had been denounced. My frequent trips between Vienna and Prague came to the attention of the authorities. They had already an agent, who still lives in Austria, tracing me. I should have been arrested, and probably would have been arrested for these spying activities. Only, I was lucky. I tell you how.

We lived in a beautiful apartment house and shared a floor with a Czech. He also had a Jewish wife. He actually ran an alcohol distillery. He made an excellent gin in his kitchen. But mainly, he was in the Resistance. You must know also something. There were various cases of treatment in the Gestapo. If you were arrested under the *Todesgesetz*—those cases where cooperation with the enemy was involved—in that case you were not only killed but you were killed in a special slow way [by hanging from a wire]. In addition, the kith and kin rule applied. That meant your whole family—children too—could be killed.

In July 1944, he [my neighbor] was arrested by the mixed-marriages department and so *they* questioned him. I have a three-page summary of his questioning. The first question was about me. They had the suspicion that we worked together in this Mafalda business.[6] But it was not the case. So when he was arrested and it was clear that they had a full idea of my activities, well I realized they arrested him because of a suspicion of me. The alcohol had nothing to do [with it]. They ignored that. But they put him in the category for mixed marriages, which is another category. When they finally arrested me, what do you think I was arrested for?

They arrested me just because I refused to divorce my wife! My wife was Jewish, remember. I had married her in 1938, as you know. Therefore the marriage was verboten; it was nonexistent! When they arrested me, they gave me the chance to reaffirm my German heritage. But I knew they were looking at me for my political actions. They suspected me of that. We had everything figured out. I should have known that such crimes like [making] alcohol are handled by a different department. The mixed-marriage violations were handled by the Prague Gestapo and political activities were handled by another, far more vicious group. So when they arrested me, on the fifteenth of October 1944, I was actually lucky. The fact that I was arrested under the prohibitions against mixed marriage meant that I got sent to a concentration camp, and I think that cooled them on the investigation of the other potential crimes, which were more serious. Since my marriage was considered a crime, and I was already in a concentration camp, they just dropped the political investigation. There was no need. I couldn't escape them. I was behind barbed wire.

But I had friends amongst these Gestapo men. You will see.

Actually, this is very funny. Technically, they didn't *arrest* me. I was *invited* to visit them. I got a postcard: "You have to be at transport on Saturday nine o'clock in the morning. You are allowed fifty kilos for a labor transport, fifty kilos of luggage." Here. This is the original document. [Otto showed me his summons.]

I got a letter from the President saying: "I am asking for your immediate statement whether you wish to continue the matrimony with your Jewish spouse, Hannah Springer, or whether you are willing to divorce her."

This letter is from the provincial president in Moravia. Moravia and Bohemia were considered Czech and Slovakia was at that time an independent country.

After I didn't reply, they stated that I am not to be regarded as a German national. Consequently, I have not acquired the German citizenship. This meant they didn't have to lock up a German. So I lost my protected status as a German. There is flowery language about being citizens of the protectorate and needing to have this confirmed by your local district office, but the gist of the language is that I lost my protected status as a German.

Q. You got this postcard in the mail to report. Did you think of just leaving, of going underground at that point?

With your family it's hard to do. Hannah was pregnant with the first daughter. We considered going into hiding. We somehow did get Hannah hidden, in her apartment. Then Hannah got this notice: "We conclude our duty to draw your attention to the fact that in spite of your pregnancy, you have so far not been excluded from the workers' transport. If you do not receive a decision to the contrary, you have to report tonight at 8:00 p.m." This is from the Jewish Central Center, sent to Hannah on the thirtieth of January 1945. But she didn't go. At that time, I was already in a camp and I couldn't help her. But she has an ingenious idea. She had a gynecologist of mixed parentage. He was half Jewish and a very good friend of ours and he helped.

• • •

So, we've talked of 1943, while I'm working as a top executive for this company and my wife is still wearing a star of David when she has to. This is all fine.

Q. What happens in 1943, when the Nazi policies toward the Jews changed?

I tell you. It got worse. We learned already about it, through an SS man who was from the same village as a friend of ours. He had to take part in a mass execution of Jews. He threw away his gun and started screaming. He broke down under this type of operation. He was beaten but was only delivered in a straight jacket to a mental institution. What he told us before he returned to the front was a really detailed report. It is something so terrible, that even when somebody tells you himself, you don't know whether to believe him. The BBC told us, and we didn't believe it. This was the first believable report, from someone who knew.

Q. Can you tell me what it's like? What do you feel at that point, what goes through your mind when you realize that what they say is true?

For me, it was very simple. There are two people: one is my wife, Hannah Springer, and the other is Adolf Hitler. Only one will survive. So simple. [Otto shrugged.] One has to work. That's why I went all out . . . I think I would have killed him [Hitler] myself. Yes. I would have killed him myself. All my political activities were the only way I could contribute to keeping my wife alive. That is it. It is that simple.

I not only kept her alive but she never spent a night in a camp. First, she had to be kept out of the German camps for Jews. Then, after the war, there were the Czech camps for Germans. Then the displaced persons camps for nearly everybody and a transit camp for embarkation to the U.S. Hannah was supposed to be in every one of them, but she did not go. This can be accomplished only with the help of Secret Services.

Q. But you *were in a concentration camp.*

I was in a camp.

Q. How did that happen that you were arrested but your wife was never arrested?

It was an action which fell upon us. All the mixed people, not only those with a wedding license dated after 1935 as we were, but all of them, all of us who got this order were transported into labor camps and the wives went on forced labor. But Hannah was lucky. She got assigned to forced labor in Prague and could stay at her home. So in the beginning, it was really like fun, well, maybe a lark, something different. But then it got worse because we were in camps which were already emptied of the Jews who have lived there. I knew that in the long run, we would follow the Jews. That is what I found out from the Wannsee conference, the one where they decided the fate of the Jews. The final solution. This conference also discussed the fate of the mixed populations, deciding that they would follow the Jews. They didn't tell *us* this, of course. Because they knew they would have much more trouble guarding people who know that they would be killed. So my wife was kept in Prague. I was kept in Camp Klettendorf in Silesia.[7] I was rounded up in October 1944. That was very late, thank God. So there were many things. I don't know whether I should go into all these details.

Q. Just tell me whatever you're comfortable with, Otto.

You know that conditions within the camps changed for prisoners in terms of the control and the treatment of prisoners from one camp to the other and also as time progressed. The Jews were of course under total control already since 1941. In the mixed Jewish group to which I belonged guard duty was less important. I knew—and they knew that I knew—that if I would escape they would simply grab my wife in Prague. In the beginning of 1945 the Arbeitsdienst was in charge of us. Everybody knew this was the least prestigious of the Nazi-party organizations. You could not expect from these people extra national socialist zeal at a time when the handwriting of defeat was already visible on the wall. I tell you one example.

I was once trapped by an Arbeitsdienst man with a small camera in my pocket. He carried a pistol and approached me and said, "What do you have in your left pocket?" I pulled out the camera. He took it, opened it and saw that it was one of the best cameras in existence at that time. He looked at it for a while, then closed it and turned around and walked off. He kept it for himself. I was saved by his greed. This happened in January 1945, five months before the end of the war. The fact that they knew the war was ending did make them a little more lenient. Oh, yes. It even changed from week to week with the reports from the battlefields. If the Germans had a victory, like the first part of the Battle of the Bulge, yes? Then the guards were strict. When they were about to lose the war, they only thought, "How do I get out of that?" You had to ride the waves.

So I was in the camp from October 1944 until I was liberated in May 1945. On May ninth, the Russians took Prague. But on May fifth already there was street fighting in Prague and our camp was liquidated. It was opened on the fifth of May. And in the meantime, the Russians came to Klettendorf near Breslau. We were marched about thirty miles to a camp named Gräditz. Gräditz was already in the direction of our home.

This was the worst time yet. For six weeks, we had absolute starvation. But then I was elected speaker of the camp and had to negotiate about our transportation into the interior as the Russians came closer and closer. So I walked with the camp physician and we came into a little town named Schneidnitz to negotiate with "the Organization Todt"[8] and we marched back. Suddenly the roads were blocked by military police and only ammunitions transports could get through. There was a transport of heavy grenades and I approached the German lieutenant and told him, "Look here. We have to march eight miles. Would you look the other way if we hopped on your truck carrying the grenades?"

He said, "I could do that but I warn you. You will see the most terrible things you can imagine. Absolutely beastly."

He was apparently no Nazi.

So we went [on his truck]. In the other direction, there was a death march. The death march of Gross Rosen camp. It skirted all the villages, and went only through fields and forests. In the beginning there were four thousand people and in Dachau where it stopped, there were less than two hundred left. They simply collapsed on the road and were killed. Some in front of me. They were shooting them. The stragglers who leaned against a tree were shot. Amongst these in the death transport is a very good friend of mine who came to Auschwitz as a boy and was in this kind of death march and survived it. He's now a professor in Sonoma University, a sociologist. John Steiner is his name. . . . I might have seen him. I might have seen him.

Q. How does one witness something like this and . . . ?

Look, it was. . . . I once had to lecture to children, ten-year-old children, who ask questions now after seeing movies about the war, like *War and Remembrance.* And one of the boys asked me, "Didn't you vomit when you saw that?" or "You could have fallen off and been killed by your grenade?"

It was true, you know. I simply. . . . I got sick, yes? Not completely. I felt it coming and then I did what Kurt Waldheim did. I turned the other way. I did the same as he did. I had a feeling I should strangle this SS man with my bare hands. But he had a Schmeisser gun and that was the only problem. Even now, I have dreams about this. Terrible dreams. I am even seeing a shrink. I do not sleep so well at night. I fall out of my bed from the dreams. I have many scars from falling out of bed. You know, I have to talk it off. I have to get it out of my system. I like to talk.

Note: The interview was terminated at this point, since Otto was crying.

•   •   •

Yesterday I told you about being on the back of a truck with the grenades, going back to the [concentration] camp and seeing the death march. What happened after that, when I got back to the camp, was another episode which was rather dramatic and which characterized how far the German Reich had deteriorated.

In Camp Gräditz, where I was returning after seeing this death march, this terrible shooting scene, we had very little to eat. We were very hungry for about six weeks. Then we were marched. The nearest railway station was already destroyed by bombing so we had to be marched about twenty or thirty miles to go to an intact part of the railroad. And guess where we were going? We were shipped in the direction of my hometown, Prague. Near it, but not quite in Prague. We were supposed to be a service detachment for a boot camp of the SS. This is something like a training camp. We were supposed to clean their toilets and so on. I think there were three hundred of us left. They crammed us in this camp near Benesov, only thirty miles from Prague.[9] But the last forty of us absolutely could not be crammed in, even according to camp standards. So we had to stand in formation for six hours. Then they told us that we would be shipped elsewhere.

They didn't have enough people to guard us so we were shipped twenty men at a clip. Two members of the labor service, who had uniforms and pistols, were going with each of these groups. We were told that two of us were selected as hostages. We had orders to stay with the guards, and if anyone from this transport would escape, we would have been shot, theoretically. I was one of the hostages. But the boys gave me their word and nobody escaped. We didn't think about escaping because they knew where our wives were. So we were all hostages. It didn't make sense to run away. They could have shot our wives. All this happened on the twenty-sixth of February 1945. It was a very grotesque situation in the camp.

I had heard some rumors that Gerbing, the camp commander, was a very reasonable guy. What he had done before that time, I don't know. But he treated us very well. You know that everybody had to wear a color of some kind, on their uniforms, denoting their crime, right? The outfit was like a pajama. Ours were green, with a yellow armband, to denote that we were labor force, slave labor force. Green was our working uniform. We were not like these prisoners who wore the triangles. We were not just slave laborers, however, we were something pretty interesting. The inscription on my armband read, "Works for Organization Todt." And then since we had to work on earth moving in the front line, we became the OT Fronteinsatz. That means front service. We were exposed to artillery fire when the Russians came closer. So now I was in this camp and I had to report as speaker to Gerbing. The SS men called me *Judenaeltester*. It means "oldest Jew." This causes some fun. In our quarters, I had a room which had previously been occupied by females and on the door there was a sign. In German, you give the gender and it was *Die Judenaelteste*. It means "the oldest Jewish woman." So this was my nickname: "the old Jewish woman."

Our camp commander complained that he had a work force and money and everything else needed to build but no building materials. I knew that if he wasn't building, then he'd have to be sent to the front. After a few days, he confessed that he was afraid to be sent to the front as a soldier. He didn't like that idea at all. So I came with an idea. I said, "What if we get some building material for you?"

I knew that two of my boys were construction engineers. One was the owner of a sizeable company and several of them were rich. So I had a conference with my boys and we bought from the black market granite, bricks, two-by-fours, and all that we needed so that we could pretend to work. We purchased materials for labor-intensive projects, like splitting the rocks, for instance. We made a sport out of it.

The people who had been there before us—they were Jews, on a transit basis—they had already started to repair a fence. We made sure to get the correct planks for a piece of our fence. It was an eight-foot-high wooden plank. On top, there was barbed wire. We unhinged one of the planks, pretending to repair it, and put real hinges on top in it so that we could pull it open without effort and noise. We got out during the night. I was several times out. We had to ration who left very carefully. We made a science out of who gets the next turn. The boys were disciplined and did not overdo it. So we would go out at night and come back in the morning. A maximum of four people a night were allowed out. We did it according to who were fathers of families, who were sick people and so on. It was a very just operation and was very successful. This was mid-March of 1945. So while I was still in the camp, I went in and out through this hinge breakout.

The Resistance wanted me to leave the camp and go and do a job for them. I said I would not do that because at this time Hannah was already expecting the child. The child was now the problem. That changed things for me, having a child. Oh, yes. I will tell you. We had planned our child for the fifteenth of April in 1945. That would have been completely all right if it would have gone normally, because it was just two weeks before the end of the war. The fifth of May was the end of the war for us.

Now, you are laughing, wondering how I could know that the war would end exactly then when I conceived the child. But that's exactly what I tried to do. I decided [to conceive the child] after consultations with Dr. Bumbala of the British Intelligence Service. I know it sounds mad, but it was so.

Q. So the British assured you that it would be okay . . . ?

No. Nobody *assured* me. But they had said several times, "Don't start a family yet." Then Dr. Bumbala said, finally, "Now you can try it." That's how it then happened.

There were several air raids on Prague. During one raid Hannah was near the office of one of my SS collaborators. He was the guy who had been a Gestapo lawyer. Hannah went across a big square when the sirens wailed. His office was on this square, so she ran there. This SS lawyer was already used to the sound of bombing and told her these are approaching bombs. They ran down into the basement. The building was all right but the neighboring house was hit by a heavy bomb; Hannah said that she had a window frame around her neck when she was dug out. But nothing happened, either to the child or to her. Remember, she is very pregnant at this point. The next day my daughter was born prematurely, on the twenty-third of March. Hannah was able to go to the Jewish hospital. This SS man chauffeured her with an official car, an official German car, and stopped before the Jewish hospital in the K_____. That alone was most unusual.

But wait a minute. There is more. We are now in K_____ Street. My daughter is born. Two hours later, I was with Hannah. They telephoned to Mr. Gerbing, to the commander of the camp. He called me and told me that I have a nice daughter. He said, "Get the rear door open. And buzz off." He told me to get out of the camp! Can you imagine?

I thought at the time that I was very lucky to have found him. Unfortunately, I don't know whether he was always as good as he was to us. [After the war,] the massacre started. He was in his uniform, so they shot him in the belly and threw him into the bunker, and he was left to die of peritonitis. Practically all SS men were shot on sight. So he didn't make it. The Czechs did this.

And then we saw the Third Reich crumble and . . . I knew we would see it. You know, people changed their attitudes completely. The guards were trying to be very, very nice and so on.[10]

MAFALDA, CHURCHILL, AND THE JULY 20 PLOT TO KILL HITLER

My conversations with Otto took place in the late 1980s and early 1990s, and included many phone calls and several visits for both taped and filmed interviews. During this time period, there was an important development that excited Otto because of its potential historical significance. I have combined Otto's narrative into one chronological story based on our conversations after this development: Otto's success in finally locating the spy known as Mafalda, a woman Otto believes links Churchill to the July 20 plot to kill Hitler. Some of this information Otto wanted kept secret until after 1995, when Mafalda's fifty-year secrecy agreement with the British Secret Service would have expired. It thus is not included in any previously published material about Otto.

Because I am not a historian, I cannot attest to the significance of this story or even to its veracity, although Otto did show me extensive documentation corroborating all that he said, and I have no reason to doubt him. One of Otto's daughters tells me Otto did not turn over his documents to the archives in Munich, as he told me he planned to do. His files now are stored with her. I am happy, through my publisher, to help arrange contact between Otto's daughters and any legitimate scholar wishing to examine Otto's files.

Now, what I have to tell you now is part of history. I have wanted to speak of this for a long time but I could not. But now I can tell it.

You may not yet know that in 1944 there was the attempt on Adolf Hitler's life. I had a very short connection to Graf Stauffenberg, who committed it. The missing link between us was a woman whose name I cannot reveal [yet] since she still lives. But her code name was Mafalda. She was in connection with the British intelligence service on one hand and also with Graf Stauffenberg. Stauffenberg wanted to have an assurance that the German areas, that is Austria and the Sudeten area, will remain with Germany if the German Resistance overthrows Hitler. Stauffenberg correctly thought that this guarantee would help encourage other people to join the plot. Look, it was natural that they didn't want to be carved up.

Now, Churchill even gave his word of honor to Stalin that he would never contact the German Resistance. But he did. That's why it is still secret. It will be secret for fifty years. But I have discovered where the woman is who was our connection! I have just learned this since the last time we spoke. I found her! You remember the last time we spoke that I told you that she is the Infanta of Portugal, Princess Maria Adelaide de Braganza.[11] She is born in 1912. I wrote her a long letter thanking her for everything, in particular, for having saved my life. Because on the day we were supposed to meet, I came to Vienna, and she was arrested by the Gestapo. But the Gestapo apparently abstained from applying the torture to her because she was royalty of a neutral country.

Let me tell you the whole story.

It was 1942 when I first heard about the Polish atrocities. I then got in touch with a very powerful group, a group that turned out to be British secret intelligence service. They had already sent a recruit, an Englishman, in 1938, just to investigate me. I was contacted by them in December 1942, when they got in touch with me, and a friend of mine named Alexander Von Moldt. He is dead already. We did what we could. Moldt had already at that time smuggled a couple of Jews via Slovakia to England. The same man who apparently recruited us, he came as a penniless student who became a language teacher. Then he disappeared from Prague and then later he returned as a correspondent of the London *Times* for Czechoslovakia and the Balkan countries. So something was already funny there. But we never learned until later what it was.

I worked a year for them. They were officially known to me as the Austrian Resistance Organization O5,[12] but some of these people worked for the British intelligence service without ever knowing. It was much easier to recruit people for an Austrian patriotic cause than for the enemy. But eventually I learned that I was working for the British Secret Service. This was not till later, though. The time of which we are speaking, I had only an inkling at that time. I don't know whether I should go into these intelligence stories to such depths but it cannot be separated.

The two people who are the original intelligence agents were trained in England: Dr. Raul Bumbala and Dr. Hans von Becker. I knew them only as Austrian Resistance people. But Dr. von Becker had already spent—I think—three and one half years in a concentration camp and Dr. Bumbala even more. Bumbala was already arrested in 1934, immediately after Hitler came in, because Bumbala was working against the Nazis rather openly in Berlin. Both of them were sent to Dachau and Buchenwald concentration camps and were let go only in 1942. When they crawled out of there, we called such agents "sleepers." They "slept" for three years and now they crawled out and they contacted me through the way I told you about already.

It was shortly after I knew already that I was working for the British [when it happens]. In early 1944—it must have been about March or something like that—I came to Vienna and I was called by Dr. Bumbala.

He said, "Here is a telephone number. Please call it and get together with the lady."

So I talked to her. And this lady was Princess Maria Adelaide de Braganza. She is the sister of the crown pretendant of Portugal.[13] Now, in the literature about this business, everybody expected that there must have been a link between Count von Stauffenberg, the assassin, and Winston Churchill. But *I know*. *She* was the person. I am convinced that Maria Adelaide de Braganza, code name Mafalda, was that person. There are several indications in the literature which seem to confirm that. For instance, we know that somebody between the twenty-second and twenty-sixth of June 1944 contacted Churchill and wanted to make a deal whereby Germany, the future Germany, should retain the German districts of Austria and maybe also the Sudetens and then they would take care of Hitler. But according to the unconditional surrender agreement, this was impossible.

Mafalda saw my friend, Dr. Bumbala, who was operating the British transmitter in Vienna, and he cabled these conditions to the British, conditions the British supposedly declined. So nothing has happened and a few days after the blown assassination attempt, I came to Vienna. All the arrests [of people associated with this attempt] had been taking place just now at that time. So I came to my hotel, which was next to the Sacher Hotel. I tried to telephone. First, numbers didn't answer. Then I got Mrs. Bumbala to the telephone and told her where I am.

"My husband will be there." So he came. Remember that this man had been already four years in concentration camps before. His health was lousy. And he got a heart attack. But, he said no doctor. He took some pills and it blew over. This is while he's in my hotel room with me! While he was sitting with me! And then he said, "These and these persons have been arrested. Everything is lost. But the most terrible thing is that they arrested Mafalda, the princess."

And he said something which I absolutely believe. He said, "I hope they will not dare"—*they* meaning the Gestapo—"will not dare to torture a royal princess of a neutral country." And apparently that has not happened because otherwise, well, he was guiding her as a superior officer in the British service and I was just to take her over. . . . You know, my trip to Vienna was planned before [the assassination attempt], which happened as a surprise. I think it is improbable that a man, having a heart attack and expecting any hour to be arrested by the Gestapo on top of that, would make up something which does not exist. That is very, very improbable. So I think that I am thanking her also for my life. If they had

tortured her, she had to spill it out. Nobody could stand that. Oh, a few
of them have though I don't know how. But she did not give anything
away.

Dr. Bumbala told me, "We cannot do anything. Keep a low profile. Go
back to Prague and wait."

That's what I did. I was overnight and half a day in the hotel and I
disappeared. They didn't make any checks on the railway and everything
went well, except that Mafalda was arrested. But after a couple of weeks,
they let her go. It was clear that she was arrested together with all the
others who were in on this conspiracy.[14]

Q. Did you have any idea what happened to her after the war?

Yes. We had a common friend who unfortunately also died—everybody
died—and who told me she had married a Dutchman of non-noble de-
scent. She is living under his name in Portugal.[15]

All that I am saying to you can be proved. The British chose very good
cover for their organization in Vienna. The leading two people, who
were trained also in radio communication in England before the war,
they were immediately suspected by the Germans. That's why they were
originally arrested and spent about three years in a concentration camp.
Now, these two people were also leaders of the Austrian Resistance,
which was a very good arrangement. You can persuade people to work
for Austria, pushed by their patriotism. But to work for the enemy, for
the British, is much more difficult to persuade. So they set up both. They
were Austrian Resistance and they were British intelligence. They were
the people who ran Mafalda, the agent, as a connection with Graf Stauffenberg. The entire secrecy about this is, I believe, to correct the image
of Winston Churchill. Why? Because Winston Churchill had given his
word to Stalin that he would never contact the German Resistance. Stalin
wanted to chop up Germany. The Stauffenberg plotters did not want
this. Nobody knows what Winston Churchill has replied. Only Maria
Adelaide de Braganza knows that. Dr. Raul Bumbala very probably told
her what to tell to von Stauffenberg. I thought she was the agent who
had talked to Stauffenberg just before the attempt on Hitler's life. I know
what she was telling him. She was telling him about the wire or transmitter in Vienna, the wire that went to Churchill. It is also mentioned by
Goerdeler, who was the highest civilian involved in the conspiracy. He
was the mayor of Leipzig.[16] He wrote it in a diary in the prison, before his
execution, that Stauffenberg assured him that his conditions for carrying
out the assassination attempt was the promise that Germany would not
be chopped up. Now I don't know exactly what Churchill has replied.
But they attempted the assassination.

Now it's only my speculation. Maria Adelaide must know something which was not good for the image of Winston Churchill and I'm curious what that is. It is very probable under the circumstances, I think, that Churchill said, "Okay, we will do something about it. Go ahead." He wanted the plot to kill Hitler to proceed. So I think that Mafalda got the go-ahead from Bumbala, who was the British agent who sent the wireless message to Churchill. Then she transmitted that message to von Stauffenberg. She must have gotten the cable then. So it's pretty interesting. [Otto later told me he believed Mafalda spent the weekend before the assassination attempt as a houseguest of the von Stauffenbergs.]

Q. How in the world did you track her down?

It was difficult, because of the secrecy in all these organizations. Many of the people I contacted were very abusive. One Resistance fighter said, "What Springer claims is absolute nonsense." Because several of the things we did, we did from impossible situations. Who would think that a man [Bumbala] who has suffered already three years in a concentration camp would be dismissed and then start to pull out his transmitter and wire Churchill! From Vienna! But it is because the Gestapo thought it is improbable, because of that that it succeeded. You will hear a few such stories.

So. One of these guys from the Austrian O5 Resistance group knew about her [Mafalda] and came up with her address. He's Count Thurn und Taxis, from a very old noble family. So this is very exciting. I have all the data here.[17] Now I am working mostly with the Institute for Contemporary History in Munich. I am leaving all my documents to them because I'm eighty-one.

Q. I see. So Thurn und Taxis helped you find where Mafalda is living now. She's still alive, I take it.

Yes. Mafalda is now living; she is married to a Dutchman. A physician named Van Uden, and in Portugal the address is Rua de _____. She is in Portugal and has many children. This I heard already. Since she was born in 1912, so she can still live . . . hopefully. At that time Thurn und Taxis wrote, he said she's living. So, I have written to her. It is a very dramatic letter. Really, it is unbelievable that I have actually found her. I have worked on that since 1982. Oh, no. Longer, longer, longer. It was very complicated. It's very exciting for me because the last time we spoke, I had no idea where she was. And just in the two weeks since then, well. . . . To get out with such a fantastic story, everybody would label me a liar. But now I have someone still living who can verify what I say. I hope only she has not lost her memory. I told her exactly how we met, and when we met and so on and so on.

It is interesting, psychologically speaking, but I absolutely have no knowledge of the date when she was arrested. I came to Vienna after the breakdown of the plot. It was either the twenty-first or twenty-second of July, I think. But I asked her now to give me the exact date. She will probably remember it.

I am under such excitement that I have simply a hole in my brain. Oh, yes. I'm very pleased. Because to have such interesting things . . . I tried, for instance, to locate her before. I knew she was a sister of the crown pretendant, Duarte. I found his address. I wrote to him. But I didn't get a reply. So perhaps the family is not so glad to have a Mata Hari. Apparently, they're not very cooperative. But she's still under the British secrecy.[18]

Even years ago already I tried. It is absolutely possible that she feels herself under obligation to the British because, as far as I know, she has signed the British agreement. Whereas I have not signed the secrecy agreement, and on purpose. Look, we have to go through my files. The thing is, when you work with the intelligence services, you get the impression that they devote 20 percent of their time to making stupid mistakes and 80 percent of the time for covering them up.

So I am now doing the following. I have real documents about this. I am sending all my documents to the Institute for Contemporary History in Munich, a highly recognized German institution. A copy of them will rest also in the Washington Holocaust museum.[19] I'm letting the Munich Institute investigate. I will tell you how things actually were but this cannot be published [yet] because I am the only living witness who has testified to that.

The Postwar Period: Being Caught by the Philby Conspiracy

Q. So. Now, it's after the war. Your daughter's been born and you've been liberated. What happens after that?

It's now May 1945. This that I will tell you was completely crazy.

You have heard about the Philby Conspiracy, yes? When I was working for the Austrian Resistance during the war, every single one of my cables was read by the British agents. You remember that the British were actually in charge of the Austrian agents. The British agent in charge of me was Maclean.[20] This I learned only later. He was number two. First was Harold "Kim" Philby and then was Donald Maclean, and the third one was Burgess. And then later it turned out that Blunt was also involved in it. He was the fourth man.

During the war, I was not necessarily what you would call a political person. I was what today you would call a person of liberal convictions. I had not been actively involved in politics. I was not a government official.

Absolutely not. But nobody could stand by when we saw these Nazis and not take part against them. So it was somehow ordained.

I could not work through any Czech Resistance groups. You must know that the Czech Resistance was crushed completely on May 27, 1942, after the Reinhard Heydrich murder or assassination.[21] And so the Czech Resistance was very ineffective. That's why I looked for something else. These people, whom I later learned had already pre-screened me before the war, they were the British. But they came as Austrians. So I thought I was joining the Austrian Resistance.

It turned out that I had to take tasks which the other Resistance people couldn't handle. Hans von Becker—the number one or number two man in the Austrian Resistance movement, they were interchangeable—he was arrested already in 1938 when Austria was occupied. So he was almost three years in concentration camps. Then they let him go, together with the other number one or number two man—Dr. Raul Bumbala. Bumbala was even longer in the camps because he was arrested before the Nazis came to power, in 1934. Just when they came to power, he was one of the first arrested. Both Bumbala and von Becker were trained in England. Since I was working under them, my cables were being sent back to England and Maclean and Blunt[22] were the ones who were reading them. There was seven people who could read my cables. Then after the war, because Philby is giving information to the Russians, the Russians realize that I was working for the British. This they knew already from these cables.

For instance, Becker telegraphed that he had hired me. In 1943, December, they broke me in completely because they needed me to travel for them instead of Becker. [Because he'd been arrested previously,] Becker had to report several times a week to the local police; therefore, he couldn't travel. So they had to take me into their confidence. That's why I know all these things. Plenty of people went through the entire war, and had not the slightest idea that they worked for the British. But I was told. At that time already, I was also told the next time I went to Vienna to bring passport photographs, samples of signatures, descriptions, anything that's needed to make a passport, and in two sets. I asked them, "Why two sets?"

"One is for false papers and the other one goes into the card index in England." And it was there. Later the Russians found it. After the war, someone in the Czech government, someone who was working for the Russians, tried to get me to work for them, too. But I said no, I was too tired; my nerves were frayed. In 1946, I decided that I cannot go on like that. I contacted a friend from childhood, a Jew with the American army, stationed in Bilden. He came to us. I told him that I was working for the British because he was working in the G2 section, the military intelligence. I told him my situation was pretty precarious.

One day he called me and said, "Otto, your sideline is economics. Would you be interested in a job in the American Embassy?"

So I was sent there and became an assistant to the economic attaché and commercial attaché with the American Embassy. I thought, "Now I am settled and nobody can touch me." Ha! Ha!

Did I tell you the story of how they approached me, the Czechs? There was already a high official. He said that he was never a communist. He was in the group that had to decide which Germans qualified for the citizenship. I knew him already from before and during the war, but only superficially. I had to do something for my parents—my parents were German—and my sisters. I saw him file my papers. Only they got "stuck" in the Ministry of the Interior. He gave me incredible papers for my parents. My parents were real anti-fascists and my father had done wonders for the Czech Resistance. So I got the permission that my parents and then also my sisters and their husbands and their entire families were allowed to leave Czechoslovakia, voluntarily and with a truckload of furniture. These were rare exceptions. Usually, the anti-fascist Germans were just driven across the border. But I was very grateful to Dr. Steiner. I did not have a suspicion yet that they were interested in me because they had heard about my reports. They decided that I'm of pretty good intelligence so they wanted to get me to work for them.

LEAVING PRAGUE

British intelligence was penetrated by the Russians, through the so-called Philby Conspiracy. It turned out that they had read every single [one] of my cables. I was ordered to see the Czech Deputy Minister of the Interior, who was the most bloodthirsty beast there was. He tried three times to get me for their service, to work for the Russians.

The Russians! There are Czechs representing them in Prague. I honestly told him, "I want to have my peace. My nerves are frayed. I don't want to continue with anything like that." So they made me a nonperson. They didn't actually take away my citizenship. No. As a German, I had automatically lost my Czech citizenship in 1945. But I was entitled to its restoration. I fulfilled all the conditions required by the law. I had actively fought against the Nazis. I was persecuted in a concentration camp. The law was there on my side. They simply held my file up in the Interior Ministry and I couldn't get a job. This is why I got the job with the American Embassy, with the economic attaché.[23]

I wanted to go back into civil life but I didn't see a possibility. So I joined the staff of the American Embassy in Prague as an economist. I stayed with them until 1948 when I had to leave, because of a big thing which happened which I will tell you about shortly.

Officially, I was spying for the Americans then. But since I was under constant supervision by the Czech secret police, I was told by the Americans to pretend to be disenchanted with the Americans. I never said that I'm a communist. It would have been too much. But I said I didn't like the amateurish ways they [the Americans] were acting here. This was true.

I said, "I want to have now my peace. I don't give a damn." And so on and so on. You know, I appeared to be neutral. I said I was disappointed by the Americans, especially by the embassy. That was my line when I talked to the communists. So the Czechs had me "turned around" for six months. You know what that means, that they had me "turned around"? That meant they blackmailed me. I should work for them against the Americans. The Czechs, I made a deal with them, which was pretty interesting. It was a contract [to spy for the Czechs] for six months. But I had told them, "Already the Americans have no confidence with me. I am afraid that I'm going to get fired. So you can't expect too much from me."

So, I was working for six months in 1948 for the Russian Intelligence Service. I was a double agent. Yes? They knew I was working for the Americans because of Maclean. But they actually caught me and forced me to work for them because of a report I had written about the Czech automobile industry. Two people questioned me. They asked several things, where I responded simply, "That's nonsense." But then came one man. "What about the report about the automobile industry?" he asked.

My name was given in the left lower corner as a source. An idiot of an American attaché had stamped it confidential. It was not confidential at all. It was from literature which was published. But this attaché had to make a big thing of it. He was the author and I was only compiling it. But the Communist secret police pulled out of their pocket a copy of this confidential report. How they got it, I don't know. I later learned. There were 103 Czech employees in the American Embassy. They put them under pressure with black market deals and then they blackmailed them. So what they did with me, they said, "Look. Anything you write for a confidential report to the American government is without doubt a crime. In your case it would be twenty years of jail."

They called in my daughter, the older one. They said, "Isn't it a pity to destroy such a nice family?" And so on, you know, threats to hurt her.

So I said, "What do you want?"

"Sign this," they said. And now here's the interesting thing. It was a time-limited contract for six months. And they kept their deal, this timed part of the bargain.

You have to understand. First of all, I was completely desperate. The fact that they could get this confidential report out of the embassy so easily meant that an American must have given it to them. Now, there are fifty-eight Americans working in the embassy. Who do I trust? I found one but we will speak of him off the record. [Name deleted for security reasons.] This man I found, a man I trusted, is my CIA friend, who is living now in Utah. He gave me material which I could give them. So-called play material. But the Czechs were pretty satisfied with that. I told the Czechs, "Now I'm fired. I'm out of the embassy."

"Oh, you have social contact with the Americans," they said. "You can continue." So fortunately I told the right things to them. After a while they came and brought my travel papers, Czech travel papers, giving me permission to leave the country. That was my deal. They kept the deal. The Americans were much worse in this respect, I must say.

But then this thing happened—a terrible thing happened. It concerned the status of the Russian atomic bomb. I learned every single detail. I sent a report with the prediction that the big bang would be a year from hence. That was in September of 1948 and my calculation was just a week off.

Let me tell you, how our spying started, with my friend who was killed.

He worked with me during the war and had a certain confidence in me. When I came back from the concentration camp, he came to congratulate me and so on. Then he said suddenly, "Look, we will not see each other for a long time. I am now a Communist. I have to live. Think of that whatever you wish. When something interesting will happen, you will see me." It was all very enigmatic.

I heard that he became a very important man as a mining engineer. He became general manager of the uranium mines in Yachinmof, the richest uranium ore in the world.[24] It was only seven miles from the American army when they stopped going east. But the American army did not know that there was something like that there. So close, and they left it to the Russians. He was now general manager of the company. He had been commanded, sometime in August or the beginning of September 1948, to go for a conference in Moscow where they then made demands on production increases which were nearly impossible. These demands meant one thing: that the bomb is not in an experimental stage but is in the production stage. He was alarmed by these figures and so got friendly with a Russian physicist, who spilled the beans completely. [Otto shrugged.] A little vodka helped.

So I just had to pick up my wife and two young children and leave in the middle of the night. The older one was five years old. The younger was almost three, just a little younger. It is not easy to do something like that. There's a lot of psychology behind that. I had luck. I had luck and instinct. This was not very rational.

Q. Let me be sure I understand. This friend comes and tells you the Russians are going into production on a bomb. You wrote this down in a memo, with his name and your name on it, and gave it to the Americans. Then the Americans show it to Maclean, who is one of the top British agents in the United States. But Maclean is secretly a spy for the Russians, and he lets the Russians know about the memo and that you and your friend wrote it. So the Russians come and arrest your friend. [Otto nodded, yes.] Then how did you learn of this, about his arrest and what had happened?

Someone comes to you. You're at home. It is long after dark. We were in bed already and she [my friend's wife] threw pebbles against our window. So I went down and there she was. "You have to leave," she says.

Now, you of course figure out immediately that someone, somewhere along the line has seen the report when something like this happens. What to do next? I calm down and think rationally. It was clear that we have to leave. But now, I tell you something truly unbelievable. My wife had certain idiosyncrasies. One of them concerned our apartment, our house and our antiques. She said, "I'm not leaving without them."

It was clear that Hannah would not go immediately. In a few days we would have solved the problem of our furniture and other belongings. But Hannah balked. "I'm not leaving without my furniture. In a godforsaken country, I want to have my roots."

Q. Weren't you angry with her?

Of course I was. But it wouldn't have led anywhere. I gave her two more days. Also, she was very logical in this respect. I know Ladia, my friend. He doesn't break down under interrogation in just two days. That was Hannah's argumentation. So we got the entire furniture out. The valuables and my documents, which you are going to see, they came with the CIA pouch. And we got out.

Q. How did you know when to leave?

I told you my friend was killed. Shortly after that cable about the bomb was caught by the British, the cable that had on it my name and my friend's name [the one shown to the Russians by Maclean], my friend was arrested. His wife came to our house at night, throwing pebbles at our window and telling me, "He's arrested. Get out." So we got out. I think that we were lucky that they went to get him first and that she was very helpful. But this was very natural since he was to them the more interesting one. He was the one who actually figured out that the Russians had the bomb, because of the amount and kinds of metal being taken from some uranium field. He was a Czech, my friend. He worked with me for the British intelligence, as a mining engineer.

But it was a year before, when I brought the Americans the news, which was directly from Moscow. This would have grave implications but it was one of the big successes of espionage. . . . The CIA in Prague was completely decimated. They told the two leading officers they are persona non grata and have to leave the country within twenty-four hours. So nobody was in charge.

Now in this situation, I got a success and I did not know. Since the Communist secret police had a confidential report, I suspected every American in the American Embassy. They had to have an American working for them and so it was difficult to get to the right person, to know who would be the right person. I cannot tell you his name. He's really secret and he's still living. He's living in Utah and I am from time to time telephoning him. He sent my cable with the Russian report to Washington and after many years—it was 1974—this top CIA person had retired already but I had his address and I saw him. I told him. "Please, can't you tell me what happened with these people?"

He had sent this cable to Washington and I asked him, "Look. I want to know. Did my report about the Russian atomic bomb have no effect at all inside the CIA?"

"It was suppressed."

"But where?" I asked him.

And he said, "I assure you it was positively judged to be genuine and real and so it went to the top." There is only one top in the CIA at the time. It was Admiral Hillenkoetter.[25] He didn't know what to do with the report. So he went to Maclean—he was still a friend who was at that time Second Secretary of the British Embassy in Washington, and on both committees dealing with cooperation in the atomic field—and showed him [Maclean] my cable, the one where my name and my friend's name were given in full, in black and white. My friend was arrested and killed and we had to leave the country rather suddenly.

So Maclean turned me in.

So, this is now what I wanted to tell you. I am actually an illegal and involuntary immigrant to the United States. I worked for the Russians for the six months. It ended on the twenty-fourth of September 1948. Masaryk was killed on March 10, 1948.[26] Then I went to Germany. The Czechs had in the meantime learned that I had betrayed them by doing this double agent thing. I brought this report to them, to the Americans. They sent an agent after me to Germany. But I was lucky. The agent defected. He was sent, not to kill me but to set me up. To set up for a kill. He had to follow me and be in contact with somebody. But he gets in Germany and he defects. So I found out that they were going to try to kill me. Now, how did this happen? I found him one day gagged and bound in my garden on my doorsteps. So I called CIC (the American Counter Intelligence Corps of the Army) and a CIC officer came.

It was army intelligence and they worked pretty well together. This man had confessed already to me that he was a double agent. I had called the CIC, but they were not fast enough. For unknown reasons, they let him sleep over in the hotel where he had been staying. Allegedly, the Communist agents had grabbed him, beaten him up, and deposited him at my doorsill as a warning. Turn the switch off now. . . .

[The rest of the conversation was deleted for reasons of security. Otto did not want to reveal anything that might hurt living CIA agents.]

Q. You were saying that in 1950 you're living in Germany.

We're living in Germany. We had no idea what they had done with the Czech agent who had contacted me. I handed him over to the CIC and never heard what had developed. They kept it secret. I never heard of him again. I don't know where he is. But, in one sense, I owe my life to him also. The CIC did not tell me anything about what happened with him but they must have concluded that his story was true because I came to be put on the list of "sensitive people."

During the Korean War, in the summer of 1950, suddenly an army alert went out for the American troops in Germany. The first step in this alert was that "sensitive people"—that means those people who were not supposed to fall into Communist hands under any conditions—had to be moved to the United States. So two CIC officers came to me late at night and said, "Mr. Springer, we are congratulating you. You have been admitted to the United States."

I said immediately, "I don't want to go." Because Hannah wanted to go to her uncle in Rhodesia.

The officer said, "Never mind. What you will do later is none of our business. Now you go to the United States within forty-eight hours." So we are involuntary immigrants to the United States. We also are "illegal" because the CIA has a very little quota of her choice people which can immigrate. At that time, I knew only of six. They are very stingy with these qualifications. So to avoid using up their small quota, they falsified my entry into the United States. It says on my entry papers that I came on the twenty-fourth of September. That is the date for crossing the border between Czechoslovakia and the American zone in Germany.

The CIA backdated these papers to May so it looked like I'd been working for them since then. That's why I am illegal, because the CIA is not allowed to falsify papers. . . . You could check on everything I am telling you. All that I tell you is true. [Otto showed me official papers.]

Q. This says that you've been working for this agency spying. And supposedly Hannah was spying also.

Yes, of course.

Q. When did your clearance expire for the British? Was that a forty-year agreement?

No. For the British, it ended with the war, in 1945.

Q. How did you manage to escape?

I have a brother in law in Holland. He wanted to take over the agency for Skoda Cars, and he bought a sample car. It was a beautiful little car, a Cabriolet. He could not wait [for the car to be ready] so he left the car to me. [That's how it happened that] during the critical time I had the car. He had entered my name already as a driver of the car in the papers so that I could cross the frontier with the car. I had British papers from the British intelligence [service]. One of my proofs [that I have that this story really happened] is a paper available with the signature of Harold Gibson, for instance, on these papers.

But now it's time to leave and I didn't know what papers to use. Should I take the Czech papers or the British papers? I decided for the Czech papers because I had a certain confidence in one of these guys. There was nothing from the Czech authorities about permission to leave the country or anything else. It was just a piece of paper which identified me as a man of undetermined citizenship. It was British—not on a letterhead—only on a piece of paper, the letterhead type, a travel identity card. But there was some kind of agreement because this same type of paper was used to leave the country and nobody was ever arrested. So I bet on the Czech papers and got out before anything was obvious. They, of course, wanted to catch me. But I was across the border before they got to me.

Q. I see. Now, let me just make sure I have this right. You didn't sign anything with anybody except the Americans. You were working for them and they're the ones that got you out of the country after Masaryk was killed. Your cables, which had gone to Blunt, had been read by the Russians and you knew you were in danger. Once the engineer you'd been working with had been picked up, you knew you would be next. So you came out then. You left Prague, and drove into Western Germany. Is that correct?

Yes. I went to the CIA in Germany. There was an overt agency called FBIS, Foreign Broadcast Information Service, and I was editor/analyst of the economic report on Germany. This was my most interesting job. I was there for two years, until 1950. Katek was my officer, the one who debriefed me. Katek has been training guerrillas for Hungary, for the uprising of 1956. The CIA fomented it [the uprising] by training Hungarian-speaking troops. They did the same thing for Czechoslovakia and Poland. I did that. It was a typical operation, like in Nicaragua. It was a Contra operation which failed and about which the lost lives are estimated between 6,000 and 32,000. The CIA was helping and fomenting [the rebellion], promising American help to the Hungarian Contras in 1956. It failed at that time and it would fail again in Nicaragua. If the voters would know what happened in Hungary, then they might have thought twice about funding the Contras. This is why the CIA did not want me to publish this one story. They did not want to remind anybody of the name Katek, although he was ten years dead. That was the name that they wanted me to delete from my memoirs.

We drove the car that my brother-in-law had given me. We packed it to the hilt and chose the biggest hotel in Carlsbad, a first-class! We stayed overnight there for our last night in Czechoslovakia.

"First of all," I said, "we cross the border as soon as they open the crossing. They will be sleeping. They will be not so attentive." So we did that. We drove to the border crossing, early in the morning. We went to sleepy border guards. I gave the guard the papers and he said something like, "I envy you that you get out." Then I stepped on the gas and I raced the car from the border. It was instinctive.

We came then to a beautiful little meadow on the right with birch trees. So I stopped. We got the children out. Let them go. And we simply breathed freely. It was wonderful. We had rest.

Suddenly Hannah asked, "Where is the suitcase with the baby things?"

We had left it standing on the stairs of the hotel! The next day, an embassy car picked it up and got it across the border. The twenty-fourth of September 1948. I have the date stamped in a passport. All the documents are here. Everything is here.

I knew then that I would never go back. Well, I did go back in 1965, but it was different. Essentially, you knew that you were leaving Czechoslovakia for good. The thoughts that go through your mind at a moment like that! Look, it was a unique feeling. Prague was absolutely unique. And it was such a wonderful life. Later, Hannah would say, sometimes when she was mad, "I will never forgive you that you forced me to leave Prague."

But for me, I had lost my home already when the Germans occupied Czechoslovakia, because I was not a Nazi. So I didn't feel at home in Prague anymore when the Communists came. It sounds funny, I know, that Hannah would still feel at home there. She was funny. She had her idiosyncrasies. When I got this job, as part of the CIA with the Foreign Broadcast Information Service, we had all the advantages of an American officer in Germany. Then Hannah didn't want to leave Germany. She's conservative. What can you do?

Q. Am I hearing you correctly? Most of what you did in terms of your political activities, your spying activities, were really connected with your love for your wife, trying to protect her against Hitler. And yet she doesn't. . . .

Right. Let me tell you one thing. When I married my wife, it was not only that I wanted to save her. But then when I had more knowledge [about] what was going on—still no confirmation, but more or less certified rumors about what's going on—about how they treated the Jews in Prague already was pretty clear. Ordinary citizens were treated terribly and Jews were treated even more terribly. But they had a special law so anyone who committed crimes to aid the enemy had to have this death. This penalty was compulsory. It was a slow death on [hung up] piano wires and so on. The kith and kin rule applied to those people. This meant that children and other family members could be killed, too. You had completely innocent people put into concentration camps by that law. So Hannah Springer and Adolf Hitler were not compatible.

Q. Did you never think during all this time or afterward, particularly when you and your wife did divorce after being married so long, that if you would not have met her, if you would not have fallen in love with her, how different your life would have been?

Oh, yes. But one thing I cannot omit. Had I not been married to Hannah, I might have had a higher probability to be killed because I would have been drafted into the German army. And not into a first-class regiment: maybe into a punishment battalion. These regiments had such losses, like the Jews.

   Someone once asked Hannah, "So your husband saved your life." And Hannah said, "Yes, but I saved also his." And it's true.

Q. I don't know if I should ask this question or not. Forgive me if I'm intruding. But after all that you and your wife went through together, you come to this country, you raise your children, just when things seem so easy, then your marriage falls apart. Do you ever think about that?

Of course. Many times. Look, it sounds a bit ridiculous. Hannah was a domineering personality. When Hitler came, she was completely dependent on me. So I became dominant. We had a wonderful time when our children grew up. But once the children were grown up and they had both already married, then Hannah's domineering personality came back and I was not ready to take that. I simply withdrew. I knew that I was guilty technically; but let's say that emotionally, my wife was guilty, too. I simply walked out and after I left her I felt liberated. But we are very good friends now. Look, we can speak completely openly, yes? If I had to start it all over again, I would do it better. . . . Now I live by myself. I have two daughters. One of them lives right near me now, with three children. The other one has two children in Connecticut. I am very close to my daughters. It's a fantastic relationship with both of them.

Why Did the Holocaust Happen?

Q. We've talked a lot about your life and a lot about what happened during the war. Last time we spoke, you said you had some things you wanted to tell me, to put things into perspective, to bring closure for you. What were those things?

We rescuers are overrated. Why? Because the Jews claim that the Holocaust is unique, which, unfortunately, it is not. It is a common, but an illogical, conclusion that if this Holocaust has to be unique and apart from everything else, then also the rescuers have to be unique and apart from everything else. This is why we rescuers are overrated. Much too much fuss is being made over us. We are again paraded as heroes. There is a guy who organized the shipping of Danish Jews to Sweden [Knud, chapter 5]. He lives nearby and is now my very good friend. Since we always get invited to the same celebrations or speaking engagements, I joke that we form a "rent-a-hero" company.

But the Holocaust was actually not unique. Other such terrible things have happened. We've all known about Cambodia. And that's why I say that the rescuers are overrated. In talking of the Holocaust, the Jews now make arithmetic the leading principle, by talking always of the number of people killed. They have now created a legend out of this giant number. It is understandable that people who lost so many are afraid that if we assume an attitude which says it has happened elsewhere and was basically the same, only the arithmetic was different, that somehow people might refute Israel's claim on their homeland.

But I think this is not the way to arrive at the truth. We have to develop mechanisms to avoid such things, even if only on a small scale, by intensive education and understanding. If you assume that the rescuers are not unique, because there have always been people like this at all times, then hopefully we will have some in the future.[27]

For me, then, the problem and the rescuers become in some ways even more important because by understanding these rescuers we can understand what it is that makes people help other human beings. The really important question is: "Why did good people become that way?" It is not enough to just say, "Good people are good, period."

Look, in order to judge these things, you have to know something about mass psychology. You learn to know the mechanism of a reaction of a crowd. When it becomes a psychological crowd, you have to watch out. Because any group of people can, under certain conditions, become a psychological crowd and commit the most heinous crimes, which they wouldn't do as individuals. One of my conclusions is this.

For instance, I think about the perpetrators as well as the rescuers. I have interviewed many SS guards. And there is one thing I wanted to tell you, one thing I learned from one of my interviews with our guards in the camp. I was always intrigued by the question: How could seemingly normal people become killers? Once, I got an interesting answer. In a camp in Upper Silesia, I asked one of our guards, pointing at the big gun in his holster, "Did you ever use that to kill?" He replied, "Once I had to shoot six Jews. I did not like that at all, but when you get such an order, you have to be *hard*." And then after a while he added, "You know, they were not human anymore."

That was the key: dehumanization. You first call your victim names and take away his dignity. You restrict his nourishment, and he loses his physical beauty and sometimes some of his moral values. You take away soap and water and then say the Jew stinks. Then you take their human dignity further away by putting them in situations where they even will do such things which are criminal. Then you take food away. When they lose their beauty and health and so on, they are *not* human anymore. When he's reduced to a skin-colored skeleton, you have taken away his humanity. It is much easier to kill non-humans than humans. [Otto paused.]

On my medal, the Yad Vashem Medal, there is an inscription. It says, "Whoever saves one life, he has saved the entire humanity." And I think the inversion of that is also true. Whoever kills one innocent human being, it is as if he has killed the entire world.[28]

Once the ice is broken, there's a psychological moment, deeply founded in genetics. Our ancestors, who hunted in a pack, they had to follow the leader. So these things are deeply rooted in instinct. One can make use of these instincts to produce amazing things.

In thinking about what makes people do these things, it is not so important whether it was one million or six million. The increase was a matter of technique and the technology of killing. Those who led the mob and fired the first shot into live flesh, those are the really guilty ones. Talking about the Holocaust in this way, just in terms of the numbers killed, this is absolutely not my view. My view is: Who breaks the barrier by killing the first Jew is guilty. To a larger extent then, the others are less guilty. It's one of my conclusions.

I think we must always remember, the first step in triggering the avalanche of group hatred is to call another human being ethnic names. It can happen again. It never will if we all observe that which, in one form or another, underlies all the great religions of the world: Do unto others as you wish they would do to you and *love thy neighbor.*

So this is my explanation for part of what happened during the war. People were able to kill so many other people, because they dehumanized them.

But not only that. What percentage in Germany were the Jews before World War II? Think. It was less than 1 percent! Absolutely.[29] Nobody knows about it because the Jews were mostly brought from Poland and from other Slav countries. In Germany, I know an exact figure only for Prussia and this was .6 percent. These Jews, of course, they were inconspicuous. There was a joke: In Mecklenburg, somewhere in north Germany, a Nazi Party boss manager cabled headquarters, "Send some Jews. Otherwise, the spontaneous pogrom cannot be carried out." Most Germans had never seen a Jew! So it was easy to tell the German people that the Jews were abominable. Because the [German] Jewish population was only 1 percent. So *this fact* one has also to put into perspective.

It is also important to understand how a society disintegrates. Le Bon describes the massacres of the French Revolution [*The Psychology of Crowds*] and comes exactly to the same conclusions as Bettelheim [*The Informed Heart*]. They both stress the psychology of a crowd. In thinking back on my own experiences, I'm coming more and more to believe in the psychology of the crowd. In a crowd, any man—university professors, highly educated people, or people from the streets—they react in a crowd always the same way. If it's the proper crowd with the proper guidance, then he becomes a mass murderer. I saw that coming. In a positive side and a negative side. It's not so much the personality; it is our misusing of instincts, about which very little is known.

When one thinks about all this, then one has to stop and think: When can it happen again? Where can it happen? And how? Because it has happened many times.

WHAT MADE YOU SAVE PEOPLE?

Q. You've thought about this a lot and you've lived through this period. Let me ask you. Why do you think you rescued people when other people did not?
Oh, because the situation was absolutely different.

Q. What was different about your situation?
I went first. I did it because I loved my wife and she was Jewish.

Q. But what if you had not been married to her? Would you have still done it?
Then probably. I would not have become a Nazi. Absolutely not. But would I have stuck my head out? If somebody would ask me, "Would you do it again today?" I would say, "Are you crazy?"

You see, I was asked this question many times. I think I just got mad, absolutely mad, because the probability at that time was already. . . . Look, the Germans had already the defensive apparatus developed for five years in Germany before they occupied Czechoslovakia. It is known that pupils were taught in school to denounce their parents. But this apparatus got much farther developed. The party grassroots organization were the janitors. In every company there were people who could get along without qualifications, just by becoming Nazis. That was so pervasive, this organization, that you never knew where you would find a Nazi eager to make a couple of bucks by denouncing you.

There is a difference also between making resistance and rescue in Germany and in occupied countries. The Danish had it much easier because the language problem made police surveillance more difficult. For instance, there were little things, such as the duty to register with police when you slept over somewhere more than one day. This had wonderful results in crime fighting but also in hunting down political adversaries.

Q. So you think the fact that you were married to your wife, that you were . . .

Of course. And I was close to her parents, I could not turn away and simply ignore what happened to them. I had really to suffer under it.

Q. What do you mean?

I loved them. I know that they were very intelligent beings. That there was no reason at all except . . .

Q. Otto, I listen to what you say. And I accept it. On the other hand, it does occur to me that there were lots and lots of other people who had many dear Jewish friends, and some were married to Jews. People who had children who were part Jewish, and still did nothing. This means there were other people who were in a situation similar to yours. They were in love with someone who was Jewish or they were married to someone who was Jewish. They had Jewish friends whom they loved. And yet they still did nothing.

It was part of my education, which was somewhat different.

Q. So it wasn't just the situation. It was also education? What was there in your education that was different?

It was a bit Victorian, the ethics of my father. For instance, all his attitudes were Victorian about sex and such things. I was educated so that I had to marry a virgin. It might sound ridiculous today but it was so.

The Jews are human beings and therefore we don't have the right at all to persecute them. That was a categorical imperative. When you see the motives of the mob and people from the mob, it was disgusting. Plenty of people had the possibility. For instance, one of my best friends had a

Jewish bride but they postponed it and then they missed the boat. It was one of the most wonderful stories, because he was not protected by a Jewish marriage. He became a German officer and went with his coast battery to Holland. When he came to say good-bye, we who were still allowed to send food parcels took care of his fiancée. When he told me he goes to Holland, I asked him to help my wife's sister who has disappeared in Amsterdam. And he did, in German uniform. He was quartermaster of his battery. A part of the German food he acquired went directly to the Jews hidden in Amsterdam. My sister-in-law survived and even bore a child while she was underground. That's a separate story.

Now this man did come back and marry his Jewish fiancée after the war. She made it through the war, too.

Q. One of the things that always intrigues me is the extent to which people make a choice. When you first decided—or perhaps I should ask, did you decide—were your actions motivated by a choice, by some sort of a conscious process of sitting down and thinking about the risks that were involved, thinking about the benefits to you? Did you go through any kind of a cost to benefit calculus or . . . ?

I have answered this question in a speech. I said that I lived in a society where we had 80 percent of Jews in our school. My best friends were Jews. My first girlfriends were Jews. And so when they told me the Jews are abominable, I could tell them I know better. That was one thing.

I started one of the speeches by saying, "I never made a moral decision I will help Jews." When it happened, then I had absolutely a compulsion to do it. The hand of compassion was faster than the calculus of reason.

Q. It wasn't actually a decision that you'd made?

It was not a decision. It was just part of my character. Something that I felt. But it was also part of my education generally. Yet I did things which can only qualify me as being crazy. I got crazy sometimes, like when they took [Hannah's] parents away, for example. I did things where the probability of surviving was very, very small.

Q. And you never thought about that? You never thought about the fact that you were risking your life?

No. But also I examined myself whether it wasn't part of showing off, and it was.

Q. It was part of showing off?

Yes.

Q. Was it anything more than that?

Of course.

Q. What else was it?

Outrage, I would say. There was a component of craziness, which I just mentioned, that had its roots in an outrage. And then, of course, my wife got pregnant. She carried my child when she was supposed to go to Auschwitz. So all that combines into a very strong motive. But nothing is simple, you know? It is a combined thing and now you come and ask what percent of this and what percent of that.

Q. I recognize that it is very complex. I think the distinctions are quite subtle that have to be drawn here. I agree with you, however, that if we do want to understand why it is that some people will be altruists and others will not, why most will just think of their own self-interest, it's important to try to make the distinctions. That's why I'm asking you a lot of questions that may seem irrelevant sometimes to you. I'm just trying to understand the process that led you to act.

So let me be sure I understand what you are saying. In general, the activities that you did with the Jews, you said partly that it was simply you were in love with your wife. You loved your in-laws. You had had an education and a kind of moral upbringing from your father and it was part of your personality. Is that what I'm hearing you say?

Yes. Right. Absolutely.

Q. Then were there other times in your life when you did things to help other people? I mean, helping Jews during the war is not the only incident?

Oh, no. There were others. Once I have saved a seventeen-year-old boy. I jumped into the high water of a river and I rescued a drowning man. Then I rescued another during a skiing trip in the mountains. He lost his way and we tried to find him in bad fog that developed into a terrible storm. It was difficult but we rescued him. I'm trying to be self-critical with the show of things. I wanted to impress also the girls with my courage. Definitely.

Q. How about duty? Was duty a factor? Did you feel you had a duty?

Look, the moral laws, the categorical imperative was there. And that is duty.

Q. What does the categorical imperative mean to you? You mentioned it before. What does it mean to you?

I have certain moral principles and I have to act morally. That means that—I don't have the correct English words. In German, no, wait a minute. Leading component I would say. My behavior at any time can be elevated to universal law. But these are things which have developed from our ancestors and they are there. For instance, the leader of a group has a certain responsibility and . . . I can't analyze it better or more for you.

Q. You do feel though that you have certain responsibilities to other people?
Of course. Especially to my child.

Q. How would you define your own identity in relation to other people? Do you see yourself as someone who comes out of a Gemeinschaft *world? Or are you more a* Gesellschaft *person? Do you see the world in those kinds of terms?*
No black-and-white judgment about that. Sometimes you are this and sometimes you are that. But what is prevalent? I would say I was a leader. For instance, in the concentration camp, I was elected leader. Then in business life and so on, I was driven and I wanted a good performance.

Q. You mentioned that it was your child. In terms of your basic identity, how do you define yourself? Do you define yourself as German, Czech, a man, an engineer? I mean, if someone says, "What are you?" what do you say?
I am like a no-lands man, a cosmopolitan. I believe that as children we should all learn foreign languages because when you understand the languages better, maybe this is a very important thing in helping you understand people better. I was against any nationalism, *always*. In Czechoslovakia, where these problems were deeply rooted, it was important. When I came to the United States and saw what was going on in the South, I decided when I had the power to fire and hire that I first would hire Negroes. I had that power over about thirty people. So I hired three Negroes. I felt it my moral duty to do that and I fared excellently with them.

Q. So morality is very important to you.
Yes.

Q. You really are a Kantian. You treat people as an ends, not as a mean to anything.
Right. Right. Right. Right.

Q. Let me just ask you a few questions. Was there any particular group, or groups, that you belonged to that were important in your identity formation? Any groups when you were a child?
Groups. Look, that was the interesting thing. I lived in a society which was a competition between three nationalities. It was Jewish, German, and Czech. The internationality was important to me.

Q. International. You consider yourself a member of mankind rather than any nationality?
Definitely.

Q. Were there any important role models for you when you were growing up?
Models? For instance, I had a teacher in engineering who had an influence on me. My father, of course. Then among great personalities, for instance, Goethe. I liked his pantheism. Goethe said once that as a human being, I am a pantheist.

Q. What does that mean to you to be a pantheist?
Spinoza. I read Spinoza, Essex, and so on, and he influenced me very much.

Q. What was it in Spinoza that was important for you?
It was again the moral principle.

Q. So you've thought a lot about morality.
Of course.

Q. Do you have any particular philosophy of life that you use to guide you?
It's funny that I have no formal religion. It was interesting. My sister was two years younger and we wanted to go to confirmation as Lutherans together. We were a very well-known family in this church and it was a family affair. But then I debated with a revered teacher who was a good scientist. He researched and wrote many books. He said after our conversation, "If you think that way, you really have to refuse to get confirmed."

So my father called me and he said, "Look, are you so sure?" Now I will tell you a small story. When my grandfather died, my father called me and wanted to pray. He wanted that we should say the Lord's prayer together. And both of us had forgotten it! That's all. [Otto shrugged.] You know, he wanted to see if I feel strong enough to go it alone. And I absolutely do. I can get along without any revelation.

Q. You don't believe there's an afterlife?
Absolutely not. Not an individual one.

Q. What kind of afterlife is there?
Back into the pool. The pool consists of the forces which create life, sometimes very carelessly. I think we are a miscreant genetic experiment of god. Because all the animals have inhibitions against intraspecies killing. But where is our inhibition to press the button of a machine gun? The dog who is subdued by another dog turns around, exposes his throat, and the other dog cannot bite. This is one of many examples.

Q. Let me ask you just one more question. How much of your actions were politically motivated? I know you were very involved in the Underground and worked with the Austrian Resistance. Did you get into that for political reasons or were they . . . ?

No. My first thought was, we are too weak to do anything with this giant apparatus of evil which was against us. My situation was so precarious that I had to find channels which were rather unusual but which promised also to help us survive.

Q. So did you see your activities with the Resistance as being primarily political or primarily as a result of your humanitarian instincts?
Both. Both. Both.

Q. Do you think about why you risked all this? Have you ever thought about that?
Yes. I knew a little bit more about Nazi machinery because I was reporting for an organization who was transmitting this information. It had no effect whatsoever. They [the Allies] completely ignored all we reported in Germany and did nothing. But I knew something about their plans and was very pessimistic about the outcome. Whereas other people had still hope that it would be really only a resettlement and so on. So I came to the conclusion that two people cannot survive simultaneously—Adolf Hitler and my wife—so I had to go all the way. I replied to the same question very easily. Once I told someone, I simply got mad. It was true. I did illogical things. The risks were far too high. But I loved my wife, of course, and this was, I think, the first motive and altruism became secondary. It was not altruism. . . . Later on, I came into this machinery of secret services and so on and it became then also an obsession. But originally it was just trying to survive and make my wife survive.

Q. You said it wasn't altruism. Why wasn't it altruism?
Because I did [it out] of *my* love for her.

Q. Did you consider her an extension of yourself in some way, or that you were one person? Is it like the marriage bond that talks about "now you are one"?
Maybe. I won't speculate in this direction because. . . . [Otto shrugged.]

Q. You don't really consider it altruism?
I know an absolutely clear case. A friend of mine. A very, very intelligent gentleman. He was a bachelor. He was German himself. But when the Germans took over, he was so mad about what the Nazis were doing that he said, "Now I am Czech." And he didn't register as German at all.

Now, you may remember that for the Czechs, the Nuremberg laws came much later. The Nuremberg laws, these were the laws that made it a crime against the race to marry a Jew. But at the beginning of the war, if you were a Czech Aryan, it might be a protection for a Jew if you were married to her. My friend Kari knew this and said, "Where is a Jew that I can marry?"

And there was one. She had fled Prague and lost, in Vienna, already her husband. She was left alone with two daughters. She and Kari didn't know each other. It was very funny, because when we introduced them, you know how it is in German, you use "thou" when you get intimate. You call each other "thou" instead of "you." Usually it happens that when you are alone, you call each other by the more intimate form than when you are in company. But with them, it was just the opposite. In company, they used the intimate form of address; but when they were alone, they were formal.

Q. What was his idea to marry her? Would that have given her protection?

Yes. Still at that time being married to a German would save you.

Q. Did it work? Did they get married?

Yes. She married Kari. Let me tell you what happened. For a while Mrs. Kari was safe. But then the Gestapo came and arrested Kari's new wife, due to a stupid mix-up of names. They came at a time when only one daughter was at home, so they grabbed her, too. The second daughter, the ten-year-old child, was with friends [that day]. Kari took the little girl who remained with him and hid her in the country somewhere. Mrs. Kari—Kari Mayer was his name—Mrs. Mayer was sent already to Auschwitz with her older daughter. Ultimately, they survived. Her daughter lost her toes through frostbite but she was alive and hopefully is still. But that was later.

Now, sometime after this, everyone married to a Jew gets a summons to get divorced from their Jewish wives. If you refuse, you go to prison, since such a marriage is now a crime against the race. We had a meeting. It was of course clear that we would all refuse. But we told Kari, "Look. You don't help your wife at all because she is already in Auschwitz. To get a divorce is just a signature for you. So why don't you do it? It's ridiculous. You help nobody. And, of course, if you refuse, you risk being arrested yourself."

But Kari said, "No. Germans are sticklers. Sticklers with all kinds of procedures and rules and forms." He said, "When I get a divorce, they could look up the files and could find that they had arrested only one child. Then they could figure that the other one must be somewhere. If there is only a small risk that they will find this child, it is my duty to go on to whatever end results."

He went to the concentration camp even though his wife had already been arrested, just in order to avoid the slight possibility that the child would be discovered. *That* is a clear case of altruism.

Q. But you don't consider what you did altruistic?
Whether you want to say one person, two persons. I don't know but it was. . . . Any motivation of human beings is complex. But the primitive had certainly a strong part in my motives.

Q. The love.
Yes.

Q. It was just an emotional thing for you.
Not quite. It cannot be separated.
    Now, which way we want to turn because I can't continue one thing leading to the other.

Q. What would you like to talk about? I have a lot of questions but I don't want to push you.
Please.

Q. I think you've told me a lot about yourself. Tell me how you would describe yourself. What kind of a person are you? You said, one time when we talked, I asked you about duty. Was that an important factor? And you said, "No, I was a show-off."
Yes. Again, things are so mixed that it is difficult to separate. I think that, if I'm honest, I have a rather high opinion of myself. One thing is important. I never made a moral decision to rescue Jews. I just got mad. I felt I had to do it. I came across many things that demanded my compassion. Odette Meyers, a survivor, was on a panel with me. She was asked why the rescuers took the risks they did. Meyers shared something she heard on a recent TV interview with a German rescuer, a woman who said she was tired of hearing about her spirit, courage, and nobility. "I did it because of self-respect," she said, "a lot of self-respect."

Q. What does that mean to you?
I like the word self-respect because it is what I said before. It is one of the egotistic components in my motivation. I respect more and feel good about it and this is a very good definition.

Q. One of the German rescuers that we interviewed, we asked about the honors. Did she do it for any honors or praise or things? And she said, "Well, it was nice to get the honors afterwards." But she said, "I never made use of that. I was only proud inside, just for me." I think that's what you're saying, is that right?

That is part of it. I am now bragging about my acts and part of it is that I had. . . . Now, again, I can't remember. . . . It's a blockage. It is the post-traumatic shock syndrome again. I have to speak and get it out of my system. The more I do that, the better I feel. That is true.

So. What else do we have in the way of questions?

Q. Let me ask you about choices. I'm interested in how people behave and in particular about times when they do what really is an extraordinary thing and certainly an extraordinary political action. Was there a choice for you? Did you sit down and make a choice about deciding? You said that you realized that both your wife and Hitler could not exist in the world.

It's only part of it.

Q. At that point, was there a choice for you? You still could have walked away.

I had no choice. Because if I had had only an affair with Hannah, I could have walked out. But when I was married with her, if I had signed my divorce, it would have been murder. Active murder. Because I knew that after that Hannah would have to be transported to Auschwitz. So it was not my choice. I came into a situation where I had no choice.

Q. But other people did it.

Okay, some people have done it.

Q. But you didn't feel it was a choice for you.

No.

Q. Why was that?

My education, influences, and a certain moral quality.

Q. You just couldn't do it.

No, no. Absolutely not. There was no choice.

Q. Was it just a kind of gut feeling that I just can't do this?

Yeah. I think so.

Q. I think I'm coming to understand that. What I'm hearing people say is that a lot of what philosophers and academics call moral choices are not really choices at all. [Otto nodded.] What about your life, though? You risked death many times. Were you afraid to die?

I was fully aware of that.

Q. You knew the costs. You knew it could happen.

Yes, I was only afraid of torturing, of being tortured. I had talked to my very good friend, Hans Becker, who was one of the leaders [of the Resistance in Austria]. He *was* tortured. It was he who was tortured about giving them our names. But he didn't do it. I spoke with him afterwards. I asked him how could he endure it. He was tortured, you know, in the usual way, cigarettes burned in his flesh and so on. He was a very religious man and he said he got religious fantasies, apparitions, until he fainted.

Q. He put his mind someplace else.
It came automatically somehow. Fantasy is not the right word. Appearances or delusions.

Q. Now, you're not a religious person, are you. Or are you?
No, I am not. I'm a pantheist.

Q. Yes, I think we talked about that. Let me ask you something. I don't want this to be difficult for you. Please tell me if it is and we can stop. But as we sit here, in your room, you're sitting on your bed with the railings and you've talked about the post-traumatic shock syndrome and how you would flail around at night and hit your head and things. Are you still having nightmares about this time?
Of course. Terrible ones. For years. I had to suppress it. I went into building up an existence in America with unusual intensity. This let me suppress my first syndromes. It keeps them down. But then when I started to dig into that time [World War II], then I had for years the identical situation in my dreams: I was sentenced to death and I could not escape. Everything was open but I simply could not walk out.

Q. This is your dream.
Yes, right. And persons who had been close to me told me you cannot do that [escape]. It has been decreed. You must submit to that.

Q. What do you think all that means?
I don't know. I have tried to figure it out. You know, we had a psychologist in the family. My wife, her maiden name was Adler. She was a second cousin to the psychologist, Alfred Adler. But I still don't know what the nightmares mean.

Q. Are these the nightmares you're having now?
No, they're completely different now. Because these nightmares ended, *always*, in the moment where the guillotine came down or the contraption strangled me. At that moment, I woke up.

Q. So now you have ongoing nightmares where you're about ready to be killed and then you wake up just as the guillotine comes down, or you're being strangled or poisoned. . . .

Yes. I got from a psychiatrist a drug which is a tranquilizer and this has helped. I have nightmares but they end happily inside the dream. For instance, when in a dream I had to submit to death by poison gas, I was sitting at a table and I couldn't escape and nothing. Now suddenly I turn around and see in this gas [chamber] a sign, "exit." And I walk out.

Q. Really. So the medicine has helped you. Otto, let me ask you. Are you afraid to die? [Otto shook his head.] No?
No. Not at all. Not at all, because it's not a big deal. It could be messy but also people complicate their lives by religion. It goes into your system when you are a child: hell, angels, devil, and so on. This generates fear.

Q. What do you think will happen when you die?
I am part of the pool again, of which something new will be created.

•   •   •

Otto Springer died in February 1994.

3

John

I have to help those in need, and when people need help, then you have to do it. . . .

Q. When you say you had to do it, that implies to me that there wasn't a choice for you. Did you . . . [John interrupted.]

No. There is no choice. When you have to do right, you do right.

John worked in the Resistance during World War II and organized an escape network to take Jews and political refugees to Spain or Switzerland.

I AM A DUTCHMAN, born in Brussels, Belgium. I lived in Holland, Belgium, Switzerland, and France before I came to the United States. I traveled a lot because I was the son of a Seventh-day Adventist pastor who was assigned to several places. I lived a good part of my life near Geneva in a Seventh-day Adventist college where my father was teaching the Bible in Greek. So I know the border between France and Switzerland very well.

When we were living in Switzerland, there was a law that the children had to go to school every day of the week, including Saturday. For us, Saturday was a day we had to respect as the memorial of the creation of God. This was one of the commandments, so my father went to the authorities to ask for permission for his children to be absent from school on Saturday.

The authorities said to my father, "This is the law. If you don't send your children, *you* will have to go to jail one day a week."

For seven years, I see my father going every week in jail because of his convictions. As a little boy, that impressed me, the idea that if you believe in something that is right, you have to be able to accept the consequence of it. That also helped me take a decision during the war: I wanted to help.

As a Dutchman, I was very unhappy to see Hitler take over Holland. I had a duty to my country, and I wanted to do something. This war was not the same as other wars; it was a war of cruelty and hate. Hitler and the Nazis were teaching hate, resentment, vengeance, and violence, all the things we are so against in my own concept of life and family. The basis of our beliefs is love to our God and love to our neighbor. The way to serve the Lord was to serve your neighbor. That was the basis for our beliefs in the church and at home. That and also the concept of personal freedom and respect for human beings.

Holland has always been a refuge for people persecuted. When the Huguenots were persecuted in France in the 1500s, they found a refuge in Holland. When the Pilgrim Fathers left England, they spent their first days in Holland. The French nobility, when they were persecuted during the French Revolution, moved to Holland. That is why you find a lot of French names in Holland.

When the war started, I thought as a human being, well, that's a question: how to help people. I thought I had a way to help them. If a Jewish person could reach Switzerland or Spain, he was safe. These countries were neutral. The big question was how to reach Switzerland from Holland. Everywhere there was Gestapo, the SS, the soldiers of Hitler. The borders were closed. The border between France and Switzerland was heavily guarded, because the Nazis knew that Jewish people tried to reach Switzerland.

What did one of the Gestapo's "Most Wanted" criminals do after World War II? John (pictured here in the 1980s) ran a health food store in Pasadena.

There was a lot of watching on the border. But I knew the border between Collonges, France, and Switzerland from my days in that college, where my father taught. In setting up an escape route, I tried to avoid the roads, to find a passage from one side of the mountain to the other side, down the cliff. There, with the help of my friends, we could watch during the night and then reach the border. We could avoid the guards, cut the barbed wire, and go into Switzerland. And so we did. Not me alone. Along the escape line from Holland to Belgium to France to Switzerland, there were around twelve people at the end working with us. During the war we helped around 1,000 people to reach Switzerland or Spain. It was not easy. The Gestapo was looking for these kind of people, people like us. I was afraid that a traitor would come, that we would be caught, arrested, deported, or killed. It is not easy. We needed means. We needed money to help 1,000 people, around 800 Jewish people. American airmen who were dropped, we saved them, too. Some political people from the government of Holland, we got them to Spain.

For these four years, especially the last two years, this group, which we called Dutch-Paris, was very active. But unfortunately for us, one of our agents was caught one day. Against our instructions, she had written down the names and addresses of the people in our organization. On the day she was caught, they found a booklet with all our addresses. And she spoke.

In one day, they arrested half our group, about fifty people. Forty-two never came back. Among them was my own sister. They died in a concentration camp in Poland.

But the war went on. Even after the arrest of these people, we went ahead. At the end of the war we had the satisfaction that we fulfilled our duty.

Oh, I can tell hours and hours, all the adventure of the war. During these four years, I had more adventure than in all the rest of my life.

I come from a family of prisoners. My great-grandfather was a minister of the Dutch Reformed Church in Holland, and he asked to be chaplain of the biggest prison of Holland. My father went to jail also. He was arrested in Holland because he protested against the arrest of Jewish people, and was put into the biggest prison in Holland. My younger sister went in a camp to save a life. My other sister was deported and died in concentration camp. I have been arrested five times. I thank the Lord that every time I was able to escape.

Q. What is it like to be arrested?

I don't know what is it like when others were arrested but I can tell you one story. One day, I was in Geneva. It was the beginning of 1944. I got a call from the headquarters of General Eisenhower to reach England. They were preparing for D-Day. They wanted to discuss with me some knowledge I had. To go to England, I had to cross the border between Geneva, Switzerland, and France, go across the mountains, and go to the southern part of France to cross the Pyrenees, the big mountains between France and Spain, approximately 6,000 feet high. In Spain, I could reach Gibraltar. From there I would take a plane to England. I know this route.

But when I got the call, I was concerned. It was the beginning of '44. The mountains were full of snow between France and Spain. I had just received news from one of my friends in this organization that a doctor—a Frenchman who wanted to join De Gaulle—had tried to cross the mountains. He was taken in a big storm and died there in the snow. So I was not too enthusiastic to go this way, aside from the danger of being arrested on my way by the Gestapo. But I saw my duty and, with the help of my friends, I crossed the border, crossed the mountains, and went to a city called Nancy, to take the train from Nancy to Toulouse. One of my first contacts was a friend of ours, a member of our organization, a young medical student who knew the mountains very well. I asked him some advice and got good counsel: go out and avoid the guards and the snow.

He said, "John, I'm going to give you a present. Here is a little Bible."

I put it in my pocket. I was walking in Toulouse the next morning when suddenly five men came around me with guns and stood up. I thought it was not very wise [to fight] with five machine guns so I put my hands up. They came up to me to feel what I had in my pocket, to find for weapons. They handcuffed me and arrested me. They wore plain clothes. They spoke French so I knew I was in the hands of the French Gestapo. In France during the war, you had the German Gestapo and the French Gestapo. They were working together, like the American army and the English army. The rule during the war was not to be in the hands of the Gestapo. They could arrest you, torture you, kill you, and they had only to answer to themselves.

They brought me in a big room. "We are happy to find you. What do you have to say, Mr. Dupont?"

I was surprised. "My name is not Mr. Dupont. You have made a mistake. I never used that name."

There was a Frenchman by the name of Dupont. Sometime before, he had killed a member of the French Gestapo, had been arrested, and escaped. I had changed the appearance of my face as much as possible. Moustache, glasses—which at that time, I didn't need—combed my hair differently. I looked like Dupont. They showed his picture to me and it was my picture. He had some marks on his shoulders. He was tortured before and had marks. So they took my coat and shirt off and found no marks. That convinced them that I was not Mr. Dupont. They apologized, as much as Gestapo members can apologize. They said I could take my shirt and coat and go.

I left as soon as possible. But when I reached the door, one of the officers called out, "You never told what was your real name."

Now that was the worst question they could ask me, because if they were looking for Mr. Dupont, they were looking ten times more for John Weidner. I wanted to tell them that I wasn't John Weidner.

"We want to know who you are. You don't tell, we find out in our ways."

I knew one of their ways to torture you was to put your head in and out of water until you speak.[1] They put me in a bathtub and do this and suddenly one man rushed into the room. "That's John Weidner, Captain Weidner."

He was looking in a book from the German Gestapo, with all the descriptions, and I was a most wanted man at this time. Looking at it, he found my picture and recognized me. "Now, Captain Weidner, we are most happy to see you," they said.

I told myself, "I will not say the same to you."

I was in the Dutch army but I was not in uniform. Because of this, I had no protection whatsoever from anyone. They recognized my picture. It was there in the book. They found my name and a full description about me because people had been arrested before and they had spoken about me. The Gestapo knew everything about me. They knew that I was a vegetarian. Being a vegetarian was not a crime, even in Nazi Europe. I mention this just to say an example of how they knew everything.

"Mr. Weidner. Your whole organization in Belgium and France, we know what you are doing. We are interested in the French people who are helping you. We want the names and addresses of these people."

"No. That I cannot do. I will not do it."

They said, "There are ways to make you speak." What they meant was to torture me.

"No," I told them, "you know from my story that I have never spoken when tortured. You can do what you want. I am never going to speak."

"We can try."

"Before you do it, I would like to speak with your chief. I want to say to him something that I don't want to say to you."

They said, "It's not possible."

He was the second most important man of the French Gestapo. He was precisely in the city of Toulouse because it was such an important place.

I said, "You can ask him, and torture me later. So ask him."

"Okay."

They came to me some time later and said, "You can speak with the chief." They brought me to the office of, I don't know his name. I said, "Mr. _____. Your men arrested me. I have not killed anyone. I help people to escape. Your people asked me to give the names and addresses of the French people who are helping me. That I cannot do. It is against the honor of an officer. If I asked you, would you speak?"

He said, "Okay, I understand what you mean. I am not going to ask you any questions. Thank you very much. I need the authorization of my chief, the head of the French Gestapo and the French police. I am going to make a good report and I am sure that in a few days, you are going to be free."

He said to his men, "He is my prisoner of war. Don't ask him anything, and treat him accordingly." So I was really happy. I did not speak. I was not tortured. I was going to be free.

One of the men who arrested me came some time later and said, "I've got your Bible. I don't read the Bible myself. But I am respectful of people who are reading the Bible."

He was not of my own religion. He was my enemy of war, someone who had arrested me. But for ten days, we talked and he brought me some good vegetarian food. We became friends.

One morning, one of the guards came to me and said, "I am sorry to tell you but the order has been given by the chief in Vichy that you are to be given over to the German Gestapo. And we are going to do that tomorrow morning. They know that you are here, and are prepared for you tomorrow morning. You have some time to write your family."

I had hoped to be free. Then my friend, the one who brought me the vegetarian food, came and said, "I heard you are going to be shot tomorrow morning."

I didn't like that. "I'd like to speak to you. I need some help. I make to you a proposition. You and all your people, when the Allies come and De Gaulle comes, you are all going to be arrested. You are all going to go to jail, and you all will be shot. Help me to escape, and come with me to Switzerland. That is a neutral country. They will take care of all you need and give you money to live there."

It was a very good proposition for him.

But he said, "No, I cannot do that. I have been with these people the whole time."

"Look," I told him, "I need help, even if you don't want to escape with me. I need some help to try to escape alone."

"What do you want? Don't ask me too much, because if they find out that I helped you, I will be shot in your place. What do you want?"

"Bring me to the _____ Prison. There are some cells there. From there, I can go to the front of the building where there are some offices and I can jump out of the offices. So bring me there and give me the key to my cell."

"Yes," he said, "I can bring you there. I cannot give the key. There is only one key, and the guard of the prison has it."

"Can you give me something to try to force the door?"

"Yes. That I can do. I'll bring some tools. Don't escape when the guard can see what you are doing. And don't escape until 6:00 in the morning. There is curfew." And he left.

It was not a good situation. I don't know what God will do. But I had confidence. I prayed the Lord that I would escape. Around midnight, I started to work on the door. Little by little, I was able to open the door. There was one guard with a machine gun, who was sleeping on the floor. At the end of the corridor, there was another guard, on the floor, also sleeping. On the front of the building, I open the door to the office, opened the window to the street. There was one guard walking around the block.

I waited fifteen to twenty minutes, till 6:00. It was the longest time of my life. I was afraid every minute that they would discover that I wasn't in my cell. It didn't happen. I opened the window. I could tell the guard was on the other side of the block. I threw myself into the street. Nothing happened, no broken leg, no gun, no nothing. I rushed as fast as I could to the second block, turned to the right, and started to walk slowly, like someone who had never heard of the Gestapo.

I went to one of my friends, a member of the organization, a Dutch priest. I knocked on the door.

"John, what are you doing here? You are supposed to be shot this morning."

"You want me to go back?"

He laughed. "You can't stay here. I am Dutch and am under suspicion. I'll bring you to a French friend of mine in the Underground to hide you."

He did hide me, and in a good place. The next day, the whole city of Toulouse was in turmoil. The French Gestapo, the German Gestapo, everyone looking. John Weidner had escaped. But I was in very good place. They did not find me. Several more days and everything was quiet. The French Underground helped me to go out of my hiding place and I could reach Eisenhower. I cross the mountains, go to England, and fulfill my mission.

At the end of the war, the whole group of [French Gestapo] was all arrested and condemned to die. I went to the president of the republic and asked for mercy. When they found out that my friend, the one who helped me, was condemned to die, they went to General De Gaulle, to get him to do something. For my friend, they changed the death sentence to a lesser penalty of forced labor.

I don't believe that the Bible is good luck. You know, "Put it in your pocket and you are saved," that kind of thing. But, I personally believe that the Bible is the gift of God that He left. It give the reason for my acts, the ethics of my life. I think that in that book, I find the reason why I have done what I did in the war.

One lesson that you have to learn from the horrible Holocaust, about why such a great amount of people—not Hitler alone—why so many people did what they did. The Jewish people, six million were killed during the war! To arrest people because of race, what is the lesson? Why did it happen? It happened because people had hate in their hearts instead of love. If all these people had love and compassion, then they would have never done anything to Jewish people. If we want to learn something, and hope it will not happen again, look at hate. You have to learn that you have to love your neighbor. He can be Jew. He can be Arab. He can be an American or German, anyone. We have to love our neighbor. If our hearts are not developed, the hearts of children, to love and have compassion, and to respect human life and beings, then we will not learn very much. So my hope is that the people have learned something from this war, and it will not happen again.

• • •

Q. Did you have to kill anyone during the war?
I never killed anyone.

Q. Would you have done it, had it been necessary?
No. It is a . . . I am not an objector of conscience. No. I believe that if an enemy is coming in your country, you defend it. You have your personal responsibility to people. The Seventh-day Adventist who got the Congressional Medal, Sergeant Doss, he saved a lot of people as a medic. He was not an objector of conscience. But he did his duty for his country, as a medic. So I think we do our duty to our country. Personally I have no wish to kill someone, but I think that a country has to be protected, and everyone has to make a decision, the way you want to do it. Most of the Seventh-day Adventists are medics. Me, I was in the intelligence. I did my duty as a human being, as a soldier, without having to kill. Killing would have been very difficult for me. People ask me, since I was tortured several times, whether I never feel any anger, did never want to beat back at the people who were doing this to me. Fighting back would make no sense.

I remember one time. A group of Jewish people was arrested and deported. One of the ladies had a baby in her hands, and the baby started to cry. It made a lot of noise at the railway station. The officer told the lady to make the baby stop crying. She did not succeed. The officer took that baby out of her hands, crashed the baby on the ground, and crushed the head of the baby with his boots. At that time, if I had a gun, I would have shot. But I could not do it. Had I, I would have been arrested and then I could not help.

Q. How does someone who is a sensitive human being, who is deeply religious as you are, witness something like this, and still maintain your sensitivity, faith, and your love for human beings?
Our reason has always dominated our emotions, our feelings. My first reaction was to do something. But I won't save the baby. I won't save

the lady. And I will be out of the picture to help other people. So, to protest will give the satisfaction to my own feelings, but [it will give] no result. So I didn't do it.

At the end of the war, the German prisoners, some German Seventh-day Adventists, were prisoners of war. They asked Saturday morning for my father to preach. He had just received the news that my sister had died in a concentration camp. At the end of the war, you could not say one nice word about the Germans. If you said that, you were what they called a collaborator. But my father preached, and he preached love, forgiveness, and compassion. He said, "In heaven, you have all kinds of nations: the French, with their finesse; the Germans with their organization; the Americans with their vision. So you can make a nice statement about everyone." At the end of the meeting, the German soldiers came to my father, because he said something nice to them. They ask my father to forgive them because my father was the only one, at that time, who could say something nice.

I think that we have to learn to forgive. We may not completely forget in the sense that we don't repeat the same mistakes, or that some nation will make the mistakes. I forgive the Nazis . . . even though my sister was killed by them.

I have a lot of German friends. I have forgiven them. Not for me to judge. Six million Jews—they are not dead; they are sleeping, waiting for the day of their judgment. For me it is consolation to know that they believe the message that they will be resurrected. I have to love my neighbor.

• • •

Q. John, let me ask you a couple of questions about this whole period. Then I want to talk about your earlier life. How do you handle the stress of a situation like this? You're living underground for most of the time during the war?
Yes. We had always tension from the fear to be arrested. But I think that when you are young and you know what you are doing is right, you have the confidence. Then you can handle the stress. I came through that.

You use the stress and use the tension. For example, I was going on the train two nights, without very much sleep. Just going one place to another place. You have to do it. When you are young, you can stand it, the constant stress. They found out in Holland, especially, that many of the people of the Underground, when they become older, have some physical problems that the doctor said originated during the war, because of the stress in the war. That's possible. But I have had no problems like that.

People often ask about my head. All the surgeries, I have had many surgeries to correct what the Nazis did to me, beating on my head. I know that my injuries came out of that time period. Yes, ok, but that is not stress. That is, "We blow your head off if you don't talk," and then they beat. So, I will not speak especially about stress. I had a constant tension, I don't want to be caught. But I don't remember any particular physical manifestation. No. Nothing.

My life during the war followed a pattern. We came three or four days in the occupied countries. We go back to Geneva, take two or three days to sleep and rest, and then go back. So I think, for me, there was no special time of stress. I will say again, with confidence, I will do what I can.

Q. You used the phrase, "You had to do it." Most people didn't do it, though. How did you feel you had to do it, when other people did not?
I had to do what everyone should do. [John shrugged.] I do it.

Q. But why did you have to do it?
Because I have to help those in need, and when people need help, then you have to do it. Now, it could be that I want to help people and I don't know how to do it. But I knew how to do it, because I knew the border. I knew how to bring them to Switzerland. I had to do it. Because I had the knowledge of how to do it.

Q. When you say you had to do it, that implies to me that there wasn't a choice for you. Did you . . . [John interrupted.]
No. There is no choice. When you have to do right, you do right.

Q. When does one make this choice?
Some people just do it suddenly. One day, they say they are now committed to some principles, some ideas, some decision to take, to do it that way, to do right. For others, it takes more time.

Q. How did it work for you? Was it an early realization as a young child? Was it when the war came?
I had the privilege to be born into a family that had the idea of serving your neighbor. They taught us that ideal. I remember my father say, "There's an old lady. You help her to carry her bag." This kind of thing. The parents' education helps. At the same time, with my own mind I have the idea that I have the guardianship of my brothers. I have to help others. Don't be selfish. Help others. With this concept of ideals, when the moment arrived that you had to do something, okay, you have to do it. It was my duty. I claim to be a person to help others. [John shrugged.] Then I do it!

Q. Did you ever sit down and think about the costs and the benefits and the risks involved in what you were doing? Did you sit down and think about all these things before you undertook these "adventures" that you went on?

I don't think so. I think that it came as a natural reaction from the inside. Like a mother. Normally, you don't teach a mother how to love her baby. She has that naturally. Maybe not the father, but the mother. So your instinct that you develop in yourself is to react that way. And so it was a quite natural development. Not, "Should I do it or not?"

I remember discussing with my father, one time, he say, "Always do what your conscience tells you." And for your conscience, there is no big problem, "Am I right or not?"

Another thing, I always learned to be truthful, to say the truth, never to lie. But when I came before the German Gestapo, it was for me very natural to lie, to say, "I don't know where are there [Jewish] people." It was only after the war, did I say, "Was it right or not?"

My story is the story of many people in Holland. Maybe you know a Dutch lady, Corrie ten Boom, who helped Jewish people. She say the same thing. When the Nazis come to ask, "Do you have Jews here, Madame?" Very naturally, she lie. Only afterward do she ask, "Am I right or wrong?" And even now, I ask myself [John shrugged], and I don't know.

Q. But at the time . . . ?

No question. No problem if it's right or wrong. *It was right!* It is right. They are human beings. . . . I wasn't lying so much to save my life but to save other people.

Q. You are saying there is a higher value for you than to tell the truth?

I think sometime in life you have to make a choice between higher values. This is a very difficult question. I can't say to anyone else. . . .

Q. What was the highest value for you, the value that was guiding you during this time?

Love your neighbor. You have to help. Now you can help someone who is in the street with nothing to eat. You can hand him a dollar, and you have done something to help him. Obviously you know there are some people, some groups—what you have in Los Angeles, the Mission, the Salvation Army, the Mother Teresas—they value others, other people. A value that everyone should have. Should not be selfish. . . . That is the reason, the ideal, expressed in the Bible. In the New Testament, Jesus said, "You want to show love for me, show love in action, not just, 'I love you.'" If I just said that to my wife, and I kiss her, and never give any presents, she won't believe in my love. I have to prove it. This means action.

The big temptation in life, I think, is to develop yourself intellectually, develop your knowledge, but you don't develop your heart. You know, before the war, Germany had the greatest amount of scientists. The greatest amount. They had really great brains. Yet the Holocaust happened there. So this knowledge [they have] is not saving humanity. I think it is wise to develop your knowledge, to develop your ability, physically, mentally, and so on. But if you don't develop your heart, love in action, compassion to those in need. . . . [John shrugged.]

This is the great value of America. America has shown this respect for others, this love for others. No other country in the world has all these Rotary Clubs and other things to help people. America helps other people outside of America. America has been a generous nation, thinking about other people. Brotherhood, America. America, brotherhood. If America loses that, it is not America. The great value of America in the world is that Americans are helping other people, other nations, other groups, churches, social groups. When we have somewhere an earthquake, somewhere like Armenia, the Americans go.

Q. Let's talk about how some of the countries responded to the Holocaust, countries like Switzerland and the United States. You were talking about Americans being so generous. But the Americans did very little during the war to take anybody in, and the Swiss were not totally opening their doors to people, were they?

We have to realize one thing. What happened in Europe, the Holocaust, the real terrible facts were not known until after the war. I had heard during the war about gas but I didn't believe it. Most of the people I had known during that time didn't believe. I could not believe that even the Nazis would go so far, so low, to use that to kill people.

Q. What did you think was happening to the Jews who disappeared?

We believed in concentration camps, but not in the gas chambers. We thought that the Jews were being put into concentration camps but that was all. When they spoke about the gas chambers, we couldn't believe it. Most of the people I knew in Geneva said, "It's not possible." America didn't know it. If the president or anyone knew it, they tried not to believe it. The arrests, I have seen. I witnessed Jewish people arrested. My father saw Jewish people who were arrested. If you had seen the Jewish lady with the baby whose head was crashed. . . . I will never forget it, but maybe in one week *you* will have forgotten it.

I think that it was possible that America didn't know. Nobody is perfect. America can't be perfect. You have the population and the administration. Generally speaking, the administration has not the heart of the population. America has felt a kind of responsibility . . . to help the Jewish people. In one sense, the state of Israel, the existence of a Jewish nation, reflects a feeling of remorse.

Q. When you're talking about giving to others, then how do you decide what you can give to others and what you have to keep for yourself? You talked about being in the train station and seeing the German officer pull the baby from the mother's arms and kill it. You said that if you had had a gun in your hands, you would have killed him then. But then you also said that it wouldn't have done any good. What kind of principle does one evolve or derive in order to deal with this kind of situation?

I was young, alone. . . . My sisters, one died so maybe you could say that I should have thought about not involving my sister. One sister was arrested and deported. She died, Gabrielle. She went to a torture camp and died in Poland. She was liberated by the Russians. For ten days, she was so weak, she hadn't eaten food in so long, that she died there. When I got the news that she had been arrested, I cried for three hours. I felt I was responsible in some way. And still, I feel it's too late. Whether I involved her or not, I don't know. There are some things I have still to deal with.[2]

For me, I have a hope. I believe that the dead are sleeping, and that there is a promise of resurrection. I believe in a Judgment. So for me there is a consolation; for a few years, I don't see my sister. For a few years. But there is an eternity. The rest of my life is a short period of time, for me, for everyone. I believe in the Judgment. It gives me consolation and hope that my sister still lives.

Q. A person who is not religious would say to you, "This is a fairy tale you're telling yourself. It's something you're creating, a fantasy to make yourself feel better."

Life is possible because there are a certain amount of people who are not selfish and who believe in sharing with others. That makes life possible. If there is no love and sacrifice, no concept of others, then maybe life would be possible in some ways but it would be a terrible tragedy, that one can be killed and robbed all the time.

Q. You think there is more to life than just pursuing your own self-interest?

Even if I didn't believe in the Resurrection or eternity, I would still believe in this point of view. If life has to go ahead in this earth, it is necessary to think about others. Now, the laws of the land, they are there to protect people against selfishness of others, to conduct a life that makes it possible to live.

Q. You're talking about practical aspects of life now. Before it seemed to me that you were talking more about the meaning of life in some sense. You were speaking, if I may use that term, about what it means to be a human being. What does it mean to be a human being to you?

I have some privileges; we get in turn some responsibilities. To have the abilities of speech, of hearing. I can walk. I am thankful for what I have. My responsibility is to share with others, because [otherwise] life would not be possible. I have seen in my life people who are selfish, and not happy. People who have power, and money, and everything, and they don't have enough. Never enough. They are not happy. I have seen people who are unselfish, and happy, people who don't have very much, and are happy with what they have. My ambition, my aim is to be happy. Then [you ask], how can you be happy? By being selfish? [John shook his head.]

Q. You would not have been happier if you had simply taken all your family and sat out the war in Switzerland? After the war, you could have said, "At least my family is intact. I love them, I've been a good person, I haven't done anything wrong." You would not have been happier doing that?

You have to do what is right. You have to think about more than yourself. You have to think about yourself, certainly. You have to eat, and have a home. But you must not concentrate on that. It is not my aim, it is not my rule to say, I, I, I. I have seen others around me, Salvation Army people, they are very happy. Why? Because they are helping. I see a lot of people who are very rich, but they don't have enough. I think happiness comes through helping other people. I am convinced of that. I see it around me. I see it for myself. I am really happy. I can make other people happy.

Q. When you spoke of being given certain gifts, and how these gifts entail certain obligations and duties, you did not mention things such as being born into a wealthy family, or being born into the Dutch tradition of helping people. Instead, the things you mentioned as gifts are things such as the ability to speak and hear, things that every human being—except in rare cases—is born with. And yet, you speak of these as gifts. Are you suggesting that merely having the gift of life entails certain responsibilities?

Yes, I think so. And I am happy that I can fulfill my responsibilities. To give an example. During the war, someone who worked with the Germans and who had become very rich, he had put a lot of money in Switzerland. At the end of the war, he fled to Switzerland. But he could not go back again to Belgium or to other countries. As soon as he came out, as soon as he would step across the border of Switzerland, he would be arrested and committed to thirty years of prison.

I got an offer of five million Swiss francs just to declare that this man had given me some information about the German army that was then brought over to England. To say that he was a kind of agent, five million Swiss francs! That's a lot of money. That was at that time nearly a million dollars. With that money, you could help so many poor people. [John shrugged.] But I could not do it.

Q. Now this is very interesting to me. You're saying in this case that you would not tell one very simple lie, even to get enough money to help a great many people. But during the war, you told a great many lies, in order to save and help a smaller number of people.

It seems strange in some ways.

Q. It's not consistent. You're saying it was natural in both cases. . . . [John interrupted.]

There *is* a consistency in some ways. During the war, there were people suffering not by their own faults, but by the hate of other people. Since they were suffering, I had to help them. Here, in this other instance, there is someone who is going to suffer because of his own faults, knowing what he was doing. I don't think I was in the right position to help him. It would be getting money in an unholy way. For example, say you are a diplomat. You can cross the border. You can bring in cocaine, and make a lot of money. That is not the way to do it. I will not make money in that way.

When I lied during the war, it was not to make money. The motive was not selfish, selfish power, selfish money, or for myself. It was to help others. To make money for myself, that is different.

Q. What about people who did help Jews during the war for money? There were such people.

Yes. I met such people. . . . [John shrugged.]

Q. You actually gave away a lot of your own money during the war.

All I had.

Q. There is a story I heard about you, that you were taking someone over the mountains, and one of the women looked down and noticed that you had no socks on. You were skiing in the snow with no socks.

It was a Jewish man. He had nothing, just shoes. I took my socks off, and gave them to him, knowing that I could have socks later, somewhere else. But it's true. We have to make some sacrifices. The only way we can be really happy is to forget yourself and make other people happy. This idea comes essentially from the Bible: love your neighbor as yourself. That is what God asked us to do. I think always about the example: Christ who died, for me, in order to save me, not for himself. A deep religious concept in my life has come out. I always say, "Learn to read the Bible; it will tell you how to love your neighbor."

Q. Let's talk a little bit about religion. How important a factor do you think religion was in general for most people who rescued Jews?

I don't know that you had to be religious. An Adventist, a Catholic, or a Jew, you had to have love in your heart. How does love come into your heart? I don't know exactly. But I know I have to have love. If I don't have it, then I have to ask the Lord to give me it. I need more love, more affection, more consideration for others, and more desire to help others, and be less selfish.

Now, some people are born with money. They love their neighbor, and they can give money. So everyone has to act on his own, to give what he has. I could help people because I knew the border. I knew other people who could help Jewish people, they knew the border in Holland. Or they hid them in an attic. The means I had to find what way I have to help. What can I do? All right, I have that ability. Let me use it, not for myself, but for others.

Q. Are you saying that the critical factor in your rescue activities was not a religious one, so much as love in your heart for other people?

For myself, I was raised by a family who developed in me the feelings of life. And so, I had that privilege. I had to use that privilege for others. If I was born a millionaire, born from a millionaire family, then I would give a few millions. God won't ask you the day that you come into heaven, "How much was your bank account, and how much was your knowledge." He will ask, "What have you done with what you have?"

Q. What will you say?

I will say, "Not enough."

Q. You haven't done enough.

I could have done much more. In the end of my life, I will have to make progress.

Q. Most people will say that what you did was an extraordinarily good deed.

No.

Q. You don't see it as that?

Absolutely not. I did my duty. That is all.

Q. There was nothing unusual about what you did?

No. I don't think anything special. If you ask me why I did it, okay, I did it for love. I would never consider myself a fantastic hero or that I am a fantastic person, because, for me the one hero and one person who was perfect was Christ, and I follow his example. *He* was perfect, but nobody [else] is perfect. Even Paul was not perfect. He said it himself; he was struggling all the time. Selfishness and pride, we are born with that. I can't do it myself alone. I need the power of God.

Q. What do you feel about some of the honors you've gotten? You have a lot of honors.

I am a human being. I think it is always a good feeling that some people thank you. The Jewish people who thank me, I am happy; it give me a good feeling, when they say thank you, when they send me notes saying, "I won't forget you."

When I was in Holland, some people said nice things to me. Ego, and pride, I think that appeals to those parts of me.

Q. Did you do it in any way because you wanted the honors?

No. Never! I think that the people underground never had any idea of this! Never!

Q. What about doing it because it made you feel good about yourself?

I feel bad if I don't do what I have to do, and I feel good when I do what I have to do.

Q. Did you do it in order to feel good about yourself?

No, not in order. But, the result was that I was happy. No. You have a friend who is nice to you. Why? Because they love. Not because he expects something in exchange. Sometimes you do something, and expect to get something in exchange. But there is a natural feeling to show that I love you, and to show affection, and not to get something. Is that not so?

In the Underground, there were Catholics, Protestants, agnostics, Jews, and non-believers. But there was a yearning to serve and to help. It didn't matter what religion they had. I am convinced that on the Day of Judgment, not only the Seventh-day Adventists are going to be saved. In fact, I believe that non-believers will be saved, because the idea is to live together in harmony, based on love. Some people just show love. I can give a good example of love in action. Albert Schweitzer. He didn't believe in Christ but he did fantastic work for the people in Africa. Now if he had believed in Christ, he might have been a better example in some ways, but that is up to God to judge, not to me. I do know one thing: it is important, very important, to develop this feeling of duty to others, of respect for others.

Q. Let me ask you a question about duty. You've mentioned it several times. Do you think people have a social responsibility to help other people in need, even if it hurts them, or hurts their loved ones?

It is said to love your neighbor as yourself. It is not said directly that you love him *above* yourself. It is not said that you have to sacrifice everything. One moment, yes, you may make a special sacrifice. You see a home burning, and you risk burns to rescue the people inside. But I don't think that in your daily life that you have to always think about others and forget yourself, your wife and children, your neighbor and other people. Your social responsibility is to help, but to have also a family who is not a charge of the state. You give first to your children, I believe that, and you have to accept that other people will die because you have to save your children. So there is a question of conscience, of good judgment, and everyone would not answer the same way.

Q. What about your parents and family? Did your parents know what you were doing during the war? What if your mother had been upset and had said, "John, I love you so much. You're my son. Please don't do this. I can't bear risking your life."

First of all, my mother wouldn't ask that. Second thing, maybe God will make that my mother will never ask that. Maybe she wants to ask. I believe in God's intervention in some ways. But if my mother asked me, "John, please don't do this," I would go ahead anyway. I would not answer the request of my mother. If I put my father there, if they brought my father in and said they are going to shoot him if I didn't tell my name, I have no problem because my father would say, "John, don't speak."

Q. What if your father would have said: "Speak, save me."
No.

Q. What about a child?
I think God would help me so that I don't have to answer the question.

Q. A child would be different for you?
You know, the Huguenots, when they were persecuted in France, wives and children were tortured and they never spoke.[3] They accepted to be tortured, but they would not speak. I think that God will give you the power to accept, to suffer, in terrible ways, or make it so that you will die before you have to suffer too much. I believe that God has His plans. I trust that I can sense it. I don't ask the question too much: if, if, if. If it happens, then it happens; then I want to do what is right.

Q. But you were tortured rather badly a couple of times.
They wanted to know where I, where we had hidden several people, certain members of my organization. The first time they suspected me, they had no proof. I didn't speak, and they beat me and beat me in the head. Then they let me go. They beat me badly in the head. They beat

you with the guns, bang, and they beat you in the stomach and your head. But they couldn't get anything out of me, and they had no proof.

Q. You weren't tempted to tell them anything?
Never! Never tempted. Never! I think the moment I would have asked myself if I should tell them, that was the end. I would have spoken.

Q. It never entered your mind?
Never. I could do something. They could say, "We will kill your children, and we will save you. Your son, or your daughter, here, you are saved." Would you do it? No. If they say, "Kill one child, and others will be saved." Would you do it? No. To live all my life with the guilt that I killed one. . . . [John shook his head.] It's not right.

Q. How old were you during all this time when this was going on?
The best years of my life. Between twenty-five and thirty-two. I was born in the end of 1912. The war started in 1940. I was twenty-eight. Physically and mentally, that was the best time of my life.

Q. How would you describe yourself, as a person. After I do these interviews and go home, my husband says, "Well, tell me what this guy was like today." What do I tell him?
The truth.

Q. What is the truth?
Good question. I don't know.

Q. Do you see yourself as an aggressive person, a passive person?
I am an aggressive person. When I was a kid, I was really a naughty boy.

Q. A naughty boy?
My little sister, Annette, she came in and told what I do that day and when my father came in, bang, bang, bang. . . . [John smacked his hands.]

Q. You got a spanking?
I got a lot of spankings when I was young. I learned discipline, which is the stuff of love. If you have love and no discipline, things can go bad. If you have discipline and no love, not good. My sister never got a spanking. The fear of my mother was enough for her. Not for me. It depends on the child. Some children, you love and sweet stroke, you get good results. Another child, no. They need discipline. My father could beat me all the time. But he let me win sometime. But the same time, I got a lot of love. So that was my youth. But my young brother, he was so sweet, so nice, so kind. I say to love and discipline the right way. What do *you* think?

Q. I think you're absolutely right that children need boundaries.

They have to learn sometime by force. Sometime, you are too sweet and too nice, and they don't respect authority, the country, the laws of the country, and of the city, because when they were young, there was not discipline. Discipline is important for respect of law. But the law of God is above the law of men. In my own life, I make the decision: the law of God first.

Q. Let me ask you a little bit about how you view the world, and about how you see yourself in relation to other people.

I want to make my living, to make money if I can, but not to make money for myself. My money has to be serving others: my church, the Rotary Club, the Boys Club, everything. I have to use my means regardless of what others are doing, I have to go my way, unselfishly, and help.

I am an immigrant to the United States. My gratitude toward America obliged me to be active in the activities of the city. For example, now I am president of the Downtown Merchants Association. I am president of the Chamber of Commerce. I am active in my church. I have been president of the Rotary Club. It is my duty, as gratitude towards America. I come here, I find nice homes, nice roads; it is my duty to show my gratitude by doing something for my city.

Let me tell you something very funny. My first memory of Americans was in 1919. I was a boy of seven, and the Americans came into the city. I was hungry, and the Americans came with a lot of food. I said to myself, "Now, I am going to eat." But then I became afraid 'cause the Americans were eating all the time! I thought that nothing is going to be there for me. That was my first reaction about the Americans. They were eating a product that was unknown to me at that time: chewing gum. My first memory of Americans was of chewing gum. They kept chewing it and chewing it and chewing it and I didn't understand it. I was so hungry. Then I found out it was chewing gum. This was my first introduction to Americans, in Belgium. So, at the end of my life, I've seen a lot of things: wars, peace, liberations, and suffering. It is a world where there is no solution. In Europe, there is now a better time. I am happy that the Americans came to deliver us from Europe. I am grateful for the sacrifice she made to us.

• • •

Q. Would you have saved Hitler if he had been drowning in a lake?

Yes, I would save him. I would save him to go to Judgment. One day he will go to Judgment anyway. We all do, one day. But I would like to have him sit in Judgment now, at this earth, with the other people.

Q. Do you feel we do have free will?

Oh, yes. We have to choose right from wrong. But then, to do what is right, that is the power of God. The power in my mind to judge right or wrong, to do what is right, God has given me that power. I know that if I was going this way, I am wrong. I know if I go that way, I am right. But to go, I need the power to go this way or that way. *That* power comes from God. We can decide we want to do right, or wrong. But God is the one who helps us do it. That is what I believe. I do it myself, but I ask God to give me the power. God does not make robots. He makes free people, free to choose, and if you choose right from wrong, it is your decision, not the decision of God.

Q. God just helps you act on the choice, is that what you're saying?

The miracle of God came in helping me escape the Nazis to protect my mission. I remember one day, I took the train from Lyon to Paris. It was 10:00 o'clock in the railway station in Lyon, and the halls of people were packed with people who wanted to board the train. When the train came, there was no place for me on the train. At the end, I squeezed myself between the wagons, the first two wagons behind the engine. There was the engine, then the car, and I was between the two. I sat there eight hours. In the end of the train, there were some workers who pushed a brand-new, empty car, and the car stopped just before me at the end of the train, and I jumped into the car. Two or three hours suddenly, there was a big shock. An attempt had been made to destroy the bridge. The news came that the first engine and the first cars went into the ravine. I woke up, and saw the engines and the cars. People were crying and calling for help. I went down the ravine. All the people there were dead, crashed in the wreckage. I went back to my [original] compartment. It was full of blood.

God gave me the idea to move, because otherwise I would have gone into the ravine instead. The wagons at the back were taken away and went to Paris.

I remember one day, the Nazis decided to arrest all the families of those who were serving with De Gaulle and the French. One man (the Count of Menthon), he was in London and his wife was in Geneva. She had a boy of five years old, Olivier de Menthon, still in France. "John, please pray for my boy. I am concerned with him." I said I'd do my best.

I took the boy, and went to the border, and passed the creek. The creek was muddy, there was a lot of rain, and the creek was swollen very much. It was just near the border of France and Switzerland. Anyway, I took him on my shoulders and started to step in the water. We went down and down, and the water came up and up and up. It came just to here. "Do we swim? Do we go back?" I ask myself. And the next step, it went up, up, and we were saved. I finished . . . and I took the boy to his mother. That was the night before Christmas of '44. I said, "Here is your Christmas present."

I will say that the greatest amount of people who we helped, after the war, never thanked us. But many, many came and thanked us. I found out that Jewish people are just like non-Jewish people. You find nice people, thankful people, selfish, grateful, all kinds of people. It is not because they are Jewish that they are better people than other ones. They are all very intelligent. But what concerns behavior in life? Kindness. Some are very kind, very nice, and some are not. Just like other people.

During the Holocaust, families died in the concentration camp, in the most horrible way. . . . [John seemed lost in thought, then shook his head.] I hope people have learned something from this. We need to be more kind, more compassionate for other people. So I hope everyone has learned something out of this war.

Q. What did you learn mostly out of this war?

Principles. Take the story of Germany. Germany was a very nationalist country before the war. In their song, their national anthem is "Deutschland Über Alles"—Germany above everything. Germany was a wonderful country. The Reformation was there, and they started to print the Bible in Germany. Germany was the first country to become very nationalistic: Deutschland, Deutschland. They wanted to make it bigger. At the end of '14, they invaded Belgium and France, made the war. The Americans came and they lost the war. For a nationalist country like Germany, it was very hard to accept to lose the war. They were angry and there was not very much work.

Then Hitler came. He came out of Bavaria, and was Catholic. He said, "We have not lost the war. The Jews caused us to be defeated." That was a nice thing to be hearing for the nationalistic people. So he started in Germany a great desire for revenge and "We Germany, Über Alles," and start to have a hate against Jewish people. This was more and more and more hate developing as he worked on people. He used young people, Hitler Youth, to say, "He is the man we need." So he prepared the country. He had the army prepared to go to war against whole countries: France, Belgium, Denmark, Norway. Then he went to the east: Czechoslovakia, Hungary, Romania, and so on. He made a treaty with Russians. Then he forgot the treaty, and said, "Now I will go to Russia."

He made two big mistakes. One in Dunkirk, when the English and French were trapped, and losing. At that time, Hitler had the possibility and the force and the strength to make an invasion of England. But he didn't do it. He waited, from May to September. During that time, the Americans sent weapons, planes. In September, Hitler decided to invade

England, first by planes. Bomb, bomb, bomb. The first day, he lost planes. The second day, again, and again. So much planes lost, he decided he could not make it. That saved England. I think it was the will of God that England was saved.

The second thing, when he went to Russia, the Ukrainians loved him. They wanted to go with him against Russia. He said, "Hah." He treated them like undermen, subhuman. The second great mistake. And so, he lost there in Russia. He lost like Napoleon lost.

People are afraid of losing now in Iraq. Like Hitler, you can't discuss with Saddam Hussein. He promises something and he won't do it. The Americans are afraid to speak with him. Anyway, he promises something, and he won't do. So Napoleon, and so Hitler, lost the war. But if Hitler had gone to England, he could have dominated Europe for a thousand years. I believed that God has made miracles there.

• • •

Q. You were telling me earlier about carrying the young boy across the river and taking him to his mother in Geneva and saying, "Here is your Christmas present." You said this was one of the nice things that happened. Are there other nice stories that you remember from the war?

Not so much that you want to hear.

Q. What was the worst thing that you saw during the war?

There was a government in France during the war, very controversial. Half of France was Vichy under General Pétain. But what was very bad with Vichy was that they had a legal agreement with the Germans that the Jewish could be arrested by the French and given over to the Germans. The Dutch Jews, in the southern part of France, not the French Jews, were arrested and then deported. That was bad. The Jewish people were arrested and sent to the concentration camps. Again, we thought they were sent to the camps, not gassed. The people were separated, wife and husband. . . .

Q. You said that after the war, your doctor advised you to come to this country?

No. I had some friends, and they had some psychiatrist who told them I was not in good shape. I was one of many others who had the same condition. The war had shaped us. All the memories of wartime. Go to a new country and forget all that. I came to America . . . to forget . . . or at least not to see it so much. I will never forget it! But it is not the same to be at the place and see it every time you pass a place. So I went to America. Here, all is new and nice and good. I am happy with America.

But tomorrow, if a dictator came over to take over America, I fear lots of people would walk with the enemy. I have seen it in Europe. The Dutch, the French, walked with the enemy.

Q. How do you feel about collaborators?

I have nothing against them. I feel pity for them. They are forgiven. It is over. But during the war, they were even more dangerous than the Germans themselves, because we knew about the Germans, but the collaborators! They were worse than the Germans themselves, because we knew the Germans, but to betray us. . . .

Q. What about Suzy [the member of your group who was caught and revealed names]?

She made a grave mistake.[4] She had kept all the names and addresses of the other people in our group. It was forbidden. The first rule: never, never write anything down. But she did it anyway. She was arrested, by the French first and then handed over to the Germans. They told her they would kill her father and mother. . . . She spoke. . . . She spoke, and in one or two days, practically, they arrested almost one hundred and fifty of our people. But I and the four most important people were not taken. . . . We were not caught because we were always traveling, always going without a fixed address. So she could not say we were here or there because we never said to her where she could find us. So, all the people that were arrested did not know our address. We were ourselves changing address all the time. It was just the five most important people: me and four others.

Q. How did you hear that Suzy had given away names?

We heard.

Q. You heard what?

We heard that this person had been arrested. Then another had been arrested, then another, and another. . . . Why? We knew that Suzy had been arrested. We then made the conclusion: who knew this one and this one and this one? That was Suzy. She was the only one who knew all the addresses. She was the only one who had the addresses for everyone.

When she was in camp with people, they told her, "You have betrayed us." And she said, "No, no." She lied about it.

When the war was over, she came back.

Q. Came back from a concentration camp?

Yes. But we had papers from the Gestapo, papers saying what she had said. And there it was. So we knew.

She had done good work. She had made a mistake. She did not go to the Gestapo to betray us. She made a mistake. I said to the people who came back from Germany, "What should we do? I can forgive her, but I cannot forgive her for you." We talked about it and we forgave her.

Later she married, and now lives in Holland. It plays heavy on her conscience. She said that she never forgets it.

Q. Did you see her yourself, after the war? Were you there when she was interrogated?

No.

Q. Did you ever see her?

I sent my officers.

Q. Did you ever see her yourself?

No. I was a little afraid for myself. Not that I would hurt her, but of what I would say. I avoided the temptation. My father spoke with her, though.

Q. What did he say to her?

When he heard that my sister passed away, and Suzy came back from the camp . . . terrible. For three hours I cried. . . . I never cry. For three hours, I cried! And then I had to say to my mother and father . . . it was terrible. I went to Holland, I told first my father. . . . He was very ill . . . and then to my mother. I told them first that my sister had been arrested, and then the next day, I said to my father, "She passed away." She would never come back. At that time, they were afraid that my mother would lose her mind. Only a mother, I think, can really understand the loss of children. I cried with mother and father and sisters. Sad . . . my mother always had a sad look after that. But she was courageous. Then later, my younger sister got married, had two children, and that let some of my mother's joy back again.

Q. What did your father say to Suzy when she came to see him?

He forgave her. He was very nice to her. . . . He could see that Suzy was suffering. He forgave her, and wished her the best.

Q. Did your mother feel the same way?

I am not able to read all the heart of my mother. She did sign the letter of my father, saying that Suzy was forgiven. If it was possible for her to forget completely and forgive completely, I don't know. So much suffering, thinking about this. . . . A mother's child taken out of her hands by the Gestapo. How can people be so inhumane . . . beasts. Sadism. How can people be that bad? I can't believe it. . . .

Q. Do you have any thoughts on why, on what it is that can make normal people do such terrible things?

The heart and conscience disappear. The heart disappears. Some of the Gestapo people are very interesting. They had a family, they had a wife, children. Their hate was so great against the Jews, but they had a normal life. You find it is true. Many boys kill their father, mother. Anyway. These kind of things are hard to forget in some ways. But not the depression. I keep smiling, and I find I can do my best for myself, and help other people to be better.

Q. Let me ask you a couple questions about that period. Had there ever been any time before the war that you had been involved in any kind of rescue activities? As a youngster?

Nothing special that I know. I know watching my father, seeing him spend the afternoon to feed the poor people, to speak with them, to visit hospitals, all that developed a heart for me. A feeling for suffering. You know? I could not see a fish on the line without that I suffer for the poor fish.

Q. So your feelings about the value of life seem to extend beyond human life into the animal world?

Yes, I am a vegetarian. One of the reasons I am a vegetarian is because I don't like to kill. But again, suppose that I had nothing to eat. I would kill, rather than die. I am more important than an animal. God has made the animals for me. But I can't kill them for the joy of killing, just for hunting. I can even avoid it for eating and so. But if I had nothing to eat and it was cold, then I would think that my religion should say, you have the right, and if you want to use it for yourself, your wife and children, then kill them. But I don't need it, and I stayed a vegetarian. My sister was a vegetarian, but when she was in camps, she started to eat meat. When I was in a camp for a few days or so, I exchanged my meat against the vegetables of the other prisoners. That Gestapo meat was so bad, they always got sick with dysentery, and I was not sick. But I will eat meat. I will kill if it is necessary.

Speaking about killing, many people are against using animals in laboratories and medical research. I think that many of these medical research are made in an inhumane way with animals. We should always have it done in such a way that the animals will not suffer. But I will not go to the extreme to say we should never use animals to make experiments because, if we need to save human beings, then I think we should use animals in a way to save lives. But use them with compassion even then. Make it so that they suffer as little as possible. A lot of people have no compassion for animals and they will just treat them as nothing, instead of being very careful not to let them suffer.

Q. When you were rescuing these people, did you do any of that because you were trying to expunge guilt for an earlier time when you had maybe not done something?

No.

Q. Nothing to do with that?

In our home, we were always taking out of the Scripture the idea of payment. For me and my family, it was not important. God forgives us. Don't think about it any more. You don't need to pay anything. No need for guilt anymore. God has forgiven us. So, if I had done something wrong in the past, it is over. Rescuing was not to pay or get in good grace with the Lord. No, it was not to forget or forgive what I had done in the past. If you steal money from someone, you give it back. Now there is something maybe that you can never give back. Some things that are very important, maybe when you are young, but are not that important later. But I never had a feeling of guilt, that I had to pay for something done earlier.

Q. You've talked a lot about judgment and the Judgment Day. Was there any kind of conscious thought in your mind that maybe rescuing Jews was going to buy you a better spot in Paradise?

Oh, no. Never. All that concept of paying to get something better in the future, no. Yes, I would like to participate in the new earth. I'd like to be saved. But, I don't, *absolutely* I don't do something because I will have a better position in heaven, no! The *idea,* that I would do something in order to get something better, it wasn't like that! It was my duty, I had to do it. But not to gain something out of it.

Q. You talked a lot about your father and your mother. Were they important role models for you when you were growing up?

They were models for me. I saw love, discipline, and caring. I've never seen my father and mother discuss anything. Never. My father will spank me, not my mother. But I never saw my mother disagree or argue with father. If my father has an opinion, and my mother opposing it? Never.

Q. You never saw your parents fight?

Never! Always united. Later my mother told me that when my father spanked me, she would cry and go to her room. She could not stand it. But she let my father do it, because she knew that he had authority, had reason to do it. But I never saw a difference of opinion between my father and mother in the home. I could not switch from father to mother, mother against father. If I was guilty, my mother would say, "Father's coming home tonight." I think that it was such a wonderful family life, with such great respect for parents, and so much love and respect, because I think they were logical in their own life, in their beliefs.

Q. They were also religious people?

Very. But, they were not dogmatic. Not full of rigid principles. Consider baptism. We think that people should make their own decision, and that babies are not making their own decision. So before you are baptized, you must be at an age when you can make your decision. My mother and father was very interested that I become a Seventh-day Adventist and baptized, since my father was a Seventh-day Adventist minister. But when I was fourteen years old, my father took me to the Catholic priests, to the Mormons, and we discussed their religion. He would take me to several religious groups to discuss religion, so that I could make my decision on my own, knowing what I was doing.

Even though he was a Seventh-day Adventist, he would take me to other groups to discuss religion. Always my father would say, "I'd like you to discuss your religion for my son. The one thing I want is that we take the Bible as a basis of discussion." So I knew what I was doing. I was not just following the religion of my father and my mother. I knew what I was doing. My father was very wise.

Q. If your father was a role model for you, did you feel in any way that had you not lived up to his expectations of you, that you would have been letting him down?

I was more concerned that I would do something that would make the heart of my father and mother very sick.

Q. So their possible disapproval was important to you?

Yes.

Q. When you think about your rescue activities, did you ever think about the fact that "this might be me" in a situation, that you might need something sometime, and that you would want someone to help you?

No, I was not preparing the future for myself.

Q. Was there ever a critical period in your life, emotionally, where you just felt that you needed help, desperately, where you felt that you were alone or needed help?

When my sister passed away, and I had to go to my folks and say it. What should I do? How should I do it? But, otherwise, I don't remember especially.

Q. How did you handle that? Was there someone there for you who helped you?

Yes. Someone who had been deported, who was in the same camp as my sister, she came back and told me of the end of my sister. She was there at the end.

Q. So she was able to help you emotionally?

I think that nobody could really help me at that time. I cried and cried. Some friends came. I didn't want to do anything with them. I was on my own. Big shock.

Q. You weren't able to do what a lot of people do to handle things like this, in different ways. Maybe they go out drinking with someone or they have a lover who is helpful. You didn't do any of these things?

No. It would have been impossible, I think. If I had been a smoker, maybe I would smoke, smoke, and smoke. I could have drank and drank and drank, but not for me.

Q. Not for you. Let me ask you about people who chose not to help during the war. What do you think about those people?

It depends on the reason why. I cannot automatically say that someone who does not help is bad. Someone might have his wife and children to worry about. He is afraid to help. Most of the people in Europe who did not help were concerned with what could happen to themselves. People didn't help because they did not know how to do it. I will not condemn such people who do not help. It would be difficult to say. America did not help with refugees. They were not in direct danger themselves.

Q. You don't judge anybody else?

No, I will not judge.

Q. Do you think people are basically good or bad, or self-interested? Do you think there is a norm?

Basically good. Good and bad. Some with conscience, some with more, some with less. Some people have more ethics naturally than others. They are born with that concept.

Q. Born? Ethics are born within us?

With some, yes, I think so. Not so much with others. We are all not born equally. We're not all born equally in terms of our ability to make moral judgment, or equally in other ways. We are all born equally to right of choice—that, yes. But one is born poor, one is born more rich. One is born indigent. One is born not indigent. One is born with four fingers or five fingers. One is born with illness. But we are not born equally. Women are women, men are men. Each has something mentally, physically. Each has to work together. The men need the woman to have the baby. So each has to work together. Because of inequality, it is my duty to share the thing that I have. If I don't have it, I cannot give it. But it is my responsibility to work [with] what I have. If I have more money than another one, and the other one does his best, and does not have the money to live, I have to share with him.

Q. But how do you account for the difference in terms of moral choice, for some people's ability to make better moral choices than others?

I think that some people are born with a better notion of what is right and wrong. Some people are born with the privilege of parents who are wise how to educate their children in a way that they can be useful to society. God is not going to judge a person only on his act, but also on other things around him. A poor guy who has a piece of bread, if he steals, well, I will not judge him so much as God will judge him. I cannot read the hearts of everyone. Think about some people. For some reasons, even though they make a big effort, they just can't make it because they don't have the ability to do it. So be nice, and don't be harsh. They do their best; be nice to them. We are born unequally, and society has to try to bring the best we can to make the equality more apparent, to get less inequality. The rich have to pay more taxes than the poor, because that is the way to help. It is important for the people to be not too selfish.

Q. Do you think you were changed much by your rescue activities?

Basically, I don't think so, no. I think mostly I've learned to love people on the better way. For example, we have a poor guy who hasn't worked. I helped him to find a job, so he can learn a job. When he knows the job, then I have helped to learn the way to be helpful.

Q. So you learned how to be more helpful through your rescue activities?

How. How to be more helpful. I learned *how* to do it. But it didn't change me basically. Basically, no. The desire to be helpful is there. God asked me to develop that feeling. How to do it, that is where my brains are coming in. God gave me the lightning in my brains, the understanding to do so and so. Take the Chamber of Commerce or various organizations. If I am the president of the Chamber of Commerce, I never say I am a Seventh-day Adventist, never. I do what is right and wrong. I will be guided by my conscience. But I will never say my church teach me that and that.

Q. But what would you consider your basic identity?

My identity is to fulfill my function on the way that I know is best. And so I think that if you can help someone with conscience, knowing right and wrong and the power of the decision . . . having the ability to give good judgment, that is what I like to do. I fulfill my function.

Q. Your accent sounds French to me, not Dutch. Is French your first language or is Dutch?

No, Dutch. Dutch is my first language. I am Dutch. My mother could not speak French. I was raised part in Holland, part in Belgium, part in France, and part in Switzerland. I was raised in both big and small cities. Brussels is a big city. Then I lived not far from Geneva, in what was not more than a little village.

Q. Was there anybody else in your life when you were growing up who was a particularly important influence on you, other than your mother and your father?

No. My teachers and school, through their teaching and their example in their life.

Q. Was there anybody who encouraged you to become a rescuer in particular?

Not especially. It came naturally. With other friends who shared opinions and worked together to help. . . .

Q. When you did these rescues, did you usually initiate them yourselves? Did people come to you and ask for help? How did it work and what goes through your mind when you do it?

Most of the people that I helped, for example in Lyon, there was a Dutch consulate, and the Dutch people who came to the consulate. Now, the consulate was closed. There was an officer there who would tell people, "We can't help you very much, but go and see Mr. Weidner." These people could have friends and family who would say, "Go and see Mr. Weidner."

Q. But how did you know how to trust people, which people to trust? There is a story in your book about a family that had gold hidden away?

Yes, I remember this story. They were Jewish people. They told me they had no money. During the war, it was not easy. You had to find shelter for them. Where do you do this? Who is going to pay for their food? This needs money. So this Jewish family came, and the lady said she had nothing, When we came to the border, she had hidden in the bread, a gold bar. The Swiss took it but they gave it back to her.

We needed to use judgment and ways to be sure that someone was really good. One day we found out that one of the men was a spy. We found out, but we didn't tell him. We sent him to England. In England, they followed him. He went to all kinds of addresses. After that, they arrested him, and they arrested all the other people, also spies. So I never had really a betrayal from one of our men, except Suzy, but even that is not a betrayal. In that we were lucky, to have succeeded, not to have dangerous people.

But the Americans! One day they were sent to England. The next day they were flying over occupied countries, and they were shot down. One time a group of ten Americans was shot down. We took five with one group and a group of five with another part of our rescue group. At Toulouse, we crossed a street, and there were the first five. One turned and called out, "Hey, Joe!" Whew! Sometimes Americans were very naive. I told them always, with cigarettes or with forks, always keep it the other way. I would always tell them. I had to use a lot of improvisation to tell them how to avoid to be taken, or if you were taken, what to say and how to come out. I was not trained for that.

Q. Let me ask you about this period. When you're in this kind of situation, do you consider the possible repercussions of your actions before you act, specifically about how it might affect you later? About possible consequences for your family or friends? Things like that?

I don't think so. I think during the war there is just one idea: win the war.

Q. Did you have any expectation about how people would respond to your actions. Did you expect people to say, "Oh, you did a wonderful thing."

No. No gratitude, nothing. I never expect that. But what we expected [politically], after the war, we thought it would be paradise. All the people, all the Nazis, would be out of the way. I thought we'd be left with a nice society, of nice people who helped the Allies and worked against the Nazis. I thought we could incorporate the Nazis, start again to make money. Build a concept of justice. We were wrong. Human nature was there. It doesn't change.

Q. What is human nature?

Selfish and pride. That is a characteristic of human beings.

Q. You say that's the norm, that most people are selfish and think about themselves.

Basically. I think that basically people have the tendency to be selfish. A little baby is selfish. He thinks about himself. What to drink, what to eat, when to cry. He is not concerned with you. He grows up, then you teach him, "You can't do this. You can't do that." Education. There is always that self-preservation. That's normal: selfishness.

Q. But that's so different from the way you are. The mixture is so different in you than it is in so many other people. How do you explain the wide variance that we have in people?

Birth, education, and the decision to turn to the power of God, to change things that have to be changed. I don't go to God and say, "Please take the desire of smoking away from me." I know some people who do that. But I don't do it. I only ask God for more important things, important for me. I never asked the Lord to take me away from this earth on narcotics.

Q. If we wanted to have more people like you, what would we do?

I don't know. I don't think myself an example. I don't want to take me as an example. You can just say, "He is a person who wants to be a good Seventh-day Adventist. He believes that he has to follow the instruction of the Bible. To follow the instruction, God gives the power to do it. That's John Weidner. But he makes a lot of mistakes. Lot of faults, because he is not perfect." On this earth, complete perfection cannot be completely attained, because we are human beings. We are imperfect by nature. I cannot see right. I cannot speak right. So, I have to learn my imperfections, and live with them, and ask the Lord to help me in some ways.

Q. You think there are reasons for everything?

He prepares me for eternity, not for this earth. You have a child whose teeth do not grow right. You go to the orthodontist, he makes braces. That child is not happy at all. He suffers. Why do you do it? Because later, in twenty years, that child will be thankful. So God does something now, he knows that later that we can be happy. I can't understand it. I don't know [why it happens], but He has his reasons. Just like that child doesn't understand you. Why does he have the brace? It's not nice for mother and father to have to do this. But you love that child; you are ready to let that child suffer now in some ways for his later welfare.

Q. So you don't blame God because you lost your leg, or because your sister had to die, or because the whole war happened.

He could have saved my sister. He could have saved the Jews. But do I know the will of God? The state of Israel exists. Do you know why? Because six million Jews died. The Americans and so many in the world feel responsibility for that, and so they create the state of Israel. Suppose God wanted to make it that way. Six million Jews had to be sacrificed to make the state of Israel. I don't know. Good can come out of bad things even though I don't always know why.

You know the story of Job. Job had all kinds of tribulations. He lost his wife, he lost his children, and he was sick. Why? He never came to the Lord and said, "Why?" Job stayed faithful. Job was an example for all the universe. All the angels for all the universe stayed faithful.

Q. But did you never lose your faith at all during this terrible period?

No. Some people have said that they lost it. They cannot explain what happened, and then they couldn't believe in God anymore. "What kind of god could permit the Holocaust?" I know some people who say that. "I can't believe in God because of the Holocaust." When Eisenhower landed in Europe, he was a man sending out young, strong people, who would be shot down and killed. What would a man on the moon say, who did not know what was going on? "This person is crazy. He is sending all these young people and they are to be killed? [That makes] no sense." But Eisenhower did that because he wanted to save Europe, and save America. That was his plan. For that, he had to accept some sacrifices. Why are young people and the innocent people being killed? Why has God permitted the Holocaust? He has His reasons. I have faith in Him, because the past proved that He has a plan.

Q. You never had any dark nights of your soul?

Never. There was a Dutch woman who was in concentration camp. She was very religious, and she believed that there were always reasons for things. She went through a period where she felt like the war, everything was so bad. She was arrested, and then she was in a building that had bed bugs. The bed bugs were almost too much for her, and she cried out, "Why do we have to have bed bugs on top of everything else?" Now, after the war, she get out of prison and she find that the guards would come in the women's camp at night and rape the inmates. But they never come to her barracks because of the bed bugs.

Q. Is there anything I haven't asked you that I should ask you? Anything that you would like to say?

Not especially. You have asked me more than anyone in this world has asked me about the wartime. But I am happy, and I say you can ask me any question, and I will answer you.

Most of the people who were rescued were just hiding. They needed someone with instinct, the love instinct, without thinking about risk. The people like me, who did it [helped them escape], they had to do it.

Q. That simple. Was it really that simple for you? You just had to do it.

Yes. In the book about me, in the introduction, the author made the statement that when the situation arose, it was very natural for me.[5] Very simple, I had to do it, and it wasn't special. Basically, my parents raised me in such a way that when the time came, God was able to use me to help some people.

It made me happy. I helped Jewish people. Many people—the Minister of Justice of Holland—I helped him to go to Spain. The one who became the Minister of Justice of France, the Count of Menthon, I helped him.[6] I helped people who later had important positions in the government or in social life. That makes me happy, that these people are of value, that they have been helped.

Q. Did you take people across the Pyrenees as well as through Geneva?

No, I had guides. I went once on my own, to Andorra. But with the Pyrenees, there were some special guides I knew, and they helped me. I paid for that.

Q. Do you remember the day the war ended?

It is hard to remember my own birthday, but let me think one moment. No, I don't remember. I don't remember the day that I found out Hitler was killed. I don't remember those days specifically. Interesting, isn't it? Do you know that when you are in surgery, they put you asleep, and that the drugs affect your memory? I had this head surgery three times because of the beatings to my head during torture in the war. So my memory is very bad about names and dates because of the surgery on my head. I think it is called narcosis. Three times. Dates are hard for me. Not events, and people, maybe. But names and dates are very hard. But I remember now that your name is Kristi because my wife has a niece who had a baby, her name was Christine.

Kristi, you are the first person who asked me very good questions that I myself had not thought about, about why and what happened. I don't analyze myself too much because I do not concentrate on myself. But I know my weakness, my problems. I can be jumpy if something is not right, instead of keeping it easy. I am sorry about my wife.

Q. Are you a political person at all?

No, never.

Q. Do you consider what you did during the war political?

No. I don't think a soldier who fights actually in Kuwait or so is doing a political action. He is doing his duty as a citizen. That is independent of politics. Belonging to the Chamber of Commerce, and helping people, that is not political. That is humanitarian. You do something as a Mother Teresa, or the Salvation Army, that is not political. With the Rose Parade, in Pasadena, this year the Seventh-day Adventists will have a car, for peace. I feel I want to be a consequent Christian, not just in theory but in practice. Then we have to show love and action. To love your neighbor, that is a consequence of being a Christian, to love your neighbor.

Q. Is your neighbor God? Is it all part of the same?

Yes. I have to show to God I can do something for him. Observe Saturday as a day of rest in memory of his creation. But I can show my love to God, to love his Scripture. He created you and me and I can show to God.

Q. Is it that, or is it that we are all part of God? Is God us?

No. I was created by God. It goes through the Bible, "In the beginning, God created the earth and heaven. He created Adam and Eve." He created. We are not a part of him. But he created us in his image. So God is like us. He can see. . . . [John shrugged.] I can't understand God. Because He had no beginning. Can you understand no beginning? Suppose there were no God. Could you understand no beginning of this earth? It has to start somewhere. I cannot understand God. But I have faith because I have seen Him. Christ came on this earth to reveal God, and I can have an idea what is God.

• • •

According to the Simon Wiesenthal Center, John was one of the most wanted men on the Gestapo's list and saved over 800 Jews and 100 Allied airmen through his escape network. John described this network as comprising "all kinds of people. Catholic, Protestant, Jews, agnostics, everything. I was the head, but my right and left hand were two Jews." After the war, John served as an officer in the Dutch army, prosecuting those who had helped the Nazis and screening these people to decide who should be punished, and how. John did this for three years but became disillusioned when he realized how many collaborators eluded punishment or received slight punishment and then returned to their former positions. "I realized then that anyone who believed in pure justice is always disappointed because it does not exist." To escape painful memories, John came to the United States in 1958, where he met and married his wife, Naomi. When I knew him, John Weidner was running a health food store in Pasadena, an occupation I found touchingly surprising for the man at the top of the Gestapo's Most Wanted List.

John died in 1994.

4

Irene

I did not ask myself, Should I do this? But, How will I do this? Every step of my childhood had brought me to this crossroads. I must take the right path, or I would no longer be myself.[1]

Before she was forced into slave labor during World War II, Irene (pictured here at age seventeen) studied nursing in Poland.

I AM A SURVIVOR. I am alone.

I was born in May 5, 1918. In Poland. In the little town of Kozienice.[2] I was the first child. And my own life was saved when I was very young. It was a beautiful spring day, and somehow I had crawled out from the house. Nearby was a little brook, full of snow. I was just running for that brook, downhill as fast as I could go. Our dog knew that it was a danger for me because of the brook. He ran after me and with all his little power, he pulled me back by my dress. All the while, he was yapping, and that alerted my mother and she came running. That little dog was a big hero at our house, for he saved my life.

I think about that later and I guess I believe that maybe the Lord knew I had something else to do with my life. And that's why he saved me.

My parents were young. My father was an architect and chemist, and my mother was a wonderful woman. She was a saint. That may be why I was able to do the things I did later during the war, because Mama never sent anyone needy from her door. There were Gypsies in the forest near our home. I remember one time my mother took a Gypsy woman into our home for two weeks because the woman had pneumonia. There was always someone coming home with us. We all, all five of us children, always brought home from school a bat, a dog, or cat, whatever needed help. My mother always knew what to do.

My father had many understudies in his architectural firm. Some were Polish, some were German, and some were Jewish and Russian. They had children, so we children all played together. All kinds of mischief we did together. But we learned to live together. They were my friends. There was not the difference that "this is Jewish" or "this is Catholic" or "this is whatever." We lived and played together.

When I finished high school, I wanted to be a nurse. That was my life's desire. So my father signed me for the best school in Poland, which was in middle of Poland, in Radom. At that time we [my parents] lived close to the German border where my father had built a ceramic factory. Just when I was starting my school, Hitler declared war and invaded Poland. So I was right away separated from my family. I could not return home, because my parents were already taken by the Germans. So all of a sudden I am alone and there was a war and unbelievable horror unfolded before my eyes. Hitler was moving and the aeroplane was throwing bombs. Everywhere there were fires and explosions. There were people dead and wounded. The screaming for help was horrible. I was on the way to the hospital, because I worked and studied in the hospital. There was so many wounded, we tried to help; but Hitler at that time with the blitzkrieg, he was moving with the speed of light! And in a couple of days he was almost at the middle of Poland. The Poles didn't really have time to retreat.

After the marriage of her daughter, Irene dedicated her life to telling young people about the war and the Holocaust. Here she speaks to the author's class in the late 1980s.

Being alone, a young girl, not yet a nurse, just a young student, I attached myself to other nurses, and we joined the Polish army. We went for three weeks on the run, with Hitler pursuing us. In three weeks, when we were almost to the Russian border, the war was over. Hitler and Stalin had made a pact. They divided my country. There I was, a little girl far away from home, on the Russian side. I didn't know what to do or where to go. The Polish generals said the war is over, anybody can do whatever they want. So I went with a couple of the nurses and some of the army, and we escaped to the forests.

Q. Why didn't you try to go back to your family?

Because there were Germans there. Oh, my God, there was terrible confusion. Remember, I was only eighteen years old. I did not know what to do. So we escaped to the forest; we were merely trying to survive.

Just before Christmas of 1939, a big Russian patrol overtook us, and I was brutally violated. I was raped and beaten, and left in the snow to die. [Before that] I was not even kissed by a boyfriend. You see, life was different then. Then, too, I had developed tuberculosis in my teens, so I did not develop physically like other girls. I developed late.

Well, I survived. Somebody found me and brought me to a Russian hospital. I remember waking up in the hospital and I could not see because my eyes were swollen and I thought I was blind. I was screaming, "I'm blind, I'm blind." I was calling for my mother and at that moment I felt two arms around my shoulder and a woman's voice was speaking to me. But with a language that I could not understand. Still, it gave me the feeling that there was somebody that cared. It was a Russian woman doctor that took care of me. She felt like mother figure. I started crying, and maybe because of that I am normal. She gave me the help, not just medical but also emotional. She gave me the help my own mother would.

Then in the spring of 1940, there was the exchange of the population between the Germans and Russians. I was one of the first to try to go back, but I could not go back to my hometown because that was now in Germany. So I went back to the town where I had done my nursing. And I was alone. I did not have any means to support myself. Anything I did, what I had, was on my body. I had not been in a prison camp in Russia. No, I was in a hospital. I stayed in the hospital the whole time.

It was in December that I was picked up. In February was the exchange, so it was a short time. But the woman doctor, when I did start feeling better, she assigned me to the hospital duty. She took me under her wing. I would maybe have stayed longer, but they had a war with Finland at that time and she was assigned to go to Finland, and a man was supposed to take her place at the hospital. I wanted to see my family. So that's the reason I was the first to report to go. Luckily, in Radom I found a girlfriend I'd been in school with. Since she lived in Radom, she offered to let me stay at her home.

At that time I was weak. I started feeling very bad. I guess I was anemic. Then one Sunday we went to church. The church was surrounded by the Germans. They let all the people with children go. They let the older people go. But all the young people, they put us on the trucks. They brought us to a special confinement, and we were told that we would be sent to Germany to work in fields and in factories.

This a slave labor camp. They sent their own people to the front. The Jewish people from Germany were brought to Poland. Then they took the Polish people. So I made a peace with myself that I would be going to Germany; there was no other way I could get out. But just before my transport was supposed to leave, a group of German officers came to the camp. One was an older man in a raincoat, a major, and he started picking people at random. He picked about ten people, and I was one that he picked out. We did not know for what or where we would go. They took us in trucks, and they brought us to an ammunition factory in Radom. I was assigned to put the ammunition in the boxes but the smell of the chemical they used to make the ammunition was very bad for my lungs, since I had had tuberculosis at the beginning of my life. So one day I fainted. Right in front of the major when he came to inspect. I just fainted.

When I came to, I was scared. I started using my best high school German to explain that I want to work but I am just returned from the Russian side and I am weak and sick. I guess he took pity on me. Maybe because I was blond and blue-eyed, maybe because my name was Gut. Because I remember, he asked me, "Are you German descendant?"

"No, I don't know about that. My name is Miss Gutowna."

And he said, "You are very honest." Because I did not jump to say, "Oh, yes," you know, to save myself. He said, "Okay, I will give you another chance at another work." So he assigned me then to work in the diner. He was in charge of about thirty officers and about twenty German secretaries. He needed someone to serve breakfast, lunch, and dinner for them. Well, the work was nice. There was enough food. It was clean. And I started feeling better.

But going to work one day that winter, I went a different way [than] usual. And I came face-to-face with a real nightmare! The streets were barricaded with barbed wire. There were so many people. They were all yelling, screaming, shooting into air. The Germans did not allow anyone to cross the street or stay and watch. I was petrified. I ran. With the uniforms and guns, it was just awful. I ran and there was a house right by the street, an empty house with boarded windows, probably a Jewish house. I went in to find a hiding place. From the first floor of that house I witnessed a death march. I witnessed unbelievable things. Oh, there was so many SS men. They were yelling, screaming, kicking, pushing, beating, pushing masses of people from beyond the barbed-wire encampment. There were old men and old women and there were people on crutches. There were pregnant women. There was children, all sizes. The little ones, they were screaming, "Mama, Mama." They were going along because their parents were strong enough to be a slave. One was wounded and her little girl was holding her. Oh, it was unbelievable.

Then I saw a young woman with a baby in her arms. It was hard to hear what transpired, but the SS man pulled the baby and threw it with its head to the ground. The mother's scream penetrated even to my hiding place. I will never forget her inhuman scream. She leapt to save her child, and one bullet went to her head. She was dead, lying next to her child. It was unbelievable. I felt like I wanted to jump out. I was young and I wanted to strangle them with my bare hands. I was afraid. I was scared. I was petrified with fear. And I could just stand and cry and say, "God, where are you? What's happening? Why will you watch such a nightmare?" But it was worse, because it was true. I could only stand there, helpless, and furious and scared. Then I guess I just lost my faith; I threw a tantrum against God. Later on, when I was calming down, I could hear shooting from far away, and I knew that each shot was aimed to kill another human being. . . .

But you know, in war you don't make decisions; they are made for you. In the beginning of 1941, the Germans were fighting Russia, pushing them almost to here. The major was responsible for delivering ammunition, guns, and transportation for the German front. The whole plant was moved behind the advancing German army and the old major assigned to me this same job but in the new location, Ternopol.[3]

The major was not in the Gestapo. No. He was in the [regular] German army.[4] I think he was a civilian German engineer drafted into the army. They put the uniform on him because of what he knew to do. In the town of Ternopol, he had many officers, many more secretaries, and three hundred Jewish people working under him. In the meantime, the major gave me another responsibility. He liked me. So he gave me the responsibility of caring for the laundry room for the German officers and secretaries. There I met twelve Jewish people. They were once people of means. There was a lawyer, a doctor, a nurse, an accountant, a tailor, and a dressmaker. There were twelve of them. They did not know me. It took a while for us to become friends, but we did become friends.

When I was serving dinner, I noticed quite often that the local head of the Gestapo was sitting by the table with the major. So I start making sure that I would be serving the table where the major and Gestapo[5] man were sitting. I began to listen to their conversation. Even after I started to listen to the conversation, I at first did not know what I was hearing; but I then started making sense of it. The Gestapo man was making plans for raids on ghettos and war shipments. See what they did, they separated the strong men and women. These were not put in the ghettos. [They] built a barracks outside the ghettos, and that was under the command of the Gestapo man, Rokita. There were many factories that were taken over by the Germans. When they needed workers, they called Rokita. He said, "I need fifty people, Jewish people; I need one hundred people." So the major, because his work was important for the war, you know, because of his making the guns and ammunition, he had three hundred Jewish people working for him. Now the major, because of his work, more or less protected many Jewish people, because he [told the Gestapo], "I need the people. I don't want you to take them for the night exercise." And he got it.

When they were sitting [talking in the diner], I realized what was going on when Rokita said, "Major, next week, say Wednesday or Thursday, don't count on the Jewish people to work."

Major was mad. He said, "What you mean? My job is important! I have trained people to do repairs. You know that we need them for the front. Yet you go and take the people away!" He was always mad.

I started carrying the information to the laundry room, and we created a grapevine information center, without knowing what we were really doing. It was not planned. It was not that smart. But then, when I told them, "Next Thursday or Wednesday will be a raid," or whatever, then I became the ears and the eyes of the Jewish people working there. I could not go to the factories, you know, because that was not my place. But *they* could meet with the workers in the barracks. Oh, they told me awful stories. How during the night the Gestapo, [well,] you know. They'd wake them up in the middle of the night; tell them to stand straight; if they moved their feet, they'd hit them. It was awful.

So they would spread the news, but we needed help so that they would not be captured. What we did was to take the laundry room, which was just one room with a whole wall of shelves, and we made about ten of the shelves very shallow. We just put little blankets on them so it did not look contrived. We made a place behind the shelves for a hiding place so if something happened, the Jewish workers in the diner, they don't need to go to the ghetto. I tell you, there were many times when the raids occurred when these twelve Jewish people stayed the night, hiding behind the shelves in the laundry room. . . .

One day a worker in the diner, a young girl named Franka, who was my age, went to the ghetto to get her parents. Two days passed and there was a raid, and she did not come back. I loved Franka. I was worried. So I pleaded with the major.

"She was a dressmaker," I said. "She took three dresses for the German secretaries. They had the fabric from Germany, and Franka had to go to make buttons on a special machine. She did not come back and now the girls have come for measuring." I made up this story, and pleaded with the major so that I could go and get Franka. He gave me a pass. He got a pass from the Gestapo man.

Anyway, I went to the ghetto. I tell you, this is a nightmare, going the day right after the action. There were bloodstains on the streets, the houses. Everything was so quiet. You could see that somebody was moving by the window, but it's spooky. Finally I came to the house where one of the girls at work had told me Franka lived. I opened the door and it was dark. I call "Franka, Franka, Franka." Nobody answered. Finally, when I was passing by the stairs that lead upstairs, she grabbed me. She was hiding underneath the stairs. There was an enclosure that she opened up. She said, "Irene, what are you doing here? It is a raid. They will kill you!"

I had a hard time quieting her down. She was not herself. Then she said, "My parents are dead. My parents." They picked up her parents at that time, and she did not want to go with me. She said, "That's it. I give up. There's no way." I give her a hard time to convince her not to do this. I said, "Franka, you're young. You have life." I was holding her in my arms and kissing her and trying to quiet her down.

I said, "Now get a basket. We'll put some dresses in a basket." I had the permit for myself and the dressmaker. So Franka walked behind me. I told her not to say a word. I was always playing on the fact that my name is "Irena Gut," a German name, and because I spoke German in those days. Now I cannot speak it [German]. Psychologically, I just cannot make myself do it. I understand it but it's hard for me to speak. So I brought her in.

I was assigned a little room by the diner. Inside the ammunition plant the whole four walls were fenced off, and there was a guardhouse. They were bringing the workers back and forth. Only through the guardhouse and only the officers have an entrance from the dining room into the diner with a separate entrance. I usually did not go anyplace. I was just sitting in my room or working.

I had earlier met a Polish girl named Helen. I asked Major, since it was a holiday, if I could go to church. This Polish girl was with her mother; they were destitute. They were alone. At that time I didn't know anything about the final solution or anything, but I was aware what horrors are happening. I am terrified for my family. You know, how I was alone. So all this created a close feeling between us. She said that her father was killed by the Germans. Because some partisans had killed Germans soldiers, the Germans picked up some Polish men and killed them in retaliation. We started talking, and Helen said that she is married to a Jewish man. They had been rich once. He was now an orderly for the Gestapo man, who selected Helen's husband because he was a man of the world. The Gestapo man promised Helen's husband that when the end will come, he will let him go.

So, finally the time came when I overheard them say that the liquidation was coming. The first time I heard the talk was in May 1943. I told the workers in the laundry room that they'd have to go. They were so scared, and said, "Irene. Help!" But what could I do? I did not have a home. I did not have family.

So anyway, when the time come for the total liquidation, Helen came over and started crying. She said that her husband had been ordered to go to the ghetto. The Gestapo man didn't keep the promise. She told him, "Then we'll go together, and that's it."

Then in early June, one day when I felt so helpless cause I did not know what to do, there came this miracle. In the beginning of June, the major said that he has just taken a villa, and [asked that] I be his housekeeper. Even though I hadn't seen the villa, I just knew that there is the place! I felt it so strongly that God put me there, in the right time, and the right moment, and the right place. Now I have a place for my friends.

Q. Do you think the major knew that you were going to hide Jews when he asked you to be in charge of the villa?

No. The front was very strong, and he got so many more officers from the German soldiers, he wanted to have more place for them. So he had to have the villa. He wanted to be separate. I don't think he knew what I was doing. He knew that I was sympathetic to the Jews. He knew that it hurt me that I could not help. I did not sit with him and talk, like you and I do now, but I talked with one soldier. His name was Schulz. Short, fat, with the red cheeks. He was Wehrmacht. He showed me his wife's picture, and his children. He was always saying, "That dumb war. I want to go home and see my children." When he saw that sometimes the Gestapo did something wrong, he'd say, "They're fighting the women and children instead of going to Russia and fighting." And one time when I witnessed such a cruelty and was standing like a statue, I asked Schulz, "What is happening? What is happening?"

He took my arm and he says, "The officers are coming. It's not good for them to know you are Jew lover." He lead me away and out of trouble. He was just one of the ordinary soldiers. Just an ordinary soldier. But he was put in charge of that dining room. He was over me; he was the supervisor.

I know that when the time come then for the total liquidation, I wanted to help so badly that I did not even pay attention to what will come. I had no experience. The villa was there. There were two families living there, one Polish and one Ukrainian. The Polish people moved right away. But the Ukrainian family, they had a permit from the major to stay longer.

[Irene interrupted herself.]

Let's see, this is wrong; this is long story. But I want to make straight to you how it was at that time.

The time was short. It was June the twentieth. It was already the day that Jewish people were not supposed to come anymore to work. And six of the twelve Jewish people left to go to the forest. I helped them. I helped them to get out because they didn't want to be caught at the last minute. So they went.

Now I still have six in the laundry room. When the day came, the day when the Germans were taking all the Jewish people from the factories and bringing them to the transports, I locked my six people in the laundry room behind the shelves. I was thinking, "Okay, next day the Ukrainians move, and I somehow will get them there."

So what happened? I was serving dinner that night, and Schulz said that the theatrical group from Berlin came, so all their officers and secretary will go to theater and dancing. But when I was serving dinner to the secretaries, there were three girls sitting and talking. The one said to the others, "Tomorrow be sure to dress nicely."

The other said, "Why?"

"Because there will be so many young SS men here."

"Why?"

She said, "Well, you know where the Jews are working, the next day the Gestapo will come and search all the premises."

I heard that. And I said, "Oh, my God, no! What am I going to do?" My feet buckled, because it was such a crudely made hiding place. They would find it, there's no question.

So, it comes evening, and I didn't know what to do. I was beside myself. Well, I did not know what to do, how to tell them. I was scared to leave them there. Ida, her husband, and then Franka, Zimmerman, Dr. Lifshitz, all of them there. But I went about my business.

Upstairs, on the second floor, was the major's little suite. I quite often cleaned there. That day I am cleaning and I splashed water in the bathroom hot water heater. I had brought water in so many times to that room, but never before came to my focus a little window above the bathtub. It was like an air vent above the bathtub. The air vent was in the big hotel-type of walls, very thick. You know, the old-fashioned building. There was about maybe a five-foot by four-foot opening, with a little mesh screen. Why at that time it comes to my focus, I don't know. I took a chair. I climbed up and opened the screen. I saw that it was maybe five or six foot, and there was another window. So that was an air vent for circulation. That gave me the idea that there is where I will hide them, in the major's bathroom. So I went downstairs. When it was dark, I opened the laundry room. I sneaked two men upstairs because I did not know what that easement could hold in terms of weight. Lifshitz was a young man, and he went up first. Well, thankfully it was made from a wood, not metal, because metal would make a noise. One by one I brought all six of them there and brought them water, and some crackers and bread. I told them to be careful that they don't fall asleep, because the major will come. He will use the bathroom though he was very hard of hearing.

Well, finally I finished everything and I went to my room downstairs. About 2 o'clock in the morning the Germans started coming from the party. I knew that they all were drunk because they were slurring their words, and laughing. A real noisy crowd. I did not sleep that night, that's for sure. But next morning I was early in the diner, waiting for Major and everybody else to start coming. They all had hangovers. Nobody wanted to eat anything. Just coffee. Finally the major came in. He was very cranky because he had a hangover. He wanted only coffee. And I knew that he had not discovered anything. He went to the office and the officers and the girls started to go out.

But I looked through the window and like cockroaches, the SS men, they were crawling everyplace. Everyplace. Here. There. They went to my little room. They were allowed to go search everyplace, you know. Well, I talked and I was waiting, so impatient. I wanted to go upstairs. Finally I saw they did not see any of them. I told Schulz that I'd go to clean the major's apartment, the major's suite. I took the pail and put in some bread, something to drink and some towels on top. I was going through the little kitchen, down in the little hall to reach the bathroom [where they were hidden], when the door opened and a young Gestapo man came out from the bathroom. I thought, "I am dead." I mean, I was just faint. And he apologized. He said, "Excuse me, Fräulein, that I startled you." He treated me well because I didn't look Jewish. He didn't expect me to be a worker.

I said, "I am Major's housekeeper. I came to clean it up." So he went out. I locked the door and I opened the door to the bathroom. There Ida was sitting like a Buddha. You could see the outline of her body. I mean, if you looked for it, you could see it. But the Gestapo man had not been in to search the bathroom. He just went in for his physical need. He went in to use the bathroom himself. That's the reason. But I came in at that moment, so he just opened his pants, went, and did not look around. He just used the toilet. He went in for his physical needs, that's all. When he went, I locked the door to the major's suite, and opened the grill.

They thought the Gestapo man had been me coming, because they were sitting there since the raid started about 4 o'clock in the morning. They heard the shooting and explosions. They heard the Germans exploding the vestments. The Jewish people were making hiding places where they live. When they saw me, they told me they would go down and give themselves up.

I say, "Look, we almost died. My life is dependent here, too. Stay this evening. During the day the Ukrainian family will be moving out. This evening you will be in the villa." So they came down to use the bathroom. Then I closed it again and went downstairs. I went to the villa to see if the Ukrainian family had moved out.

But I was thinking now, "How will I get them down?" You see, I was so young. I wanted to help, but I didn't think. I didn't plan ahead. It was like when you see a child drowning in the water; you don't think if you can swim; automatically, you want to do something. You jump. That was exactly my way. I knew it was wrong what they did, the Germans. I knew that I had to help. I wanted to help so bad, but I just didn't make plans. And so, I was finally thinking now, about how will I do it.

Well, you wouldn't believe what I did. Today I am laughing about it. I did not want to tell the Jewish people what I came up with, because it would scare them more. They had already gone through so much. So I waited until after dinner to tell all.

The Germans were still sleeping, because of the drinking the night before. They went early to sleep. Major had an awful headache. He told Schulz, "I am so woozy. I have a hangover. I feel so bad. Get me some medication." It was like an aspirin only a little more so it would work like a sleeping pill.

I knew that when the major went upstairs to bed and Schulz went someplace to get the medication for him, the major would ask me to bring it with something to drink. So I brought the medication. I noticed that at that time he was taking out from his pocket the keys, and he put the key on the night table with a bunch of keys. But I knew which key was for the door because many times they opened it. So I waited about a good two hours, maybe an hour and a half, and I went upstairs in the night, tippy-toe, and sneaked into his bedroom. While he was asleep! There was nothing else to do. I took the keys, and I locked him in his room. I don't know why I did that. Maybe for security, because I feared he could wake up and make a noise. The bathroom was not off his bedroom. It was down a hall. So then I let the Jewish people out, one by one, down two flights of stairs, while I'm watching. I opened the door and then I would have to watch because there was a guardhouse. The guardhouse protruded a little to the street. So I had to watch to make sure the guard was not looking. I let them out, one by one into the night. I could not go to escort them. They knew where the villa was, since I had explained that before. One couple, as a matter of fact, was from the town. The major had earlier told [me] to go out and look over the villa. I had left open the window to the coal chute, the wooden chute that they put the coal in. And during the night, one by one they came there. That night, everybody left the diner and went to the villa.

Irene had another scare when she later heard that the SS would inspect the villa.

They told me the villa was built by a Jewish architect, and that he was finishing it as the Germans went from Germany to Poland to Ukraine. We thought there must be a hiding place in that villa, because of the Jewish architect. So we had that thought in the back of our mind.

The next day, after the breakfast, the major said to Schulz, "Can you spare Irene from the diner, from breakfast to luncheon, because I want her to go to the villa to let in the soldiers who will come to clean and paint the villa."

Now he's telling me! I did not know about that. More problems! So I went like lightning, to the villa. But instead of six Jewish people, there were twelve people. Six people that I don't know came along. They just saw the other people and came along. Well, I guess they were friends. Helen's husband was one. That was seven. There were other people that I did not know. They were working in the plant, though I was not close to them. But they were close to the people I saved. And you know, when you're dying, when you're drowning, you grasp at any hope.

There was no time to get acquainted or anything because I knew that the soldiers would be there pretty soon. We decided the dirtiest place was the downstairs, so I put the Jewish people in the attic. The attic was hot, since it was almost the end of June. There were no windows, just little openings in the ceiling. And no toilet. Nothing. But I could not do anything else. So I had to quick take them from the cellar and take them there and lock them in. By the time I was finished, the soldiers were right behind me to see what had to be done. It took a couple of weeks for them to finish painting and cleaning. It was a nightmare. If I don't believe so strongly that God put me there for a reason, why in the last minute the villa became available, I would have died. Because they were in the attic. The major did not want to move in until the villa would be finished. He was traveling here and there.

Schulz brought a little cot for me to sleep on at the villa. I know Schulz knew something. He never spoke of it. But he brought me food, water, bread, everything. He'd say, "Instead you running back and forth to the diner, you have it here."

Since the major was not there, we used every opportunity at night to look for the hiding place. Finally, we found it! It was underneath the coal chute. It was a wooden post made like a little wall, made from wood. There was a box. When you removed the box, it exposed an opening. It was not big. You could not stand. But you could crawl. Behind the house was a gazebo. Underneath the gazebo was a hiding place. The Jewish architect who designed the house must have constructed the gazebo as he was finishing the villa. He must have known by then about the coming persecution.

I never heard anything about him, about what happened to him after the war. Nothing. Nobody knows what happened to him. I guess maybe he had money. I like to think he got away, because what he did was a blessing. We were so thankful.

By now, Irene assumed all was well after all these preparations, so she was shocked to hear that the major intended to have an orderly live in the villa.

I didn't even think about that. When I heard that, I almost fainted. How stupid I was! There I was just sitting like a mother goose on her eggs. I said, "All that work for nothing." Because if somebody moved there, how will I get to the cellar? They cannot live underneath in the darkness; though if it had to be, it had to be. But right away I said, "Oh, Major, please. I will do everything. I will clean your shirts and boots and everything. But don't bring any men here to live." I said, "You know I was raped by Russian soldiers, and I am so scared of men." I opened my heart and I told him.

And he said, "Well, I can now understand why pretty girl like you don't go out, have a boyfriend."

Finally, the major said, "Okay, but I want to tell you that I will have many parties, and I don't know that you will be able to do everything." But I pleaded with him, and he said, "Okay, okay. I give you a chance." So that's how we were surviving. . . .

Helen, the Christian wife [of one of the Jewish men hidden in the villa] took and managed a farm for one of the [German] officers. The Germans had taken it since it was a Jewish farm. Helen was hiding Jews in the forest while she was managing the farm. So many times she came to visit her husband with the horse and buggy or the sleigh in the winter. She said she had a cold and carried a handkerchief, and walked in the house. I put the ham in the handkerchief, and she brought the potatoes and blankets, whatever she can organize and I organize. I was busy talking to all the German officers and secretaries, telling them that I have a family. I have sisters. I have a cousin. I have friends that are hungry. So they would give me the ration tickets which they didn't need. When the major had parties, he needed liquor; he needed all kinds of goods. Schulz would take me to the German military store. With the ration tickets, I bought shoes. I bought all kinds of things that were needed by the Jews Helen was caring for in the forest. Sometimes I'd put on Helen's handkerchief and coat and I'd go to the forest. And Helen would have time alone with her husband in the cellar.

One day about seven weeks after they were hidden in the villa, another couple, Ida and her husband, came to me. "Ida is pregnant," they said. So the doctor, he told me, "You get this and this. We have to do something because we don't know how long we'll be hidden."

I had seen the children going to death. I remembered that. And I pleaded with them. I said, "Don't. Hitler will not have that baby. Let it be. You'll see. We'll be free by that time." And that's just how it happened.

Q. So you did not give Ida an abortion?

No. I pleaded with her. I said, "No way. Hitler will not have that baby. Please, Ida. Don't do anything." I pleaded with all of them. We were liberated March 15, 1944, and a little boy was born in May 1944. So Ida was living there during all this time like the rest of the people, most of the time in the cellar. When there were more Gestapo in the area, I would put them under the gazebo. But once Ida got too heavy to crawl through the tunnel to the gazebo, I put her in the attic with her husband.

· · ·

One day in September, the end of September, I was in town. Suddenly, out of nowhere the Gestapo was pushing everyone from the streets to the marketplace. They forced us to witness a Polish couple with two little children and a Jewish couple with a child being hung in the middle of the marketplace. They forced us to watch to see what happens when someone befriended a Jew.

I closed my eyes. I could not watch. But you can hear the breathing, the cries of the children. I was like a zombie, numb. There were signs on every street corner saying, "This town is Jew-free. Whoever will help escaped Jew descendants is dead." So I knew what could happen. But that doesn't matter. I mean, they were human beings. I knew I didn't have to help; I took the responsibility. I believed so strong that for reasons God put me there so everything will be fine. I did have such a strong belief in that. But I was shaken that day, seeing those children hung.

Coming to the villa, I opened the door. I closed the door. I even locked it. But I pulled the key out. Usually I pulled the key and put it in the inside lock and turned it in the lock, so when the major would come home he could not walk in; he would have to ring the bell. But that day I was so shaken up that I took the key and walked straight into the kitchen. I put the things down. I came back with something, put it on the sink, and I was looking white like the snow. I was trembling. Four of the girls came out, as they usually did when I was alone in the kitchen. The door was locked and we had a warning system. They knew I was not normal and they asked me what happened. I said, "I'm catching cold." I could not tell them what I had witnessed because it would put a guilt in them. I could not do it. I was standing with the door open and the major walked in on us.

Q. And he saw you?

He saw me. He saw the four girls. He was just standing. His eyes was unbelieving. His skin was shaking. He looked like he'd seen a ghost. Without saying one word he turned around and went to his library.

Well, I did have to go and face him. There was not any other way. He knew [some of] them from the laundry room. When I went in, he began to scream and yell at me. "How did you dare to do so? Behind my back! I trusted you. I give you home. I give you protection. Why?"

By that time I was crying. I said, "They are my friends. Nobody has a right to kill. I didn't have a home of my own to take them to. Please forgive me." I kneeled down. I was kissing his hand. I was holding to his knees. I was praying and pleading. I said, "It's my fault. Let them go. I take the punishment." I did see something in his eyes, you know. Just a moment of hope. But he said, "I have to go now. When I come back, we will talk."

I locked the door and I ran as fast as I could downstairs. They wanted to run away. We were all desperate. But it was during the day, and if they went then they could be picked up. Because the front was so close at that time, there was a curfew. I did not know if the Gestapo was coming or even if the major had called Gestapo. So we decided that they would go underneath the gazebo. We would prepare food for three days. And I said, "If in three days I do not come and get you, that means I am dead or arrested. Then you're on your own. You have to go to the cellar and through the window and to the forest, one by one."

There was nothing else I could do. Poor Ida was in the attic. I could not take her because she was too big. She could not crawl anymore. Time was so short. I did not know.

About midnight the major came home. He was so drunk. He went to his room. I had to go and face him. There was not any other way. I was standing in front of him, and he reached and pulled me onto his lap. He started opening my clothes and he said, "I will keep your secret but you have to be mine, and willingly." There was nothing I could do. I was trapped. So many lives depended on me.

Q. So he said he would . . . ?

Keep my secret. He did not want to know who else was in the house. He never asked. He got used to the girls. They could come out when he was there.

Q. But the deal was that you had to be his mistress?

Yes. He was an old man. And I guess he loved me. He said, "Is that so bad? I help you and you give old man the last joy in his life. You're beautiful," he'd say.

I had to give in. There was nothing I could do. It was horrible for me because first I was raped by Russian soldiers and that left a scare and fear. And second he was an old man, you know, and German.

[The tape was turned off at this point. It was turned on again only at Irene's suggestion.]

Anyway, the time then came late in January [1944], when the major said the villa had to be evacuated because the front is coming. The Wehr-

macht has to retreat and then the front-line soldiers will take the villa. I
knew that I cannot leave them [the Jews] underneath the gazebo because
in war you never know how long things will be. So I went to the forest
and made an arrangement with the people there to bring my people to
the forest. I would try to bring the men first. I was to leave them just
outside the town and then they will be picked up and taken to the forest.
That was the best arrangement we could make. Luckily, the major had to
leave for two days to go to a neighboring town.

Helen's husband, who spoke beautiful German and had been working
for that Gestapo man, he put on the major's hat and the major's coat.
Helen brought a horse and a sleigh because it was winter. We put three
men in the sleigh and covered them with blankets. We put in some things
like shawls because they would have to build a bunker. We drove through
the town. There I was, sitting next to Helen's husband and the soldiers
were saluting. It was not too hard because it was the beginning of
March, and everybody was running. We could already hear shooting from
the front. The war was almost at our door. We looked like everybody
else, running. So that's how I came to the forest with the women. And I
remained with them. One day the major came back and I was just gone.
I was not there. He came back and I was not there.

Q. Did you ever see him again?

No. I did not see him. But I did see his pictures. And Roman, Ida's little
boy [the one conceived in hiding], told me about him. But that's another story.

At this time, in the forest it was very cold. I was so worried about Ida
and her baby. But on March 15 the Red Army liberated us. So now my
friends were free to start a new life, another life. In May, the beginning of
May, the little boy was born. They named him Roman.

I did not want to stay with the Russians. I wanted to find my family. I
missed them so much. My responsibilities were over. I had fulfilled them.
So I said good-bye and started inching towards my home. I joined the
partisans because that was the only way I could go. So we were fighting
the retreating Germans and the Russians who were advancing. We were
right in the middle. Naturally, I was not fighting. I was just a messenger
girl sometimes, but that's all. Almost on the door of my home in 1945,
Russia took all of Poland and I was arrested by the Russians because of
my association with the partisans. I did not know anybody there who
would help me, or anybody who would even know whether I am arrested. I was scared to say anything. I was in a Russian and Polish military
place. I was not in a jail. Before they put you in jail they have a special
place for interrogation. They want to find out what I know. They will
wake me up every night to do something. That day they brought me to

an octagon building. A young man brought me. He felt sort of sorry for me since he's Polish. I say, "Gee whiz, I am not a German. I am Polish! What do they want?"

He opened the door and there were about twenty men standing in their undergarments. You know, I got so mad! My Polish blood got cooking. So I said, "Look, I will do what you want me to do but I don't need to stand and watch you undressing." Then I just turned and marched out.

Well, behind my back, the windows were open. The bars were far apart. Without thinking what I was doing, I squeezed myself through the bars. I squeezed my body through and I jumped. Luckily, I fell behind the fence. I fell like a cat on all fours. I did not even kick off my high heel shoes when I jumped. I could not stand on my feet. They were like rubber from the jump. There was an early spring. To this day, I remem ber. The feeling that I am free gave me the strength.

I knew Ida's family, with the little boy Roman, were on their way to go to Germany. I did not have any place else to go, so I went there. I remember coming to the building. They lived on the fourth floor. I pushed the button and I was standing at the wall and by this time my feet were swollen like balloons, since I'd broken some veins from the jump. I pushed the button next to their name. Then the door opened and a Russian soldier came out. I looked at him and he looked at me. "Are you Irene?"

"Yes."

He was a brother of Ida. His whole family was killed by the Germans. So he took the Russian uniform and went with the Russians. He was visiting, and he said, "What happened? What you doing here?"

"Well, I escaped."

"Irene, we knew about you. We tried to do help. We tried to help you." But it was too late for me to say I am sorry, so he took me into the laundry room in that building, and he went upstairs. Ida came and said, "Irene, what did you do? You could be free, since we were talking with the commissar. Now they will come here to find you."

Q. Ida's family had arranged to have you released, but you had escaped before you could be released. Is that right?

Yes. Because of that, they could not keep me. So the brother, because he had a Russian uniform, he rented a car. He took me in the car and brought me to Krakow. There I was for a couple of weeks, with Dr. Lifshitz [another of the people I had hidden], with my feet up. I was like mother; a little here with this, a little there.

In the meantime, I found out that my mother was arrested. My family did not know anything about me because I didn't even have time to get to them. But my Jewish friends went to the house where we lived before the war. They found out that my mother, with my four younger sisters, were arrested by the Russians because of me. My father was killed by the Germans, just before Russia took over. That's what I found out.

I wanted to give myself up. I didn't want my mother and sisters to be hurt. But they did not allow me, my friends. They say, "Wait. You're hurt." Then, by the time I felt better and my friends went back to check it out, my mother had been released with my four sisters. They had all disappeared. That's what the neighbors told us. They told us that my mother was released, but we could not find her. They just disappeared.

Q. You couldn't find your sisters either?

No. They were little girls; I was the oldest one.

Now I could not be in Poland. I was wanted in my own country! Because of the Russians that I had escaped from! So at that time my Jewish friends wrote my story down and left it with the Jewish Historical Committee in Krakow. We did not write because we did not know if we would ever see each other. They smuggled me out. I dug out the false name: Sonia S_____. They made my hair black, and they smuggled me out to Germany, to a Jewish repatriation camp. That was 1946. I stayed there until 1949. I took my name back and my hair grew out. I looked so funny, with black and blond splotches and red from the dye!

I met my husband in the camp. In 1948 a group of men came. My husband was with the United Nations. In 1948 they came to the re-patriation camp to check it. The Jewish people were very proud of me. I was one Catholic living in the Jewish camp. So they wanted the Americans to interview me. The problem was that I spoke Polish, German, Russian, and Yiddish and he spoke French and English. Between us, we knew six languages, but had not one in common. So somebody had to translate.

There was no romance or anything at that time. My husband is American, third-generation American. His grandfather was the first Republican mayor of New York City during the Civil War. He told me at that time that America would be very proud to have me as a citizen. But there was not a romance or anything. In 1949 I came to United States.

Q. Just to visit, not as his wife?

No. We said good-bye in the camp. There was nothing between us. He was just admiring a young woman who did what I did. I came to the U.S. by myself, without money, family, marketable skills, not one word of English. When I came, a Jewish organization gave me a hotel room to stay in the first night. They told me [that] if I wanted something, to call. That's what I remember.

But the wonderful feeling of being free after so many years! I put the biggest sign on my memory, "Do Not Disturb." I did not want to remember the war or anything. Forget! I wanted to give myself a chance to know America. I wanted to have the normal life I never had before. And in five years, I become a United States citizen. I pledged allegiance to America, to the land of the free.

I had met a Jewish girl from Warsaw, and she wanted me to work with her, as a dressmaker. So I met her in New York and worked with her. One day she sent me for something near the United Nations building. After I bought the things she told me [to buy], I stopped at the automat. I loved the automats cause it was so easy to order. But I knew how to get already my cake and coffee, and sitting by the table, a gentleman come to my table, and said, "May I sit down, please?"

Well, when I opened my mouth, he knew I had an accent. So he started, "Parlez-vous français?"

"No, I do not speak French. I am Polish. I am Polish and I was in Germany."

He look at me. Then he started telling me my story. It was the man who interviewed me in the repatriation camp! I mean, that whole time, I think that God just made a plan, A-B-C, and that's how it went. So, he started telling me my story. He was a widower. He invited me to dinner, then another dinner. And in six weeks we were married. Then my little girl was born. I now have a family of my own. Then we moved to L.A.

It was a year and a half when we moved in here. My husband got a job with the newspaper and I met Alex, who was Jewish and from Poland. We became very good friends. We were the best of friends. He was a Polish survivor. He had lost his whole family. I am rescuer. And I am from Poland. But he didn't speak and I didn't speak. We wanted to forget. So we never spoke of it.

It wasn't until my daughter married and his daughter was the best maid, and I started feeling sorry for myself because I am alone. One morning, I read a newspaper. Usually I was not interested in the newspapers. I was too busy. Well, in the newspaper there's a story that the Holocaust never happened; it is all Jewish propaganda. Well, you see, God again in this moment told me, "You raised a child. I gave you time. Your job is not finished."

It stabbed me so! I was so mad, I say, "How did they dare to say so? I was there!" And I started speaking. I wanted to be a witness. My husband was bragging about me to his Rotary Club. So they invited me to speak. The first time I spoke, I opened my heart. I cried every five minutes. It was so hard from the subconscious to bring all the memories. There was a newspaperwoman that I did not even notice. She made a picture of me, and she gave me front-page story. A rabbi read the story.

He called me. I showed him the letter from my Jewish friends in Poland. I dragged out the papers that the Jewish people wrote many, many years ago. I had never even opened them to read it, you know. I wanted to forget. I showed him the paper. We talked. We become very good friends. He sent my story to Jerusalem to Yad Vashem. From there I received three letters from people I had saved. And the first one was from the young man.

Q. From the little boy?

The little boy. He called me dear mother. I still did not know anything about my family, but I was just so happy. And in 1982, I was invited to Jerusalem. My story was confirmed and I received a Medal of Honor.

Now who do you think paid for my trip? Alex. My friend. He was so thrilled. He told me, "I've known you for so long, and I never knew!" When this story came out in the newspaper, it was the first he had heard it. So he paid for it, for my trip. Because otherwise I could not go. I could not go. See this, too, is a difficult road. Many of the people, the rescuers, are invited [to Jerusalem]. But their trips are not paid for. Many of them cannot afford it. But Alex even went with me. I planted the tree overlooking the New Jerusalem, and I prayed at that time. I prayed for Israel. I realized the importance of Israel. That like good mother, it brought thousands of people. It brought them spirit and body. It gives them a reason to stay alive. A feeling of belonging. And you know, the knowledge that this is a homeland for the people that were so persecuted! If Israel as a state would have existed before the war there would not have been a holocaust. And that's why I am still speaking now, to Jewish people, and Christian people, at churches, organizations, schools, saying that Israel is important.

And now, the new Hitler's blueprint is in the news everyday. The skinheads, the terroristic organizations. Let us pay attention. Because you know Hitler's *Mein Kampf* was published and assimilated before the Holocaust. But nobody believed! Where were the human nations then? He rose to power, and six million of Jewish people, millions of other nationalities, were all killed. Even when the news started coming through different organizations about the persecution, we still did not believe it. The nations, the human nation, still did not believe. Nobody helped.

So that's my point. To speak, for the children to learn. To learn to listen. I think that if I were Jewish my story would be published already. But I am being discriminated against because I am Polish. People don't realize that Poland was for 150 years cut, pushed, taken by Russia, Prussia, and Germany. Why did the Germans put the crematoria in Poland? Why? Because the Germans wanted to kill Poland, too. That's the reason they did it. Poland was tied up and bled. So I am between the hammer and the nail. From one side are the Jewish survivors. From this other side the Polish Catholics. I've never been invited to speak to the Polish Catholic churches. The survivors don't want to see me because I'm Polish. You know what bothers me also, when I am speaking? Sometimes the Jewish survivors say, "You are only one." That's not true! There were many like me. Many are dead, many who helped.

Q. So what you're also saying is that there are a lot of people there who gave tacit help, like the German soldier Schulz?

Yes, although he really didn't do much, still he did know. *Many* in that time found the courage to care.

Q. Did you ever find your sisters?

Yes. That was also one of those miracles. I had tried through the Red Cross for many years [to find my family]. But nothing. I have a Jewish friend in New York, who was saved by Polish people. She was traveling to Poland, back and forth. She knew me very well and we were talking. I ask her, "When you go to Poland, maybe you can ask your friend about my family." So one day she went there. Her friends have a little store, a Mama-Papa store in Poland. She told them about me, that she has a friend in Orange. Her name was Irena Gut, and she had four sisters and now she's alone.

There was a woman in the store. "What did you say was the name? Irena Gut?" Then she said, "That's my sister. That's my sister!"

It was my second sister, Janina. My friend gave my sister my address and she sent a telegram. The telegram looked to me like it was something that you throw away, just one of those advertisements. But I glanced at it a second time and there were three Polish words that mean: "Come. I wait. Janina." When I read it, I cried. Oh, my God. This was in 1985. And it is the first time I received a letter! I did not have the patience to wait for three months to send a letter. I wanted to go! So I got a passport. There I was, on the way to Poland. I went to Krakow. Going down the plane I remember searching with my eyes, looking; but I didn't know how my sisters looked because I hadn't seen them since they were little. Now they were married. In one corner I noticed four women, four older women, just standing. It did not dawn on me. I just looked over them, not paying attention. One of that group stepped out and say, "Irena?"

I turned. It was such an unbelievable meeting when we first held each other in our arms. Now, from not having anyone, I have thirty-one in my family. My sisters married and had children, and their children have children. I am the oldest one but I look the youngest. Because you know, it's hard, living in Poland. And they had an awful time. I asked them how they disappeared. My mother was so scared when they let them out, scared that they would arrest them again. She didn't know what or why, so she took a false name and went to a village, another city completely with my sisters. And then she died in 1957, my mother. She never knew what happened to me. So the first thing, I went to visit the grave. And I cried. Oh, it was so unbelievable.

They told me that my daddy was shot. My father was killed by the Germans. The Germans took him into German territory.[6] He wore a band with the letter "P," because he was Polish. Though he could say he was German, since his name was German. Maybe his forefathers were German. But he would not say it because he was not raised that way. He was raised Polish. Two drunken soldiers killed him. Papa was walking on a sidewalk and they told him to go walk on the street. I guess he was a proud man and he gave them wrong look. They took gun and shot him. That's all. So that's how it happened with my parents.

When Germany took over they forced my sisters to work. There was a place where you take the clay from the ground; my father used it in a ceramic factory. So they forced my sisters to dig the clay in the winter and my littlest sister's hands are crippled because she was so young and was digging with her hands. They told me horrible stories.

· · ·

In every nation there are good and bad people. Because the Germans took the country and forced them to do some things, there is no reason to blame everyone. Because that is creating hate. I am a witness to that. I am an innocent bystander. But I am not with Polish. And I am not with the Jewish survivors.

Q. You see yourself as apart?

I *am* alone. When I ask the ADL [Anti-Defamation League], I say, "Why am I not asked to speak by you?" Because I know that many, many Jewish survivors go into schools and speak.

And they say, "Oh, there are so few who helped!"

"I don't care. I am one. I have a right and I want it," I tell them.

Q. What about the German major? Did you ever hear from him again?

Oh, the German major. Would you believe that he was like a grandfather for the little boy Roman? Roman, the little boy conceived in hiding and born just after the war? The little boy, Ida's boy. He told me that the major's children threw him out because he was a Jew lover. His big boys were with the Nazis. He did not have a home. His wife had been dead a long time. And these two boys threw him out. Not only because he was a

Jew lover but because he had a Polish girl, too: me. They knew [about me] before the war ended because right before the war ended the major received letters from Berlin to send me away. The German secretaries were jealous, so they were doing some spying on the servants.

Ida heard all this and went to look for him, to look for the major. When she found him, he was at a house that was bombarded. He didn't have a room. He didn't have anything to eat. He was so poor, an old man. So Ida went to the Jewish organization and said that he knew they were hidden in his house and he did not say anything. They testified for him and the authorities assigned him a little room, and he was coming to visit Ida. To little Roman, he was like a grandfather. Would you believe? So you see. I forgive him. I don't—I did not hate him for what he did to me. That's life. You see. Life from different angles. It's not black and white. It has all different colors and angles. My destiny was to meet him. There was a God that put me in the place, and there was always somebody, like the Russian woman doctor, always somebody was there.

Q. What happened to Schulz?

Schulz was killed by the Russians when they were retreating. Ida felt very bad about that. We all knew that he knew. He knew about us but never said a word. But he was always bringing things and helping.

Q. What I'm hearing you say is that it's very difficult to maintain the kind of human communication during a war. That because of the situation, individuals are forced to choose up sides of one kind. But that you and the people you associated with were able to reach across those barriers and find some kind of human communication, a bond. The major. Ida and her little boy. A major who could have turned you all in, who did something in some ways which was very unfair to you, but which was motivated out of love and affection.

Yes, because it was. I mean, he did really love me. I cannot say that he was brutal. He was not beating me or anything. He was very direct, very allowing, expressing himself. He would say, "Irene, is that so bad? I keep your secret. I will help you. And you give old man the last joy in his life."

Q. Then after the war, the people that he had helped, in turn helped him, and he becomes a grandfather to the boy.

You see! It is such a story I wanted to tell. That there are bad and good people. I am not trying to put hate on any particular group. The time is for us to reach to each other. That's the only way we can be safe, even now. That's all. That's the reason that I am doing this. I feel sometimes hurt because of the aloneness. I understand the suffering of people. I am sometimes hurt by it. That they could not reach and understand. I know the pain. I know the feeling. I was there, too. I went through hell. I was persecuted, and I also am a survivor. I lost my contact with my family and I was alone. And that's what is hurting sometimes.

· · ·

In 1989, Irene's husband, suffering from the early stages of Alzheimer's illness, had a stroke. He could no longer care for himself without full-time aid and Irene had neither the financial resources nor the physical strength to continue alone, especially given her increasingly busy schedule of public appearances. Desperate for help, she turned to her Jewish friends. In violation of all the rules, a Jewish home took in her husband "out of respect for what she did for us during the war."

The last time I spoke with Irene, she asked me to be sure that anything I published about her made clear her closeness and gratitude to the Jewish community.

Irene died on May 17, 2003.

5

Knud

I'm often asked why we in Denmark reacted so humanely and positively against the discrimination and arrest of the Jews. I don't know why. But maybe it was . . . respect for our fellow man and humanity in general.

As a wartime policeman, Knud took part in the extraordinary national effort that saved 85 percent of the Danish Jews.

I WAS A RECOGNIZED rescuer of Jews. But since the Danish people as a whole saved Jews—a unique phenomenon and one very specific to Denmark—we never received any individual honors. The Yad Vashem put up a special monument for the entire country.[1] There is a hospital in Jerusalem and a special forest planted for the Danish rescuers. So we have been honored plenty.

There are some people today who claim that there has been too much emphasis in speeches, books, and TV on the Holocaust horrors and the Nazi concentration camps. But witnesses to what happened over fifty years ago are "over-the hills," so we who are still alive and able owe it to society to tell our stories, because society must learn from past mistakes.

I have told my story so many times that I turn off my hearing aid, as I really don't want to hear the story again about myself.[2]

I was able to help some Jewish families, many Danish saboteurs, politicians, German deserters, Baltic refugees, and British and American airmen to avoid being captured by the Gestapo by taking them by boats to Sweden. We were lucky that Sweden was so close. I was just fortunate enough to be at the right place at the right time, at the age of twenty-five. I never considered myself a hero for what I did. I'm speaking now for friends, who were not as fortunate as I, but who were caught and suffered or died in the hands of Gestapo.

I'm born on the twenty-eighth of March 1915, in a small town called Vorup, outside Randers in Jutland, Denmark. I was baptized there as Knud Olsen. My father was in the printing business. My grandparents on my mother's side were blacksmiths and farmers, and my grandparents on the other side were coopers. Coopers, you know, make barrels. A long time back in the family, they made barrels for herrings and for pork sides or whatever. People would salt these things in beautiful wooden barrels.

When I grew up, even from when I was a very small child, my parents would be yachting. We would sail on the fiords of Denmark. Some of my best experiences as a child were being on the sea. I grew up a rather proficient sailor. The season in Denmark is very short for yachting. It's only from about April to the end of October. In the wintertime, we would have gymnastics and make shows and have fun in general, but we also learned something about navigation and the splicing of rope ends, the technical aspect of sailing.

I have one brother, nine years younger. I was in school for about ten or eleven years. At that time, I had decided that I liked my father's trade as a printer. So I became a typographer, actually an apprentice typographer. I did pretty well and I came out with flying colors and some medals at the time of my apprenticeship.

In those days in Denmark, when you were eighteen or nineteen, you'd have to appear in front of the Commission for Selecting of Soldiers. At

Knud (pictured here with his Yad Vashem Medal) now
lives as a retired inventor in northern California.

that time it was compulsory. They'd come in and you have to stand in
front of these people, stark naked, while they would look you over. I
went for this inspection and they chose me for the Royal Guards. It was
the custom to choose two good-looking fellows from each county to
serve as Guardsmen. It must have been a bad year for good looks, because I was chosen to serve as a Guardsman for King Christian X. So I
started as a Guardsman when I was twenty or twenty-one years old. That
was of course interesting, not only to be a Guardsman but also to come
into Copenhagen, which is where we Guards served. First of all, you go
through a military service. You were to be completely trained in a fighting
company service. Later on, you at the same time are instructed in the

actual Guard Service for the Castles. And that was naturally very interesting. All this was in 1937.

In 1938 we were called in again to the Guard Service because the Germans went into Alsace-Lorraine and the Sudetenland. So we were stationed up in the northern part of Sjaelland (Zealand) as a fighting unit. But nothing happened with Denmark in 1938.

One of the interesting parts of this period for me was that we were stationed at a small town on the Rungsted, outside of Copenhagen. I was stationed near the estate of Karin Blixen, the one who wrote *Out of Africa* [under the name of Isak Dinesen]. She would serve us tea in the evening and tell us stories about her life.

After the Guard Service in 1938 and 1939, it was clear to us that something had happened in Europe that we didn't like. In 1937, I was yachting in Germany, near Kiel, with some people from my hometown. We could already feel the difference since the National Socialists came into power. We were invited in Kiel to visit one of the pocket cruisers called *Köningsberg*. We knew what was happening. In that part of Europe, we could already feel that there was a lack of foreign news. For my own part, printing had fallen on lean years. You couldn't get a good job. So the government asked some of the Guardsmen, because we had the size and were probably brought up right, to come into the police force, as an extra police force. Because of the general political climate, they [the Danish government] were concerned. They didn't want anything to happen in the Danish population. So they added to the police force in 1939 and 1940. That's how I became a police officer. This was not my chosen profession. This was just [something that happened] as part of what eventually became the war.

On the ninth of April 1940, the Germans went into Denmark. Early in the morning, I woke up in Jutland, with the noise of hundreds of German airplanes over our sleepy heads. Instead of bombs, we received flyers of cheap paper with the message, in faulty Danish language, that we were what they called a protectorate, and that they would respect our king, our government, army, navy, police, and judicial system. To resist in the flat and small country of Denmark against the enormous German war machine would have been a dramatic farce, [so the Danes did not resist,] whereas Norway, invaded the day later, fought bravely for some time, and consequently suffered a great deal.

They occupied Denmark. Actually the resistance in Denmark was very small because the Danish administration had made a nonaggression pact with Germany a couple of years earlier. There was fighting for only about a couple of hours. The Germans allowed both the Danish administration and the king to stay in power. We had our own army, navy, police force, and judicial system. Compared to other countries, we lived a very normal life in Denmark the first two or three years of the war. And the Germans behaved quite nicely. As a police officer, I could actually arrest Germans. This was highly unusual in Nazi-occupied Europe. When Hitler decreed that the Jews had to carry the star of David, Denmark was the only country in the world where it wasn't even suggested [that Jews be made] to carry the star of David.

From 1940 to 1943, life was relatively easy in Denmark. I can't tell you for sure, of course, why this was the case. Partly, I think it was a respect towards the Danish attitude. The Germans knew that we considered the Jews as Danes and nothing else, the same as we did Catholics or anybody else. But in some respect it was a kind of German snobbishness towards the Aryans, the blue-eyed blonds and Nordic types. Then, too, the Germans needed all the products they could lay their hands on, and they needed the railroads for the transportation of their troops up to Norway. But also they needed not only the food products that Denmark produced, but some occupied country which they could hold up as a kind of outstanding example of their generosity. Even the German soldiers at that time were not allowed to do things in Denmark that they did in the other occupied countries all the time. I'm talking now about the first two and a half years.

But then we got to know what was going on all over Europe and we got tired of the lies of the Germans. We got tired of having them utilizing and taking our food products. We never starved in Denmark. There was enough food for us, too. But we got tired of seeing the Germans buying or exporting or stealing things. Even if they paid in Danish money for what they got, we still saw that we were getting ripped off.

With almost everything being expropriated by the hungry occupiers, including paper, there wasn't much work in the printing industry and I had to look for another job. The state police department was short of manpower in a difficult situation, and they had an opening—especially for a former Guardsman—to join the police. So I applied and was accepted after a training course at a police academy. We were supposed to keep the generally unhappy population away from anti-German behavior, and especially from sabotage of factories. The Danes were forced to work with the Germans, while these military occupiers robbed us not only of the merchandise but most of all of our independent Danish pride and dignity.

It was quite a balancing act being a police officer: on one hand make the Nazis believe that we wanted to keep peace and order, and on the other hand, assist the fast-growing resistance. We were able to supply members of the Underground with some weapons and instructions on their use. It was small acts of sabotage to begin with. Like, we would drive in a police car, and throw bricks through the windows of the Nazi office trying to hire manpower for them. Then, innocently, we would report back to the police station that some "irresponsible" individuals had made a silly act of anti-German behavior. Somehow, while this was going on, one of the very few "Quislings" [informants] reported me to the German commander, General von Hanneken.

Q. Is it true that the Danish king wore a star of David at some point? I've heard that story and then I've also heard that it isn't true.

No. It isn't true. That's a lovely story about the Danish king saying that he would wear a star of David. But it is absolutely just a nice beautiful story, because the Danish Jews were *never ordered* to carry the star of David. But now this is something that's very interesting. What the king actually did was something that was a lot more important in my opinion. At the time when that Himmler and Hitler had decided to purge the Jews in Denmark, they sent the king a letter saying they wanted to solve the Jewish problem in Denmark. "Do you accept?" they asked. And the king sent a letter back. "We don't have a Jewish problem in Denmark. We are all Danes." This was on the twenty-ninth of September or the first of October.

Actually, I have to tell you something else. In August 1943, the Germans gave the Danes an ultimatum about our behavior because at that time we had started a lot of sabotages and a lot of anti-German activities. So they came up with a kind of an ultimatum to Denmark. This, the Danish government would not have anything to do with. The government said: "We cannot accept your ultimatum." There was a prohibition against allowing more than five people in the street, and there was a curfew put into effect. Other things like that. This started a folk strike, all over Denmark on the twenty-eighth of August. The people simply stopped. Even electricity and gas and food. All the production stopped. And again, strangely enough, the Germans gave in and said, "Alright. We are pulling back on that ultimatum." The country was at that time under the government by Dr. Werner Best of the Gestapo and of General Hanneken of the army.[3] They tried to form a new Danish government, which didn't really come off. They took over the Danish army and navy. The navy sank most of their ships. The Germans then interned the Danish army and navy, as they did not trust them. The army did small acts of resistance, and the navy personnel managed to sink most of their ships before the Germans could get them. Even the submarines went down to the bottom of the harbor—but this time to stay there and not come up again. On Amalienborg Castle the Guards defended themselves and gave Germans a heavy loss, until they decided that they really did not want the king as a prisoner.

As the anti-German sabotage and resistance grew, Hitler and Himmler became upset over the happenings in the otherwise favored "protectorate" to the north, and they demanded a different, more cooperative Danish government and much tougher laws against the Resistance. This resulted in a 100 percent folk strike that lasted eight days, before the Germans realized that they would have to forget some of their demands to get the country back to normal. Many of the Danish sailors escaped to Sweden. But we still had the police force.

Then on the twenty-ninth of September, just before Rosh Hashanah, we found out from a German shipping expert in Denmark—a German friend of Denmark, Georg Duckwitz—who warned a member of the Danish government about the impending raid, and the news spread like wildfire. There were 300 or 400 police troops from Germany coming into the port of Copenhagen on a ship called *Cometa*. They were sent to arrest all the Jews in Denmark. Duckwitz informed the Danish prime minister, Hans Hedtoft, about it. We had many, many underground newspapers organized by the Resistance, and all the underground papers found out about it at the same time so we knew everything that was going on. There were roughly 7,500 Jews in Copenhagen, and people got all of them out of their own apartments. It was a lot of trouble because [in 1943] the Danish Jews didn't believe the Germans would do such a thing. They didn't believe it was serious because they had heard it in so many rumors before, and nothing came of these rumors. But at this time, the papers said: "*This* time we *know* it's going to happen."

Even with all the police troops coming in from Germany and the Gestapo working and everything else, the Germans caught only about 256 Jews on the first night.[4] The Gestapo had obtained most of the addresses of the Jewish families by stealing the names from the synagogue in Copenhagen. The oldest was a lady of 102, and the youngest a baby of two years. Most of the 7,500 were moved into apartments of friends, into churches, into schoolhouses, into anything as long as it was out of their own homes. Almost all the Danish population worked in order to protect the Jews. During the next ten or fourteen days, we managed to send most of them over to Sweden. That was where I as a person started my "export service" of Jews. I became a rescuer.

I was at the police department in Frederiksberg, just outside of Copenhagen, when a friend of mine came over. "I have to help some people," he said. "I'm sorry I can't do it myself but you know your way around. You're a yachtsman." And he said, "There's a family that we want to take down and send them over to Sweden."

"That's fine with me even though I'm in service [on duty] too. But I'll go up and ask the police commissioner whether I can take a few hours off."

I was still in uniform when I went up to the police commissioner. I said, "My grandmother is dying again and I've got to take her to a hospital."

And he said, "I'm so sorry about your grandmother and certainly you can take off. And don't you think she would appreciate a police car?"

"I'm sure she would." But I didn't use it because we had to be very careful in Copenhagen at that time. My friend Frej and I were colleagues at the police station at Frederiksberg. I wasn't surprised when he asked me to assist one of his neighborhood families—Jews—to flee to Sweden. Frej and I were yachtsmen, and he knew that I had earlier helped some saboteurs out of Copenhagen North Harbor (Nord Havn). We set up a meeting place at a local chocolate store. Then I met these Jewish people. In the evening, I met a grocer, Valdemar Jacobsen, and his family and several others. Of course, they had brought far too much luggage with them. With all their suitcases and boxes they looked like tourists going for a long trip. With plenty of warm clothes on and with the baggage, it would not be hard for a Gestapo man to see what looked like a Jewish exodus. I took the whole big family in; I don't remember how many exactly. At first, all were on streetcars, later on by taxi. We split up in smaller groups with contact people, so that we would arrive at the same station about the same time, using buses and streetcars. Finally we hired some "good" taxi drivers, until we came to a point not too far from the harbor. We huddled together in the small wooden sheds, where some commercial fishermen I knew kept their tools and their nets. We all had to hide in their little sheds that they had down at the port. Then we had to negotiate with the fishermen because there were quite a crowd of people down there.

There were two reasons why it was easy enough to get people out. First, in early October, the weather was pretty bad. If the Germans had issued this order in the summertime, when it's light almost till 12 o'clock at night, we couldn't have done a thing. But fortunately, it was late in the year and the weather wasn't too good and everything was dark and fairly miserable. Second, the police department were also coast guards. Of course, the Germans had their navy and Gestapo boys running around. But the Danish police had a coast guard watch at the ports. Of course, being another policeman and being a colleague, we could find out from the coast guard police force where the Germans were stationed. Every time a patrol would go out or in, we would know all about it. So we could send the boats with the Jews over at a time where it was fairly safe, when there'd be no patrol boats.

Unfortunately, we had to negotiate on payments. In a situation like this, when you have a lot of people who are scared of not getting out, there were some people who unfortunately flashed money to get on the first boat. Some would pay a fair amount of money to leave. But others didn't have any money at all. We had to spread them about and get all of them out. We really had to be careful that none of the boats took off without having a full load of people in it. That is where we could be most useful as policemen. We couldn't do anything official, since everything we were doing was against the laws the Germans were enforcing, but we could at least talk terms with the fishermen. Of course, I never blamed the fishermen—and I *don't* blame them—because they were transporting people instead of going fishing. So we had to see that at least they didn't suffer any loss.

Every time I came to the police station, there were "secretive" phone messages from more people who themselves needed a trip or who had friends who needed a trip on our boats. Meeting Jews whom you had never met or even heard of before the fall of 1943 was a strange experience. Sometimes not even catching their names and family relationship, because it was immaterial to the mission we set forward to accomplish.

Outside our meeting place at a chocolate shop, German soldiers, three together, steel helmeted and with loaded machine guns in their arms, patrolled the streets night and day. More upsetting still were the Admiral and Mercedes automobiles, with Gestapo and Gestapo helpers in civilian clothes. Oh, they had brutal ways in surprise arrests, usually followed by painful interrogations or indiscriminate killings. We never knew whose names were in their little black books, or who or what got them there.

Later on, it was arranged with our friends over in Sweden that fishermen would get, oh, just a very little money. In fact, it was something like $40 or $50 for a round trip, no more. It wasn't much. But at least we made sure they didn't suffer any loss. We also found out that the Germans sometimes would have spies in the Swedish ports. So some of my Danish friends established an office in Malmö, Sweden, and from there on they bought boats. Thanks to help from a lot of Jewish people in Sweden and Danes in Sweden, we had enough money to buy our own boats in Sweden. These boats from Sweden would go out and meet our boats from Denmark at the territorial border of Denmark and Sweden so that the Danish boats didn't have to go all the way into Swedish ports. I'm just talking about what happened these first eight or ten days, during the time period that established my own part in the rescue activities.

None of the boats I sent over with Jews was caught, but two fishing skippers were caught with mail and news items, and their boats were destroyed. Four helpers in the Danish-Swedish Refugee Service, to which I belonged, were killed.[5]

After the exodus of Jews I was kept busy with five to six fishing boats to carry saboteurs, politicians, deserters, or Allied airmen, together with news, books, intelligence, and photos. At this time we had our own arrangement on the Swedish side, and they would meet us halfway at the territorial borders, so that our boats would not have to enter Swedish ports unless we lost a meeting at sea. It wasn't easy, especially in bad weather or dark nights.

Sometimes our fishing boats were kept so busy with our underground transports that they often did not have time to fish. So we had them buy a catch from Swedish fishermen in order not to come back without fish!

Actually, the help to the Jews, I would say, was a minor part of my rescue activities. Later, using five or six fishermen plus the contacts established in Sweden that we used until the finish of the German occupation in 1945, we got lots of human exports; we took saboteurs, deserters, information and intelligence service, and everything else. But transporting the Jews was the start of our human exporting business, establishing routes from Denmark to Sweden. That's really how I got into this because of helping, at least let's say that was the start of it. On occasions, we had sent a saboteur over to Sweden, somebody who I knew was in danger. But from October 1943, we had much more assistance sailing back and forth. I really don't want to be a special hero on this. Much later in 1944, you would be shot or you would be sure to get put into a concentration camp were you caught. It was then that it actually was, in my opinion, much more dangerous.

For the five or ten days in 1943 when most of the Jews came over— well, of course, there were still some left who didn't come over—but during that time we had a good establishment with some of the fishermen. They were very helpful in many ways. There were many ways we could get Jews over, partly because we knew where the German patrol boats were. Sometimes we sailed our boats over low water, where the German patrol boats couldn't follow us. Of course, the Germans could have stopped all fishing, or even stopped all sailing in the Danish waters, but it would have been detrimental to them because the Germans needed the food products they got from Denmark that way. They needed the fish products. There were still a lot of other ships, because Denmark is mostly islands, 300 or 400 islands beside the peninsula at Jutland. So in order to keep communication between the various islands, you had to have ferries going all the time. This is *in addition to* the small fishing boats that I'm talking about. It's just that it is the fishing boats that were my particular domain. They are what I used most. Some other people, on occasion, could use larger boats. For example, we had some beer boats come from Elsinore, sailing to the island of Bornholm. The beer cases would be stacked up so there was an empty room in the middle of it where you could transport about twenty or thirty people. Many things like that were done at that time.

You get some funny things that happened, too. One of my fishermen, he had to buy the fish over in Sweden because he didn't have time to fish himself. At one time he had an old codfish that he'd carried so long that it almost got hairy with seaweed. He had that fish so long that it almost knew him. Another fisherman we had helping would always carry a side of Danish bacon that he would give to the German inspectors who came on board to inspect his boat. He would cut a piece off and give it to them. Then he would very politely ask them about their position the next day, where they'd be because, he said, "If you want some fresh fish or more bacon, I'll drop by and give you some." So the Germans would give him their position on the next day. I don't know whether they ever got the fish or not but I doubt it. [Knud laughed.]

You know, this was not the only funny thing that happened. When we started the rescue, hundreds of Jews were evacuated by ambulances and brought into hospitals, where they were put to bed in various wards, even though they were perfectly well. One nurse asked what kind of sickness she should use for the hospital record, and the doctor told her, "German measles."

This was the kind of thing that let us get so many people out of Denmark. I'd say we got out about 7,500 Jews. But all total, there were 20,000 Danish refugees helped over the waters to Sweden.

There was a lot of sabotage of factories working for the Germans. There were 700 railroad sabotages. The Germans got more and more unhappy with the conditions in Denmark. In 1943, I was finally reported to the German General Hanneken for anti-German activities. I was personally reported. The Germans issued a warrant for my arrest and I went underground. I had to live in many different places, always in hiding. But I stayed in Denmark instead of getting over to Sweden. And I still worked at the police department.

In all this time I still functioned as a police officer, until September 19, 1944, at which time the Germans realized that they could not trust the Danish police to stop sabotage and railroads being blown to pieces by saboteurs. The Gestapo, enforced with army and German police troops, on that day surrounded all Danish police stations and arrested 1,900 officers, from top to bottom. They were put on trucks and transported by a ship *Cometa* and thereafter cattle cars in Germany to concentration camps in Buchenwald and Neuengamme, where many suffered sickness or died.

Fortunately, I had left the station early in the morning. When I returned I found it surrounded by Germans with small cannons and machine guns, and I saw my colleagues being pushed onto the trucks.

Q. You continued working for the police even though the Germans had issued a warrant for your arrest?

Surprising, isn't it? I know. Despite this warrant for my arrest, they just let me work there. [Knud laughed.] I always got paid.

But then on September 19, 1944, the Germans got tired because they couldn't trust the Danish police. They knew that some police were actively involved in sabotage and other anti-Nazi activities. I wasn't the only one, you see. So the Germans sent in the Gestapo and the German army into Denmark. They surrounded all the Danish police stations on September nineteenth and took over the police department. I'm sure that my dear friends at the police station—about 1,800 of them in all—they probably thought that they would be interned in a Danish camp in the southern part of Jutland. But they were taken into a ship. That ship was the *Cometa,* the ship that took the Danish police department down to Germany. My police colleagues ended up in Neuengamme and Buchenwald, in the concentration camps. About 150 of them died, although they were only there from the fall of 1944 to May 1945. It was very sad, especially after all the police had done. But fortunately again, I escaped.

I had been sent home from duty at six o'clock in the morning. When eleven o'clock came, the Germans blew the air alarm, the air warning in Copenhagen, which at that time was to be sounded to call all the policemen who were sent home to come back on duty again, so that we would have a double force during an important air raid. I was in bed when I heard it. After turning around in bed a few times, I finally got on my bicycle and tried to bicycle out to the station where I was posted. I had on my policeman's uniform but I had put a raincoat on over it. I had to pass two or three police stations on my way to my station, and I could hear shooting. I saw what was going on. I realized on the way that the Germans were taking over the police force. I saw that there were small cannons and machine guns in front of the police station so I knew something was up.

We had an annex to our police station. I figured that this annex, the Germans probably didn't know about. So, instead of going into the main station, I went over to the annex. I filled a sack full of passports, driver's licenses, and permits to go out on the street during curfew, all kinds of legal forms that we could use later. I filled a sack with all these things. I couldn't transport the sack on my bicycle so I had to take a taxicab to get out of there. In those days, you weren't allowed to travel without identification [Legitimations Kort]. All of a sudden, the taxi cab driver turns around. "Do you have your identification card?" he says.

"Yes!" I told him. "I have five hundred of them!"

The cab driver figured out what's going on. He was like most of the rest of the Danish people, not too keen on the German occupation. So he told me, "There's a raid going on right down here by the Germans. We'll have to get the sack up on the top of the car."

So that's what we did. We put the sack with the permits up on top of the car. We go some other way where they didn't have a raid. And we got through. We kept all these documents from falling into German hands.

Then later, during the war, we used them for Jews, or for other people who needed them, whenever they needed a new passport or anything like that. Some of these forms are still shown at the Freedom Museum in Copenhagen.

I certainly don't take credit for all the illegal things that were done. This was just my own little adventure.

From then on, after they took all the Danish policemen away and put them into camps, I'm really living underground. At that time, I had "shipments" three or four times a week to my friends in Sweden. We had an organization that would get all kinds of letters and information, all the secrets about official business—and about ordinary people—in Denmark. We had a lot of mail and we had material from eighty intelligence services that we brought over in microphotographs. At the same time, from Sweden we received a few weapons. Not too many, because the Swedes had to walk very carefully; they didn't want an invasion from Germany. So they had to try not to openly support what we did, but they certainly did support it in many other ways.

I was contacted by a courier from the Danish-Swedish refugee organization in Sweden. They had lost a lot of people in the transportation and they were short of boats. They wanted to know whether I could help them. We had quite a meeting with the courier. I told him that if they would take care of the money matters, so I could pay the fishermen just a small payment—not much, mind you, but something—and if they would meet them over in Sweden, or at the border between Denmark and Sweden, where the waters between Denmark and Sweden meet, I could send them elephants if they would pay for it! This was just to show them that we could do anything as long as they supported it. So we agreed that we would get an arrangement started with at least three or four transports every week. And we did that.

In fact, in some respect we carried more mail than in peacetime. We had appointed people in Denmark to collect important mail for the press all over the world. Not just spying material and photographs. More practical things were sent back and forth as well. Things like a ladies' new upper plate. What do you call it? Her bridge. Maybe the bridge was unusual, so it had to be made special. We'd send things like that. There were money affairs and many correspondences between Denmark and the rest of the world went over to Sweden. So we continued to work on that. They would send me information back at various ways where the fishermen would meet them at preset meeting points on the high seas. It all worked beautifully, and we had up to five or six connections a week. At that time, there were very few Jewish people left [in Denmark], but occasionally we would have a Jewish person or an Allied airman or some foreigners we could send over to Sweden. For example, I sent over four or five Germans who had been international circus artists and who didn't want to go to the Russian front. They asked us to be interned and sent to Sweden. In that case, we did it.

During all this time, I was living underground. But at the same time, fortunately, the Finance Department in Denmark made an arrangement so I got my police pay even though I was underground. After the police were taken over [by the Gestapo], the checks were still deposited in the bank. I don't know how they did it. The Finance Department just did it. So I still had my pay. I guess in all that I lived in about sixteen different places. I wasn't married during this time. And I'm not going to tell you about my love life during the war! [Knud laughed.] Usually I would just spend the night wherever I was. As the war was ending, I also was connected with the intelligence service of the Danish navy and sent about eighty different miniature intelligence films over to Sweden in capsules, microfilm in capsules. That was the kind of work we did with the Resistance.

Oh, I could tell you lots of stories about things that happened during the occupation [of Denmark]. For example, during the folk strike in 1943, the German army placed a couple of armored tanks in the middle of the Townhall Square of Copenhagen. Early the next morning when people went to work, they were all laughing, enjoying signs at the bases of the tanks, saying in Danish "Saelges" [for sale].

Well, after so many visits of the fishing boats from Denmark into Swedish ports we learned that the "visits" sometimes were being reported back to Gestapo in Copenhagen. This problem was solved by our own people on the Swedish side by obtaining our own "Swedish" boats, and meeting the Danish boats halfway between Denmark and Sweden at the territorial borders. But . . . it wasn't always easy to meet at night or in bad weather, and skippers and crew from both sides spent many hours out on the water, waiting for "contact." Most of the time, the latest "contact" would get the position and time for the next planned meeting. When this didn't work we tried some other "underground" communication method. With good friends at the railroad terminals in both Denmark and Sweden, we found that the German troop transports (in sealed cars) could help us, and our helpers placed messages in a designated spot under the third railroad car, counted from the locomotive or diesel. This message was then picked up by friends on the receiving end.

During most of the war, the Germans still had diplomatic connections to Stockholm by air. Irregardless of whoever piloted the airplanes, our "friends" at the airport were sure that just before the planes took off, they succeeded in a most ridiculous task of putting the wheel stop blocks onboard the departing plane. The blocks were hollowed by a woodcarver, and we got a few important messages carried this way, when other methods failed. Taking the blocks with them, oh, the Germans must have thought that this idiotic Danish custom was a strange one.

After one of "my" fishing skippers were caught by Gestapo and painfully interrogated, I knew that the brutal treatments wouldn't stop until the interrogators had a satisfactory result in finding out where the skipper received his orders and "deliveries." I rented a small empty apartment close to the harbor. This apartment would daily be filled with information that was up to date, but of very little importance. Nobody would stay very long at the place. All the helpers and couriers would be told to disclose this "contact place" when they felt that the Gestapo had brutalized them more than enough. The apartment could only be used one time, but it was easily replaced.

• • •

Oh, I could tell you stories for days. Once, a police colleague and I, along with a third man from the Resistance, had arranged a meeting at a Vesterbro Hotel, where we understood that we could meet someone with hand grenades "for sale." Unfortunately, I had been delayed, and when I came to the hotel, some strangers informed me that the Gestapo had been there and had picked up some Underground persons. Fortunately, it was not my friends, who had arrived just *after* the visit by the Gestapo. But my colleague avoided me for a long time since he thought I had been there early, and had failed to warn him, instead of the other way around. This kind of misunderstanding, relating to dangerous situations which were wrongly interpreted, could bring trouble on both sides.

Another time, I had a meeting at a very popular restaurant in Copenhagen called the Skandia. The Skandia had good food and a full band for lunch and dinner. The owner was a man named Mikkelsen. The inspector, what you'd call the maitre d'hôtel, was Henning Petersen. The bandleader was Merriman and the singer was Eddy Russell. They were all very active in anti-German activities, and consequently many prospective saboteurs and resisters frequented the restaurant. I became best friends with Henning Petersen, along with a couple of the charming waitresses. Petersen had contacts who claimed to be able to obtain weapons from the Germans. In an afternoon we were going to meet these people—opposite Skandia. As Petersen and I went out of the door, I observed something. You know, sometimes I think I had a "radar-eye" to detect suspicious informers. Anyway, I saw two groups of people of the "wrong kind" on each side of our meeting place. I said to Petersen, "Let's skip the meeting, and see what happens?"

I had to take off for the police station, and later was called by a crying waitress, who told me that Petersen had just been shot through the neck and had died on the floor of the restaurant. Later it turned out that Petersen had been shot in a so-called clearing murder, because he often turned down reservations by German officers. The owner of Skandia was arrested by Gestapo later at a meeting with Underground leaders. He suffered greatly during imprisonment, so I was just lucky that time.

Q. What was it that motivated your activities? Was it your patriotism? Was it your humanitarian desires?

Denmark wouldn't have been free if we hadn't fought the Germans for two thousand years. Being a small country to the north and having an aggressive nation like Germany nearby, we would always be under pressure. If we hadn't defended ourselves for thousands of years, Denmark would have been Germany. My grandfather and his great-grandfather had fought in the wars between Denmark and Germany. There was one in 1848 and one in 1864. My grandfather told me, quite frankly, to hate all Germans. Period. But, of course, I couldn't do that. During World War II, we were all living under pressure from Germany, so my Underground work was primarily because I didn't want to be occupied by a German force and we wanted to resist the Germans regardless of what they did. The rescuing of Jews was connected to that feeling and it was also just a humanitarian feeling. We considered them not as Jews as such but as Danes. They were our people and they lived in Denmark. They were adopted by Denmark. It's a very homogenous society and the Jews in Denmark, even if they had a completely different religion, we found it interesting because we didn't have a lot of minorities. So the ones we had, we could take care of.

I'm often asked why we in Denmark reacted so humanely and positively against the discrimination and arrest of the Jews. I don't know why. But maybe it was because although the Danish living standard was fairly high and people in general lived well, the Danes live in a rather miserable climate. It's a country without many natural resources. No iron, coal, or minerals, until long after the occupation, when they found a good supply of oil in the North Sea. Because of the necessity of importing most raw materials, the Danes have to work hard, be inventive, and in general be resourceful, show respect for values and minimize waste. So, what we experienced was not only respect for material values, but also respect for our fellow man and humanity in general. In schools and in the home we were taught to act responsibly, individual responsibility . . . and *not* to be intimidated by extreme political or religious zealots. Our religious traditions did not allow for any extreme standards, and certainly not for discrimination.

I went back to the police force the day the war ended on the fourth of May. Of course, we had shortwave radios but we heard on the BBC from

London that the Germans had surrendered in Denmark and Norway at eight o'clock on the morning of May fifth. We knew that the foreign press was coming over from Sweden, on our boats to visit us in Denmark and to report what it was like when Denmark was free. So we were quite busy running around, receiving some of our friends from Sweden and from London. At the same time, the British troops came. There was this English General Dewey. He and his troopers came into Copenhagen. The Underground forces had an armband on our sleeves. It was blue and red and white. It was just given out to Resistance fighters to denote that we belonged to the Underground organizations, to the Resistance.

We were quite busy not only receiving our friends but also arresting the collaborators. That was quite an affair because the files on them were lacking so we had to take the Underground assistants' word for those things. Arresting collaborators wasn't so difficult for me because, being in the police force, it wasn't unusual. It was difficult sometimes because all of them, of course, would claim that they were innocent. We would have to depend only on various witnesses and neighbors or people who would bear witness against the people who had been collaborators. Fortunately, we didn't have that many in Denmark; we had very few Quislings, but we did have some. Most of the Germans behaved pretty nicely. They were tired of the war. Of course, they knew what was coming. The Gestapo resisted the peace. Some of the Danish collaborators who were in uniforms were also quite obnoxious. But it didn't take long for the Underground to quiet everything down.

In the meantime, we had the Danish Red Cross and the Swedish Red Cross coming up on the fourth and fifth of May. They were on white buses, transporting people from the concentration camps of Therezienstadt and Neuengamme.[6] This was quite an experience, to see the people who came on those white buses of Count Bernadotte, the Swedish count who made it possible for them to come. He made an agreement with Himmler that they could pick up the Danish and Norwegian concentration camp population and bring them into safety in Sweden.

Really, what he did was one of the most outstanding examples of humanity! The Swedish Count Bernadotte made an agreement with Himmler whereby he could pick up all the Danish Jews from Therezienstadt and from Neuengamme and bring them into Sweden so that they would be protected from the invasion, that is from the invading Americans and English.[7] But in fact, mostly they would be protected from the Gestapo, which would have blown up the concentration camps and killed all the people to eliminate the evidence of the inhumanities that had been done to them. Count Folke Bernadotte, with hundreds of buses, picked up these people and brought them in through Denmark on ferryboats over to Sweden from the last days of April to May fifth. He saved more than ten thousand people during those last few days. Unfortunately, he was killed, presumably by the Israeli Stern Gang because somebody said that he was pro-English and pro-Palestinian, which is absolutely not so.[8] I'm telling you all this because I feel he was a rescuer. He was very much a rescuer. I think that even if it hurts somebody, he should be recognized as a rescuer. Now, Raul Wallenberg is being promoted somewhere.[9] They want to know all about what happened to Raul Wallenberg in Russia. It's about time that we also know all about what happened to Bernadotte at that time in Palestine.

I know this because I actually saw these people as they were coming through. I certainly did. [Knud hesitated, then spoke in a lowered voice.] You know, we had heard about it. We had seen some. But we had only heard about their sufferings and their sicknesses. Here you could see it. Even if they had already been treated better and had some food, it was still a misery to hear about their experiences, to see your friends who had lost hundreds of pounds.

Q. How do you react to something like that? How does a sensitive human being deal with such things?

You either react or you just drop your hands. You do something and you help them! We helped them with food. We got them installed in various schools and hospitals. We got them into homes again and they were treated by doctors in hospitals. There were some non-Jewish refugees who came up, too. We couldn't distinguish between the Danes and Norwegians and the German and Jewish refugees from other countries; but we certainly took care of all of them.

After the war, I went back to the police department for a little while. I think I stayed with the police department about three-fourths of a year.

Then you know, after you've been in Denmark, all closed in, almost imprisoned in the Old Country, for five years, we wanted to get out. So I had applied for a visitor's visa to this country [the United States] in 1946. That's what I received. I came here as a visitor and I ended up staying. I had a patent on photo engraving. I have had several other patents, besides the one for an object that you probably have on your desk, the paper clip container. I designed the one with a magnetic top. I'm also an inventor. I thought that the gold was easy to find on the streets in this country. But I'm still looking.

So I became, first of all, an import/exporter. Later on, I was in printing again. I became a supervisor in a print shop. But this has nothing to do with the Jews.

It took a lot of years before I ever thought about the rescue operation and the Underground. The Yad Vashem in Jerusalem had honored a lot of people in Europe for their actions during the war and for saving Jews.

But then in 1984, when they started the Holocaust museum in Washington, D.C., all of a sudden a wise guy said, "Yeah, but are you sure you honored the people who immigrated from the countries in Europe?"

Then they had to say, "No, we did not. We forgot those." So they invited about seventy or eighty of us, from many nationalities, not just Denmark, to an opening. Really, it was quite an affair, in Washington, D.C., in 1984. They honored us and took interviews for the State Department of what we had done during the war. At the same time, I found here that they also had connections to the local area press and I found myself in pictures and articles on the front pages on newspapers and on three different TV stations. That made a lot of things get rolling. So I have been making speeches or presentations and being honored in various ways. I gave some small speeches at the colleges and universities and high schools. However, due to the very specific things that happened in Denmark, where almost everybody helped, the Danish Underground organizations and the Resistance organizations claimed rightfully that we don't want to have any individual honors from Israel but to be honored in total, for all of Denmark. So there's not only a hospital called Christian X in Jerusalem but there's also a park devoted to all the Danes.

· · ·

In what became a rather abrupt end to our filmed interview, Knud suddenly became very emotional and muttered something like, "That's it! That's all you get!" as he walked off camera.[10] I sat there a minute, afraid that he was somehow offended, although there had been nothing in his demeanor to indicate this distress prior to his abrupt exit. He then returned a few minutes later and somewhat self-consciously shoved something in my hands, explaining, "If you really want to understand, you can read this." After reading his document, I asked Knud if I could include it in anything that was published about him and he agreed.

People always ask me to talk at these gatherings. I don't have much to say. I can read you something I wrote once. It's for the end of my autobiography—which I'll probably never write—but I wrote this first 'cause it says what I feel. Let me read it to you.

"When I look back on my life—I'm seventy-four years young—if I were looking for an explanation of life on earth, what's the purpose or why are we here—and this I am *not*—I would say that our life experience here on the good earth is an almost indescribable, beautiful, phenomenal, anonymous gift, presented to mankind as a most intriguing but completely natural miracle. It's a gift to be valued and enjoyed, unless adverse circumstances like sickness, pain, and suffering make it impossible for the individual. It's a gift to be shared equally with fellow human beings, and animals as well, in peaceful coexistence, in a harmonious, loving, altruistic, nonbiased, nonviolent and nonexploiting way."

"We have today so much scientific knowledge about the physical and biological world of ours. I think some of the old traditions, philosophical and religious beliefs should gradually be replaced with more intelligent, simplistic rules of behavior. These should emphasize respect for our common natural habitat, for all fellow human beings and for the animal world, and should emphasize all the necessary obligations and responsibilities."

"Nothing, no religious beliefs, philosophies, or even fantasies are as intricately wondrous and beautiful as the gift of existence here on earth. From an inexplicable explosion in time, our globe became solidified, whirling around in a fairly even geometric pattern in its preordained, gravitationally forced place in the galaxy. Thanks to continuous energies deluged on our earth from the nucleic active sun, our globe developed gases: hydrogen, oxygen, nitrogen, helium, and many more inorganic and organic substances, as in an unbelievable fairy tale. Even more unbelievable is the evolution of biological life from all of the above; the end result is the human species and our ability to see, hear, feel, taste, and sometimes remember, think and communicate. Not because of any great energy output or cunning by ourselves, but because our chemical-electronic-magnetic brain cells are working naturally, or naturally working. It's all there. And with little training and learning, it's a part of us. It's the miraculous gift: the curlicue strains of protein DNA and RNA work, and so do the inherited chromosomes, hanging around like apples from a tree branch. This is our inheritance from nature. We are nature; nature is us. We are definite substances in a natural continuity."

"I am thankful and happy that I have been part of this physical and biological miracle, this life on earth. I'm starting to burn out or wear out, which is also a part of the adventure of being. I haven't been able to make the earth a much better place, but I hope that I've not made too much damage either. I've left a few chromosomes of mine as a handful of genetic traits with my daughter. I hope she takes good care of them. They are, after all, from way back in time. And they are a valuable gift from the marvelous miracle which is life on earth."

• • •

The rescue of the Danish Jews was an exceptional historic event. In most other occupied countries, the Germans found it relatively easy to round up and deport Jews. Of the approximately 7,000 Jews living in Denmark in October 1943, most escaped to Sweden. Estimates vary on the numbers of

Jews captured. Knud estimates 256, while other experts say as many as 431 were captured and sent to Therezienstadt. Even then, the Danes successfully convinced Eichmann, via Werner Best, to keep the Danish Jews away from the death camps, and the Danish church and civil service groups sent more than 700 packages of clothing, food, and even vitamins to Jews in Therezienstadt. Because of the Danes, it is estimated that nearly 96 percent of these Danish Jews survived the war. Many Danish Jews returned home after the war to find their homes, personal belongings, even their gardens and pets taken care of by neighbors.

Georg F. Duckwitz, the German shipping clerk who alerted the Danes to the October 1943 raid, was honored for his part in the rescue and served as Germany's ambassador to Denmark in the post–World War II era. He died in 1973. Hans Hedtoft, the Social Democrat who helped organize the Resistance, became Minister of Social Affairs in the first postwar government in 1945. He headed the Social Democratic Government in 1947–50 and became prime minister in 1953. He died in Stockholm in 1953, while attending a meeting of the Nordic Council.

In Jerusalem, a monument in the shape of a boat was erected on the twenty-fifth anniversary of the Danish rescue. One of the small boats actually used in the rescue is prominently displayed in Yad Vashem. It is placed on the Avenue of the Righteous as a tribute to the Danes who brought hope and life and trust in the human spirit.

Knud did not speak about his Resistance activities for more than forty years. In the spring of 1991, Knud was invited on a trip to Israel.[11] On April 19, 1991, on a sun-filled day at Yad Vashem and surrounded by fifteen fellow rescuers, including his friend Otto, Knud received a Yad Vashem Medal and plaque, in honor of all those who died during the Holocaust, and in honor of people like Knud who tried to save them. Knud now lives alone in Northern California.

6

The Complexity of the Moral Life
and the Power of Identity
to Influence Choice

*To be a rescuer, under these circumstances, it took a
unique person. Someone who had the deep-seated conviction . . . that they had to do it. And they were not people
who were making choices on reflection. They just simply
had to do it because that's the kind of people they were.*
—*Immanuel Tanay, survivor*[1]

MOST OF US, at some time in our lives, come face-to-face with that most
basic concern of ethics: how we treat others. We find guidance from
religion or philosophy in the form of general principles, while literature
and biographies provide more concrete intimate illustrations of how our
fellow human beings wrestle with moral dilemmas, illuminating the pit-
falls and rewards of the moral life in a manner we can relate to our own
lives. At a more personal level, we learn about morality by observing the
behavior of those around us, although here both social convention and
the particular nature of our relationship with those observed often inhibit
our ability to ask the difficult questions we might like to pose. Rarely do
we have the opportunity to speak as frankly and engage in a dialogue
with people who are as morally commendable as the rescuers we have
just met. The rescuers' stories thus take on a particular value. They help
us think about our own lives in terms of ethical issues, and it is to such a
consideration that I now turn.

Taken as a whole, the rescuers' stories focus attention on three important points. First, we are struck by the complexity of the moral life. A
wide variety of forces influenced rescuers; no single factor can be said to
have caused their rescue behavior. Duty, socialization, religion, an innate
moral sense, even the explicit mention of Kant's categorical imperative—
all these factors were mentioned by one rescuer or another. The driving
force behind moral action thus seems both complex and multidimen-
sional. It is not as simple as following rules or moral principles, even

those as widely accepted as the Golden Rule or the prohibitions against lying or treating people as only a means to an end.[2]

Second, we are struck by the remarkable extent to which none of the rescuers agonized over what to do. This insight is significant, given the tendency, in both Western philosophy and literature,[3] to think about moral action in terms of agonistic choices that are conscious and soul wrenching.[4]

Third, instead of moral dilemmas and agonistic choices, we find identity. The rescuers' sense of who they were, and how they saw themselves in relation to others, so limited the range of actions the rescuers perceived as available that they literally did not believe they had any other choice than to help Jews. Identity played such a critical role in shaping their treatment of others that their extraordinary actions seemed matter-of-fact, unremarkable, and unnoteworthy to the rescuers themselves. Moreover, this influence from identity appeared to operate through a cognitive[5] process that consistently drew particular parts of rescuers' complex identities to the fore.

If we analyze rescue behavior, we thus come to the importance of character[6] and perceptions as a motivating force behind ethical behavior. To understand why our sense of self exerts such moral force, we need to understand how people see the world and themselves in relation to others. We need to decipher how their minds work, to ask how they take in the myriad bits of information that bombard us all daily and piece them together to make sense of reality. By understanding how people construct their frameworks for analyzing reality, how they select and group other people into categories—good versus bad, trustworthy versus threatening—we may begin to determine how the moral psychology works to exert such a powerful influence on behavior.

Once we move beyond the interesting specifics of the rescuers' stories and make a more systematic consideration of *how* the rescuers' moral psychology worked to influence their actions toward Jews, we are led to a host of questions that need to be answered.[7] How intricate and interrelated were the factors that contributed to the rescuers' moral life? Why didn't the rescuers explain their actions using the language of choice? How did their sense of self in relation to others constrain the range of options they found available? Can we figure out *why* rescuers' sense of self had such importance in constraining choice? Is it that rescuers' characters were uniformly altruistic, or do we need to determine how different parts of a complex identity are called forth in response to particular events in the external world? Can understanding someone's perspective— the way one sees oneself in relation to others—offer a compelling explanation for the individual variation in moral action, one that a reliance on constant character cannot offer? These are large questions to which the answers presented in chapters 6 and 7 can provide only a thought-provoking beginning.

The Intricacy of the Impetus toward Moral Action

A consideration of each of our rescuers suggests how variegated are the forces underlying moral action. Given the intricacy of human beings, this finding should not be remarkable. It becomes noteworthy, however, given both the scholarly and the popular propensity for clear, simple explanations, and the construction of moral maxims or systems of ethical rules and prescriptions. Because such an unifocal approach offers the advantage of straightforwardness it is perhaps an understandable result of a human need to classify and simplify in order to instruct and inculcate ethics. Nonetheless, this approach carries with it obvious drawbacks when we ask whether real people act this way.

We can see this problem clearly in the analysis of the behavior of the rescuers discussed in this book. Consider Otto as an example. Otto suggested that a variety of factors motivated him, from self-respect and a sense of duty to outrage and a desire to show off.

Otto: I examined myself whether it wasn't part of showing off, and it was.

Q. *It was part of showing off?*
Yes.

Q. *Was it anything more than that?*
Of course.

Q. *What else was it?*
Outrage, I would say. There was a component of craziness, which I just mentioned, that had its roots in an outrage. And then, of course, my wife got pregnant. She carried my child when she was supposed to go to Auschwitz. So all that combines into a very strong motive. But nothing is simple, you know? It is a combined thing and now you come and ask what percent of this and what percent of that.

Q. *I recognize that it is very complex. I think the distinctions are quite subtle that have to be drawn here. . . . I'm just trying to understand the process that led you to act. . . . In general, the activities that you did with the Jews, you said partly that it was simply you were in love with your wife. You loved your in-laws. You had had an education and a kind of moral upbringing from your father and it was part of your personality. Is that what I'm hearing you say?*

Yes. Right. Absolutely.

Q. Then were there other times in your life when you did things to help other people? I mean, helping Jews during the war is not the only incident?

Oh, no. There were others. Once I have saved a seventeen-year-old boy. I jumped into the high water of a river and I rescued a drowning man. Then I rescued another during a skiing trip in the mountains. He lost his way and we tried to find him in bad fog that developed into a terrible storm. It was difficult but we rescued him. I'm trying to be self-critical with the show of things. I wanted to impress also the girls with my courage. Definitely.

Q. How about duty? Was duty a factor? Did you feel you had a duty?

Look, the moral laws, the categorical imperative was there. And that is duty.

Q. What does the categorical imperative mean to you? You've mentioned it before.

I have certain moral principles and I have to act morally. That means that—I don't have the correct English words. In German, no, wait a minute. Leading component I would say. My behavior at any time can be elevated to universal law. But these are things which have developed from our ancestors and they are there. For instance, the leader of a group has a certain responsibility and . . . I can't analyze it better or more for you.

The above excerpt typifies Otto's discussion, which touched on many of the frequently cited influences on moral action: duty, education, moral principles, and socialization. Such a complex of motivating forces was evident for other rescuers as well. I found it especially striking that even in discussing a single influence—such as religion—the rescuers spoke in terms of multicausality when discussing the impetus toward moral action.

Religion.   Let us consider the example of religion since this is often said to provide an important source of morality. Theorists crediting religion as the origin of morality frequently adopt a threefold argument. (1) We need an external deity to create absolute standards of "right and wrong." (2) We need religious institutions and sacred books to help us know what is right and what is wrong, to guide us as we determine what is moral action. (3) We need religion to force us into doing what is right by making us frightened of punishment by a powerful deity. Some variant of these views is found in most of the world's major religions.[8]

Yet this kind of explanation was not evident in any of the rescuers' discussions of religion. Indeed, nowhere is the complexity of the moral life more evident than in rescuers' conversations about religion. For example, John was perhaps the most religious rescuer I interviewed, and his narrative makes it very clear that religion was central to his life. But John did not make religion the critical factor in his own explanation of rescue behavior, although John did make frequent references to God and the Lord, and identified the Bible as his guide for life: "I personally believe that the Bible is the gift of God that He left. It give the reason for my acts, the ethics of my life. I think that in that book, I find the reason why I have done what I did in the war." This is about as explicit a statement as any researcher will ever hear, and I was tempted simply to explain John's behavior through religion, until I recalled other parts of John's narrative, including John's own reluctance to identify religion as the impetus behind rescue behavior.

Q. Let's talk a little bit about religion. How important a factor do you think religion was in general for most people who rescued Jews?

I don't know that you had to be religious. An Adventist, a Catholic, or a Jew, you had to have love in your heart. How does love come into your heart? I don't know exactly. But I know I have to have love. If I don't have it, then I have to ask the Lord to give me it. I need more love, more affection, more consideration for others, and more desire to help others, and be less selfish.

Irene also described herself as religious and my conversations with her touchingly illustrate the complex role played by religion in rescue activities. Irene began our first interview (chapter 4) by telling a story about how she was saved by a little dog, who pulled her back from a brook when she was a child.[9] "I think about that later and I guess . . . the Lord knew I had something else to do with my life. And that's why he saved me." While describing her rescue activities, Irene later says, "I felt it so strongly that God put me there, in the right time, and the right moment, and the right place."

Irene experienced some of the horrors of the Holocaust firsthand, and our conversations were filled with difficult discussions and emotional moments. At times Irene would break down and cry and I would suggest turning off the tape recorder. Irene accepted this offer only once, saying, "What I have to tell you now is so horrible that you have to turn off the tape recorder." Somewhat alarmed and wondering what on earth Irene could tell me that was worse than what I had already heard, I complied. Irene told about going to confession and revealing to the priest that she was sleeping with the major—a man she was not married to—but that she was doing this in order to buy his silence about the people she was hiding. The priest figured out what was going on and told Irene she was endangering her mortal soul. He said she should immediately stop sleeping with the major and turn in the Jews. "I walked out of the church and never went back," Irene told me. Of all the things that happened to her, Irene considered this the worst. Only later did she tell me it was all right to use the story.

I did not interpret Irene's difficulties with this event as indicating a lack of religious faith. But I do believe Irene's response indicates that something even more important than religion drove her rescue activities. When confronted with a choice between saving human lives and doing what her church told her to do—turn in the Jews and stop sleeping with the major to buy his silence—Irene saw no choice. In this regard, Irene's attitude typified the views of other religious rescuers; the sanctity of human life and the desire to protect that life was a more fundamental impetus than religion. If the two conflicted, religion was less important than human well-being.

If John and Irene are emblematic of religious rescuers, Otto illustrates rescuers with no formal religion. Otto was quite clear that he believed in no afterlife, and he classified himself, at different times during our conversations, as a pantheist and as a Kantian.

Q. Now, you're not a religious person, are you. Or are you?
Otto: No, I am not. I'm a pantheist.

Q. Yes, I think we talked about that. . . . Do you have any particular philosophy of life that you use to guide you?
It's funny that I have no formal religion. It was interesting. My sister was two years younger and we wanted to go to confirmation as Lutherans together. We were a very well-known family in this church and it was a family affair. But then I debated with a revered teacher who was a good scientist. He researched and wrote many books. He said after our conversation, "If you think that way, you really have to refuse to get confirmed."

So my father called me and he said, "Look, are you so sure?" Now, I will tell you a small story. When my grandfather died, my father called me and wanted to pray. He wanted that we should say the Lord's Prayer together. And both of us had forgotten it! That's all. You know, he wanted to see if I feel strong enough to go it alone. And I absolutely do. I can get along without any revelation.

Q. You don't believe there's an afterlife?

Absolutely not. Not an individual one.

Q. What kind of afterlife is there?

Back into the pool. The pool consists of the forces which create life, sometimes very carelessly. I think we are a miscreant genetic experiment of god. Because all the animals have inhibitions against intra-species killing. But where is our inhibition to press the button of a machine gun? The dog who is subdued by another dog turns around, exposes his throat, and the other dog cannot bite. This is one of many examples.

Margot's religious views also tend toward the informal. Although at certain points Margot describes herself as religious, her conversation seemed to edge into discussions of an innate moral sense, as did conversations with John and Otto. Margot also highlights the important role of emotions and feelings in driving rescue actions.

MARGOT: I'm a religious person. But I don't go to churches. Look what happens with Reverend Swaggart. He goes to bed with somebody. All that holy doings! You don't have to show it that you're so holy. I don't really have any particular faith so to speak. I am baptized but I'm just as well Jewish. I know the Jewish religion very, very well. I know the Catholic religion very, very well. I know everything. I learned it.

Q. What kind of faith do you have?

I believe in God, in one God. But not in falling down on the floor. In Spain, when I studied, I had a teacher. She told me: "Nobody can learn it [faith]." There are lots of things that you can't learn. You can feel things. Some people want other people to talk about it, to tell you what is in them or what they feel. Either I think, "Uh oh, there's something wrong," or "Everything's all right." I *feel* them. You cannot learn certain things. You have either compassion with these people, or you think, "I couldn't care less when they drop dead."

Q. Where does it come from though, these feelings? It must come from someplace.

I think it's born in you. That's what that Spanish teacher said. It is in you. You feel things. I feel an enormous lot of things.

Margot continued, articulating a kind of moral sense theory in her discussion of her actions toward Jews.

Q. Let me see if I'm understanding what you're saying. Are you saying that you think that people are born, or at least some people are born, with an ingrained sense of compassion, of right or wrong?

I think so.

Q. Is everyone born with it?

No. Well, could be. But some people, already at home they have such a terrible home life that they get angry at everybody. You cannot learn some things in life. But there are lots of people that do you harm and they are disagreeable and they hurt you. Then you just leave them alone and think, "Oh, to hell with them." But on the other hand, you can't help everybody in life.

To my surprise, Margot was not the only rescuer to speak in terms that would be familiar to a moral sense theorist. Comments such as these raised the question of a sense of right and wrong, born within us but nurtured and shaped by society through others. This concept is what some philosophers and evolutionary biologists have argued is an innate moral sense, possessed by both humans and other animals.

An Innate Moral Sense.   Moral sense theory is a somewhat obscure theory of morality, largely dismissed by ethicists since the eighteenth century. Its essential argument is that human beings are born with an innate sense of right and wrong, much as we are born with the sense of touch, smell, sight, etc. How this sense develops and its precise contours—what is considered foul or good smelling, morally prohibited or praiseworthy—will vary from culture to culture. But the basic claim is biological: some sense of right and wrong is born within us.[10]

John joined Margot in speaking about the importance of developing the moral sense that is born within people. In this regard, John's discussion of Germans makes clear that a moral sense is distinct from the development of intellect or knowledge, just as a sense of touch is distinct from a sense of smell.

You know, before the war, Germany had the greatest amount of scientists. The greatest amount. They had really great brains. Yet the Holocaust happened there. So this knowledge [they have] is not saving humanity. I think it is wise to develop your knowledge, to develop your ability, physically, mentally, and so on. But if you don't develop your heart, love in action, compassion to those in need. . . . [John shrugged and continued on this theme later in our conversation.]

Q. Do you think people are basically good or bad, or self-interested? Do you think there is a norm?

Basically good. Good and bad. Some with conscience, some with more, some with less. Some people have more ethics naturally than others. They are born with that concept.

Q. Born? Ethics are born within us?

With some, yes, I think so. Not so much with others. We are not all born equally. We're not all born equally in terms of our ability to make moral judgment, or equally in other ways. We are all born equally to right of choice—that, yes. But one is born poor, one is born more rich. One is born indigent. One is born not indigent. One is born with four fingers or five fingers. One is born with illness. But we are not born equally. . . . [E]ach has to work together. . . . Because of inequality, it is my duty to share the thing that I have. If I don't have it, I cannot give it. But it is my responsibility to work [with] what I have. If I have more money than another one, and the other one does his best, and does not have the money to live, I have to share with him.

John seems to argue that a moral sense, like other inherited traits, may be distributed differentially and that the environment has a critical impact on its development. This suggests an innate, phenotypic quality to morality.[11]

Q. But how do you account for the difference in terms of moral choice, for some people's ability to make better moral choices than others?

I think that some people are born with a better notion of what is right and wrong. Some people are born with the privilege of parents who are wise how to educate their children in a way that they can be useful to society. So God is not going to judge a person only on his act, but also on other things around him. A poor guy who has a piece of bread, if he steals, well, I will not judge him so much as God will judge him. I cannot read the hearts of everyone. Think about some people. For some reasons, even though they make a big effort, they just can't make it because they don't the ability to do it. So be nice, and don't be harsh. They do their best; be nice to them. We are born unequally, and society has to try to bring the best we can to make the equality more apparent, to get less inequality. The rich have to pay more taxes than the poor, because that is the way to help. It is important for the people to be not too selfish.

John links an innate moral sense to socialization, suggesting we all can have hate and love in our hearts and that love has to be developed.

> JOHN: To arrest people because of race, what is the lesson? Why did it happen? It happened because people had hate in their hearts instead of love. . . . You have to learn that you have to love your neighbor. . . . If our hearts are not developed, the hearts of children, to love and have compassion, and to respect human life and beings, then we will not learn very much.

This emphasis on an innate sense of morality was also expressed in response to my more explicit questions about John's decision-making process. John's answer made me wonder if, and how, an innate moral sense may be related to the lack of choice also found when the rescuers discussed their wartime actions.

> *Q. Did you ever sit down and think about the costs and the benefits and the risks involved in what you were doing? Did you sit down and think about all these things before you undertook these "adventures" that you went on?*
>
> I don't think so. I think that it came as a natural reaction from the inside. Like a mother. Normally, you don't teach a mother how to love her baby. She has that naturally. Maybe not the father, but the mother. So your instinct that you develop in yourself is to react that way. And so it was a quite natural development. Not, "Should I do it or not?"

Otto aptly captures the view of many rescuers in suggesting the importance of deep-rooted genetic influences in leading us toward moral actions rooted in instincts.

> OTTO: On my medal, the Yad Vashem Medal, there is an inscription. It says, "Whoever saves one life, he has saved the entire humanity." And I think the inversion of that is also true. Whoever kills one innocent human being, it is as if he has killed the entire world.
>
> Once the ice is broken, there's a psychological moment, deeply founded in genetics. Our ancestors, who hunted in a pack, they had to follow the leader. So these things are deeply rooted in instinct. One can make use of these instincts to produce amazing things.

We find the concept of a moral sense intertwined with John's emphasis on the sanctity of human life. John's conceptualization of ethics as corresponding to a natural, ingrained sense of right or wrong is reflected in his discussion of his own deviation from any code of ethics, which troubles John but which underlines his sense that the sanctity of human life is the most fundamental value.

> JOHN: Another thing, I always learned to be truthful, to say the truth, never to lie. But when I came before the German Gestapo, it was for me very natural to lie, to say, "I don't know where are there [Jewish] people." It was only after the war, did I say, "Was it right or not?"
>
> My story is the story of many people in Holland. Maybe you know a Dutch lady, Corrie ten Boom, who helped Jewish people.[12] She say the same thing. When the Nazis come to ask, "Do you have Jews here, Madame?" Very naturally, she lie. Only afterward do she ask, "Am I right or wrong?" And even now, I ask myself [John shrugged], and I don't know.
>
> *Q. But at the time . . . ?*
>
> No question. No problem if it's right or wrong. *It was right!* It is right. They are human beings. . . . I wasn't lying so much to save my life but to save other people.
>
> *Q. You are saying there is a higher value for you than to tell the truth?*
>
> I think sometime in life you have to make a choice between higher values. This is a very difficult question. I can't say to anyone else. . . .
>
> *Q. What was the highest value for you, the value that was guiding you during this time?*
>
> Love your neighbor. You have to help.

This exchange again emphasizes the complexity of John's moral views. John rejects both prior socialization and deontological[13] or rule-based ethics by rejecting the learned prohibition against lying, saying explicitly that he was always taught not to lie, always to tell the truth, but that he lied to the Nazis and knows it was right to do so. At the same time, John seems to acknowledge the power of such deontological systems and socialization by his confusion and concern, even when we spoke, that he had deviated from what he had "always" believed was right, from what he had been taught was right.

Other rescuers exhibited this same pattern. Irene knew absolutely that what she did was right to save Jews, even if it meant that she had to violate her religion's sexual moral code in order to buy the major's silence by sleeping with him. And she was quite firm about her response when her beloved Catholic Church told her, through the person of an anti-Semitic priest, to stop endangering her mortal soul and turn in the Jews: "I walked out of the church and never went back!"

Margot also rejects the idea of rules—the critical component of the deontological approach—when she tells how she was taught not to lie but did so during the war. It is striking that John and Margot employ similar language and examples in rejecting the Kantian prohibition against lying.

> *Q. Do you have any particular ethical credo that has guided your life? Any system of ethical beliefs?*
>
> MARGOT: No. You don't steal. You don't hurt anybody. You don't lie. Well, I lie sometimes. When I was in the Resistance I lied a lot. When I was in Prague and I had to translate, you should have heard what I told them! I didn't believe it myself.

> *Q. How did you develop your ethical beliefs?*
>
> [Margot shrugged.] That was me. I don't know.

Creating a Moral Character.   Many philosophers, advocates of religion, and psychologists all note the importance of teaching ethics. In every rescuer we can clearly detect the importance of socialization, whether in the form of explicit exhortations to do good or in the form of mentors or role models who inspired them. For example, John's father was a critical force in John's life, a minister who impressed upon his children the importance of following your conscience. For John's father, this meant undergoing short but regular periods of time in jail because he refused to send his children to school on the Sabbath, which is Saturday for the Seventh-day Adventists.

> JOHN: As a little boy, that impressed me, the idea that if you believe in something that is right, you have to be able to accept the consequence of it. That also helped me to take a decision during the war: I wanted to help.

Sometimes John's socialization took the form of role modeling, as in the above example. At other times the importance of family influence came through more explicit exhortations.

> I had the privilege to be born into a family that had the idea of serving your neighbor. They taught us that ideal. I remember my father say, "There's an old lady. You help her to carry her bag." This kind of thing. The parents' education help.

The ethical principles—such as helping others and doing your duty—that were acquired through role modeling and socialization processes eventually merged into identity, shaping John's character in the manner suggested by Aristotle and described in both the philosophical literature on virtue ethics[14] and in the psychological literature on altruistic personalities.[15]

> I have the guardianship of my brothers. I have to help others. Don't be selfish. Help others. With this concept of ideals, when the moment arrives that you had to do something, okay, you have to do it. It was my duty. I claim to be a person to help others. [John shrugged.] Then I do it!

At other times, however, John's sense of who he is seems to be the result of a more proactive process on John's part, as if he has consciously reflected on who he is, where he comes from, and what this family legacy means to him. "I come from a family of prisoners. My great-grandfather father was a minister of the Dutch Reformed Church in Holland, and he asked to be the chaplain of the biggest prison of Holland." This discussion suggests the complex intertwining aspect of constructing a moral life and the ongoing nature of this process, much as is described in virtue ethics.[16] This process was apparent during John's discussion of his father's going to jail in protest against the arrest of the Jews. It was evident when John talked about his younger sister's being sent to a concentration camp because she saved Jews and, even more poignantly, when he discussed how his other sister was deported and died in a concentration camp. The circular pattern of influence is evident in John's discussion of his sisters' rescue activities, since they were inspired in part by John himself. The fact that his father and his sisters worked with John also highlights the circular fashion through which identity is formed and reinforced by others, as pebbles tossed in a brook create continuing and intersecting ripples. John's family was a critical influence on him, even as he, in turn, was influencing different members of his family.

> *Q. Was there anybody else in your life when you were growing up who was a particularly important influence on you, other than your mother and your father?*
>
> No. My teachers and school, through their teaching and their example in their life.
>
> *Q. Was there anybody who encouraged you to become a rescuer in particular?*
>
> Not especially. It came naturally. With other friends who shared opinions and worked together to help.

Q. Let me ask you a couple questions about that period. Had there ever been any time before the war that you had been involved in any kind of rescue activities? As a youngster?

Nothing special that I know. I know watching my father, seeing him spend the afternoon to feed the poor people, to speak with them, to visit hospitals, all that developed a heart for me, a feeling for suffering. You know? I could not see a fish on the line without that I suffer for the poor fish.

Like John, Margot was influenced by her father as a critical role model. Although Margot noted the importance of other people in her life, her main influence clearly was her father, from whom Margot felt unconditional love and with whom she had a good relationship. But Margot does not draw an explicit line between this influence and her rescue activities.

Q. Was there anybody else, other than your father, who was particularly important to you when you were growing up? Anyone who influenced you?

MARGOT: Oh, I had lots of friends.

Q. But it was mostly your father. [Margot nodded, yes.]. . . . When you were growing up, were you conscious of the fact that your father was an important and powerful man?

Yes, I think so. Because wherever I went, they'd say, "Oh, are you related to Hans Scharff?"

"Yes," I said. "That's my father." And people bent over to help you. . . .

Q. Was that important to you in your later rescue activities?

No. It was not important. . . .

How about your role models? People that you emulate. People that you admired a great deal.

I only liked my father because he was smart. He helped everybody. I wish I were as smart as he is.

Q. You said he was very affectionate with you.

Not affectionate, no. He never hugged me or so. But he said if I have anything, I should come to him, and whatever I had, worries or so forth, I came. . . . I made every year a trip with him. . . .

Q. He gave you a lot of attention though?

Yes. He did. Because when I had something, I came to him.

Q. Did you feel you had unconditional love from him? Did you feel he loved you without any conditions or reservations?

Yeah, he loved me.

Like the other rescuers, Irene's actions reflect a variety of influences, including socialization and role models in the form of her parents. And like John, Irene speaks of not having a choice, of acting out of her sense of self, and of being compelled by a strong sense of human connection.

> IRENE: My father was an architect and chemist, and my mother was a wonderful woman. She was a saint. That may be why I was able to do the things I did later during the war, because Mama never sent anyone needy from her door. There were Gypsies in the forest near our home. I remember one time my mother took a Gypsy woman into our home for two weeks because the woman had pneumonia. There was always someone coming home with us. We all, all five of us children, always brought home from school a bat, a dog, or cat, whatever needed help. My mother always knew what to do.
>
> My father had many understudies in his architectural firm. Some were Polish, some were German, and some were Jewish and Russian. They had children, so we children all played together. All kinds of mischief we did together. But we learned to live together. They were my friends. There was not the difference that "this is Jewish" or "this is Catholic" or "this is whatever." We lived and played together.

We thus come to a major leitmotif running throughout the rescuers' narratives: Regardless of its origin or the nature of its development, we encounter identity. Let me first, therefore, demonstrate how identity short-circuited agonistic choice. In chapter 7, I then construct a more detailed consideration of identity as a concept to ask why identity might constitute so important an influence on morality.

A SENSE OF SELF CONSTRAINS CHOICE

Identity Trumps Choice. As we listen to the rescuers' stories, we hear them mention many different factors driving rescue behavior: duty, socialization, religion, and so on. What we do *not* hear mentioned is choice. This omission is significant, given the emphasis on agonistic choice in the philosophical literature and rational choice theory.[17] Consider Margot's narrative.

Q: You started out, really before we even started the interview, talking about making conscious choices, and you said you didn't really think you [did that].[18] Was there really a conscious choice that you made?

MARGOT: I don't make a choice. It comes, and it's there.

Q: It just comes. Where does it come from?

I don't know. I don't think so much because I don't have that much to think with. That was what the professor said: "Take your first feeling and don't think." And I said, "I got nothing to think with."

Q: Do you think it comes from the basic—what I've heard other people say, and I'm asking. I don't want to put words in your mouth here— what I've heard other people say when I've asked them this is that they didn't think they could live with themselves if they'd done something other than that [help Jews]. Is that true for you?

It has nothing to do with it.

Q: It was just totally unconscious?

Yes. You don't think about these things. You can't think about these things. It happened so quickly.

Q: But it isn't really totally quickly. There's a tremendous amount of strategic planning that has to be done.

Well, I was young. I could do it. Today, I don't know. I'd have to try it. But I was thirty-two years old. That was pretty young.

Q: You didn't sit down and weigh the alternatives?

God, no. There was not time for these things. It's impossible.

Q: So it's totally spontaneous. It comes from your emotions.

It's pretty near impossible. You couldn't do that. You wouldn't understand what it means. Suppose somebody falls in the water, as I said before. You want to think, "Should I or should I not?" The guy would drown. You know, that's no way.

Q: Was empathy a part of it at all?

Meaning what?

Q: Feeling that this could be me?

No, never even thought of it.

Q. No. How about feelings of duty? . . . Did you feel sorry for the people? Pity?

I don't know. I don't feel anything, to be honest.

Q: How about the repercussions of your actions. Did you think about what might happen because you were doing this?

You don't think about it. No way.

Q: You didn't worry about possible consequences for you, for your family?

No. No way.

Q: Did you have any expectations about how you thought people would respond to you? You're shaking your head no. No anticipation about what your father might have thought?

No. My father helped wherever he could. No way. No.

Q: Now, many people would say that what you did was an extraordinarily good deed and that you should be rewarded.

That's what they say now. The hell with it. I don't want any reward.

Q: Were you honored by Yad Vashem? [Margot nodded.]

Yeah. But I didn't even know it until I got a letter from Professor Oliner [a scholar interviewing rescuers],[19] who said that he heard about me and he would like to interview me or would send somebody to come interview me. I didn't even know what he wanted. So I wrote back, "Dear sir, I don't even know you. What is it all about?"

Q: So you didn't even know about the Yad Vashem Medal?

No. I wrote back to Oliner. Because I'm unlisted, I have my phone number on my letter paper. And he called immediately. He said he was in Jerusalem and he heard about me. I said, "You did? What a surprise!" I didn't know.

Q: Now, you said you didn't talk about this for a long time.

No. I didn't talk at all except when he [Oliner] came into the picture.

Q: So this has been about three or four years ago [mid-1980s]?

Yes. I never told anybody.

Q: So you went for almost forty years without talking about it [the war]?

Never even gave it a thought to tell anybody.

Q: Did you talk about it with your husband?

No! He [Ted] didn't know anything. He said, "What is that all about?" Then when I was asked to go to Washington, D.C., for the opening of the Holocaust museum, he said he'd come along.[20] But he paid his own way. I was invited.

Q: Forty years without talking about this at all. Why was that?

Never. I didn't think anybody was interested. Besides, I wanted to write something down once. When I started, a lady said, "Oh, that's so long ago. Nobody's interested." So I forgot it again.

Q: Has it been painful for you to talk about it? To drag up memories?

Yes. After a while I was a little bit—I am very much inclined to depression. I'm very often depressed. But that has nothing to do with this. It's my nature. I'm depressed and I thought, "Oh, God, so many friends died." Now many friends die because they're so old. . . .

Q: That's amazing, that you went for that long without talking about it. But a lot of people I've spoken with said the same thing. They didn't want to think about it.

We don't want to talk about it. There's nothing to say.

Q: If you knew now exactly what was entailed in rescuing Jews, would you do it again?

Yes, at once.

As we think about any ethical decision-making process, and ask whether rescuers engaged in such a calculus, we find a closely related theme in ethics, one that suggests the merits of the people helped are relevant to the decision to help others. This was not, apparently, the case for rescuers such as Margot, who reinforced her insistence that her acts were not the result of conscious choice in which considerations of merits or worthiness entered a calculus.

Q. How do you decide whom to help then?

Well, I didn't decide. There's no decision. It's not like you say, "Oh, well. It's five o'clock. The people come and the judge will come in and so forth." No. There is no decision. You either help or you don't. . . .

Q. Do you feel you have a choice here? [Margot shook her head, no.] It just happens? That's just the way you are?

Yeah. You don't just stand and think. You have no time to think if something happens. Suppose somebody drowns. If you stop [to] think, "Shall I? Shall I not? Eeenie, meenie, miney, mo." You can't do that. You either help or you don't.

Q. Do you think it's just a disposition that some people have toward helping others?

[Margot shook her head, no.] You don't walk away. You don't walk away from somebody who needs real help. But some people who are real nasty. . . . Now, suppose something would happen to Hitler. I often thought, would I help him? Because I never believed that he was dead. Now I believe it more, but at the time I didn't really think he killed himself. But would I help this guy, after what he did? But on the other hand, people didn't have to do it.

I found it interesting that Margot's ambivalence about helping Hitler is not evident in John, who explicitly says: "I would save Hitler. I would save him to bring him to justice."

The spontaneous, non-calculating aspect of their acts was strikingly evident in all rescuers.

IRENE: I wanted to help, but I didn't think. I didn't plan ahead. It was like when you see a child drowning in the water; you don't think if you can swim; automatically, you want to do something. You jump. That was exactly my way. I knew it was wrong what they did, the Germans. I knew that I had to help. I wanted to help so bad, but I just didn't make plans.

Both rescuers and survivors insist, in study after study, that this was the case.[21] The people I interviewed are not atypical in this regard. "There was no decision to take," a French rescuer told Rittener and Myers, a finding echoed in other studies of rescuers.[22] This sentiment is reinforced by survivors, whose testimony becomes extremely compelling both because survivors were there to assess rescuers at the moment of action and because survivors have no need to justify rescue behavior.

To be a rescuer, under these circumstances, it took a unique person. Someone who had the deep-seated conviction . . . that they had to do it. And they were not people who were making choices on reflection. They just simply had to do it because that's the kind of people they were. (Emmanuel Tanay, Polish survivor in Rittener and Myers 1986)

Perhaps because I began my scholarly life as a political economist— trained to look for explanations of human behavior that emanate in a rational calculus designed to further people's perceived self-interest[23]—I found this empirical finding especially difficult to assimilate. I kept re-turning to query the rescuers on it in different ways, trying to make sure I was, in fact, hearing them accurately and was not misunderstanding what they were saying.

> *Q. Let me ask you what really is the hardest question for me, the hard-est to understand. What do you think it was that made you able or willing to risk your life, when so many other people did not?*
>
> MARGOT: Well, I think it's just me. I would risk it now. I wouldn't care.

Beyond this emphasis on identity, Margot seems to suggest that her acts were predestined.

> *Q. Margot, let me ask you. I'm a mother, and I think about the things that you did. One of the things that would be primary in my mind, I think, would be how this would be affecting my children. Forgive me for asking this. When you think about what you did, and you think about some of the costs that you paid. . . .*
>
> *[Margot interrupted.]* Money?
>
> *Q. No. The estrangement with your daughter. The fact that your fi-ancé was beaten to death. Do you think of that now?*
>
> I think of it very often, but I cannot help it. I believe that things are predestined. That's the way it had to come. You can't help it. . . .
>
> *Q. You said you believe in fate. In predestination. Do you think man can control his fate?*
>
> No, you cannot control it because when you control it, that's your fate, that you should control it. It is your fate that you do it like this. For instance, if I want to push you, it's my fate that I push you. You know what I mean?

Irene echoed this idea, saying, "You know, in war you don't make deci-sions; they are made for you." We find this same view expressed by Otto.

> *Q. One of the things that always intrigues me is the extent to which people make a choice. When you first decided—or perhaps I should ask, did you decide?—were your actions motivated by a choice, by some sort of a conscious process of sitting down and thinking about the risks that were involved, thinking about the benefits to you? Did you go through any kind of a cost to benefit calculus or . . . ?*

OTTO: I have answered this question in a speech. . . . I started one of the speeches by saying, "I never made a moral decision I will help Jews." When it happened, then I had absolutely a compulsion to do it. . . .

Q. It wasn't actually a decision that you'd made?

It was not a decision. It was just part of my character. Something that I felt. But it was also part of my education generally. Yet I did things which can only qualify me as being crazy. I got crazy sometimes—like when they took [Hannah's] parents away, for example. I did things where the probability of surviving was very, very small.

Q. And you never thought about that? You never thought about the fact that you were risking your life?

No. . . .

Q. Let me ask you about choices. I'm interested in how people behave and in particular about times when they do what really is an extraordinary thing and certainly an extraordinary political action. Was there a choice for you? Did you sit down and make a choice about deciding? You said that you realized that both your wife and Hitler could not exist in the world.

It's only part of it.

Q. At that point, was there a choice for you? You could have still walked away.

I had no choice. Because if I had had only an affair with Hannah, I could have walked out. But when I was married with her, if I had signed my divorce, it would have been murder. Active murder. Because I knew that after that Hannah would have to be transported to Auschwitz. So it was not my choice. I came into a situation where I had no choice.

Q. But other people did it.

Okay, some people have done it.

Q. But you didn't feel it was a choice for you.

No.

Q. Why was that?

My education, influences, and a certain moral quality.

Q. You just couldn't do it.

No, no. Absolutely not. There was no choice.

Q. Was it just a kind of gut feeling that I just can't do this?
Yeah. I think so.

Q. I think I'm coming to understand that. What I'm hearing people say is that a lot of what philosophers and academics call moral choices are not really choices at all. [Otto nodded.] What about your life, though? You risked death many times. Were you afraid to die?
I was fully aware of that.

Q. You knew the costs. You knew it could happen.
Yes, I was only afraid of torturing, of being tortured. I had talked to my very good friend, Hans Becker, who was one of the leaders [of the Resistance in Austria]. He *was* tortured. It was he who was tortured about giving them our names. But he didn't do it. I spoke with him afterward. I asked him how could he endure it. He was tortured, you know, in the usual way, cigarettes burned in his flesh and so on. He was a very religious man and he said he got religious fantasies, apparitions, until he fainted.

Otto articulates this idea again later, when he describes his identity as closely tied to being a person with certain kinds of moral values and actions.

Q. In terms of your basic identity, how do you define yourself? Do you define yourself as German, Czech, a man, an engineer? I mean, if someone says, "What are you?" what do you say?
I am like a no-lands man, a cosmopolitan. I believe that as children we should all learn foreign languages because when you understand the languages better, maybe this is a very important thing in helping you understand people better. I was against any nationalism, *always.* In Czechoslovakia, where these problems were deeply rooted, it was important. When I came to the United States and saw what was going on in the South, I decided when I had the power to fire and hire that I first would hire Negroes. I had that power over about thirty people. So I hired three Negroes. I felt it my moral duty to do that and I fared excellently with them.

Q. So morality is very important to you.
Yes.

Q. You really are a Kantian. You treat people as an ends, not as a mean to anything.
Right. Right. Right. Right. . . .

Q. So you've thought a lot about morality.
Of course.

In discussing this lack of choice, all the rescuers edged into discussions of identity as imposing constraints on their actions. Often, these discussions ended by the rescuer trying to articulate the notion that they simply could not have lived with themselves if they had not helped people. Otto articulated this in the context of his love for his wife, and suggested how that love was woven into his self-respect in a way that suggests the traditional dichotomy between protecting one's own self-interest and helping others made little sense for him.

Q. So did you see your activities with the Resistance as being primarily political or primarily as a result of your humanitarian instincts?
Both. Both. Both.

Q. Do you think about why you risked all this? Have you ever thought about that?
Yes. I knew a little bit more about Nazi machinery because I was reporting for an organization who was transmitting this information. It had no effect whatsoever. They [the Allies] completely ignored all we reported in Germany and did nothing. But I knew something about their plans and was very pessimistic about the outcome. Whereas other people had still hope that it would be really only a resettlement and so on. So I came to the conclusion that two people cannot survive simultaneously—Adolf Hitler and my wife—so I had to go all the way. I replied to the same question very easily. Once I told someone, I simply got mad. It was true. I did illogical things. The risks were far too high. But I loved my wife, of course, and this was, I think, the first motive and altruism became secondary. It was not altruism. . . . Later on, I came into this machinery of secret services and so on and it became then also an obsession. But originally it was just trying to survive and make my wife survive.

Q. You said it wasn't altruism. Why wasn't it altruism?
Because I did [it out] of *my* love for her.

Q. Did you consider her an extension of yourself in some way, or that you were one person? Is it like the marriage bond that talks about "now you are one"?
Maybe. I won't speculate in this direction because. . . . [Otto shrugged.] Whether you want to say one person, two persons. I

don't know but it was. . . . Any motivation of human beings is complex. But the primitive had certainly a strong part in my motives.

Q. The love.

Yes.

Q. It was just an emotional thing for you.

Not quite. It cannot be separated. . . . Again, things are so mixed that it is difficult to separate. I think that, if I'm honest, I have a rather high opinion of myself. One thing is important. I never made a moral decision to rescue Jews. I just got mad. I felt I had to do it. I came across many things that demanded my compassion. Odette Meyers, a survivor, was on a panel with me. She was asked why the rescuers took the risks they did. Meyers shared something she heard on a recent TV interview with a German rescuer, a woman who said she was tired of hearing about her spirit, courage, and nobility. "I did it because of self-respect," she said, "a lot of self-respect."

Q. What does that mean to you?

I like the word self-respect because it is what I said before. It is one of the egotistic components in my motivation. I respect more and feel good about it and this is a very good definition.

Q. One of the German rescuers that we interviewed, we asked about the honors. Did she do it for any honors or praise or things? And she said, "Well, it was nice to get the honors afterwards." But she said, "I never made use of that. I was only proud inside, just for me." I think that's what you're saying. Is that right?

That is part of it.

Instead of choice, then, we find identity. All the rescuers I interviewed referred to the spontaneous and reflexive aspect of moral action, as they depicted their behavior toward Jews as part of a broader decision concerning the kind of person one was.[24] Although other factors also contributed to rescue behavior, this insistence on the ordinary aspect of their acts suggests rescue activities were not considered agonistic moral choices so much as the natural steps on a path chosen by a prior molding as a certain kind of human being. The question then becomes, why does identity so effectively short-circuit choice by limiting the options perceived as available? It is this finding that traditional moral theory leaves us at a loss to explain. In the next chapter, I will argue that the answer lies in the political psychology of identity and the importance of perspective in evoking critical parts of that multifaceted identity.

7

How Identity and Perspective Led to Moral Choice

The deep love of two beings melted into one is the ultimate fulfillment. The hardships that teach understanding form the character within one's self. The injustices against the innocent are the experience and knowledge of grim reality. Above all, there is the ability to help and alleviate the pain of fellow human beings. This I believe is the ultimate goal of our short existence on this earth.

—Margot Scharff Lawson

WHY DID IDENTITY SO EFFECTIVELY influence moral choice for rescuers? To answer this question, we must explore the rescuers' moral psychology. We must ask how their minds worked and what made someone like Margot and the other rescuers we have met different from other people. Is it simply that rescuers had an altruistic personality? If so, what produced this personality? Was there an altruistic perspective at work, in which external stimuli triggered the altruistic parts of rescuers' identities? If so, what activated this perspective and how did it relate to identity? What role did an underlying worldview and self-concept play in this process? To answer such questions, we must explore the possible linkages between identity and moral action.

The first part of this chapter thus begins with a consideration of the concept of identity itself and asks *why* we might expect identity to influence moral choice. Part 2 asks *how* identity works to influence moral acts. In doing so, we explore the philosophical and psychological literature on the ties between ethics and identity, work that locates the linkage in the human need for consistency and self-esteem.[1] Part 3 suggests identity exerts its moral influence through a psychological process in which certain moral values are integrated into one's sense of self; it is the integration of these values, rather than merely a looser subscription to such values, that appears to influence moral choice. Part 4 asks how the external environment calls into play different self-concepts, especially what we might think of as a moral or an altruistic self. Analyzing rescuers suggests it is the cognitive classification of others that influences our treatment of them, through a process in which moral salience is accorded to the needs of others. The chapter concludes by asking if an emphasis on perspective—for all its analytical value in illuminating the process by which identity may draw forth different aspects of a self that is multifaceted and complex—risks leading us toward moral relativism and all the thorny issues associated with that concept.

IDENTITY AND THE SELF: TERMINOLOGY

Throughout this book, I have used the terms *identity* and *self* more or less interchangeably, since this usage reflects both everyday discourse and the scholarly terminology found in political science. Conceptual distinctions do exist, however, and a brief consideration of such differences can help illuminate substantive knowledge of the general phenomenon into which both terms tap.[2]

In general, identity refers to those characteristics that describe one particular object or person. For example, Catarina Caterleigh is an American anthropologist with Social Security #358-20-0093, born on February 25, 1953, in Walnut, Illinois, to Robert and Verna Caterleigh. These particular characteristics distinguish Catarina from all other women. They identify her. Similarly, Catarina's car is a white BMW 525i, made in 1999 with serial #55893.[3] No other car has these identifying characteristics. They distinguish Catarina's car from all other cars. They identify it.

The concept of *self* can easily be differentiated from *identity* if we consider two critical dimensions on which Catarina and her car differ: self-awareness[4] and agency.[5] Catarina can have an awareness of herself and can independently initiate action, but her car cannot. Both Catarina and her car have physical embodiment, but only sentient beings can have what we think of as a self. The term *self*, then, refers to both the physical and the psychological being, with feelings, thoughts, and attitudes socially validated though multiple identities in a complex matrix of social relationships.

Psychologists generally agree that all people share the experience of reflexive consciousness. Reflexive consciousness means that people are self-aware. The human mind can think about its own identity, focus on some aspect or property of the self, and compare it with some goal or standard. This comparative aspect of self-reflection is part of an evaluative function, the process by which we think about our self-worth. Thus we speak of humans as having both self-awareness (knowledge about the self) and self-esteem (the evaluative dimension of self-knowledge).

The self also exists in a nexus of groups and relationships. This gives the self an interpersonal aspect and makes us social beings. We do not create who we are in social isolation or only by looking inward. We learn about who we are by thinking about our connections to others (Catarina is the daughter of Verna and Robert Caterleigh) and about how our behavior sets us apart from others (Catarina is the only Caterleigh daughter who is an anthropologist).

Finally, the self is able to make choices, to exert control over itself and the world through initiating action. This executive function of the self provides Catarina with another critical difference from her car; the car can be known to others but it cannot do anything of its own free will. We do not use the terms *agent* or *agency* for a car. For human beings, however, we speak of self-regulation, self-defeating behavior, decision making and choice, volition, and the quest for control and autonomy.[6] Only for sentient beings do these concepts have relevance.[7]

So there are important conceptual distinctions between the terms *identity* and *self*, and yet in both everyday discourse and much of social science the terms are used interchangeably.[8] How do we resolve this dilemma? My approach is to use the terms *identity* and *self* interchangeably and define both to refer to my sense of who I am, both as a person who takes action and as someone who is self-reflective.[9] This captures what lies at the core of most everyday discourse conceptualizations of identity: the perception, which begins to grow early in childhood, that we are agents and self-reflexive people who think about who we are, and that we also are objects who can be thought about and liked or disliked by others.[10] This definition of *self* and *identity* thus refers to our physical bodies and to the interconnectedness of our minds and our bodily experiences. It takes account of our *intra*personal emotions and attitudes, including our knowledge, perception, and conceptualization of our selves, all of which are qualities that reflect our *inter*personal experiences as part of a community and as individuals engaged in social interaction.

Analysts since John Locke have noted identity's complex and multifaceted nature, in which a person is defined as "a thinking intelligent being, that has reason and reflection, and can consider itself as itself, the same thinking thing, in different times and places."[11] The multiple aspect of identity is aptly captured in what William James[12] referred to as the one-in-many-selves paradox, a term that seeks to capture the apparent contradiction between our desire to maintain self-continuity over time while nonetheless acting out different roles in what amounts to effectively changing personalities, situation by situation.[13] Freud's[14] discussion of the id, ego, and superego and Mead's[15] work on the subject and the object self also contributed to what has now become the commonplace recognition of the multiplicity[16] of identity.[17]

How do others enter into the construction of identity? Most contemporary discussions of identity reject the idea of the self as a thing apart from the physical person, recognizing that the mind is embodied and therefore subject to physical constraints whose importance we are just beginning to decipher.[18] Current thinking suggests there is a genetic component to identity that we have only begun to make sense of, with certain personality traits being inheritable, if only via tendencies toward certain dispositions.[19]

We do not possess the self so much as become a self, then, through a complex process of genetic predisposition, socialization, and development.[20] This process contains both a cognitive or thinking component and an emotional component.[21] The cognitive aspect of identity is important because it allows us to regulate our behavior, coordinate activities, and plan activities in anticipation of the actions of others.[22] But the self is not merely a mental construct located just inside one's head. Most conceptualizations of identity assume human beings have both biological needs (e.g., for sleep or food) and analogous social needs (such as security, respect, or prestige).[23] As such, humans are biologically programmed to be social beings, with the ability to engage in symbolic communication and self-awareness. As social beings,[24] we do not develop in isolation but in a social context.

Thus we find the importance of "the other" for the most basic construction of identity. Parents and grandparents give us our genetic makeup and shape our early lives through childhood socialization. Culture enters via social groups, schools, the nation, the historical period, etc. Those around us influence and shape us everyday through our immediate interactions with them, and so on.[25]

Unfortunately, we know too little about the precise manner in which others' perceptions of who we are feed into our own sense of self.[26] Classical psychoanalytic approaches, stressing the family and critical others, tend to privilege early childhood experiences that construct one's basic personality, or at least provide critical shaping for any biologically determined personality predispositions. A more extended time period in which others influence an individual's sense of self is featured in the now classic formulation of identity by Erikson.[27] Analysts since Erikson have tended to stress four essential aspects of identity: (1) our conscious sense of individual identity; (2) an unconscious striving for continuity of personal character; (3) the extent to which ego synthesis is ongoing or developmental; and (4) the maintenance of some kind of inner solidarity with the ideals and identity of a group. The contemporary work on identity[28] thus suggests we need an internal sense of continuity or sameness, and that we need to feel others share our concept of what this essential character is.[29]

What happens when the need for self-consistency conflicts with the need for self-enhancement? The evidence on this is not definitive, with some analysts arguing that the drive for consistency is more powerful than the need to feel good about one's self and other analysts arguing the counter position.[30] Both motives seem important, and I believe both the need for consistency and the desire to feel good about one's self provide critical keys to understanding identity's relationship to ethical behavior.[31]

ETHICAL IMPLICATIONS OF IDENTITY

Philosophical Works on Character and Virtue Ethics.   One of the most extensive discussions of the ethical implications of identity—or character, as philosophers often prefer to call it—exists in a body of literature known as virtue ethics.[32] Also called virtue-based ethics and agent-based ethics, different forms of virtue ethics predominated in Western philosophy before the Renaissance and are evident in the works of Aristotle, Plato, the Stoics, and Aquinas. Essentially, virtue ethics argues that the foundation of morality is the development of good character traits or virtues. Someone is good if he has virtues and lacks vices.[33] Virtue ethicists place special emphasis on moral education since character is shaped in our youth. This gives the community and adults a special responsibility in molding the young. Minus such shaping, the young will grow up acquiring vices, such as cowardice, vanity, and insensibility.

With the growth of social contract theory, utilitarianism, and Kantian ethics, virtue ethics fell out of philosophical vogue until the 1950s when contemporary virtue ethics can be said to have originated in a 1958 article by Elizabeth Anscombe titled "Modern Moral Philosophy."[34] Part of Anscombe's critique focused on the preponderance of duty-based ethics and the problems with this approach, which makes ethics a matter of principle, rules, and acts. Anscombe's critique spawned an impressive renaissance in the contemporary philosophical literature.[35] But Anscombe's call for better detection of the moral psychology remains largely unfulfilled, and it is to this challenge that I address my remarks.

What is contemporary virtue ethics and how is it relevant for our concerns? Contemporary virtue ethics builds on Aristotelian discussions of character and morality. Virtue ethics is not explicitly designed to address the question of moral motivation but rather to ask what constitutes a moral character and a moral life. This means virtue ethicists[36] tend to focus on character rather than on discrete behavior or individual acts. While an individual with good character might articulate particular rules that guide her behavior, it is not the principles themselves that are an ultimate source of justification. Instead, these principles are justified only in so far as they endorse conduct that would be found in, and encourage the growth of, the character of a virtuous person.

The end goal of virtue ethics is human flourishing. What precisely is meant by human flourishing is the focus of much philosophical discussion. For example, the flourishing may refer to the flourishing of the actor or to someone else who is the recipient of the actor's virtuous behavior. This recipient could be an individual, a group, all humanity, or even sentient life in general.

Proponents of virtue ethics argue that the value of a virtue ethics approach to ethics lies in its grounding of morality in facts about human nature or the development of particular cultural traditions rather than in focusing on morality in abstract principles of reason or subjective preference. They also argue that virtue ethics more fully captures the psychological forces that are critical for ethics: relatively stable dispositions, habits, and long-term goals. In doing so, virtue ethics thus presents us with a rather comprehensive and unified conceptualization of the moral life, one that helps us think about our wants, goals, likes, or dislikes, and about what kind of a person one is and wants to be. In this sense, virtue ethics is seen as less narrow than rule-based ethics.

Virtue ethics is not without its critics, however, some of whom argue that virtue ethics is circular; that is, it defines "right action" in terms of acts that create virtuous character, and then defines virtuous character as character that leads to right action. Virtue ethics is further accused of being arbitrary, since there is no widely accepted standard of what it is that constitutes human flourishing. (Different cultures and historical periods, for example, provide particularly divergent definitions in this regard.) Nor, critics argue, do we know what virtues will lead to human flourishing. Virtue ethics is further indicted for focusing too much on the individual rather than on those affected by one's acts. Finally, it is charged with being fatalistic insofar as it makes morality a function of luck, luck in genetic predispositions and happenstance of birth, parents, upbringing, and opportunities.

My purpose here is not to engage in a scholarly evaluation of virtue ethics but to take what we can from this important body of literature and ask how virtue ethics can help us better understand the relationship between identity and ethics.[37] Reading the virtue ethics literature with this goal in mind, I find several points of extreme interest.

I begin with the fact that virtue ethics emphasizes characteristics of persons, not moral rules. In doing so, it de-emphasizes explicit choice in favor of habit and a person's typical ways of viewing the world. The development of habits and certain forms of behavior both reinforce and form character.[38] When the habits are "good," the person naturally, almost without thought, does the "right" thing. To explain rescue behavior, a virtue ethicist might argue that the right thing became "natural" to people like the rescuers because rescuers had developed virtuous habits[39] that gave them the moral sensitivity required to recognize moral wrongs and to know what was the right thing to do to correct these wrongs.

In this regard, virtue ethics provides an incredible match with our rescuers. All rescuers exhibited similar worldviews. These worldviews were ones in which all people were valued equally and in which the sanctity of life and human well-being formed the foundation for value systems. The process and mechanisms by which individual rescuers' value systems might have been instilled could differ, ranging from religious instruction to duty and an innate moral sense, as we saw in chapter 6. But the basic contours of the worldview were the same. This worldview is captured in Margot's comment in the epigraph at the beginning of this chapter, about the ultimate goal of our short existence on earth.

Furthermore, the habits of caring for others had become so integrated into rescuers' sense of who they were that these habits created the kind of altruistic personality that made rescuers' incredible wartime behavior spontaneous. Their moral sensitivity was so heightened to the plight of others that rescuers' actions seemed natural and automatic, as in the insistence that no one could walk away from such suffering, even though rescuers knew that most others did, in fact, do just that: walk away.

But virtue ethics does more than just offer an explanation for the rescuers' attitudes, that is, for their insistence that there was no choice and that their acts were "normal" or what any "ordinary" person would do. It also helps us understand our admiration for rescuers. We admire such people and would like to become the kind of person who is able to perform these acts in the same generous spirit.[40] Listening to the rescuers makes us aware of a different way of perceiving, thinking about, and assessing the situation; in doing so, it helps increase our own moral sensitivity.

Other critical elements of the virtue ethics explanation are found in rescuers' narratives. For example, John suggested that happiness is tied to fulfilling one's responsibilities, to achieving a kind of consonance between behavior and internal standards.[41]

> I have some privileges; we get in turn some responsibilities. To have the abilities of speech, of hearing. I can walk. I am thankful for what I have. My responsibility is to share with others, because [otherwise] life would not be possible. I have seen in my life people who are selfish, and not happy. And I have seen that people who are unselfish are happy. I have seen people who are selfish, who have power, and money, and everything, and they don't have enough. Never enough. They are not happy. And other people don't have very much and are happy with what they have, and are happy. My ambition, my aim is to be happy; then how can you be happy? To be selfish? [John shook his head, no.]

We also find the link between one's own happiness and caring for others in rescuers' narratives.

Q. You would not have been happier if you had simply taken all your family and sat out the war in Switzerland? After the war, you could have said, "At least my family is intact. I love them, I've been a good person, I haven't done anything wrong." You would not have been happier doing that?

You have to do what is right. You have to think about more than yourself. You have to think about yourself, certainly. You have to eat, and have a home. But you must not concentrate on that. It is not my aim, it is not my rule to say, I, I, I. I have seen others around me, Salvation Army people, they are very happy. Why? Because they are helping. I see a lot of people who are very rich, but they don't have enough. I think happiness comes through helping other people. I am convinced of that. I see it around me. I see it for myself. I am really happy. I can make other people happy. . . . We have to make some sacrifices. The only way we can be really happy is to forget yourself and make other people happy. . . . Do that.

We find constancy of character. All the rescuers said they had not been changed by their rescue activities. John expressively captures this view and then follows it with one of the core ideas of virtue ethics: the idea of character development that then makes moral action flow "naturally" from who you are. In doing so, John alludes to the circularity between behavior and identity; one's actions emanate from one's character but also feed back into who one is, shaping, changing, or reinforcing the basic identity.

Q. Do you think you were changed much by your rescue activities?

Basically, I don't think so, no. I think mostly I've learned to love people on the better way. For example, we have a poor guy who hasn't worked. I helped him to find a job, so he can learn a job. When he knows the job, then I have helped to learn the way to be helpful.

Q. So you learned how to be more helpful through your rescue activities?

How. How to be more helpful. . . . But it didn't change me basically. Basically, no. The desire to be helpful is there. God asked me to develop that feeling. How to do it, that is where my brains are coming in. God gave me the lightning in my brains, the understanding to do so and so. . . .

Q. But what would you consider your basic identity?

My identity is to fulfill my function on the way that I know is best. And so I think that if you can help someone with conscience, knowing right and wrong and the power of the decision . . . have the ability to give good judgment, that is what I like to do. I fulfill my function.

Rescuers also illustrate the virtue ethics link between character and moral development, as most rescuers saw a connection between their wartime deeds and family relations and socialization that shaped their habits of virtue. John, Margot, and Irene spoke of their parents teaching them, by their instruction and by their example, to care for others.

IRENE: My parents were young. My father was an architect and chemist, and my mother was a wonderful woman. She was a saint. That may be why I was able to do the things I did later during the war, because Mama never sent anyone needy from her door. There were Gypsies in the forest near our home. I remember one time my mother took a Gypsy woman into our home for two weeks because the woman had pneumonia. There was always someone coming home with us. We all, all five of us children, always brought home from school a bat, a dog, or cat, whatever needed help. My mother always knew what to do.

Margot credited her father with much of the inspiration for her rescue activities, noting both his ingenuity in outwitting the Nazis and his willingness to use his own position and wealth to help others.

MARGOT: My father was wealthy. I told you. He kept the whole convent. He bought coal on the black market. He bought food on the black market. He bought everything on the black market. My father had all the connections. We had papers forged. We forged things you wouldn't believe: passports, other documents [the Germans wanted]. We had once a guy who was terribly afraid. He came to my father. My father made him a Swiss citizen, and wrote from the American Embassy that the Germans should take care of him because he was a special man. Now, my father knows the German mentality, too. So he sent several unimportant papers, just newspaper clippings, to a family we knew in Switzerland, just casual friends, not people we know very well. Then right after that we sent them a letter, saying that by mistake we sent you some papers. Please send them back. They did. And so we got the envelope with the Swiss postmark. When my father showed the Germans the letter, the forged letter making this man a Swiss subject, the German official said, "Yeah, you can show me a letter. But where's the envelope?" And we had the envelope! Our friends had sent it all back.

> My father did this kind of thing for everybody. You wouldn't believe.
> There was nobody who came that was not helped. And he was never
> arrested. He was never caught.

Finally, John noted the importance of his father's example of conscience
in going to jail each Saturday rather than sending his children to school
on the day that was the Sabbath for Seventh-day Adventists.

At the same time, rescuers' narratives also highlight a potential limitation of a virtue ethics' account of moral motivation: its emphasis on character instead of behavior.[42] Virtue ethics assumes character predicts behavior, or at least that the two are highly correlated. But what happens
when one engages in "uncharacteristic" behavior? World War II presents
many acts of moral courage and valor from people who were, throughout
most of their lives, scoundrels and rogues, just as it presents too many
instances of otherwise virtuous people turning a deaf ear to suffering or
even participating in the evil. (Consider the wartime behavior of Oskar
Schindler or the failure of religious leaders such as Pope Pius XII in this
regard.[43]) John speaks directly to this issue.

> Jesus said, "You want to show love for me, show love in action, not
> just, 'I love you.'" If I just said that to my wife, and I kiss her, and
> never give any presents, she won't believe in my love. I have to
> prove it. This means action.

This emphasis on action separates rescuers from the traditional virtue
ethics view in which possessing a virtuous character is an end in itself,
apart from the moral acts this virtuous character might produce. Presumably a Jew in hiding from the Gestapo cared less that he was being
saved by a virtuous person than that he was being saved at all. The priest
who told Irene to stop endangering her mortal soul and turn in the people she was hiding, although perhaps a virtuous man in other regards,
quite properly had his advice rejected by Irene. The rescuers thus focus
us on an important critique of virtue ethics: Why do we want to develop
a moral character if that moral character is not then reflected in moral
acts? And if the disjunction between character and acts continues, at what
point do we say one's character has changed?

Rescuers also show us a second potential weakness in a virtue ethics
account: despite its emphasis on cultivation of good habits, virtue ethics
also emphasizes the strength of character necessary to "do the right
thing." Yet all the rescuers I interviewed insisted their acts were "no big
deal," that it was natural to perform such deeds. Rescuers did mention
logistical difficulties in putting together the actual rescue. But no conversations ever indicated any need for strength of will to perform a task

considered onerous and unwanted. There is a difficulty, then, in putting together virtue ethics' insistence that acts emerge naturally out of character with the virtue ethics' emphasis on strength of character necessary to do "the right thing."

The naturalness of moral action was sometimes expressed through rescuers' insistence that there was "nothing special" about what they had done or that they were not extraordinary people.

Q. You don't see yourself as anything special?
MARGOT: No, I'm nothing special.

Q. You don't think you did anything extraordinary?
No. Definitely not.

Q. How can you say that?
Because I *didn't* do anything extraordinary. Lots of people help others. No, I certainly didn't. No, absolutely not. I didn't do that much.

At other times, this view was reflected in the rescuers' insistence that their acts were "natural" or spontaneous, as in Otto's explanation that "the hand of compassion was faster than the calculus of reason." John echoed this view.

Q. Was it really that simple for you? You just had to do it.
Yes . . . when the situation arose, it was very natural for me. Very simple. I had to do it, and it wasn't special. . . . It made me happy.

John captured the sense, expressed by all the rescuers I interviewed, that what they had done was natural.

Q. Did you ever sit down and think about the costs and the benefits and the risks involved in what you were doing? Did you sit down and think about all these things before you undertook these "adventures" that you went on?
I don't think so. I think that it came as a natural reaction from the inside. Like a mother. Normally, you don't teach a mother how to love her baby. She has that naturally. Maybe not the father, but the mother. So your instinct that you develop in yourself is to react that way. And so it was a quite natural development. Not, "Should I do it or not?"

Finally, the inevitability aspect of these extraordinary acts is reflected in the rescuers' insistence that they had no choice in what they had done.

IRENE: I did not ask myself, Should I do this? But, How will I do this? Every step of my childhood had brought me to this crossroad; I must take the right path, or I would no longer be myself.[44]

The above quotes support the virtue ethics notion that there is a natural inevitability, springing from identity, to rescuers' acts. But there is no strength of character required. This suggests a potential tension in virtue ethics. If moral action is a natural outgrowth of character, how can these acts require strength of will? This tension between cultivating virtuous habits that then naturally lead to right action and developing the strength of character necessary to "do the right thing" is a potential contradiction I leave to virtue ethicists to resolve.[45] The empirical evidence from the analysis of rescuers, however, suggests that strength of character is the far less important of the two.

Even if virtue ethics leaves some critical aspects of rescue behavior unexplained, the virtue ethics approach is nonetheless extremely helpful in revealing the links between identity and ethics, especially in highlighting the importance of character and the importance of deciphering the moral psychology. For further insight on why identity is so important for our moral life and how its influence is conveyed, let us now turn to recent psychological work on the moral psychology to ask why and how identity impacted and constrained choice for rescuers.

MORAL PSYCHOLOGY: INTEGRATION OF MORAL VALUES

Psychologists count the desire for self-esteem a fundamental human need.[46] Most consider the preservation of this self-esteem critically related to maintaining identity. This need seems a basic part of human nature; indeed, the reason people view the world the way they do often can be traced to this underlying need to maintain a favorable image of themselves. Given the choice between feeling good about themselves and representing the world accurately, people often take the first option.

Continuity of self-image is also important.[47] When there is a significant discrepancy between perceived self-image and one's behavior, people experience a cognitive dissonance—a sense of discomfort and uneasiness—which they try to minimize, either by modifying their behavior or by shifting their underlying values in order to achieve conformity.[48]

Recent psychological work has built on these twin ideas—the need for both self-esteem and continuity of self-image—to explore the relationship between identity and moral action. For example, Colby and Damon[49] asked people engaged in morally exemplary works (such as setting up charitable organizations or helping the poor) how and why they had become involved in the projects that defined them as moral exemplars. The Colby-Damon research is particularly interesting because it focuses on individuals who resemble rescuers but studies them while they were involved in their morally exemplary work. It thus avoids—or at least minimizes—a potential methodological problem of concern to analysts of rescue behavior: doing a good thing at one point in time then may produce changes in personality or worldview that seem causative to the analyst who is speaking to the subject years later.

Colby and Damon's work underscores my own empirical findings on the importance of identity as a constraint on choice. What is interesting about their work, however, is their suggestion that moral exemplars differ from other people not because of the particular moral beliefs that they hold but rather by the high degree to which these values are integrated into the participant's sense of self. For Colby and Damon, it is the integration that is key. What predicts behavior is the extent to which moral beliefs become a part of how the person sees him- or herself.[50]

We all know that many of us fail to live up to our ideals much of the time. What Colby and Damon suggest is that our ability to live up to our ideals is largely a function of the degree to which these ideals are integrated into our identity, our sense of who we are.[51] Their work thus focuses attention on the integration of moral commitments that then become the core of our sense of self. When such integration occurs, breaking with these moral beliefs can constitute a turning away from one's own essence that is psychologically damaging.[52]

Further support for this link is found in a cognitive structuralist model of identity development by Blasi.[53] Blasi asks how identity can link the explanatory gap between moral thought and moral action. To answer this question, Blasi returns to Festinger's[54] work, noting that people avoid self-*in*consistency. For Blasi, the need for self-consistency is the product of several phenomenal qualities of the self. In particular, Blasi notes that the self, at the phenomenal level, is the experience that one is the agent responsible for all of one's actions; this includes mental actions. By positing a single entity that possesses and is concerned with both actions and thoughts, we can clearly see the need for consistency between thought and deed. For Blasi, it is the drive to have consistency among beliefs, thoughts, and actions that becomes the engine that drives moral action. Where moral beliefs are integrated into the self, immoral action threatens to render the self incoherent.

Thus both the Colby-Damon study and Blasi's work provide one explanation for the rescuers' lack of choice: doing anything else would have produced an inconsistency that would have rendered the self incoherent. What was at stake for the rescuers, then, was their very sense of self, their core identity.

This insight is helpful in illuminating identity's importance for moral action, but it raises a host of further questions. First, the relationship between identity and morality is probably more complicated than the mechanical relationship suggested by this formulation. People have different responses to their compromises between moral beliefs and actions. Some feel shame, while others appear to experience relatively little remorse.[55] We need to understand the *nature* of the integration, not merely ask whether someone has integrated moral beliefs into his or her sense of self. Second, we still need to determine *how* the integration of moral beliefs with the self results in differing possible outcomes.[56]

Let us return to the rescuers with the above remarks in mind. Doing so lends new significance to the comments from rescuers suggesting that their values were not so much a reflection of values chosen in a rational sense but values that had become so integrated into their sense of who they were that these values formed an integral part of rescuers' identities. John provides one example of this, as he outlines the distinction between the choice of action and the choice of the kind of human being one wants to be, a distinction noted in philosophical discussions of the relationship between the self and choice.[57]

> JOHN: I have the idea that I have the guardianship of my brothers. I have to help others. Don't be selfish. Help others. With this concept of ideals, when the moment arrived that you had to do something, okay, you have to do it. It was my duty. I claim to be a person to help others. Then I do it.

Irene speaks of this same process in her autobiography, noting that "every step of my childhood" had led her to a point where she had to "take the right path, or I would no longer be myself."

The link between sense of self and lack of choice has been discussed by analysts concerned with impulsive helping, works suggesting the amount of time spent in cognitive processing is between twenty seconds and one minute.[58] Given the amount of thought that had to go into finding extra ration tickets, medicine, a hiding place, and so forth, rescuers must have engaged in a certain amount of cognitive processing; but the rescuers' cognitive processing appears to have had only one track—the track that led to helping.[59] This process seems more intense than socialization. It suggests there is an integration of moral values into one's sense of self in a manner that forms a master or core identity, an essential self that is the mainstay of one's self-concept. It appears that values inculcated through socialization must fall on fertile soil to become the critical integral part of one's core self.

Ironically, we can see the distinction between socialization and integration of values most clearly when we look at how rescuers deviated from the socialization they received from their parents and critical others. This distinction was articulated by Knud, who highlights the extent to which values that are socialized are not always the ones rescuers acted upon: "My grandfather told me, quite frankly, to hate all Germans. Period. But, of course, I couldn't do that."

Knud's description of his grandfather's admonition to hate all Germans and how he moved away from this warning also alerts us to a problem with an approach based only on the integration of moral values: What of the nature of the values that are integrated into the self? After all, studies of Nazis suggest many Nazis genuinely believed their despicable policies were a moral struggle to rid the German body politic of a crippling disease.[60] Unless we designate the nature of the moral values integrated into identity, we produce a model driven by the need for self-consistency but with no direction inherent in the model itself. Nor is it clear how the developmental approach solves the problem of self-consistency.[61]

Overall, then, the literature on moral psychology is extremely helpful in advancing our understanding of why identity constrains choice. In particular, this literature suggests that if we want to understand *how* the integration of moral beliefs with the self works to motivate us to act morally, then we need to determine how the external environment triggers critical values that are integrated into the sense of self in a manner that leads to moral action. For further insight on that, I turn to what I call the altruistic perspective. This perspective plays a critical role through the process of cognitive classification and the according of a moral imperative to act to help another.

The Altruistic Perspective and Moral Action

Our perspective consists of the mental categories by which we sort the various stimuli from the external world and organize them to make sense of reality. Perspective can be defined as our point of view, outlook, or perceptions of reality, or as our underlying cognitive frameworks. Perspective affects the way we see ourselves, how we see others, and how we then classify others. (The concept itself is a rather simple one; indeed, it is reflected in much everyday language, as when we say someone is an optimist, who always looks on the bright side of things, or a pessimist, who expects the worse and finds it.) Since perspective flows from our underlying predispositions and our identity, its influence on identity is subtle and difficult to disentangle. Our concern here is to understand how perspective affects identity to influence moral action. Analyzing rescuers suggests the following process.

Much of identity does develop over time and in the fashion described above by both virtue ethicists and developmental psychologists, and it is reasonable to think of identity—or character or self—as something enduring, continuous, and with a central core. But we also know that identity is complex, more like a diamond with many facets than a simple flat slate. We observe a range of behavior from the same individual. Much of this variance can be explained by the power of the situation to shape both our perspective on the world and how we see ourselves at any particular point in time, and thus draw forth different aspects of a complex identity.[62]

I believe this is the process through which perspective affects behavior in general. In terms of perspective's role in leading to moral action, however, I believe the external environment taps into the self-concept to trigger *moral* action through creating a sense of moral salience. Let me present evidence supporting this conclusion.

The Self and Others: The Literature. The admonition to love your neighbor lies at the heart of most moral and religious systems. The question is: Who is your neighbor? Both humanistic texts and social psychological work suggests that in practice this moral admonition frequently becomes interpreted as loving those who are like us.[63] Since people demonstrate a ubiquitous tendency to favor in-group members and discriminate against out-group members, how we define others becomes critical to our treatment of them. The rescuers make us aware of the ethical and political implications of this psychological process and focus us on the importance of moral salience. They force us to ask how the external environment—through factors as diverse as other people and political institutions or laws to the framing of situations or the memory of past events—works through our perceptions to evoke one part of a multifaceted identity as opposed to another.[64]

We can use this knowledge to ask if ethical behavior emanates from our basic character or if the critical factor is instead our character as it is perceived *at the moment of action*. The evidence presented from the rescuers seems to point to character as perceived at the moment of action. It suggests that all of us are, at least occasionally, influenced by the situation, by how others act and by what we perceive as social, political, and ethical constraints. This finding encourages us to focus on understanding how the immediate situation shapes behavior; it suggests a strong component of ethical motivation resides in what we might call our social psychology, that part of our psychology focused on the extent to which our thoughts, feelings, and behaviors are influenced by others, either through their imagined or their real presence.[65] In particular, this social psychological approach may provide valuable insight on how the cognitive process of perspective serves as the link between identity and shifts in moral action.[66]

Because this linkage is not specific to the Holocaust or to the particular individuals interviewed here, we can draw on the general literature in social psychology to inquire about the ability of the situation to tap into different parts of our basic personalities. Studies on altruism are particularly suggestive in revealing how our basic tendencies to help strangers vary greatly in response to the actions of others around us. In particular, Latané and Darley found a variety of factors were significant, from our friends warning us that helping others may endanger our own life or ridiculing us for being soft-hearted to suggesting that the person in need may be undeserving.[67]

Findings about the ability of others to influence whether we help or ignore people in need are drawn not just from studies of altruism; they are reinforced in a variety of broader social psychological studies. These studies often inquire about the interactive process between the concept of a constant character and the ability of the external environment to tap into different aspects of a complex self. Indeed, two of the most famous experiments in social psychology illustrate the power of the situation to work on the self-concept and thus affect behavior: Milgram's experiments on obedience and Zimbardo's Stanford Prison experiments.[68]

Prompted by concerns about obedience to authority after World War II, Milgram performed a series of experiments in which two individuals agree to participate in an experiment on learning. One person—I shall call her Gracie—is the designated student or learner and is strapped in a chair with an electrode placed on her arm. The other is the teacher—call him George—who reads a list of two word pairs and asks Gracie to read them back. If Gracie gives the correct answer, George goes on to the next word pair. But if the answer is wrong, George is instructed to administer an electric shock to Gracie. Shocks begin at 15 volts and continue in 15-volt increments, eventually reaching as high as 450 volts. In reality, no one in Milgram's experiments received shocks and all the designated learners (such as Gracie) knew about the true purpose of the experiment, which was to determine how far people (like George) were willing to go in inflicting pain on another person.

While Milgram theorized that only the sadistic fringe of society would agree to inflict such pain on another person, this was not the case in his experiments. Roughly two-thirds of all Milgram's participants were "obedient" subjects. Milgram's experiments thus suggested that the great majority of people—in America, not Germany—would willingly participate in activity that harmed others when apparently necessitated by nothing more intimidating than the demands of scientific authority as embodied in the form of a rather non-threatening person wearing a white lab coat.

Milgram later explored these findings in other works, trying to allow for cultural differences and race but again found that people tend to follow the instructions of an administrative figure. Milgram found his results extremely disturbing, since they suggested that character cannot be counted on to insulate people from brutality and inhumane treatment at the direction of authority figures.

The Stanford Prison experiments also explored the importance of the situation for our treatment of others. Zimbardo and his assistants divided twenty-four college student volunteers into two groups: prisoners and guards. All students who volunteered for the experiments were screened in advance and all were judged free of psychological problems, medical disabilities, or a history of drug abuse or crime. Individuals in this group of relatively normal, middle-class males were randomly assigned to play roles for the purposes of what all participants knew was only an experiment designed to ask what happens when you put good people in a situation fraught with potential for abuse. Both the students playing the part of guards and the students acting the role of prisoners lived in a prison constructed from a corridor in the basement of the building housing Stanford's Psychology Department. Within a surprisingly short period of time—six days—the volunteers playing the guards became so abusive to their fellow students (even though they knew the game was just an experiment) that Zimbardo terminated the experiment. As with the Milgram experiment, Zimbardo's students lost their sense of who they were because of situational factors that then led them to engage in behavior that was undesirable from an ethical point of view.

Work on the power of the situation to affect action through influencing self-perceptions becomes directly relevant for our concerns since—ironically—the impetus for these experiments arose, in part, from a desire to understand why the Holocaust had occurred in an otherwise modern, politically and scientifically developed country like Germany. How could civilized human beings allow such atrocities to occur? One immediate postwar answer to this question lay in what was widely viewed as the German tendency toward authoritarianism and its importance in allowing a few madmen to intimidate a civilized but obedient people who were willing to comply with orders.[69] Here is where the work on rescuers makes a significant contribution to the scholarly literature.

Prior Work on the Altruism of Rescuers. The dominant tendency in early work on altruism was to explain away altruism as a disguised form of self-interest, arguing that altruism provides psychic gratification or is designed to encourage reciprocal altruism.[70] Much of the best work on altruism was based on experimental laboratory work, such as Batson's work on empathic altruism.[71] But experimental work cannot fully simulate the more complex interactions in the political world. This is where political analyses, even those based on small samples, provide rich insight.

For our purposes, it is fortuitous that when we move outside the laboratory, the best literature on altruism often focuses on rescuers of Jews.[72] Much of the early work is autobiographical, by rescuers[73] or survivors,[74] and consists of anecdotal portraits designed to document rescue activity.[75] There was little work directly focused on rescuers' motivations until London's 1970 work. The initial social science works on this topic were correlational and inquired about a wide variety of sociocultural factors, such as religion,[76] social class,[77] or gender.[78] When analysts considered the psychological aspect of rescue behavior, they tended to focus on general psychological factors, such as the thrill of adventure involved in rescuing or a sense of social marginality in which the rescuer felt an empathic bond with the persecuted because of the rescuer's own perception of being an outsider.[79]

The first important systematic analysis of rescuers established personality as the critical explanation of rescue behavior.[80] *The Altruistic Personality*, by Sam and Pearl Oliner, was the largest survey of rescuers ever conducted, including 406 rescuers, 126 non-rescuers, and 150 rescued survivors throughout all of the Third Reich.[81] It found that an altruistic personality, in which habitual behavior, encouraged by parents or other significant role models, led to habits of caring that effectively became structured as an altruistic personality.[82] These habits always included tolerance for differences among people and a worldview characterized by the Oliners and their European collaborators[83] as "extensivity" to refer to rescuers' more extensive conceptualization of the moral community.

The Oliners' project is the first important one to focus specifically on what we might think of as identity. Its findings are reinforced by those of Tec, another survivor writing around the same time. Tec focused on personality factors, arguing that rescuers had a strong sense of individuality or separateness.[84] Tec concluded that rescuers were motivated by moral values that did not depend on the support or approval of other people so much as on their own self-approval. At about the same time, a filmed documentary, interviewing survivors as well as rescuers, argued that rescuers "had to do it because that's the kind of people they were."[85]

The psychological importance of reinforcing empathic and humane behavior was noted by a generation of younger scholars, such as Fogelman, the child of survivors.[86] Fogelman's work stressed certain psychological factors related to the sense of self. In terms of identity, Fogelman found rescuers undergo a transformative encounter that effectively creates a different self, a rescuer self, which allows otherwise normal people to lie, cheat, or even kill if necessary. This transformed self is critical for Fogelman, providing rescuers the ability to maintain a kind of double life. This transformation, however, while designed to help save life, often means the rescuer engaged in what would generally be thought of as unethical behavior.

How do we put together these findings on the importance of the self with findings on the power of the external world to key into critical aspects of a complex self, thus calling forth certain types of behavior, even, as Fogelman suggests, to create a transformative self? What do our rescuers—who lived through the actual historical period, not a laboratory experiment or a computer simulation—suggest about the relative power of the situation to influence behavior toward others?

At some level, the rescuers must be counted as illustrating the constancy of character, not the situation, since they were the ones who did, after all, withstand the incredible anti-Semitic pressures of the political environment and the behavior of their fellow citizens. They acted out of their sense of self and refused to be people who were "just following orders." At least for the rescuers I interviewed, it was not that their identities were transformed, as Fogelman seems to imply, so much as that they were people whose core selves judged lying or cheating immoral political authorities less important than saving human life.

Yet, as we also have seen, rescuers were influenced by critical others, either via their initial acceptance of values of caring that then became ingrained into their character or, occasionally, in terms of networks of people with whom they worked. How do we evaluate this aspect of rescue behavior? Is the answer to the debate over character versus situation more complicated than it first appears?

Categorization and the According of Moral Salience. In probing more deeply, we need to determine the nature of the stimulus from the external environment and to ask what part of identity was triggered by external stimuli. In doing so, I found the German rescuers particularly instructive. They had no nationalistic pride to support them in their resistance to the German governmental policies of genocide and, after the war began, their resistance to the Nazi regime became treason. The existence of war increased the patriotic pressure to support their government, no matter how bad its policies.[87] There was little in the external environment to encourage German rescuers, and much to inhibit their desire to help. Why did they resist this pressure?

Otto's narrative notes the importance of the cognitive process of categorization for understanding why people engaged in genocide. Otto turns to the power of the group noted by social psychologists and calls into question the kinds of character explanations offered by virtue ethics. In particular, Otto seems to suggest that given appropriate external conditions, most of us will succumb to our baser natures.

OTTO: It is also important to understand how a society disintegrates. Le Bon describes the massacres of the French Revolution [in the *Psychology of Crowds*] and comes exactly to the same conclusions as Bettelheim [in *The Informed Heart*]. They both stress the psychology of a crowd. In thinking back on my own experiences, I'm coming more and more to believe in the psychology of the crowd. In a crowd, any man—university professors, highly educated people, or people from the streets—they react in a crowd always the same way. If it's the proper crowd with the proper guidance, then he becomes a mass murderer. I saw that coming. In a positive side and a negative side. It's not so much the personality; it is our misusing of instincts, about which very little is known.

Otto's analysis suggests the desire to follow others is part of our genetic predisposition. And Otto is very clear in arguing both that the Holocaust was not the only genocidal activity the twentieth century had seen and that it can happen again if we are not careful to protect against mob psychology.

When one thinks about all this, then one has to stop and think: When can it happen again? Where can it happen? And how? Because it has happened many times.

Otto again emphasized the instinctual aspect of immoral acts in referring to the herd aspect of genocide.

In thinking about what makes people do these things, it is not so important whether it is one million or six million. The increase was a matter of technique and the technology of killing. Those who led the mob and fired the first shot into live flesh, those are the really guilty ones. Talking about the Holocaust in this way, just in terms of the numbers killed, this is absolutely not my view. My view is: Who breaks the barrier by killing the first Jew is guilty. To a larger extent then, the others are less guilty. It's one of my conclusions.

What is especially useful in Otto's discussion of perpetrators' wartime activity is the importance of the situation and others in drawing forth different aspects of our complex identities.

Look, in order to judge these things [perpetrators' behavior], you have to know something about mass psychology. You learn to know the mechanism of a reaction of a crowd. When it becomes a psychological crowd, you have to watch out. Because any group of people can, under certain conditions, become a psychological crowd and commit the most heinous crimes, which they wouldn't do as individuals. One of my conclusions is this.

Much of what Otto describes above could be interpreted as emphasizing group identity or character. Does Otto's explanation still focus on character or identity as a static phenomenon? Is Otto merely shifting the level of identity to the group (not the individual) level, but still maintaining the concept of identity as fixed? I don't believe so, and the rest of Otto's discussion becomes critical as we attempt to discriminate between the two concepts: identity as static or identity as responsive to the environment.

Otto appears to suggest he is not describing group behavior as an entity that exists and takes independent action so much as he is describing how the group's behavior evolves out of the group's identity *in interaction with others*.[88] In particular, Otto effectively describes how perspective—our way of seeing the world and other people—works to categorize and classify people into certain slots from which differential behavior then flows naturally.

> [W]e must always remember, the first step in triggering the avalanche of group hatred is to call another human being ethnic names. . . . So this is my explanation for part of what happened during the war. People were able to kill so many other people, because they dehumanized them.

But Otto's discussion of the situation for shaping human behavior occurs in the context of explaining behavior of perpetrators, not rescuers. This raises the value of a comparative analysis, since any behavior may come into sharper focus when analyzed in a broader context that allows for more contrasts. Otto's discussion of perpetrators nonetheless moves us toward what I came to believe is the critical factor in linking the lack of choice and identity to what we know is great variation in behavior toward others. This critical factor is the power of the situation to shape both our perspective on the world and how we see ourselves at a particular moment in time, through calling forth different aspects of an identity that is complex and multifaceted.

Otto focuses us not so much on other people but more precisely on perspective as the psychological factor that shifts our cognitive categorization and classification of people in response to a wide variety of external, situational factors. This is most poignantly captured in Otto's recollection of a conversation with a concentration camp guard, a man who explains to Otto that he had not wanted to kill Jews, but did so anyway.

> I have interviewed many SS guards. . . . I asked one of our guards, pointing at the big gun in his holster, "Did you ever use that to kill?" He replied, "Once I had to shoot six Jews. I did not like that

at all, but when you get such an order, you have to be *hard*. And then after a while he added, "You know, they were not human anymore."

That was the key: dehumanization. You first call your victim names. . . . You take away soap and water and then say the Jew stinks. . . . Then you take food away. When they lose their beauty and health and so on, they are *not* human anymore. When he's reduced to a skin-colored skeleton, you have taken away his humanity. It is much easier to kill non-humans than humans.

Otto was not alone in identifying the importance of perspective for categorization and classification. For example, John noted the importance of the classification process when he spoke about killing. In this, John resembled other rescuers in suggesting he saw the humanity in non-human life forms. John explicitly links this perspectival ability with his treatment of animals, saying that because he is able to see their "humanity," John not only treats animals differently than he otherwise would; he treats them better than he would if he did not see their value as life forms, as part of a life force animals share with humans. The importance of categorization is further evident in John's recognition that there are gradations in this life force and that human beings have more rights than "lower" animals because, presumably, they share more of this basic life force.

JOHN: [M]any people are against using animals in laboratories and medical research. I think that many of these medical research are made in an inhumane way with animals. We should always have it done in such a way that the animals will not suffer. But I will not go to the extreme to say we should never use animals to make experiments because, if we need to save human beings, then I think we should use animals in a way to save lives. But use them with compassion even then. Make it so that they suffer as little as possible. A lot of people have no compassion for animals and they will just treat them as nothing, instead of being very careful not to let them suffer.

The subtle gradations in valuing life were reflected in another conversation with John. John expressed great pride not just in doing his duty during the war but in doing it *as a human being who did no harm to others.* "I did my duty as a human being, as a soldier, without having to kill."

We know that people have to use categories to organize reality and make sense of it. The vast literature in social identity theory makes it further clear that we categorize ourselves in relation to others and then compare ourselves with these critical others.[89] But there are many ways in which we can compare ourselves to others. This means that those of us interested in moral questions must ask not just how people construct categories but how they accord moral salience to these categories. Rescuers, for example, did draw distinctions between Jews and Nazis. But they did not accord moral salience to these categories. Both Jews and Nazis were supposed to be treated as human beings. Instead, rescuers constructed a broader or an alternative category that was deemed morally salient. For rescuers, the morally salient category was the human race, not ethnicity, religion, or political affiliation.

This raises a further important question: Is it the recognition of common membership in a category that is necessarily relevant, as social identity theory would seem to suggest?[90] Or is it merely that shared membership in a category makes it *more* likely that one will treat other members of the same category well? It may be that the cognitive recognition of a shared category tends to accord moral salience, but this may not *necessarily* be the case. I discuss this more fully in chapter 8, but the empirical evidence from rescuers does suggest that a modification of social identity theory may be in order. It is not enough to say that people divide the world into in-group/out-group. We have to ask how the categories are first constructed and then how the categories are accorded moral salience.[91]

While this conclusion is somewhat speculative, I would argue that perspective may play a critical role here. Perspective seemed to affect how rescuers classified or categorized people; tremendous moral implications for behavior flowed from this categorization. For example, Knud notes the importance of categorization. But in doing so, Knud provides an interesting study in how humanitarianism sometimes works against socialization, with the categorization schema Knud developed himself being more important than the categorization framework he was taught to observe as a child.

Q. What was it that motivated your activities? Was it your patriotism? Was it your humanitarian desires?

KNUD: Denmark wouldn't have been free if we hadn't fought the Germans for two thousand years. Being a small country to the north and having an aggressive nation like Germany nearby, we would always be under pressure. If we hadn't defended ourselves for thousands of years, Denmark would have been Germany. My grandfather and his great-grandfather had fought in the wars between Denmark and Germany. There was one in 1848 and one in 1864. My grandfather told me, quite frankly, to hate all Germans. Period. But, of course, I couldn't do that. During World War II, we were all living under pressure from Germany, so my Underground work was primarily because I didn't want to be occupied by a German force and we wanted to resist the Germans regardless of what they did. The rescuing of Jews was connected to that feeling and it was also just a humanitarian feeling. We considered them not as Jews as such but as Danes. They were our people and they lived in Denmark. They were adopted by Denmark. It's a very homogenous society and the Jews in Denmark, even if they had a completely different religion, we found it interesting because we didn't have a lot of minorities. So the ones we had, we could take care of.

Knud's own categorization schema is evident in his refusal to classify either Germans or Jews as bad. "[There is] no distinction between Germans and Jews, etc." He sees Denmark as a victim of an aggressive neighbor against whom they had to fight to protect themselves. But he does not hate the Germans. And while rescuers recognized Jews as being in a different category, assigning Jews to one category did not seem to affect their also being placed into other categories since Knud refers to Jews "not as Jews as such but as Danes," as "ours" and as people who need to be protected.

In part, rescuers seem to have adopted superordinate categories, thinking of all people as the same and thus deserving of equal treatment. This extensive categorization process searched for the common ties, not distinctions that separated people. Margot's response typified the extensivity of rescuers' categorization.

Q: Was there anything in common about the people you helped?
MARGOT: No. They were just people.

The rescuers' categorization schema seemed to be one in which all people could exhibit individual and group differences but also could still be placed into the common category of human being. This common category took on a superordinate moral status in which all people deserve to be treated with respect and dignity.

I conclude that the cognitive process[92] by which rescuers viewed others—their categorization and classification of others and their perspective on themselves in relation to these others—played a critical role in identity's influence on moral action. The cognitive process included an affective component that served as a powerful emotional reaction to another's need. This reaction in turn provided the motive to work to effect change.[93]

Tapping into a Particular Self-Concept. A critical part of the process by which perspective influenced moral choice involved the manner in which the external environment tapped into the rescuers' core self-concept, a self-concept distinguished by its self-image as people who cared for others. Perspective linked the rescuers' self-image to the circumstances of the Jews by highlighting the Jews' situation in a way that then accorded a moral imperative to the plight of others. By tapping into this particular self-concept, the suffering of others became morally salient for the rescuers, in the way that the plight of one's child or parent would be salient for most of us.[94]

Because the value of caring for others was so deeply integrated into the rescuers' self-concept, it formed a self-image that was the underlying structure for their identities. This meant the needs of others were frequently deemed morally salient.[95] This self-concept translated and transformed rescuers' knowledge of another's need into a moral imperative requiring them to take action. Their self-concept became so closely linked to what was acceptable behavior that rescuers did not just note the suffering of others; the suffering took on a moral salience. The suffering of Jews was felt as something that was relevant for the rescuers. It established a moral imperative that necessitated action.[96]

The fact that the rescuers felt a moral imperative to help is evident most strikingly in statements that reveal their implicit assumptions about what ordinary decent people should do. In *The Heart of Altruism*, I referred to these as canonical expectations about what is acceptable behavior.[97] The unspoken expectations are embedded deep in a rescuer's psyche but are revealed in rescuers' description of what was—and what was not—in their repertoire of behavior. As Margot said, "You don't walk away. You don't walk away from somebody who needs real help." Or Margot's statement that "[the] ability to help and alleviate the pain of fellow human beings . . . is the ultimate goal of our short existence on this earth." Other rescuers employed similar phrases, almost as if reading from a common menu of moral behavior available to them. Witness Madame Trocmé's question: "How can you refuse them?"[98] John's insistence that "when you have to do right, you do right"; and all the rescuers' insistence that "there is no choice."

For rescuers, all people within the boundaries of their community of concern were to be treated the same, and their circle of concern included all human beings.[99] This perception of a shared humanity triggered a sense of relationship to the other that then made the suffering of another a concern for the rescuers.[100] Significantly, this extensivity included Nazis, with the rescuers demonstrating extraordinary forgiveness of Nazis.[101] I believe it is this role of perspective to classify and categorize people and then to work through a cognitive process of salience that provides the link between the lack of choice and identity on the one hand and the variation in our treatment of others.[102] But more complete empirical evidence on this requires analyzing bystanders and perpetrators, and a full description of this project requires another volume.[103]

What we do have by way of clear empirical evidence linking identity to moral action are the following critical concepts: (1) the desire for self-esteem and the need for continuity of self-image; (2) core values stressing the sanctity of life and human well-being, values that then are integrated into our underlying concept of who we are; and (3) external stimuli that trigger critical aspects of our multifaceted and complex identity in a way such that we notice and accord moral salience to the suffering of others.

Let me conclude with a brief discussion of the relation between perspective and critical core values to make clear that an emphasis on perspective is not misinterpreted as advocacy of moral relativism.

Perspective and Moral Absolutes: The Core of a Universal Morality as Human Well-Being and the Sanctity of Life

If how we see things is so critical to moral action, are we left in the world of moral relativism, in which there are no absolute standards concerning right or wrong and everything is subjective? Moral relativists might argue that we have to accept the Nazis' values and respect them, even if we do not share them. They might argue further that since the Nazi policies were adopted legally, according to laws passed by the German people and their duly-elected representatives, we therefore do not have the right to impose our own values on Nazis. Must we accept this view, and the Nazi genocides, as part of moral relativism, given the importance of perspective for our rescuers? No.

In reality, analyzing rescue behavior yields several insights on why moral relativism is an untenable ethical position. When faced with genocidal laws and the human suffering that these legally passed laws produced, it was the rescuers who effectively said, "This is wrong, and the fact that the laws were passed legally is irrelevant." Using rescue behavior as a lens through which to examine moral action during the Nazi period clearly shows that there are cultural standards that do *not* rest on objective standards of right and wrong. Rescue behavior thus rejects national laws or local custom as justification for the wholesale slaughter of human beings. Rescue behavior shows we can value different cultures without subscribing to the view that our moral values stop at our own national borders or at the limits of our own culture.

Indeed, rescuers encourage us to believe there are more important values than those that rest simply on culture or local laws. A consideration of rescue behavior thus reminds us that we also must focus on the nature of the values integrated into our sense of self. It returns us—briefly—to a consideration of whether or not there are core values that are universal and, if so, what these values are. The moral exemplars we met here revealed that, indeed, there are core values that transcend time, place, culture, and any kind of particularity. For all the rescuers, these moral values were woven into both the rescuers' self-concept and the particular worldviews—what psychologists would call their underlying cognitive frameworks or cognitive construals—which rescuers used to understand and make sense of the world and events around them. An analysis of rescuers thus yields several important insights on the moral psychology.

First, the core of a universal morality has to do with human welfare. Time and again, this is the value that trumps all others in the rescuers' value system. Second, in thinking about ethics, we must focus on behavior that promotes the interests of people who are affected by the action, not merely on the motives of the people who take the action. Third, if human welfare is the core of ethics, then this core provides a standard for our legal rules and cultural norms. Governments, laws, and cultures must be evaluated in light of this absolute standard. There may be difficult moral issues to be dealt with in the face of genocide—should we kill in order to stop the killing, for example—but our discussions of morality should hold them separate from the broader issue of whether we are right to disapprove of others' behavior. The rescuers tell us that human welfare is the core of ethics and that when governments, cultures, or laws violate this central core, the moral individual will resist.

8

What Makes People Help Others: Constructing Moral Theory

> *Unfortunately, the Holocaust was not unique. There have been other instances. . . . For me, then, the problem and the rescuers become in some ways even more important because by understanding these rescuers we can understand what it is that makes people help other human beings. The really important question is: "Why did good people become that way?" It is not enough to just say, "Good people are good, period."*
>
> —*Otto Springer*

STORIES ARE A RICH SOURCE OF information about how people think about moral issues.[1] Can they also inspire us to think more deeply about these issues? Are there broader theoretical implications to be gleaned from what we have learned from the rescuers, as Otto suggests? In this chapter, I present initial thoughts of a more theoretical nature about the process by which identity and perspective work through the moral psychology to influence our treatment of others.[2] To do so, I present the outlines of a moral theory intended to fill a gap in existing ethical theory. The theory is empirically grounded and locates the impetus for morality in identity, not religion or reason. Instead, it explains morality as a fundamental correlate of the human capacity for intersubjective communication and the need to distinguish boundaries via categorization. In articulating the critical parts of what we have discovered so far about the moral psychology and weaving them together into a theoretical statement, I focus on the following points about a basic human nature.[3]

All individuals are motivated by a need to protect and nurture the self. This manifests itself not only as the drive toward both self-interest and sociability but also through desires for predictability, control, and cognitive consistency. A basic self with core values develops early in childhood and reflects both genetic predispositions and later life experiences.[4] This self is shaped by culture and has a central core but is multifaceted, with different aspects coming to the fore in response to external events and cognitive framing. Moral situations are perceived from the perspective of the core values and the self-concept into which these values are integrated. This self-concept is part of, and will be reflected in, the cognitive framework that helps produce the actor's perspective, her sense of her self in relation to others. Moral—or immoral—behavior thus emerges as an outgrowth of the self-concept as tapped into by cognitive framing and perspective.

In trying to specify more clearly the psychological process underlying the development of a moral perspective—and not one morally neutral or immoral—I draw on my own empirical analysis of rescuers;[5] but I also situate my analysis in the broader context of recent work in moral psychology to build on several key findings. (1) Moral exemplars are distinguished from other people by the particular values they hold and by the unusual degree to which these moral beliefs are integrated into the actor's sense of self. (2) This integration motivates moral action by making the integrity of the self dependent on consistency between moral action and moral identity. (3) The need to protect and nurture the self as a general psychological process appears to turn an individual toward good, rather than evil, when situational factors contribute to an objective assessment of one's self that causes the individual to think about universal entitlement to humane treatment. (4) This perspective must become integrated into one's own concept of self, working through the actor's need for self-esteem and cognitive consistency, in order to provide moral salience to the perceived needs of another.

The chapter begins by discussing the critical components of a theory emphasizing moral perspective. It then considers the moral psychology and asks how we might construct moral theory utilizing identity and perspective to explain the moral psychology. In doing so, several caveats are in order. I am not arguing that rescuers are paradigmatic of all moral actors. Nor do I suggest that rescues never were performed for other than moral reasons.[6] And certainly it would be foolish to assert that analyzing only a handful of human beings, at one particular point in time, can be anything more than suggestive. Suggestive it can be, however, and one thing it suggests is the need to supplement traditional explanations of moral choice with a theory that emphasizes identity and perspective, as outlined below.[7]

CRITICAL COMPONENTS IN A THEORY OF MORAL PERSPECTIVE

I situate my theory of morality in a broader intellectual context that assumes there are central tendencies in human behavior and that moral theory must allow for and build on these constants. What are these constants? I would argue that human nature is complex but that there is a basic human need to protect and nurture the self.[8] This means both self-interest and sociability are critical, but neither is dominant.[9] Our selfish individual desires are balanced by less self-centered—although often still individual—yearnings for the social respect, affection, and memberships that provide limits to the selfishness that may accompany self-interest. Because self-interest and sociability form crucial links to the concept of self that affects moral action, each should play a central part in the construction of moral theory.

Beyond this, the psychological literature suggests people also desire predictability and control. These desires relate directly to cognitive dissonance through the need for cognitive consistency, which provides a key source of an individual's psychic comfort and the maintenance of identity.[10] This returns us to the concepts of identity and self, discussed in chapter 7. I thus construct a theory of morality that uses the self and identity as the intellectual mortar to bind together my thoughts on general theory with the literature on morality found in virtue ethics and moral psychology and with my own analysis of the people whose narratives are presented in this book.

In constructing this theory, I argue that ethical political behavior flows naturally from our perceptions of self. Culture provides the initial range of self-images available, and actors gravitate toward different images according to both genetic propensities[11] and situational/contextual factors.[12] Ethical acts emanate not so much from conscious choice but rather from deep-seated instincts, predispositions, and habitual patterns of behavior that are related to our central identity. These in turn emanate in factors as diverse as genetic programming, social roles, and culturally inculcated norms. We need not be consciously aware that we possess this instinctual moral sense; nonetheless, this sense can be more powerful than any conscious calculus.

To this skeletal discussion of how identity shapes and even supersedes consciously held moral values[13] I would add that adherence to moral values evolves out of one's core identity, an identity that is effectively preset for most adults.[14] We may modify our core identities later in significant ways but only with great psychological effort. This means we should speak of adults as agents discovering rather than creating their identities.[15]

Can we weave these findings into a theory that captures key aspects of the moral psychology, especially one that specifies more clearly how actors are turned to moral acts, and not to acts that are immoral or morally neutral? This topic lay beyond the scope of my earlier work on altruism and provides the challenge for us now.

The Moral Psychology

To understand the moral psychology, I begin by accepting the concept of a self that is complex and multifaceted but which has core values that constitute a master self that seeks consistency between acts and values that have been integrated into this central identity. I assume, however, that even core values may war with each other and that these moments will be the ones which present individuals with difficult moral dilemmas, as in the agonistic choices found in traditional moral theory.[16] To parse our way successfully through such difficult moral situations and to understand how identity can lead to moral action, I turn to the concept of a shared humanity as the core of a moral identity. This concept, in turn, lays the foundation for the belief that all are entitled to decent treatment merely by virtue of being born human. The core values of a shared humanity and the commitment to human well-being provide the critical foundation for the moral perspective.

Because identity is so multifaceted and because it is malleable in response to external stimuli, we all will engage in differential treatment of others, within the constraints imposed by our master identity and depending on which aspect of our identity is triggered at certain points in time. This is where the moral perspective and moral salience enter. How we see each other in relation to others will determine the range of possible choices available to *us*, not to others. This perspectival link between self and moral values is the piece of the puzzle that has so far eluded moral theorists. It is this moral perspective that triggers moral salience, the sense that another's need is relevant for us, that it is important that we take action to help, not just feel empathy, concern, or sadness at the plight of others.[17]

Let me now use the analysis of how identity and perspective constrained choice in the morally exemplary rescuers to sketch the essentials of a moral theory that locates the impetus for moral action in a complex interrelationship among identity, fellow feeling, universal boundaries of entitlement, and a perspective on self and others that focuses the actor on seeing our common humanity.

Character and Identity.   Our moral actions emanate, in part, from our sense of who we are. Certain actions will be ruled out automatically, and others prescribed, by our self-perceptions, by the kind of person we believe ourselves to be.[18] This is evident in the need—noted by psychological studies of rescuers[19] and other moral exemplars[20]—to minimize the discrepancy between how one conceptualizes one's self and how one then acts. Our activated self-concept may change, however, in response to external stimuli. One influence on this may be the degree to which our actions correspond with our self-concept, and whether we align actions with our sense of self or modify our self-concept in response to actions that deviate from our initial self-concept. Everyone has some sense of a core self, however, and this is a critical influence on behavior.

This was evident in rescuers' explanations of their behavior. As one Dutch rescuer noted, "There are times when we all wish we had done something and we didn't. And it gets in your way during the rest of your life."[21] Other rescuers also articulated this tie between moral action and sense of self.

> You asked me earlier if I would have been able to live with myself if I had not rescued these people. No. The possibility was that they should have a very hard situation, and you have the feeling that if you send them back, you don't forget it for your life. So I don't think I could have lived with myself. (Bert, Dutch rescuer)

This emphasis on character echoes both the psychological studies noted earlier and the literature in virtue ethics. It differs in several important ways, however. First, it focuses our interest not on character itself so much as on the relationship between character and behavior, particularly the extent to which character predicts behavior. Second, it assumes our self-perceptions will vary and that external stimuli can trigger various aspects of our self-perceptions; we thus allow for variation in action by avoiding treating character or identity as static, even though there will be a central core to character. These two distinctions allow us to explain the praiseworthy acts of someone like Oskar Schindler, for example. In Keneally's fictionalized account (1982), Schindler's character was multifaceted, and his actions toward both Jews and his first love—money— changed over time in response to shifts in his perceptions of himself in relation to these particular others.

Universal Boundaries of Entitlement. The moral perspective assumes all people are entitled to certain humane treatment simply because they are born human. This rejects the emphasis, found in virtue ethics and social identity theory, on community ties, a tendency that can result in privileging communitarianism as a morally superior form of sociopolitical organization.[22] Instead of personalistic or group ties, the rescuers demonstrated a universal worldview in which the boundaries of those people toward whom one evinces a tender regard are drawn so broadly as to be all encompassing. I would argue that this constitutes the second critical component underlying moral action.

We can understand the importance of such universal boundaries by considering the narrative of Tony, one of the most articulate rescuers on this topic.

> I was impressed with the individual of Jesus as a man, just like you or me, ahead of his time. . . . Whenever they said, "You're the Christ," he refused [to take the title]. When they said, "You're the Son of God," he'd tell them, "We are all sons of God." Now, if you think of God as creation, then we *are* all part of creation. We *are* all sons of God. And I realized, simply and without getting too deep into these philosophies, that Christ, Buddha, Gandhi, they're all the same person. They are all the hero with a thousand faces. That's what I've learned. It's helped me.

Tony reiterated this thought later.

> I was to learn to understand that you're part of a whole, and that just like cells in your own body altogether make up your body, that in our society and in our community that we all are like cells of a community that is very important. Not America; I mean the human race. And you should always be aware that every other person is basically you. You should always treat people as though it is you, and that goes for evil Nazis as well as for Jewish friends who are in trouble. You should always have a very open mind in dealing with other people and always see yourself in those people, for good or for evil both.

Tony's extension of rights to all, even the Nazis, echoes the approach of natural rights theory. His universal boundaries of entitlement are reflected in his insistence that the Dutch not do to the Indonesians what the Dutch have just fought the war to prevent being done to them. This provides something akin to the objectification requirement underlying the moral theory of Smith and Hume via the impartial spectator; it contains similarities with that part of Kant's categorical imperative in which an act should be taken if the world would be better or worse if everyone did as we are about to do. The moral impetus of rescuers such as Tony differs from Kant, however, both in omitting any basic decision rule and in rejecting Kant's emphasis on duty and rational calculus.

The rescuers' moral perspective appears to accord all individuals basic human rights, even as it allows for tremendous variation in individual differences and for human failings. It draws moral boundaries universally, rejecting the claims of groups as the foundation for moral salience. For example, several of the rescuers could easily have claimed special treatment because they were German (Margot and Otto) and hence members of the privileged group. They refused to do this. Other rescuers (Irene) explicitly rejected the kind of entitlements behind a Rawlsian veil of ignorance, arguing that even if they knew they would benefit from special treatment they would not design such a society because it was morally wrong.

Fellow Feeling. The shared humanity component of perspective locates the impetus for moral action in fellow feeling. "We all belong to one human family," Irene said, a thought expressed by all the rescuers interviewed. A Berlin rescuer (Bethe) echoed this sentiment. "When one knows that one is bound into a bigger entity, then one cannot really act otherwise." It is this fellow feeling that appears to make another's plight relevant for the rescuer. This felt relevance is what then leads to action, according moral salience to another's suffering.[23] This moral salience, which is related to developing the moral sensitivity emphasized by virtue ethics, appears to work through three stages: (1) There must be recognition of another's need for help. Rescuers did not ignore the deplorable situation for the Jews, as many bystanders did. They had the moral sensitivity to recognize the suffering of others. (2) Rescuers felt able to provide help. While this might be thought of as a specialized form of efficacy, it was quite specific to the occasion and need not necessarily correlate with the rescuer's general level of efficacy. (3) Rescuers felt the needs of others were relevant for the rescuer; it was not enough for rescuers to feel generalized concern, empathy, or sadness in the face of another's misery. Their sense of fellow feeling meant *they* felt compelled to act to alleviate this suffering.[24]

Fellow feeling echoes themes found in both of Smith's books[25] and in Aristotle's *Nichomachean Ethics.* Such feelings may be inculcated by many different factors, some of which are described by Aristotle and Smith. (Culture and socialization forces such as parental exhortations or religion are two obvious examples.) But it simply may be born into people. In this regard, perspective resonates with moral sense theory in saying that an inherent aptitude for knowing right from wrong is innate in all human beings. This is illustrated by an exchange with John, in which he describes fellow feeling as being related to the feeling—expressed by other rescuers—that their extraordinary actions were "natural."

Q: Did you ever sit down and think about the costs and the benefits and the risks involved in what you were doing? Did you sit down and think about all these things before you undertook these "adventures" that you went on?

I don't think so. I think that it came as a natural reaction from the inside. Like a mother. Normally, you don't teach a mother how to love her baby. She has that naturally. Maybe not the father, but the mother. So your instinct that you develop in yourself is to react that way. And so it was a quite natural development. Not, "Should I do it or not?"

The idea of humans being born with a moral sense resonates with two important ancient Greek concerns: (1) the idea that we must nurture the development of inborn dispositions to care for others and (2) that the development of this capacity is part of what makes us human. This emphasis on fellow feeling and the mutuality of humanness as central parts of a moral identity brings us to the last critical component of my thoery.

Perspective and Moral Salience: The Link between Suffering and Helping. Virtue ethics discusses the importance of the capacity to see and recognize moral wrongs. For the virtue ethicist, developing this moral sensitivity is a critical part of becoming a moral individual and constitutes a prerequisite for moral action. After all, one cannot be expected to correct a wrong of which one is unaware.[26] The importance of this moral sensitivity is evident when we contrast the stance of bystanders with that of rescuers and underlines the importance of the moral salience mentioned above.[27]

I am exploring this theme more systematically in a book contrasting rescuers with bystanders and Nazis on this dimension. But it is perhaps instructive to note just one example here, a woman I shall call Beatrix, who was a bystander and the cousin of a rescuer I interviewed. Beatrix was very close to her cousin, and knew he had spent all but a few months of the war in hiding, condemned to death because of his rescue activities. During our interviews in 1992, Beatrix told of having been afraid that her husband might be drafted. Since Beatrix and her husband had a large home, they had built a hiding place for him. Fortunately, Beatrix told me, they never had to use this.

"Did you ever think about using it for someone else, other than your husband?" I wondered.

A look of bewilderment crossed Beatrix's face, as if she had never thought of this in the fifty some years since the war.

I tried, gently, to pursue this line of questioning.

Q. Did you know what was going on? What was your impression of what was happening [to the Jews]?
Did I know?

Q. Yes. What did you think was the situation for the Jews? You said a lot of them that you knew went to Africa. . . .
Yes. And they went to a camp in the neighborhood.

Q. What kind of camp was it?
Those camps. There was no gas, but they had a very bad life.

Q. So it was a work camp?
Yes.

Q. Did you know about the concentration camps during the war?
Yes.

Q. Did you know that the Jews were being gassed?
Yes. I can't tell you who told this, but my husband heard a lot when he worked in the hospitals.

Q. How did you react?
You couldn't do anything.

Q. There was nothing you could do?
No. No.

Some critical aspects of the moral psychology become evident if we examine Beatrix's explanation of her wartime behavior. The first is her view of herself as a helpless person who could do nothing. Indeed, "There was nothing I could do" was her reply whenever I queried her about her failure to help others. But putting this response together with her efforts to help her husband is instructive.

Virtue ethics alerts us to the notion of moral sensitivity, a sensitivity that is important to cultivate; indeed, some philosophers argue it is as difficult to develop and maintain this moral sensitivity as it is to develop and act on the will to take action necessary to correct the moral wrong. Contrasting Beatrix with the rescuers fleshes out our understanding of this psychological process and highlights the importance for moral psychology of our perspective on self in relation to others. It wasn't that people like Beatrix did not recognize the existence of moral wrongs and the need to help those persecuted by the Nazis. Their inaction occurred because they did not recognize the moral salience of these wrongs *for them*. Beatrix knew that Jews were being gassed; she neither denies nor minimizes that knowledge. Similarly, she knew her cousin had been unjustly condemned to death, just as she knew her husband could be drafted into the German army. What was different was that she failed to see what the perilous situation of her cousin or of the Jews had to do with her, while she did recognize the relevance of her husband's far less precarious situation.

The psychological process of helping another involves the recognition of another's need. It entails the actor's belief that she can take action that will alleviate another's suffering. And it requires the acknowledgment of moral salience, the recognition that another's need is a concern *to the actor*. Making the connection between one's self and the other, identifying the relevance of another's plight to one's self, is a critical part of the moral perspective. Before we condemn bystanders, however, we should think about the moral salience of innumerable problems of which most of us are aware. Moral salience probably explains why so many of us— people who are reasonably ethical human beings in our everyday lives— do so little to alleviate problems like the genocide in Bosnia or Rwanda-Burundi, or even human suffering in our own country. Like Beatrix, we do not recognize the situation as something directly relevant for us. We then conclude that it is not a situation that we can affect very much. "There is nothing we can do," to paraphrase Beatrix.

The importance of moral salience is evident in Keneally's fictionalized account of the wartime behavior of Oskar Schindler.[28] Keneally tells how, as the war is ending, Schindler shifts his base of operations west, spending the last of his money to bring his Jews into his factory so they will be protected from the vicissitudes of war. During the move, some of the Schindler Jews—the Schindler women—are mistakenly shipped to Auschwitz instead of to Schindler's factory. Schindler learns about this and races to Auschwitz to bribe the camp commander to free the carload of the Schindler women. The commandant quickly takes Schindler's diamonds. He notes that releasing these particular women will be difficult but says he can easily reroute the next trainload of women to give Schindler other women to work in his factory. Schindler protests. He wants these particular women. Although not stated explicitly, the commandant seems to find Schindler's concern ludicrous, suggesting, in effect, that one Jew is as good as another. At some level, this view is obviously true; one human being *is* as good as another. But Schindler had seen the humanity of these particular women and that was what moved him to take action.

This incident underscores the importance of perspective in evoking a sense of moral salience. If we do not see the humanity of the persecuted, if we do not extend our circle of humanity to include particular others and instead draw the kinds of group lines that communitarianism emphasizes, then we can look away, as Beatrix did, and as Schindler did in many other instances.[29] Seeing another's need is a critical part of moral salience. But so is the recognition that another's need is of direct concern to me. This recognition of relevance plays a crucial role in making the conceptual effort to find a way to help.

Empathy and Perspective.   This importance of recognizing moral wrongs also picks up on some of Hume's work on morality and returns us to the shared aspect of human entitlement discussed above. Hume and Smith argue that the ability to make moral choices emanates from the ability to pull out of one's immediate situation and to put oneself in another's place through a process of sympathy, or what we would frequently now call empathy.

Empathy is a commonly cited explanation for altruism[30] and is usually said to contain both a cognitive and an affective component. The cognitive aspect of empathy is what provides the viewer with the ability to grasp what another person is feeling and to discriminate among various behavioral cues necessary to assess that person's emotional state. Work such as Hume's seems to imply that this cognitive ability to put one's self in the place of another is critical for ethical treatment of the other.[31]

But in thinking about this further, we soon realize that the cognitive ability to understand how another feels also can be used to manipulate and torment, much as the Nazis did to their victims. We thus need some mechanism that moves us beyond empathy as a narrowly conceived cognitive process and joins empathy's cognitive component with an affective mechanism in which the observer is emotionally aroused by the feelings of others in a manner that encourages a desire to attend to their needs.

For the rescuers, the cognitive aspect of empathy appeared to enter through the structure of knowledge that formed an expectation of a coherent sequence of acts and events in a given situation. These sequences appeared to have been stored in the rescuers' memories, often subconsciously, both in the form of scripts about how one treated those in need or in the form of schemas about how one viewed one's self. These important self schema, the existence of such scripts and schematic frameworks, explained the rescuers' habitual, spontaneous, and nonconscious or reflexive altruism. The behavioral consequences of such scripts and schemas were the rescuers' automatic help for the weak and their continuing habits of caring.

The self-concept thus was critical. But the perspectival aspect of the self was crucial in providing the affective element to a generalized cognitive empathy. Perspective thus appears to have been critical for the rescuers in one significant regard. Rescuers seem to have accorded everyone, including themselves, the entitlement of certain basic human rights and decent treatment because of a perspective that made them see themselves at one with all humankind.

The process of universally according all people these entitlements had an important and ironic consequence. It prevented rescuers from becoming sacrificial martyrs since rescuers also are included in the family of man.[32] It enabled rescuers to see the humanity in everyone, even the perpetrators, and the human weakness in everyone, even themselves. This provided the impetus to act to help the needy, and to forgive the guilty.

For the rescuers, allowing and cherishing the humanity in others was closely related to the ability to fully claim the humanity in themselves.

This process of perspective works in some way as the impersonal ratiocination process does for Hume, Smith, and Kant, who need objectivity and impartiality both to derive universal rights and to give the actor the right to claim rights for her- or himself. Certainly perspective makes us aware that there are different ways of seeing things. But there is a warmth of fellow feeling to the altruistic perspective that seems missing from the kind of objective rational calculus of rights in opposition that we find in alternative theories.[33]

Let me now try to take these components of the moral psychology and weave them together into an empirically based theory that explains what drives moral action.

Constructing Moral Theory Utilizing Identity and Perspective to Explain the Moral Psychology

Consistency and Identity.   Identity is complex and multivariate; it is critical that an individual—and the world—have the sense that the individual who is here today is also the same individual who was there yesterday and the individual who will be there tomorrow. Longitudinal congruence provides a key source of an individual's psychic comfort and the maintenance of identity.[34] Consistency thus plays an important role in identity maintenance.

This is clearly illustrated by the literature on cognitive dissonance. Cognitive dissonance refers to the feelings of discomfort that occur when we hold two or more inconsistent cognitions or when our acts deviate from our stated beliefs. This discomfort becomes especially acute when our actions do not accord with our customary, typically positive self-conception.[35] Originally, theorists thought this dissonance was caused by any two discrepant cognitions.[36] Later work, however, suggests that not all cognitive inconsistencies are equally troubling. Dissonance seems most powerful and upsetting when we behave in ways that threaten our self-image, because such behavior forces us to confront the discrepancy between who we think we are and what our actions reveal about our character.[37]

But how does a drive toward consistent behavior—that is, behavior in line with our concept of ourselves—get us to moral behavior? After all, unrepentant Nazis would have no problem reconciling their acts and their self-image, yet few of us would find them morally praiseworthy. If a Nazi is content being a Nazi and is fully aware of this identity, even though she does not recognize the immoral aspect of this ideology and her support for it, can she not spend her whole life behaving in ways that are fully consistent with this self-image and never approach moral action? Of course. Consistent behavior alone will not get us to moral action. Since my interest is in specifying a theory that drives us toward morality, not just one that explains how people end up at varying points along a moral continuum, we need additional mechanisms. So far I have addressed only the human need for consistency between action and self-image. Let me now relate the need for self-esteem to boundaries and categorization.

Self-Esteem, Boundaries, and Categorization.   If the psychological literature clearly establishes that all humans have a need for consistency of identity, it is equally clear that the desire for self-esteem is an innate part of human nature[38] and an important part of identity formation.[39] Can we think of innate needs for self-esteem being tied to concerns with leading a moral life? Is there a relationship between my own need to feel good about myself and my humane treatment of others?

We could construct a logical argument linking self-esteem to universal morality.[40] Indeed, the reciprocal granting of entitlement has a long history among philosophers. Gewirth argues that an individual's drive toward self-fulfillment will logically lead that person to accept the requirements of universalistic morality.[41] The essence of Gewirth's argument suggests that it is logically impossible to conceive of ourselves as purposive agents without also recognizing what is a critical condition for successful action: an entitlement not to have our freedom arbitrarily restricted. And logically, if we as prospective purposive agents have such rights to freedom, then we also must acknowledge that all other prospective purposive agents have similar rights. Gewirth uses logic to forge this linkage, however, and although he does consider the vast evidence suggesting that people can behave immorally without feeling a lack of inner peace, his argument remains foundationalist, not empirically based.

Empirical evidence now exists to support this logical argument, however, and I draw not only on my own empirical work on rescuers but also on work in psychology and linguistics to support my claims. I begin with research on children. Research on self-recognition among toddlers suggests self-recognition develops around two years of age[42] but continues throughout our lives, gradually becoming more complex.[43] Although there are important gender and cultural differences that researchers are only now beginning to document, for most adult humans a sense of self is said to serve three basic adaptive functions on which most psychologists agree: managerial, emotional, and organizational.[44]

Managerial functions inform us of our relationship to the physical and social world and help us organize our behavior and plan for the future.

The emotional function of the self helps us determine our expressive responses.[45] The organizational function helps us create schemas, the mental structures around which we organize our knowledge.[46] We use these schemas to interpret and recall information about both the social world and ourselves. One of the most important schemas is the self-concept, and the information we notice, remember, and think about is often organized around how we view ourselves.[47]

How do these broader psychological needs for self-esteem and consistency serve to develop and protect a sense of self? An inborn narcissism[48] exists in infants and includes the important aspects of a social being to which Aristotle alerted us. Narcissism originates in the infant-mother relationship, and analysts now believe infantile narcissism is an inherent universal capacity that evolves throughout the life cycle.[49] Narcissism thus is now viewed as an essential quality of maturation, not just a neurotic self-love.[50]

The dynamics of narcissism as a positive force affects entitlement through the person's need for self-esteem. The process of individuation is one in which the individual begins to separate from the mother and acquires a sense of otherness, in order to establish boundaries between the infant and the mother. In a healthy process, these boundaries lead to a kind of categorization in which the infant—let us call her Rosie—can distinguish between herself and others. Without these boundaries, Rosie will feel a sense of being overwhelmed. Her ontological security is threatened, and Rosie will experience personality stress and disintegration.[51] In a healthy process, this narcissistic need for self-esteem works through the establishment of boundaries in a manner that helps move Rosie toward a sense of entitlement, of being worthy of and due certain rights and treatment. To get from Rosie's individual sense of entitlement to her moral treatment of others, however, we must turn to work on linguistic categorization to link equivalent treatment of others to our own sense of entitlement.

The Psyche's Need for Individuation and Boundaries: Language and Categorization. The healthy psyche's need to differentiate itself from others leads to the drawing of boundaries.[52] But how does a need to differentiate ourselves from others get us to universal entitlement? My argument here draws on Smiley's pragmatist moral theory and Chomsky's theory of universal grammar to reject cultural relativism and arrive at an empirically grounded understanding of universal entitlement of rights and treatment.

Smiley (1992) argues that moral rules "exist" by virtue of their practical application or embodiment. We see our morality in the actual procedures we use for moral evaluation. Smiley argues that in order to make rational sense, these procedures have to rely on either community standards or some concept of god as the ideal moral judge. Both these foundations frequently are absent from our modern sensibility. God cannot serve as our foundation because many of us are atheists or agnostics, because those who do believe in a supreme deity (or deities) cannot agree on one particular vision of god, and because our social order—at least in post-Enlightenment Western society—depends on a separation of politics and religion.[53] Nor can community serve as our foundation since we recognize that we live among a multiplicity of cultures and communities.[54] This means we need a foundation for judgment that can transcend particular group allegiances or local boundaries. Can we find such a foundation? One possible route may be through reference to Chomsky's theory of language.[55]

Chomskian linguistics provides one possible solution to the problem of cultural relativism that confronts universal moral theories. According to Chomsky's model, there is a fundamentally rational structure to the human mind. This rational structure is embodied in basic grammatical structures and underlies the universal human ability to learn and use language. Because the language use of all linguistically competent humans conforms to certain describable parameters, and because these parameters can be demonstrated to be implicit in the genetically inherited learning capacity of all[56] human children,[57] by referring our standards of rational judgment to these basic universal capacities we can assure ourselves that they transcend cultural boundaries. Then, because we can find a capacity for rational judgment inherent in the universals of human language, we can apply this capacity to standards of moral or political behavior, uncovering hypocrisy, faulty reasoning, and parochial prejudices to arrive at truly universal standards of moral judgment. This argument for universalism resembles traditional rationalism, but it is rationalism grounded in the fundamentals of human language capacity rather than in introspection. As such, it should be empirically verifiable.

Even in the absence of shared communal standards, then, we can argue for universal practices of moral evaluation. We make this argument if we think of community in largely linguistic-consensual terms.[58] Doing so requires us to formulate a universal understanding of linguistic consensus.[59] If we accept as valid the Chomsky arguments regarding the nature of language use and speech communities, then the only coherent understanding of moral community that we can reasonably form will be a universal one. This is because community standards (of whatever sort, not merely moral standards) are a type of linguistic rules and rule following itself is both a universal and an individual property of humans that transcends the boundaries of community and culture alike.[60]

Much of Chomsky's reasoning regarding the connection between language capacity and universalism consciously relies on connections already drawn in Kant's epistemological and ethical writings. Chomsky's universal grammar parallels Kant's a priori categories. The ethical duty to accept reasonable and universal standards of fairness and justice, which motivates Chomsky's political activity, stems from this universal grammar in a manner roughly analogous to the relationship between Kant's duty-based ethics and Kant's account of knowledge of the world. Kant's introspective philosophy has been critiqued by relativists—such as Heidegger, Foucault, and Derrida—for being too dependent on Kant's historically and culturally specific subject position. Chomsky's theory, in contrast, makes reference to a notion of reason that is as broadly based in the diversity of human languages and cultures as possible and thus frees universalism of the culturally bounded critique.

Chomsky and Universalism.   Chomsky's reformulation of Harris's structural linguistics sought to explain the transformational structures catalogued in Harris's extensive work.[61] While Chomsky's reformulation is nominally an empirical theory about the workings of the human cognitive capacity for language learning, its significance extends far beyond the empirical study of language or cognition. By restoring the Cartesian[62] interest in universal grammar, Chomsky also restores the possibility of a universal, rational ethics based on principles inherent in the common structure of all human language.[63]

According to Chomsky's theory, human children are born with an inherent capacity to rationally organize sensory information into discrete and manipulatable symbols (words) that can be recombined according to a finite set of rules (grammar) into a potentially infinite number of sequences (sentences, and so on). Children do not need to induce the rules of grammar from the speech they hear around them; rather they actively construct a grammar based on their innate capacities and then modify this based on their interactions with other speakers, quickly becoming competent speakers of the language(s) spoken around them.[64]

Evidence supporting Chomsky's theory comes from Bickerton's investigations into the structure of Creole languages.[65] Such languages lack general standards of grammar and are independent of the native languages of their various speakers but nonetheless always form a coherent grammar of their own. The grammar in question is virtually identical in structure across all Creole languages and is mirrored in the experimental grammars formed by children learning a language for the first time.[66]

Chomsky's work on the active role of children in language acquisition and the relationship between the competence of individual speakers and what comes to be standardized as the accepted language of a speech community has a particular relevance for us. First, Chomsky's work demolishes the myths of essential racial and cultural difference. It thus attacks the idea of coherent communities as self-contained grounds of truth, an idea that accompanied the rise of modern nationalism and the Romantic reaction to modernity. Second, Chomsky's critique of the ideal speaker-listener problem is analogous to the problem in moral theory of the ideal blamer. The importance of this is critical, as can be illustrated by reference to Smiley and the problem of universal morality.

Smiley wants us to find a communal basis for judgment that can be philosophically coherent in the face of a lack of cultural consensus.[67] Thus Smiley has clarified the central problem for us: how to rationally justify moral blame within a modern worldview. She also has made clear why the problem matters: as a matter of practical existence, human beings find the practice of moral evaluation indispensable. This raises a further challenge: offering a satisfying account of how we can address this problem to our own ethical satisfaction in the face of all these pragmatic considerations. The critical question thus remains open: how might a moral theory recognize, rather than paper over, these contradictions, without surrendering a claim to rational foundation?[68]

Categorization and Universalism.   The answer lies in the psychological process of categorization and reciprocation. We can turn to a wide variety of sources presenting evidence suggesting that an innate drive to categorize, as noted through both the linguistic and the psychoanalytic work described above, leads to universal moral values and ties one's own self-esteem to similar treatment of others. Wittgenstein's work on the problem of other minds, for example, suggests that if it were not for language we would lack any knowledge of other minds. The thing that causes us to recognize other minds is the fact that before we get to the problem of other minds, we use a sentence whose structure is reciprocal. The statement "I can see you" implies "You can see me." So there is something in the structure of language that makes people both an "I" and a "me," a distinction reified in psychological work on the self, as discussed in chapter 7.[69] The statement "I can see a car" does not imply "the car can see me," however, since the car does not have language. Because both Bert and Rosie (for example) speak language, Bert and Rosie are both subjects, in the Kantian sense of sentient beings, and all subjects have the same rights. The reciprocal nature of language puts all those who use language into the same category of sentient beings.[70] We thus can use the reciprocity of language to get to reciprocity of treatment in an ethical sense. This link between linguistic and ethical reciprocity is reinforced by the psychoanalytic work on categorization, which suggests that we are "the other" to other people, just as they are "the other" to us. Thus there is an inherent reciprocal aspect to our human natures because of the psychological need for boundaries and the linguistic need for categorization.

CONCLUSION

Does the moral psychology described above capture—or at least allow for—the empirical reality for people like the rescuers? I believe so. Certainly the literature on the Holocaust suggests that rescuers of Jews during World War II spoke constantly of both Jews *and* Nazis as "people just like us." Utilizing common categorization seemed to require equal treatment of both groups, regardless of how the rescuer felt about the individual Jew or the particular Nazi. Similarly, genocidalists appeared to psychologically distance themselves from neighbors once considered friends, relegating them to the subhuman category in order to justify mistreating them. Reclassification and recategorization seem to be critical parts of the psychological process by which other human beings are declared "unworthy of life."[71] At different points in time, many discriminated groups—Jews, Muslims, Armenians, American Indians, African Americans—have been categorized as less than human by those who persecuted them.[72] These are but a few illustrations of my point that people's categorization influences their treatment of others, a point also supported by the vast experimental literature on self-categorization and social identity theory.[73] I encourage others to examine further instances of the treatment of others—from prejudice, ethnic violence, and genocide to altruism, cooperation, and collective behavior, including wars and domestic and international policymaking—through the lens of identity and categorization.

The empirical evidence found in the rescuers' stories thus is supported by linguistic, psychoanalytic, and social psychological work on categorization suggesting both that people do categorize and that such categorizations are a universal part of human nature. Once people create such categories, furthermore, they seem to feel as if they must accord equal treatment to all individuals within such categories. This suggests that the drive toward morality may emanate in our basic human psychology. Human beings who wish to be treated well must recognize and honor the humanity of others if they wish to claim it in themselves.

A Different Way of Seeing Things

IF THERE IS ONE POINT I hope to convey in this book it is the power of identity to shape our most basic political acts, including our treatment of others. How we see ourselves, and how we see others in relation to ourselves, has profound implications for our behavior. This often works in subtle and unconscious ways.

I have delayed publishing this book much longer than I should have. I began my interviews with some of these people in 1988. Even allowing for the everyday distractions of life and the demands of scholarship, sixteen years is a long time. I can explain some of this simply: I could not bear to part with the rescuers. Holding onto their stories was a way of keeping the rescuers close to me, and I held off sharing them in the way one clings to that private time with a lover, before he is introduced to your friends or family and the sweet intimacy takes on a new and more public dimension.

But there was something else as well, something that even now eludes my ability to articulate or even comprehend it fully.

I have spent hours poring over the rescuers' stories, listening to the tapes again and again, trying to make sure I had captured each rescuer's voice, had understood what the rescuers had entrusted to me. Trying, with limited literary skills, to convey a sense of the interaction, when so much of their message was too subtle and elusive for me to be sure I grasped it myself.

Academics are taught to be analytical and impartial. The rescuers taught me something different. They forced me to leave the safety of the scholar-subject relationship and challenged me to become a friend and a repository. I was not prepared for this, and it changed me.

One rescuer, a German Jew who is not considered here because he wished to be interviewed "off the record," explained why he had remained steadfastly optimistic, even cheerful, throughout the war. He spoke of the pain and confusion felt by refugees and Resistance workers after the fall of France. "There were many suicides," he said. "For most of us, it was like the fall of civilization. As if the barbarians had taken over the world we once knew, and there was no hope."

"I couldn't be that way," he said. "I was always happy. If I had given up my optimism, I couldn't have lived."

This sense—that one had to look at life realistically, not ignore its ugliness, and yet still smile in order to live—resonated at a deep level for me. It is to this kind of message in the rescuers' stories that I would like to turn now, even though the message may be deeply personal and poorly understood.

In doing so, however, I do not want to minimize the other important parts of the rescuers' stories, and perhaps any accounting should begin with the more obvious and easier to understand implications of the rescuers' narratives.

The stories of individual rescuers have historical significance, the importance of which should be neither overlooked nor minimized. In his preface to *Divided Memory: The Nazi Past in the Two Germanys,* Jeffrey Herf notes: "History is the realm of choice and contingency. Writing history is a matter of reconstructing the openness of past moments before choices congealed into seemingly inevitable structures."[1] The rescuers' stories have a freshness that captures this openness of the past. They remind us that other options were available, that the Holocaust need not have occurred.

Each story documents specific events, and this documentation becomes more valuable as witnesses die and—incredibly—a pernicious revisionism seeks to deny or minimize the existence of the Holocaust.[2] Some stories touch on controversial historical issues, as does Otto's suggestion that Churchill was in contact with the German Resistance and knew in advance about the July 20 plot to kill Hitler. If Otto is correct that Churchill promised some kind of conditional surrender in exchange for Hitler's removal, despite his assurances to the Allies that he would never agree to such a plan, historians will have to revise their assessment of Churchill's wartime activities.[3]

Other stories focus on the role of the ordinary German in supporting the Holocaust. In this regard, the stories of the German rescuers carry particular weight by reminding us that there were Germans at all points along the moral continuum. Not all Germans were Nazis, and not all Nazis were German.[4]

As a corollary to this, the rescuers' stories send the strong message that good and bad exist in all people, and that we must constantly fight those forces that draw forth the bad and encourage those that speak to the better angels of our nature. Ironically, it is the rescuers who insist that this is as true for Nazis as it is for the rest of us. As one Dutch rescuer said:

I don't feel that the Nazis are monsters. I never felt that way. The Nazis were normal German people who, through education, training, cultural thinking, and greed, ended up where they were. And

tomorrow it's our people. And the day after tomorrow, it's somebody else. History teaches you that the minute you destroy an enemy, you look behind you and he's standing there in your own ranks.
You have to many times look in the mirror to make very sure that he
hasn't crept into your head. . . . We have to watch for the old "yellow gooks" mentality. It is much easier to shoot at or burn the "yellow gooks" than to shoot at and burn some other farm boy just like
yourself. But the evil and the good can be in all of us. Good and bad
is in all of us. You have to look in the mirror. We're always looking
in the mirror. (Tony)

In an age plagued with ethnic violence, sectarian hatred, and a tendency
toward isolation in the safety of our own groups, this message may not
be a popular one. Certainly it is not comfortable to be reminded that
each of us carries within us the seeds of prejudice and the ability to harm
others, if only through insensitivity, inattentiveness, or cowardice. But it
is important to remember that genocide, ethnic violence, discrimination,
and stereotyping can occur anywhere, among any people. No one group
is immune.

The rescuers' stories yield further insight into broader issues of ethics
and morality. As we saw in chapter 6, the rescuers' stories reveal both the
complexity and the multiplicity of forces driving the moral life. As we
read the rescuers' stories, we find many different factors contributing to
their moral acts: duty, outrage, religion, an innate moral sense, socialization, role modeling and mentors, even a desire to show off. It is true that
all of these factors provide impetus for moral action; but the many times
when such influences are absent makes it prudent to conclude that these
forces constitute facilitating but not necessarily essential drives toward
doing good.

What is perhaps more striking, as we sort through the myriad possible
forces driving morality, is one startling omission: the lack of choice. Instead of the agonistic choice that lies at the heart of traditional explanations for much of ethics, we find identity. This is not to discount the
importance of other influences on the moral life; it merely suggests the
tremendous and too frequently overlooked role played by identity in
shaping our actions. Character counted more than the influences traditionally said to provide the impetus behind moral action, and emotions
and feelings trumped the cool and impartial calculus of reason.[5] The opportunity to spend time with the rescuers, to walk around inside their
heads, if you will, provides us with closely drawn cognitive portraits of
moral exemplars. This exercise provides empirical foundation for philosophical accounts of virtue ethics and for our more general understanding
of why it is so important to develop good moral character.

In this regard, it is perhaps significant that character is not all. Indeed, it was the sense of one's self *in relation to other people* that seemed the decisive factor for these rescuers. A critical aspect of this sense seemed to center on perceptions.[6] It is not just identity but also the perception of the relationship between the rescuer and "the other" that supplied the moral imperative to act. Because the rescuers saw themselves as people strongly committed to certain moral principles, because they did not accept the Nazis' characterization of the Jews as in any category other than the one to which all human beings belong, and because they felt all human beings were entitled to decent treatment merely by virtue of being human, the rescuers genuinely could not "see" any other option than to help their fellow human beings. To do otherwise was, literally, unimaginable.

This leads directly to a point close to the heart of any discussion of ethics and morality: what constitutes moral action. For the rescuers, the core of a universal morality was human welfare, not religious exhortations, systems of moral rules, or adherence to abstract ethical concepts such as fairness or justice. It was this belief in the sanctity of human life that was so integrated into the rescuers' sense of self. The integration of this particular moral value then left rescuers with no other option, even when presented with what appeared—at least to others—as agonistic choices. It meant rescuers would discard their learned rules of behavior when necessary to save a human life. For the rescuers, the moral choice was a reflection of their most fundamental identities, and these identities were intricately defined by the belief in the sanctity of human life and well-being.

The rescuers shed light on what we might think of as the moral psychology. Their stories suggest a process by which universal and possibly innate human needs for consistency[7] and self-esteem[8] provide a foundation for moral action that may be related to but not dependent on religion, reason, or externally imposed rules or laws.

How does the moral psychology operate? Much of this process remains speculative, but certain critical factors are clear and suggest the following components play vital roles: (1) the desire for self-esteem and the need for continuity of self-image; (2) core values stressing the sanctity of life and human well-being; (3) the integration of these values into our underlying self-concept or sense of who we are; (4) external stimuli that activate those parts of our multifaceted and complex identity that relate to this basic self-concept; and (5) an emotional component to the way we notice the needs of others so that we feel a sense of moral imperative to respond to another's suffering.

Perspective—the way rescuers saw themselves in relation to others—thus created a sense of moral salience. It did so through activating the rescuers' self-concept that in turn triggered a sense of moral imperative so that rescuers felt the needs of others were relevant for them.

If we wish to extrapolate from this empirical analysis—to understand how linking the needs of another to our sense of self creates the moral salience that leads to moral choice—then listening to the rescuers suggests something like the following process in which how we categorize and classify others influences our treatment of them.

Each of us wants to be treated well. Once we recognize that other people have a similar need, we are led to extend these universal rights of entitlement reciprocally, treating others as we ourselves wish to be treated. The moral psychology is reminiscent of tenets found in both religious teachings (for example, Christianity's Golden Rule) and philosophical systems of ethics (for example, Kant's categorical imperative). Insofar as this ethical reciprocity is a fundamental correlate of the human capacity for intersubjective communication and the psychological need to distinguish boundaries via categorization, however, such an ethical reciprocity appears more basic than an intellectualized sense of duty or religious doctrine. Indeed, the power of such religious or philosophical admonitions actually may emanate from their resonance with the basic moral psychology. It is possible that the moral psychology originates in a kind of innate moral sense, which then develops differentially in phenotypic fashion, depending on external forces in the environment.[9] This theoretical conclusion is speculative, however, and must await further empirical examination.[10]

Finally, the rescuers' stories underscore the tremendous power of identity as an influence on behavior toward others. For the rescuers, certain moral values had become so intricately integrated into their basic sense of who they were that their commitment to these values—human life and well-being—shaped the core of their identity. It thus became unthinkable for rescuers to intentionally engage in behavior that would contradict the essence of their identity.[11] The incorporation of these values into the rescuers' sense of self effectively created boundaries in their self-image that then limited and foreclosed any debate about transgressing these values. Because the particular moral values discussed above were so integrated into each rescuer's core identity, these commitments took on a quality of unquestioning quasi-finality, as witnessed by John's statement about never even considering whether he would reveal information under torture.[12] The extent to which these values had become integrated into the rescuers' identities is further illustrated by the extent to which rescuers performed similar altruistic acts both before and after World War II. It is evident in the degree to which rescuers' acts were not marked by any of the inner battles or hesitations we frequently associate with agonistic moral choices. And the integration is evident in the lack of choice and the absence of calculation of risks, costs, and benefits.[13]

This influence from identity is thus complex and subtle but extensive. It should not be ignored by social and political theorists. In part, the rescuers show us an alternative way of viewing one's self, one at odds with the current vogue in both academic circles and public discourse, which tends to posit a dichotomous view of an individual's relationship to others.[14] This dichotomy has appeared in many forms at different points in time[15] but essentially juxtaposes the individual with the group or community, and poses a tension between following individual self-interest versus caring for others.

Regardless of how analytically useful this dichotomy may be, the rescuers suggest this tension may be more an artificial construct than it is an innate part of the human psychology. Certainly, the rescuers raise interesting questions for us concerning our ties to others and what we need to flourish as individuals.[16] We cannot separate the question of identity from a search to understand how human connection relates to human flourishing.[17] The psychological literature tells us how basic and fundamental is our need for recognition and acknowledgment. We are not merely atomistic individuals, and our need for others is more than our need for their cooperation in our own individualistic enterprises or even for help in ensuring individual survival. It is instead a fundamental part of our human nature to crave acceptance, validation, and affirmation from others. We can find self-esteem and self-respect only when others help us claim it.[18] The challenge is to figure out how this connection is made and with whom. This is the point at which the rescuers' message becomes more elusive, although perhaps even more important.

What do the rescuers tell us about this connection? For the rescuers, any "choice" to save Jews was described as part of a broader decision concerning the kind of person one was. Rescuers' insistence on the ordinary aspect of their acts suggests rescue activities were not considered agonistic moral choices so much as the natural steps on a path chosen by a prior molding as a certain kind of human being. To have turned away from the Jews would have meant turning away from one's self. By showing us this, the rescuers remind us how important our relations with others become in preserving our own identities.[19] As one rescuer said, "I think that we all have memories of times that we should have done something and we didn't. And it gets in your way during the rest of your life" (Marion).[20]

Identity constrains action, but acts, in turn, shape and chisel at one's identity as we construct a life. It is this insight that offers us a different way of seeing things. By providing us a close, personal view of this moral perspective, the rescuers reveal an alternative way to view the self, one that recognizes the link between our treatment of others and our own sense of self-worth. For the rescuers, identity and perceptions were critical factors in their treatment of Jews. It was the rescuers' sense of human connection that caused them to risk their lives for other human beings. But this human connection also provided rescuers with something critical to their own well-being.

I said in the introduction that this was a book about loss and love, and that to understand moral choice during the Holocaust we would have to enter those dark places of our own souls, places we avoid much of the time. I meant this in part as a caution that the rescuers' stories take us to a terrible time in history, one that is deeply disturbing for most of us to read about. But perhaps an equally unsettling aspect of these stories is the extent to which examining the lives of these people forces us to ask troubling questions about our own lives.

World War II was a period when people could not avoid difficult questions. They had to confront the unimaginable. It was a time when people had to be their big selves. They could not easily evade issues of character. But character did not always predict behavior. Good people were not always the ones who rose to the occasion, and scoundrels sometimes did.

The rescuers met the challenge. When tested, they showed themselves to be people who were morally exemplary. Indeed, we still find ourselves filled with awe and admiration for them. But—and perhaps this is as important—they are exemplars who are easy to love. They have foibles, eccentricities, failed marriages, bumpy relations with their children. Their very humanness makes them more endearing, more accessible, more like us. And therein lies both their value and their ability to disturb our moral composure.

One incident with Margot sticks out in my mind, a visit when Margot showed me the book she had written about her beloved fiancé, Alfred. I interpret Margot's efforts in this unpublished book as her attempt to deal with the powerful emotions left from the war. I was struck by Margot's touching ambivalence about revealing writing that so fully captures who she is and how she thinks. The fact that Margot wrote the book in the third person, and was so tentative about sharing it with me. Her phrase: "I'd like you to see it but I can't give it away." All these indicators are subtle and I may be reading too much into them, but they seem evidence of how deeply felt is Margot's need for connectedness and the powerful force this bond, established with Alfred, still holds for Margot fifty years after his death. As painful as it was to lose this relationship, Margot's book also suggests the importance of human connection in enabling a decent and sensitive woman to hold on to her sanity, to maintain a sense of self that is wounded but not destroyed by the horrors of war.[21]

The introduction to Margot's book seems to represent Margot's attempt to understand or at least to reflect on the meaning of her life:

> It has been said many times that one might be able to relive one's past. I don't believe this. However, if it were at all possible, I hear people say that they would return to Mother Earth as the very same person they are now. But they would change most of the events and occurrences that happened in their lives. They swore that they would not repeat the mistakes they had made but would instead alter the flow of happenings and thus reconstruct the course of history. Impossible. I believe in all the wonderful and tragic moments and would never change one instant in my life, even if I could. The trials, errors, heartaches, delights, and ecstasies are part of life itself. The deep love of two beings melted into one is the ultimate fulfillment. The hardships that teach understanding form the character within one's self. The injustices against the innocent are the experience and knowledge of grim reality. Above all, there is the ability to help and alleviate the pain of fellow human beings. This I believe is the ultimate goal of our short existence on this earth.

This passage eloquently communicates the subtle but powerful aspect of human connection in providing not just friendship and the pleasures of sociability—valuable as these are—but also a fundamental human need to find meaning in life and to discover a sense of ourselves through others. It captures the power of human connection in providing the rescuers not only with the ability to save others but also with the awareness that their recognition of another's humanity was part of what gave meaning to their own lives. The end of this book, in which Margot puts some of herself on paper—in a manuscript she wants to give me but still can't bear to part with because it represents who she is—reads:

> All at once, she felt a hand on her shoulder. She looked up but saw no one. Yet she could feel her beloved Alfred beside her saying, as once he did so long ago, "Do not stand on my grave and weep. I am not there. I do not sleep. I am a thousand winds that blow. I am the diamond in the snow. I am the sunlight on ripened grain. I am the gentle Autumn's rain. When you awaken in the morning's hush, I am the swift uplifting rush of quiet birds in circled flight. I am the soft stars that shine at night. Do not stand at my grave and cry. I am not there. I did not die."[22]

Margot's moving expression of the value of human connection was not unique. I experienced similar exchanges with other rescuers. As Irene related her full story, talking about how some of the people she had saved during the war later came back into her life, I asked what she had learned of them and of the other people she knew during the war. Had Irene been able to make sense of all these events, I wondered. Was she able to find any meaning in what had happened to her?

Q. What I'm hearing you say is that it's very difficult to maintain the kind of human communication during a war. That because of the situation, individuals are forced to choose up sides of one kind. But that you and the people you associated with were able to reach across those barriers and find some kind of human communication, a bond. The major. Ida and her little boy. A major who could have turned you all in, who did something in some ways which was very unfair to you, but which was motivated out of love and affection.

Yes, because it was. I mean he did really love me. I cannot say that he was brutal. He was not beating me or anything. He was very direct, very allowing, expressing himself. He would say, "Irene, is that so bad? I keep your secret. I will help you. And you give old man the last joy in his life."

Q. Then after the war, the people that he had helped, in turn helped him, and he becomes a grandfather to the boy [Ida's son].

You see! It is such a story I wanted to tell. That there are bad and good people. I am not trying to put hate on any particular group. The time is for us to reach to each other. That's the only way we can be safe, even now.

Human connection was the key. Their sense of being connected to the Jews through bonds of a common humanity was what drove the rescuers to do the impossible, to save people from the clutches of an all-powerful state. "For them, it was a natural thing to save people, to remain human. And they didn't know it, but in doing so, they changed history."[23]

The rescuers gave, gave generously and with no thought of repayment, to be sure. But this spontaneous giving had an unexpected consequence. Caring for others helped *them* remain connected, not just to others but to themselves. The fact that these rescuers—very human people all, not plaster saints—were able to remain aware of these bonds, even in the midst of unrelenting societal and political pressure to ignore such attachments, shows us both the power and the value of a different way of seeing the world. This way is not the simple calculus of self-interest we find in the Darwinian world of dog-eat-dog. It is not the scholarly world dominated by rational choice theory, or the policymaker's world of simple cost/benefit analysis. Nor is it the communitarian's world of groups, in which the mental image of "us-versus-them" can too easily turn "different from" into "better than," as it did for the Nazis.

Resistance to genocide is not just an affirmation of universalism in which every human being is entitled to rights and equal treatment by virtue of being born human. It is more than simply seeing the humanity in the Jews, more than seeing the bonds that connect us. It is also a cherishing, a celebration of all the differences—individual and group— that allow for human flourishing, set firmly within the context of universal worth. This is what the rescuers protected for all of us when they resisted genocide, prejudice, and ethnic violence. Their very ordinariness, their very humanness, encourages us to look deep within our own souls and ask if we, too, do not possess this possibility.

Narratives as Windows
on the Minds of Others

I HAVE ARGUED HERE that it is critical to understand how people see themselves, particularly in relation to others, if we want to understand their actions. The question then becomes how best can we do this, given that we can never enter into another's mind? In this appendix, let me suggest one route I found useful, give the particulars of this tool as a methodological instrument, and discuss both its strengths and its limitations as a part of social science research.[1]

Narratives—the stories people tell—provide a rich source of information about how people make sense of their lives. Narratives yield insight on how people collect and assemble the myriad disparate facts with which we all are bombarded.

Consider one trivial example illustrative of the manner in which the salience of facts may shift. The sky is blue. The grass is green. The car is yellow. The car is careening fast down the middle of the small country road. Which of these myriad bits of information is significant? How do I register each of these observations in my mind so that each becomes meaningful for me? How do I weave them together cognitively into a pattern that allows me to make sense of reality? In this trivial example, if I am picnicking in the middle of a huge meadow overlooking the country road, I may care about the weather and the terrain. If I am walking on the country road toward the meadow and see a car speeding toward me, I am less interested in the color of the sky or even the color of the car than I am in the fact that I may be about to be killed.

Listening carefully to how people construct the stories of their lives—their narrative analysis—is particularly useful in providing insight on the cognitive process and on the role of culture in shaping any human universals. It is especially helpful in detecting the moral psychology, the subject of this book. Let me provide a brief discussion of this technique since some of these issues may be of interest to other scholars.

I begin by defining narrative as a concept and as a methodological tool in social science. I then provide a brief intellectual background on how narrative developed in literary theory and how it since has come to be applied in cognitive analysis. This section also discusses narratives as sites of cultural contestation and the role of narrative in the construction of social theory. I conclude on a note of caution, suggesting the need for care when interpreting narratives and drawing inferences based on faint clues. This is a problem confronting all analysts dealing with any traumatic memories held by people who are now elderly. It is not particular to the Holocaust.

Narrative: A Story. A narrative is essentially a story, a term more often associated with fiction than with political science. Yet narrative also refers to the ways in which we collect disparate facts in our own worlds and arrange them cognitively into a design that helps us find order, and perhaps even meaning, in our reality. Narrative thus becomes an invaluable tool in navigating the myriad sensations that bombard us daily. Insofar as narratives affect our perceptions of political reality, which in turn affect our actions in response to or in anticipation of political events, these narratives help us understand ourselves as political beings. In a similar sense, when we create and use narratives to interpret and understand the political realities around us, narrative plays a critical role in the construction of political behavior. We do this as individuals and we do it as collective units, as nations or groups.

As a research methodology, narrative finds many applications in a multitude of disciplines, from anthropology and literary theory to history and psychoanalysis. Narrative is utilized as one of the most widespread and powerful forms of discourse in human communication. It differs from other modes of discourse and other modes of organizing experience in several important ways. (1) Narrative generally requires agency. It involves human beings as characters or actors. These human beings have a place in the plot, a role in the story. When narrative emphasizes human action that is directed toward goals, it provides insight on how different people organize, process, and interpret information and how they move toward achieving their goals. (2) Narrative suggests the speaker's view of what is canonical. What is ordinary and right is discussed as the matter of fact. The unusual and the exceptional are what are remarked on. For example, a contemporary speaker would find it quite remarkable to come across instances of societies believing in the divine rights of kings or brother and sister marriages among members of the royal family, yet these practices were widespread and normal to a member of Tudor England (divine rights of kings) or ancient Egypt (brother-sister marriages). Narrative thus provides data for analysis not only in spoken responses but also in the spaces and silences. (3) Narrative requires some sequential ordering of events, but the events themselves need not be real. The story constructed may be indifferent to extralinguistic reality; it is the sequence of the sentences, the way events are recounted (rather than the truth or falsity of any of the particular sentences or of the events recounted), that reveals the speaker's mode of mental organization. How the speaker organizes events to give meaning to them is what becomes important, for it is the process of organization that reveals much about the speaker's mind. (4) Narrative requires the narrator's perspective. It cannot be voiceless. It thus moves beyond mere reporting; it suggests how the speakers make sense of the commonplace. It reveals how the speakers organize experience and reveals the distinctions people make in their everyday lives. The speakers create the context to be analyzed by drawing in what they consider relevant cultural influences. This makes the narrative contextually thick. It provides a sense of speakers' cognitive maps of themselves, both in relation to others and in the specific contexts of their described behavior.

Narrative is especially useful in revealing the speaker's concept of self, for it is the self that is located at the center of the narrative, whether as active agent, passive experiencer, or tool of destiny. In at least one sense, narratives function as autobiographical accounts given by the narrator in the present about a protagonist who bears the same name, who existed in the past, and who blends into the present speaker as the story ends. The story explains and justifies why the life went a particular way, not just causally but, at some level, morally. The narrator uses the past self to point to and explain the present and the future. This is as true on the individual level as it is on the macrolevel, when groups of people describe a common past suggesting why they have a collective identity that should be recognized as legitimate by others.

When we interpret narratives, we can perform the kind of linguistic analysis that a cognitive scientist or linguistic scholar might perform, focusing on lexical and grammatical usages or counting types of structures. Alternatively, our interest in interpretation may be less technical, focusing primarily on how people conceive of themselves and of themselves in relation to others. The narrative thus becomes an invaluable tool for political scientists concerned with how such issues as identity—group or individual—influence behavior.

Irene's story illustrates this aspect of narrative in a most touching manner. Irene was one of the first two people I interviewed. Although I had taken notes during our interview, I had not remembered what struck me quite vividly when I first read the transcribed interview. The words in black type jumped out at me from the page: "I am a survivor. I am alone." The fact that these were the first words of our interview, the way Irene chose to begin our conversations, seemed a significant revelation about how she saw herself. But Irene's story also illustrates the shifting aspects of narrative, a phenomenon that makes narrative particularly rich in that it captures the extent to which real people have multiple dimensions to their personalities, dimensions that are not immediately evident but that often will reveal themselves over a long time period. People often change, as Irene did during the time in which she was speaking with me.

Over the course of the next years that I spent with Irene, as my conversations with her continued, Irene increased her speaking engagements, telling of her experiences during World War II, so that people would know what had happened during that time. She was particularly concerned that young people know how pernicious ethnic stereotypes could be. Unfortunately, as Irene's traveling schedule increased, her husband became ill, suffering a series of strokes and the onset of Alzheimer's. A story about this in a local paper prompted a Jewish home for the elderly to make an extraordinary gesture. They would take in Irene's husband, even though he was not Jewish and despite the fact that their policies forbade them from taking stroke patients who could not care for themselves. "We owe her," the director said, in explaining why he was breaking the rules.

Irene was extremely touched and grateful and asked that anything I publish about her made it clear how much she owed the Jewish people. What had been true for Irene throughout most of our interviews—the sense that she was in no-man's-land, distrusted by the Jews because she was a Polish Catholic and unwelcome by the Poles because she had helped the Jews—was eased and, perhaps, changed. Irene felt she was no longer quite so alone.

This shift in self-concept, subtle though it may be, illustrates the changing aspect of narrative and suggests the shifts in the interview process that give an asymptotic quality to our knowledge of other human beings. It also underlines how fraught with difficulties is the scholar's task in understanding complex human beings.

The Use of Narrative in Political and Social Science.   Since the origins of narrative as a contemporary method of analysis in social science is inextricably entwined with the idea of story, as a methodological tool it became unavoidably imbued with the aura of fiction. This position can be uncomfortable for political scientists for whom the drive for scientific rigor can serve as a wedge between the discipline of political science and innovations in the humanities. Nonetheless, narrative has been gaining a foothold as a useful concept in the social sciences in recent years as a methodology for rigorous research.

Martin (1996) traces the emergence of recent theories of narrative to attempts to establish the novel as a valid area of literary study. During the earlier half of the 20th century, the dominant theory argued that the aesthetic value of a literary piece lay in the perfection of its form and technique. Poetry and drama were seen as valid areas of literary study due to their attention to form and technique, whereas novels were not because of their apparently haphazard and disorderly nature. The attempt to overturn that dominant line of thought and to establish the literary value of the novel led to theories of form, structure, and technique in the novel. If the value of poetry and drama lay in form, it was argued, then the way to demonstrate the value of the novel was to show that it, too, could be subjected to critical analysis of form and technique. As this perspective took hold in the late 1940s and 1950s, other scholars argued that the value of the novel lay not in its form but in its content and effect on the reader. From either perspective, however, the realism of the novel was paramount. Accomplished novels were judged to be those in which the world or the mind was portrayed accurately and in which the author did not intrude or make his/her presence known. The distinction between form and content was thus generally accepted, even as their relative importance was being disputed.

Are There Universals in Narrative, or Is It All Cultural?   Challenges to the primacy of the realistic novel and its emphasis on impersonal narration opened the way for a shift from theories of the novel to theories of narrative. During the 1960s, the study of narrative became both international and interdisciplinary. French structuralism drew on linguistics as a model for theorizing a basic underlying set of principles connecting all narratives.[2] One of the most influential scholars to demonstrate the applicability of linguistics to other social sciences and other forms of narrative was anthropologist Levi-Strauss (1967). Levi-Strauss distinguished between surface structure (the unique details of particular action sequences) and deep structure (universal oppositions, such as life/death, that are manifest in the surface structure in particular ways depending on culture and context). In addition to linguistics and anthropology, influences came from Russian formalists, notably Propp (1928/1968), Bakhtin (1975/1981), and Shklovsky (1990). Structuralist work in a variety of disciplines demonstrates that narratives contribute to our understanding of subjects as disparate as anthropology and history or theology and psychoanalysis, even though the narrative forms in these areas differ significantly from those in the novel. Despite theoretical differences, many structural anthropologists (Levi-Strauss 1967), French structuralists (Frye 1957), and Russian formalists (Propp 1928/1968) argue that all stories are variations on a few universal plots and that the study of such narratives can provide insight into universals of human nature and experience.

The idea that there are universals governing narrative structure, as well as the structure of language or the structure of consciousness, has been challenged by post-structuralists such as Lyotard (1984), Derrida (1967/

1976, 1972/1981), and Foucault (1976/1980, 1984). Post-structuralism largely rejects any attempt to seek out universal structures of human nature, culture, history, or language. Derrida, for instance, uses the method of deconstruction to argue that spoken or written language (signifier) is never a perfect reference to a knowable object (signified), because neither signifier nor signified remains fixed or stable; they are always shifting. Foucault challenges historical methodologies that provide coherent and seamless narratives, especially those viewing history as the story of progress toward some final goal. His alternative—genealogy—is a method of history that allows for ruptures without explanations and that emphasizes history as an assemblage of moments rather than an unfolding, unbroken chain of events in which one link leads necessarily to the next. Hence, Derrida and Foucault challenge narrative in all its forms, to the extent that narrative suggests a coherent, unbroken, and totalizing theory, that is, a depiction that appears "total," without lapses, discontinuities, erasures, or contradictions.

So why is narrative so frequently associated with postmodernism? Perhaps because narrative is also associated with a kind of knowledge that post-structuralists champion. Post-structuralists seek to subvert grand, universal, totalizing theories through reference to knowledge that is local, specific, and popular. One of the characteristics of postmodern cultural practices is a blurring or rejection of lines that divide popular and high cultures. Theoretical practices echo this maneuver by drawing on popular forms of knowledge to challenge more officially sanctioned ways of scientific knowing. Narrative, which plays an important role in local, everyday knowledge, becomes part of the challenge to universal theories. Hence, post-structuralism, which cannot propose a totalizing theory of narrative, nonetheless makes use of narrative in various ways. It challenges the illusion of coherence created by narrative form, and it uses knowledge that often takes the form of narrative in culture.

Bearing Witness, an Oral Culture.   Theories that emphasize the recurring and critical role of narrative in the construction of meaning challenge the distinctions among such narrative forms as novels, folktales, and histories. They also challenge the assumptions that separate true narratives from fictions, higher forms of literature from common folktales, scholarly writing from popular writing, and the social sciences from the humanities. Despite such challenges, the usefulness of literary theories and insights for the social sciences often remains obscure. While noting the applicability of theories of narrative to provinces other than literature, theories of narrative nonetheless remain overwhelmingly directed toward fictional prose, masking the connection between the often esoteric literary theories and the broader applications they suggest.

Let me note two important and persistent areas into which narrative theories do cross academic boundaries. The first is the discipline of history (see White 1981). The immediate applicability of the puzzles of narrative theory to history makes sense because history is concerned with assembling events into meaningful sequences, with all of the concomitant problems of deciding where those sequences begin and end, what events are to be included, and what sequence counts as the most accurate. The second is psychoanalytic theory. In this approach, the wanderings of the speaker are supposed to reveal the thoughts often blocked by the subconscious. The analyst is supposed to help the analysand make connections that then help resolve inner conflicts. This approach, widely utilized in political psychology, is often criticized as being too heavy-handed in its strict Freudian embodiment. It nonetheless remains a useful tool for the kinds of psychoethnography utilized by Coles (1967, 1971, 1989) or by scholars of personality and leadership (Glad 1990; Greenstein 1982; Renshon 1996; Winter and Smith 2000). Such a technique can be especially useful when the analyst does not have direct access to the political leader or decision maker. (Studies of Politburo statements or content analysis can be viewed as a form of narrative.) Narrative is also widely utilized in creating personality profiles useful for understanding decision making, foreign policy relations, and terrorism. Lately, it has been utilized to understand marginalized groups, such as religious fundamentalists (Kreidie 2000) or people moving between two cultures (Lerner 1992; Rudolph and Rudolph 2002). These are just some of the many connections between narrative theory and other disciplines.

Narrative and Ordinary Discourse: A Cognitive View. Narrative plays a central role in cognition, in organizing our perceptions of reality into a coherent and meaningful pattern. One of the founders of artificial intelligence, Bruner has recently (1996) criticized psychology and cognitive science for underemphasizing the role of narrative in human affairs, arguing that narrative is critical in the meaning-making of everyday life. He connects narrative with the project of finding one's own place in the world. Both Bruner and Martin (1996) underscore the human need to locate oneself in a story about how the world progresses and how one fits into it. This need is clearly illustrated by how children play at being grown up and suggests how children enter into a culture and how they use stories to wrestle with the emotional difficulties accompanying maturation. Children act out difficulties with toilet training, adjusting to school, or accepting the birth of a sibling. They imagine growing up, finding jobs, and leaving home. Child's play thus becomes a rehearsal of stories and their variations, and those stories are about fitting into the world.

We never stop telling ourselves stories because it is how we make sense of our place in the world, what came before, where we are now, and where we are headed. Even as adults, we continue to imagine our futures, families, careers, retirements, and major transitions. In a series of award-winning books, Coles has utilized stories to create a kind of psychiatric ethnography in which stories are employed to capture and explicate the reaction of children and adults to a wide variety of stress, sometimes induced by political situations such as the civil rights movement in the South (1967), sometimes by economic disaster such as endemic poverty (1971), and sometimes merely by the everyday adjustment to the demands of professional life (1989).

The stories we tell are profoundly influenced by what is possible and what is valued within our culture. In a high-tech media age, an array of possible stories is provided by television shows and movies that display glamorous, exciting, and naughty alter egos or, for those weary of the fast pace, bucolic pastorals where life is simpler and more peaceful. Bruner (1996) notes the critical psychological function provided by alternative narratives—and thus alternative selves—within a culture where some people are excluded or mistreated by the dominant modes of imagining lives and progress. When narratives of culturally acceptable success are not available or are beyond imagination for a particular group, subcultures provide alternative ways to make sense of one's place in the world. (Folktales provide one obvious instance of this. Indeed, nationalist movements often make use of folk stories in their attempts to unify a people.) The importance of having such culturally available narratives, and the danger of not having narratives of success available, partially explains the insistence of marginalized groups that their stories also be represented within the mainstream media, such as efforts in the United States to include more minority heroes in history books.

Bruner is aware of the skepticism with which social scientists may view something as apparently imprecise and dependent on interpretation as narrative. He addresses this skepticism in a discussion of narrative's role in epistemology by contrasting the process of interpretation with that of explanation. Bruner argues that although explanation and interpretation are not synonymous, neither can exist without the other. Explanation involves causal statements that can be proven or disproven, such as scientific hypothesis testing. Interpretation, on the other hand, is concerned with understanding, which Bruner defines as "the outcome of organizing and contextualizing essentially contestable, incompletely verifiable propositions in a disciplined way" (1996: 90). What can be explained through falsifiable hypotheses is necessarily limited. What can be explained also must be interpreted and understood. One of the most important tools for interpretation is narrative.

Bruner defines narrative as a sequence of events that carries meaning and is justified, at least in part, by the fact that it somehow violates what is normal or expected. We do not narrate all the details of any circumstance; what we choose to narrate is generally noteworthy because it stands out by posing a problem or exception. The point of the narrative is to resolve the imbalance or uncertainty of the problem and to restore equilibrium. As such, all narratives are essentially normative, even when the voice of the narrator is well hidden. By suggesting both what is a norm and what is a departure from the norm, all narrative suggests an interpretation of what the state of the world ought to be. Using a similar argument, historian White (1981: 23) makes an even stronger claim, suggesting that all narrative moralizes judgments.

When the subject of narration deals with the common or everyday, narrative serves to both highlight and call into question what we take for granted in our daily lives. It provides a way to see from a new perspective what we otherwise overlook. Hirschman's (1977) splendid discussion of the tacit assumptions underlying a historical period illustrates how the shifts in such assumptions were critical for understanding the cultural shift preceding the European transition to capitalism. Kracauer's (1947) creative use of films to trace the deterioration in bourgeois values in Weimar Germany and the growth of Nazi power performs a similar analysis in a shorter historical period.

Narratives as Sites of Cultural Contestation.   Narratives are important in providing both individuals and collectives with a sense of purpose and place. The shared stories of a culture provide grounds for common understandings and interpretation. But as such, they may become sites of cultural conflict when those common understandings are challenged. If narratives provide a way of understanding the world and locating oneself within the broader culture, then a movement that seeks to alter the structure of society also seeks to challenge the understanding of people within that society and, necessarily, the narratives that underpin those understandings. Challenges to such stock narratives are common as society reassesses its position on critical issues. (Note the challenge by Native American groups to the 1950s cowboys and Indians game or feminist rejection of many traditional fairy tales that depict women in passive roles.) These challenges may occur at the individual level long before the group itself shifts its view on the preferred narrative. For example, the lyrics Paul Robeson sang to "Old Man River" shifted as Robeson himself became less willing to accept the role society offered him as a black man.[3] And within the group challenging the narrative perceived as dominant, members may differ as to how the narrative should be redefined. (Sometimes these disagreements or ambivalence can focus on particular words.

Witness the shift over time as "Negro" became the preferred term, designating respect, and then later became a pejorative, as "black" came to be associated with the power of the group. The contemporary confusion and disagreement over whether "black," "person of color," or "African American" is the desired narrative label illustrates the ongoing nature of the political aspect of linguistic terminology.)

The above examples illustrate how people use folk narratives to modify and challenge particular ways of interpreting history and the existing relationships among people. Nowhere is this more starkly and politically demonstrated than in narratives of national identity. Stories about the origin and development of a nation provide a shared sense of who we are, where we came from, and how we fit together. These narratives permeate culture and are essential to any kind of collective functioning. They are passed on through the formal education system and play a significant role in the broader popular culture, as is evident in the United States. (There are, for example, clear differences among a rigorous course in U.S. history, a dramatic reading of "The Midnight Ride of Paul Revere," and a viewing of the film *How the West Was Won*, yet all three illustrate how a narrative conception of history constitutes a significant part of our socialization, via both formal and informal education.)

The political importance of commonly shared narratives means they often become the focus of political debate. The importance of the American story is reflected, for example, in the bitterness of disputes over the content of school curricula. Movies and poems are important manifestations of the American story, but schools are seen as the keepers of the most true and official versions. The drive to make school curricula more inclusive of diverse peoples and histories, or to emphasize or interpret historical moments differently, emanates not only from the desire to increase historical accuracy but also from a more fundamental challenge to that sense of who we are and how we relate (and have related) to each other. What might otherwise seem a clear-cut question of facts becomes vastly more complicated when we recognize that no history is without an implicit sense of protagonists and antagonists, no set of facts is without interpretations of what is important or relevant and what is not. Challenges to the standard curriculum are made with a sense of necessity and urgency, and these challenges are often met with a defensive and resentful reception. The particular narratives of U.S. history and identity that will prevail have profound implications for how we will proceed, because those stories produce serious material consequences. How we make sense of the world and our place in it guides how we act and how we understand other actors in our world. What is at stake in the telling of the American story has as much to do with the here and now—who we are today and where we are going—as it does with events and people long past.

Barber (1992) offers an intriguing analysis of the American story and the ways in which it is contested. He suggests that nearly all versions of the American story share an emphasis on liberty. Although different versions portray the achievement of liberty, the failure to keep the promise of liberty, or the struggle toward a free society, the competing interpretations, Barber argues, are all built on one common theme. The narrative of America thus is central in struggles for rights and the formation of group identities. Indeed, the single most important strategic decision faced by those who have felt left out of the American way of life has been whether to accept or reject the exceptionalist story; to buy into or spurn the rhetoric of rights; to try to possess the American founding, understood as the Declaration of Independence, the Constitution, and the Bill of Rights, as a story that belongs to us all—or to unmask and discard the founding as the hypocritical and deceitful strategy of the powerful seeking to legitimize their tyranny (1992: 71–72).

Hochschild's (1995) work on racial tensions employs a similar logic, arguing that a vaguely articulated but deeply held sense of the American dream provides a common identity for Americans, both black and white. When this dream is questioned, and in particular when certain groups feel the dream will never be attainable for them, the underlying unity of the country becomes threatened. In this sense, both political identity and political stability emanate from the sharing of a common narrative: the belief that in the United States all groups can eventually, with hard work, achieve some kind of success.

The relation between shared narratives and national history and identity extends far beyond the shores of the United States. The revisionist history that seeks to deny or minimize the Holocaust (see Shermer and Grobman 2000 for a review) is an attempt by certain groups to rewrite history and to rewrite their own personal narrative.[4] This effort also is evident in the developing of nationalist movements worldwide, as politicians often consciously rewrite history to achieve the political goals of the new national unit. Bruner (1996: 88) describes a visit from Russian officials struggling with questions of how to teach Russian history in the aftermath of the Communist regime. Did it make sense to portray the years of Communist rule as a mistake or deception? How should they understand and present the relationship between the telling of history and the construal of future possibilities? Postcolonial writings are full of questions about how to reconstruct historical narratives that were written to fit the purposes of colonial rulers. Spivak (1988: 198) says of the subaltern studies group, a collective of Indian historians, "They generally perceive their task as making a theory of consciousness or culture rather than specifically a theory of change."

A theory of consciousness perhaps must be implicit in any history of social change, because such a history not only tells what people did but also suggests some of the reasons why they did it. The "why" can become important and contested, especially if part of the project is to document a sense of agency and self-determination on the part of the formerly colonized. Is the history told from the perspective of resistance to colonial rule? From the perspective of the occupiers? As a story of will to self-determination? As a tale of international forces conspiring to push the occupiers to withdraw? Many versions could be accurately and meticulously documented but still be a source of contention, precisely because of the inherently interpretive nature of the undertaking and because of the interpretation's repercussions for how people understand themselves in relation to their history and the rest of the world. In this regard, the rescuers' stories, and the extraordinary way their narratives are free from the need for vengeance, are particularly instructive in showing us the political and personal importance of how we see things.

Narratives in Social Science Theory. Narratives circulate in more narrowly academic arenas just as they do in the broader culture, and they provide the foundation on which social theories are constructed. Somers and Gibson (1994) offer an argument about the role of narrative in social theories of action that is broadly applicable to the role of narrative in social science theorizing. They point out that the language and concepts of social science narratives are so embedded in our understanding that we fail to recognize them as historical products rather than as universal givens. As Somers and Gibson suggest, "Social theory is as much history and narrative as it is metatheory. In its construction all theory presumes a prior question to which the theory is designed to be an answer" (1994: 45). In other words, they argue that theory is built on a narrative of a problem to be solved. By tracing the emergence of the concepts by which we currently define our problems and shape our solutions, we gain new insights and possibilities.

This argument fits with the definition of narrative, offered by Bruner and others, as a sequence of events arranged around a problem and designed to restore equilibrium. In particular, one is reminded of Bruner's (1996) and White's (1981) observations about the normative or moralizing aspects of narrative. The concepts we use to build theory are themselves narratives, or the symptoms of narratives. Development, industrialization, the cold war, and class conflict are all built on stories about how the world has grown and changed, and they are infused with strong normative implications. This does not undermine the theoretical rigor of theories that use these concepts, but it should remind us that the very concepts on which we rely are themselves dependent on assembling events and interpreting them in a particular way. We cannot do without this kind of understanding, but we do better when we are able to reflect on how we come to understand in the particular ways that we do. (Pateman's 1988 feminist critique of social contract theory illustrates this.)

Building on the insights of such contemporary theorists as Ricoeur (1981) and Lyotard (1984), Somers and Gibson suggest a definition of narrativity with particular relevance to the social sciences. This definition contains four features. (1) "Relationality of parts" describes the need to make sense of events by placing them in relation to other events; isolated events by themselves tell us nothing. (2) "Causal emplotment" elaborates the relationship between elements. The slightly cumbersome word *emplotment* simply refers to locating the elements of the narrative in a plot so that there is a causal relationship among them. "In fact, it is emplotment that allows us to construct a significant network or configuration of relationships" (1994: 60). (3) "Selective appropriation" indicates that one chooses to incorporate some potential elements into the narrative and omit those that are less germane. The narrator must evaluate what is appropriate to include and what should be left out. (4) Taken together, "temporality," "sequence," and "place" form the fourth element of narrative, emphasizing how the elements of the plot are located with respect to each other. Somers and Gibson (1994: 59) summarize their definition as follows:

> Narrativity demands that we discern the meaning of any single event only in temporal and spatial relationship to other events. Indeed the chief characteristic of narrative is that it renders understanding only by connecting (however unstably) parts to a constructed configuration or a social network (however incoherent or unrealizable) composed of symbolic, institutional, and material practices.

While Somers and Gibson's definition resembles others, theirs offers the advantage of being explicitly suited to the social sciences and compatible with the kinds of narratives found in political science.

In addition to the above four features of narrative, Somers and Gibson differentiate among four separate kinds of narrative. (a) "Ontological narratives" are those we use to function as social actors. Although these ontological narratives are a social product, they are also our own particular stories. They help us make sense of who we are. Somers and Gibson argue that understanding ontological narratives is essential for any theory of agency. This suggests a connection between identity (understanding of self) and agency (the conditions for action). In other words, a theory of how people act to change their world requires an understanding of how people understand themselves. For example, do they understand themselves as autonomous individuals acting to uphold a principle, or as agents of some greater power? In other work (Monroe 1994a), I used this as ontological narrative to contrast rescuers with bystanders who saw themselves as passive agents, borne along on the winds of history and thus helpless to oppose the Nazi regime or shield its victims. (b) "Public narratives" are narratives of institutions or social formations. Ontological narratives build on public narratives. Who I understand myself to be will depend in part on how I understand the institutions in which I am embedded. For example, do I understand my community as a voluntary association from which I can withdraw, or do I feel bound by a greater sense of obligation emanating from group members by virtue of birth? (Tönnies 1957) (c) "Conceptual narratives," more narrowly, are those constructed by social researchers. In particular, social scientists create narratives of social forces such as path dependency, political institutionalization, and economic growth. Our challenge as social researchers, according to Somers and Gibson, is to construct a vocabulary that "can accommodate the contention that social life, social organizations, social action, and social identities are narratively, that is, temporally and relationally constructed through both ontological and public narratives" (1994: 63). In other words, our conceptual vocabulary should reflect an awareness of its historical and contingent nature. (d) "Meta-narrative," the fourth and final type of narrative, is sometimes called master narrative. Meta-narratives are the grand narratives of our time in which we are embedded as social actors, especially narratives of mastery and progress, such as economic development or the expansion of human rights. They also include epic dualities, such as the individual versus society or order versus chaos and anarchy, as was the narrative posed by the Nazis in seeking to define themselves as opponents of the Bolsheviks and the chaos of Weimar. Meta-narratives can be so ingrained in our common understanding that they are difficult to recognize and are often uncritically adopted as the central organizing concepts of our theories. Meta-narratives lack the self-awareness of conceptual narratives. They appear as abstractions and universals, erasing their own history and particularity. We can easily recognize master narratives by recalling distant historical times. The divine right of kings provides one example of a politically significant meta-narrative. Another is provided by the Nazis' construction of a meta-narrative in which the good (Germany after World War I) was vanquished by evil (decadent Jewish capitalism).

Somers and Gibson provide a vocabulary and taxonomy for making sense of the role of narratives in social theory. Somers and Gibson are interested in the problem of turning theories of social action from meta-narrative into conceptual narrative. Their vocabulary thus allows for both subjective and social forces by including ontological and public narratives, articulating both the distinction and the connection between narratives of the self and narratives of society. One might question the implicit distinction between lay narratives and the narratives of social scientists. Public narratives and conceptual narratives seem similar except that conceptual narratives are the province of those who theorize about society professionally. However, this distinction can be useful in encouraging social theorists to be more aware of the meaning-making activities in which we are engaged.

The Need for Caution: The Perils in Interpreting Narrative. The power of narrative carries with it the potential for abuse and manipulation, which suggests why social scientists interested in value-free, objective scientific analysis often find narrative suspect as a methodological tool. Understanding and interpreting a narrative is perhaps as much an art form as a methodology and must be attempted with extreme care.

Narrative as a research method usually involves the use of personal accounts of particular events or of one's entire life, as in the narratives in this book. The person telling the story is given wide latitude by the researcher in the telling of the stories. While the researcher may ask guiding or probing questions, the teller retains great discretion in deciding what to include and how to relate the story. (I discuss this more fully in appendix B.) Narrative methods therefore differ from interview methods that seek short answers to relatively specific questions or that closely structure the answers given by the speaker. Some of this unexpected aspect of narrative is what makes it so exciting for the analyst. (One German bystander's narrative illustrates this quite tellingly. I began by asking him to tell me a little bit about himself. He told me he was a Goth and launched into an extended account of how "his people" had sacked Rome, information that left me temporarily baffled and which few pre-designed survey questionnaires would have elicited [Monroe 1994a].)

Interviews are not the only source of narratives; research has been done using autobiographies, letters, and other kinds of personal narratives. Narrative interviews are useful both as an alternative to other kinds of interview or survey research and because they do not require the researcher to rely on currently retrievable documents. Narrative offers a potentially rich resource for research, but careful thought is required to determine what exactly narrative tells us and how it should be used.

Some use of narrative in research has challenged dominant modes of theorizing that either theorized badly about people's lived experience or, more likely, focused on the experience of a narrow band of the population and excluded the experience of others. Feminists[5] and theorists from often excluded groups have referred to narratives of personal experience to show how dominant modes of theorizing are inadequate to account for the experiences of members of the excluded group. In addition, feminists and others have studied personal narratives to seek out patterns of experience that can be used to build more adequate theories. And they have challenged assumptions about the authority of the academic to speak for or better than non-academics. Narratives have given voice and authority to those who may not otherwise be regarded as "qualified" to speak in academic discourse. Hence, narratives of experience have been a powerful resource for challenging established theories and methods and providing insight into the particulars of lived experience.

This is exemplified by Gilligan's (1982) re-analysis of Kohlberg's (1981) work on moral reasoning. Like most other psychologists at the time, Kohlberg used male subjects to examine the cognitive developmental process. On the basis of these studies, Kohlberg argued that the highest stage of moral reasoning comes with the ability to think in terms of abstract justice. Gilligan's work included female subjects and demonstrated that men and women think differently about moral issues. For the women in Gilligan's research, compassion had a higher value than did justice. This difference reflected a choice, however, not a less developed ability to reason about moral issues. Feminists have properly argued that this is but one of many instances in which the male narrative is used to establish a "scientific" norm for all, ignoring the significant gender differences that then affect the substantive research.

The above example illustrates why narrative cannot be taken for granted as evidence. The use of personal narratives in research is sometimes comparable to the earlier realist impulse in literature, the attempt to capture the world "as it really is." From this perspective, the words of the narrator could be unproblematically appropriated as evidence, an eyewitness account of the truth, when actually the influences of many factors should be accounted for.

Scott offers a critique of the attempt to make experience visible without analyzing the conditions producing that particular mode of experience: "The project of making experience visible precludes analysis of the workings of this system and of its historicity; instead, it reproduces its terms" (1991: 779). The fact that a group exists and has distinctive experiences does not, in itself, tell us anything about how it is constituted or its relationship to other systems. The experience itself does not necessarily explain anything; rather, the experience itself can be what requires further explanation.

Scott argues that it is not individuals who have experience, but subjects who are constituted through experience. Experience by this definition is not the origin of our explanation, not the authoritative (because seen or felt) evidence that grounds what is known, but rather that which we seek to explain, that about which knowledge is to be produced (1991: 779–80). Hence, Scott argues that experience is not the irreducible bedrock on which theory can be built. It is a starting point, something that requires explanation.

Scott points out that there are two levels of interpretation involved in making sense of experience. One, as suggested above, is an explanation of what makes that experience possible. The other level of interpretation is built into the very act of experiencing itself. An experience is not an unmediated interaction with the world, imprinting itself clearly and directly in the brain of the experiencing person. Rather, part of any experience is itself an interpretation, a recognition that something happened and the construction of a theory about what that something was. "Experience is at once always already an interpretation *and* something that needs to be interpreted. What counts as experience is neither self-evident nor straightforward; it is always contested, and always therefore political" (Scott 1991: 797). This, in part, reflects the tendency of the human brain to be an imperfect witness, to distort facts and details, to remember partially or to forget altogether. But more importantly, it reflects the extent to which our experience is necessarily mediated by our understanding of the world. If we experience an encounter with a stranger on the street as threatening or intimidating, that experience can have as much to do with our assumptions about modern urban life as it has to do with the particular qualities of the stranger. That does not change the fact that we experienced fear; the experience can be said to be genuine. But the experience contains a split-second interpretation of the stranger and the situation, hence Scott's contention that experience is both already interpreted and is in need of further interpretation.

In addition to experiences being reflective of, or perhaps constituted through, our understanding of how the world works, personal narratives also reflect a drive to render experience cohesive and coherent. One feature of narrative is causal explanation (or causal emplotment, in the language of Somers and Gibson). Hence, it is a matter of definition that personal narratives also contain within them causal explanations. However, the need for coherent narratives and causal explanations can lead narratives to create coherence where none may necessarily exist.

> When Allport, Shaw, or Lewis reported life histories—how one episode of a life leads coherently into another—that coherence was assumed to dwell within the events themselves. It is precisely this assumption which modern narratology suspends. . . . The logic with which one event leads into another is not simply "out there," waiting to be recognized by any disinterested observer. Instead, coherence derives from the tacit assumptions of plausibility that shape the way each story maker weaves the fragmentary episodes of experience into a history. (Rosenwald and Ochberg 1992: 5)

Creating coherence is part of creating a narrative; this coherence can be instructive, but it cannot be assumed unproblematically. The idea of telling an experience, or a life history, imposes the form of a narrative. It calls for the teller to decide on beginnings and endings, select events, describe relationships, and seek out causes and effects. It is unlikely that we would be able to say anything meaningful without such a form. Nevertheless, it is important to realize that the form is in the telling, in the act of making sense and rendering experience intelligible, rather than necessarily in the events themselves. When dealing with elderly people, such as the rescuers, who know they are approaching the end of their life and who have lived through traumatic events, the need to find coherence in their life may be particularly strong. This may reflect an inner need as much as a desire to bear public witness or "set the record straight."

What can be said is shaped not only by the form of narrative, with its beginnings and endings and coherent causal relationships, but also by culturally available meanings and understandings. Somers and Gibson's taxonomy is useful here. What I have been calling personal narrative would correspond with what they call ontological narrative. Ontological narratives (or life stories) depend on public narratives—culturally available explanations of institutions, systems, and relationships. Hence, what is told in the course of personal narrative draws, at least in part, on what is available in culturally shared understandings. The researcher's ability to share, or at least understand what the speaker means, is particularly important in this regard, as my interviews with Nazis often revealed. (One Dutchman explained his support for the Nazis by saying he had hoped the Nazis would return the colonies the British had stolen from the Dutch. He did not mean what I guessed—South Africa—but rather New Amsterdam.)

A final element to remember when considering narrative as a research method is what Somers and Gibson call selective appropriation or what the speaker selects to include in the story and what she or he leaves out. Silences and gaps can be as telling as what is included. What is left out is often what the teller takes to be literally unremarkable, so commonplace or obvious that it is not worth remarking on. While the precise reasons for exclusion cannot be simply assumed, omissions do provide insight into the teller's assumptions about shared meanings or about the way the world inevitably functions.[6] What is included in the narrative is what is exceptional or what stands out for some reason. In Bruner's words, what is included somehow violates our expectations of canonicity (1996: 139–40). A detail that is included is generally taken to contribute to our understanding, and it does so because the speaker assumes that that detail could have been otherwise; had that detail been otherwise then perhaps the outcome would have been different. Like Sherlock Holmes's silent dog—which did not bark because it knew the intruder—the absence of comment may speak volumes. The challenge for the analyst is to interpret what this silence signifies. The fact that none of the people I interviewed for this book employed the language of agonistic moral choice, in which we have to agonize and deliberate before we finally find the courage to "do the right thing," struck me as a highly significant omission, one discussed in detail in chapter 6.

CONCLUSION

Narratives—the stories people tell—can provide a rich source of information about how people make sense of their lives, put together information, think of themselves, and interpret their world. Narratives can be indicative not only of the experiences that people have but also of the means of interpreting those experiences that are available to them in a given culture. Narrative allows room for the teller to provide information the researcher would not generally expect or think to elicit in a more structured interview situation. Although the assumptions of the researcher still play a powerful role and necessitate both extreme sensitivity and caution in the analyst, especially in the interpretation of a narrative, these assumptions perhaps constrain the interview and the resulting information less than they would if the teller could provide only short answers to specific questions, questions that are themselves constructed on the researcher's assumptions. Despite its problematic aspects, narrative thus provides a powerful research tool in the hands of the scrupulous analyst. The freshness and complexity of oral testimonies in capturing the intricate and contradictory nature of reality can be an invaluable part of the research methodology in political science, as in other disciplines in social science.

APPENDIX B

Finding the Rescuers

WHO DETERMINES who is a rescuer? How is this done? And how did I contact and meet the people interviewed in this book?

The Israeli government established Yad Vashem to create a memorial to honor the memory of the six million Jewish Holocaust victims and "the righteous among the nations who risked their lives to save Jews." Since 1963, an official Israeli commission headed by an Israeli Supreme Court justice has been charged with awarding the title "Righteous among the Nations" to rescuers who are nominated on the basis of both deeds and motivation.

This Yad Vashem commission carefully studies pertinent documentation on each rescuer. This documentation usually includes evidence from the rescued person, survivors, or other eyewitnesses. The commission asks about the aid extended, whether the rescuer received any material compensation for the aid and, if so, the amount and nature of this aid.[1] All nominations are investigated carefully to make sure the rescue was legitimate and was not motivated by the desire for money. In most cases, more than one person has to certify the rescue although this requirement has been dispensed with over time and as witnesses die. The commission also asks about the dangers faced by the rescuer and about the rescuers' motivations.

A Yad Vashem recipient is given a specially minted medal with his or her name on it, as well as a certificate of honor and the privilege of having his or her name added to the Wall of Honor in the Garden of the Righteous at Yad Vashem in Jerusalem. (At one point, rescuers planted trees in this garden but this practice has been discontinued due to lack of space. Knud's story refers to his planting a tree in this garden.) Awards are made to rescuers or their family members, either in Israel or through official Israeli representatives in the rescuer's home country. Over 18,000 rescuers have been recognized so far but this figure includes family members who shared in the rescue of Jews so the actual number of authenticated rescue stories is much smaller, approximately 7,500. Some rescuers have refused their medals, often because they felt they did not do enough. (Several of the rescuers I interviewed fell into this category.) And, according to Knud, the Danes accepted one medal as a country rather than taking individual medals, although some Danes living outside Denmark were later nominated for individual medals.

In 1988, Eva Fogelman gave me a list of rescuers living in the United States. According to Fogelman, this list had been compiled by Elizabeth Midlarsky from the files at Yad Vashem. I read through the list of names and tried to select at random, trying to balance for gender and nationality. (I was not totally successful at this, since I had only the names and these were occasionally misleading. For example, Irene's name was Opdyke, a name I correctly assumed was Dutch but did not realize was Irene's husband's name, not her maiden name of Gut, which was Polish.)

I wrote a short letter to some fifty people, telling them I was writing a book on altruism and asking if I could speak with them about their wartime activities. Anyone who has ever done this kind of work can easily attest to how much fun it is to wait for the responses. Who will respond? What will they say? What will they be like? A few letters came back immediately, marked "Address unknown" or "Moved, left no address." A few letters came from neighbors, saying the person had died. Some of these were written by the person rescued; the writer frequently offered to speak with me about the rescuer, who had become a good friend and an integral part of the survivor's life, much as Miep Gies did with Otto Frank. All but one of the people who responded said they would be glad to talk with me. The one exception was a Hungarian man who said he was quite bitter about the war since he and his co-rescuers had been turned in by some of the Jews they tried to save, and all his friends had been killed. However, he said he would meet with me, since I sounded like a "nice young girl." (An unanticipated advantage of having a soft voice and working with older people is being viewed as young.) We arranged to meet for tea "just to chat" several times but something always came up, and I finally decided that this reflected ambivalence on his part and did not pursue the interview further.

Five German rescuers were interviewed, in German, by Ute Kingman. Some thirty other rescuers were interviewed in English by me. Sometimes these interviews were on the phone since I had two small children and did not want to travel and since the original project was something between a low-budget and a no-budget operation. Ironically, the telephone interviews may have engendered a sense of anonymity akin to the analysts' couch in classical Freudian analysis. But if I had to guess, I would attribute the rescuers' incredible openness and willingness to talk to their general character since I also did both phone and in-person interviews with some rescuers and could find no difference in the subject matter discussed. A few interviews were filmed.

In all cases, interviews were transcribed and offered to rescuers for approval before any material was analyzed. (About half the rescuers declined this offer.) Transcripts were edited as minimally as possible and then only for clarity. All of the narratives presented here follow the general pattern of conversational development over the course of the time spent together. (This time ranged from a few sessions to many months or years.) Only Otto's interview material was so extensive that I had to delete some of the historical material, and I have tried to organize his narrative by topic. All other narratives flow as one story, with issues discussed as they were raised by the rescuer. Occasionally, I include material given to me by the rescuer, as I did with Knud and Margot.

I began my research by constructing a fourteen-page questionnaire that included many questions about altruism and was designed to tap into scholarly questions about rescue activity; I quickly learned, however, that this material was more frequently discussed by the rescuer and often in a context that provided additional insight into the rescuer's response to questions. The survey itself thus was used primarily as a follow-up, to make sure I covered all questions and to determine whether differences in responses occurred depending on how and when and in what context a question was posed.

Many issues are not raised here. Many questions were left unasked that probably would have elicited much valuable information. I tried to follow the rescuers' lead, however, and did not raise issues that I felt would be upsetting to the rescuer. Partly this reflects my view of the rescuers not as subjects in a research experiment but as human beings whose privacy should be respected. Some questions were not raised because I did not think of them at the time. Only later did I realize how rich this material was and how much insight on moral issues they contained. If I were to do it over again, I would probably rephrase questions and focus on slightly different questions, in at least a few instances.

I worried a great deal about leading the rescuers, unintentionally or even subconsciously, by my phrasing of questions. I must have voiced my concern one night at the dinner table for my oldest son asked me, "Weren't these people who fought Nazis and stared down the Gestapo?" "Yes, in most instances," I responded. He looked me right in the eye, then shook his head somewhat sadly, as kids frequently do just before they let you have it. "Sorry, Mom. You're not that scary." He was right, and as I read through the transcripts now, with a more objective eye, I see how comfortable rescuers felt disagreeing with or correcting me.

When possible, rescuers or their families have seen the final version of their narratives. When differences of spelling arose, I have followed the form preferred by the rescuer, even though I believe these are occasionally incorrect or—more frequently—a localized version, such as Czech versus German or spellings that were are no longer used.

Initially I referred to people only by their first names, but I do identify all of the rescuers fully at their request or the request of their family members, in the acknowledgments. Occasionally, names of family members or friends are deleted or shortened to protect privacy.

NOTES

1. I consider the concept of identity in more detail in chapter 7. Even at this point, however, we need a working definition. For now, we might think of "identity" as containing two main components: (1) those characteristics that distinguish one person from all others and (2) a person's sense of himself or herself. Psychologists traditionally use the term *identity* to refer to the characteristics that differentiate an individual—be it an object or a person—from others. This term is then distinguished from the term *self,* which refers to a concept that includes both (1) those identifying characteristics that distinguish the object or person from all others and (2) the person's ability to have an awareness of himself or herself. Hence a car could have identity but only a sentient being can have a self. Since we use the terms *identity* and *self* interchangeably in common parlance, however, and since political discussions rely almost exclusively on *identity* instead of *self* or *self-concept,* I use the terms interchangeably and define *identity* to refer to an individual's sense of who he/she is, a concept that includes both those characteristics that distinguish that individual from all others and the individual's self-reflexive sense of who he or she is.

This definition should suffice for the general reader. For those readers concerned with concepts in political psychology, I employ the following conceptualizations. Self-concept refers to our knowledge about who we are. Self-esteem refers to people's evaluations of their own self-worth, i.e., the extent to which they consider themselves as competent, decent, worthy, etc. Schema are the mental structures people use to organize their knowledge about the social world by subjects or themes. These schemas exert a powerful influence on what information we notice, remember, and think about. Cognition refers to the beliefs, thoughts, feelings, or pieces of knowledge held by an individual, and cognitive frameworks are the organizing frameworks, or schema, with which and into which we process these thoughts, feelings, beliefs, and knowledge. See also chapter 7.

2. I define political acts as those relating to power and influence but also include in this conceptualization both non-institutional acts and normative acts, those acts that bear on the well-being of another.

3. Cognitions refer to thoughts, feelings, beliefs, or pieces of knowledge. Recent theoretical developments, particularly in personality psychology, emphasize the importance of cognitive processes. Mischel and Bandura, for example, argue that cognitive concepts—the way people differ in the way they think about themselves and about their worlds—are among the most critical for understanding personality. An interest in cognition, however, is not new to psychology, with theorists from Freud and Allport to Rogers and Maslow discussing the importance of realistic cognition as part of mental health. See Mischel 1979 or Bandura 1986, 1989, 1990, 1991.

4. In *The Heart of Altruism*, I defined altruism as behavior designed to further the welfare of another, even if doing so risked harm to one's self. I tried both to explain altruism as a substantive phenomenon, interesting in and of itself, and to treat altruism as an analytical tool, useful in probing the limitations of existing social and political theories based on the assumption of self-interest. I conceptualized altruism on a continuum, running from self-interested activities at one end to other-directed acts at the other end. I then interviewed between five and fifteen people in each of four categories of individuals: entrepreneurs (whom we might think of as typifying baseline data or rational actors), philanthropists, heroes, and rescuers of Jews, as groups illustrative of individuals gradually moving away from the self-interested end of the continuum and toward pure altruism. I then compared the empirical behavior of these individuals with the major theories about altruism.

I concluded that the heart of altruism is the altruist's perception of being tied to others through a common humanity. Only this cognitive component of altruism seems to be found in all instances of altruism. Other factors may act as triggers of this altruistic perspective, however, and this may explain many of the contradictory findings in the field, since different scholars have identified various trigger mechanisms for the critical cognitive influence. For a review of these works, see Monroe 1996 or Post et al. 2002.

5. See the discussions of Kantian or contractarian philosophy in Lakoff and Johnson 1999.

6. Much of this work is highly technical and involves brain imaging. For an accessible overview by one of the founders of this field, see Weingartner 2001.

7. In methodological terms, this technique most closely resembles what Coles (1989) calls psychological or psychoanalytic ethnography. While we never know what is in another's mind, this technique seems at least to allow us to make more educated guesses.

8. Much of the best work on altruism has been done in experimental settings. A major concern for the political analyst, then, is how robust these findings are when we move to what are referred to as "natural" settings. In a normative sense, the Holocaust is hardly what one would call a "natural" setting, but it does provide a particularly appropriate setting for allowing us to examine moral dilemmas and human nature under the kinds of stresses none of us would ever want to impose artificially, in any way.

9. There is, of course, some overlap with works in social, political, and moral theory but my emphasis in this book is on the latter. My analysis also leaves aside discussions of what constitutes ethics, a topic better left to philosophers, theologians, and normative political theorists, and instead asks what drives or causes ethical acts, a question more properly the domain of the empirical political theorist interested in testing political theories with empirical data.

10. There are various conceptual differences utilized, by scholars in diverse fields, concerning the terms *ethics* and *morality*. I leave aside these distinctions and use the two terms interchangeably. For such conceptual discussions, see Walzer 2003.

11. While this literature is discussed in detail later, the reader may wish to refer to Oliner and Oliner 1988, Oliner 2003, Tec 1986, and Fogelman 1994.

12. In scholarly terms, this means I argue that we must turn to categorization theory as discussed in cognitive psychology and linguistics.

13. I am indebted to Marion Smiley (1992) for this lovely phrase.

14. For a good overview, see Ross and Nisbett 1991.

15. For example, readers interested in the critical assumptions underpinning narrative interpretation as a methodology should consult appendix A.

16. For further details on narrative as an analytical tool and how I found and interviewed these rescuers, see appendices A and B.

17. Yad Vashem is the official Israeli agency authorized to investigate and certify rescuers.

18. In all, I have extensive interviews with some twenty rescuers. A few were conducted in a few hours; most occurred over several months and some over several years. I have spoken informally with and read the autobiographies or testimonies of many other rescuers to provide background. See appendix B.

19. Some of these questions must await a second volume, analyzing interviews with bystanders and Nazis, to be addressed more fully. See Monroe 1991, 2003.

Notes to Acknowledgments

1. *The Economic Approach to Politics: A Critical Reassessment of Rational Actor Theory* (HarperCollins 1991) and *Contemporary Empirical Political Theory* (U of California 1997).

2. This work appeared in *Ethics* (1990), the *Journal of Politics* (1991), and the *American Journal of Political Science* (1994).

3. Ironically, I have criticized this shift, arguing that the heart of economic man must be self-interest if rational actor theory is not to be reduced to a tautology in which people are said to pursue exogenously specified goals that are then revealed by the actor's behavior.

4. Their families have given permission to use their last names. I do so in order to give what little recognition I can for their extraordinary acts.

5. A note on spellings is in order. The spellings of geographic places may vary according to the language or country in which they are located. In all instances, I have deferred to the choice of individual rescuers, even though this sometimes means that the spelling may not be the one most widely utilized. Similarly, I have capitalized words like "God" if the rescuer wished it capitalized, while spelling it with a lowercase "g" if that was what the rescuer preferred. In many instances, I have left phrases in a slightly ungrammatical form, when that was the precise quote and if I thought doing so helped capture the voice of the speaker. I decided not to "clean up" oral testimonies, both because of a desire for verisimilitude and a literary desire to convey a feel for the speaker. I appreciate the permission of the rescuers and their families in allowing me to adopt this procedure, and I have followed the same policy and resisted rephrasing my own questions to make them correspond to rules of formal speech.

6. All the people interviewed here saw and approved the original transcribed notes. Only after they approved these rough transcripts were the transcribed interviews edited for clarity of presentation.

7. I had hoped to be able to release the actual tapes but realized they may contain personal material and I have not yet found the funding necessary to produce tapes edited to protect the privacy of the speaker.

8. Parts of appendix A are reprinted, with permission, from the *Annual Review of Political Science* 1 (1998): 315–31, and parts of an article in the *Annual Review of Political Science* 3 (2000): 419–47, appear in chapter 7.

Notes to Introduction

1. For a description of the sample, how I contacted rescuers, and a fuller discussion of the research design, see appendix B.

2. There is a rich literature on narratives as a source of insight for scholarly work (see Kraft 2002, Hilberg 1985, and Langer 1981 for specialized works on Holocaust memories), and the literature about the particular issues involved when dealing with Holocaust testimonies and memories as sources is particularly rich. Some historians are skeptical about their reliability (Hilberg 1985) while others (Gross 1997) argue that the nature and extent of Holocaust massacres mean we must treat survivors' stories as factually accurate until proven wrong. I leave these issues to historians. My own view is that the traditional historiographical narratives are unable to capture the kind of mass extermination, personal agony, and loss of an entire civilization that the Holocaust represents and that trying to understand how people construct a narrative to address such an experience may be equally as important as ascertaining the "truth" of a narrative.

3. I have seen some of this in an extraordinary book edited by Peter Suedfeld (2001), who asked survivors and refugees from the Holocaust to describe how their Holocaust experience influenced their later lives as social scientists. The written works differed significantly from the oral presentations I heard at two different conferences. See Langer 1991.

4. In another written version of this story, Margot does put herself into the story. According to this version, the woman who begged Margot to find her sons was Eileen Knorringa.

> I sent a large food package, together with a letter telling Werner Knorringa of the days, weeks, and months I had spent together with his wife.
>
> Many weeks later, the address barely legible, the mailman delivered a rain-drenched paper. It read:
>
> Dearest Margot,
> By twist of fate and good luck, I received your package and letter at the very moment we were shipped out to a camp in Germany. I am writing on the back of a fellow condemned, as we cannot sit down in the cattle car. I had to leave the parcel behind, but I do want to thank you so very much. Your writing gives me strength and faith. God bless you.
>
> Werner Knorringa
>
> Mr. Knorringa had thrown the paper out of a boxcar just before the train crossed the German border. A Dutch railroad worker had found it, and mailed it to me. He scribbled a slight remark along the side of the letter,

telling me how he was able to decipher the address. He said he knew that the poor unfortunates were being transported to a German camp. After their usefulness had ceased, the railroad track worker wrote, the prisoners would be gassed.

5. For some rescuers, these dreams involved being trapped and about to be killed in some way. Sometimes rescuers would be trapped in a room with no door, with gas seeping under the walls. Some times they were being guillotined or hanged. Other rescuers told of hearing screams, or of a general sense of horror and impending doom.

6. Sisyphus was a man in Greek mythology condemned by the gods to push a boulder up a hill, only to see it roll back down once it reached the top. Frequently interpreted as symbolically portraying the futility of life, I find Camus's characterization more apt. While life may be a futile struggle, we may find meaning, purpose, and sense of ennoblement in trying, nonetheless, to achieve something of value.

7. I am grateful to Susanne Rudolph for this term.

NOTES TO CHAPTER 1

1. I believe Margot refers to William Cecil, Lord Burleigh (1520–98) and chief minister for Queen Elizabeth I of England.

2. In the 1930s, the Czechoslovakian population included some fourteen million people, three million of whom were Sudeten Germans who lived in the northwestern mountainous region. Konrad Henlein, founder of the Sudeten Deutsche Partei, provided Hitler the excuse to demand the annexation of the Sudetenland. His organization asked the legislature in Prague for independence. After many negotiations, reaching the brink of war, Czechoslovakia was abandoned by the West at a conference in Munich in September 1938 and divided among the surrounding powers. The dismemberment of the Czechs' territorial remains was accomplished in the following spring. Hitler ordered Emil Hacha (president of the now truncated republic) to Berlin and told Hacha he would raze Prague unless Hacha agreed to sign an order asking for German troops to march into Czechoslovakia to keep the peace. I believe this spring invasion is what Margot refers to in her discussion. See any historical text (Botwinick 1996 or 1998) for details.

3. The German blitzkrieg armies marched into France via the Low Countries and Holland asked for an armistice in five days.

4. Tony van Renterghem, another rescuer from Holland, tells me *rits* was a slang term, slightly outdated during World War II, akin to saying "a penny for your thoughts." But neither Tony nor I could find this usage noted in any Dutch dictionary.

5 "Makin' Whoopee!" written by Gus Kahn, was a popular song in the late 1920s and refers to making love.

6. As with many of Margot's stories, the details vary from one conversation to the other. As best I can determine, the story of the apples and the disinfectant

refers to one of Margot's several incarcerations, from August 5, 1942, until the spring of 1943.

7. In later correspondence, Margot told me Elsie Hagen had taken her children to the convent. In our conversations, Margot said her father took the girls to the convent. The divergent details here and elsewhere in her narrative underline Langer's comments about oral testimonies and convey not just the fragility of memory but also the difficulty the human mind has in later making sense of chaotic times.

8. Samuel and Pearl Oliner published *The Altruistic Personality* in 1988, based on their interviews of rescuers such as Margot. See chapter 7 for a full discussion of this work and of other scholarly works on rescuers.

9. Margot is referring to the United States Holocaust Memorial Museum.

10. I believe Margot refers to a large concentration camp in the woods near Vught, near the city of Hertogenbosch in the south of the Netherlands. It was the only official SS concentration camp in the occupied part of northwestern Europe.

NOTES TO CHAPTER 2

1. Readers with an eye for detail will note slightly divergent spellings of towns, camps, etc., throughout the book. These reflect different usages depending on language (e.g., German versus Czech or Polish) or time period. Whenever a rescuer insisted on a particular spelling, I have tried to honor these requests. In this case, I believe Holubrov may refer to what is also spelled Holubkov, Czechoslovakia.

2 Otto's daughter, Irene, believes this refers to the Charles University.

3. Among other prohibitions, Jews and "Aryans" were not permitted to marry since such "breeding" constituted crimes against the race.

4. On the night of November 9, 1938, the Nazis unleased a series of pogroms against German Jews. Jewish shops, homes, and synagogues were destroyed. Because of the broken glass from shattered store window panes, this event is referred to as Kristallnacht (Night of the Broken Glass). At least 91 Jews were killed during Kristallnacht and many more were injured, with 30,000 later sent to concentration camps. Many of these died within weeks; others were released only after agreeing to emigrate and to transfer their property to "Aryans." Kristallnacht culminated the slowly escalating violence against Jews and signaled the transfer of the "Jewish problem" to the SS to solve.

5. Otto: "I had a sworn statement from the police liaison in the Jewish community. The Jewish community had a complete organization and they had also police references for contact with the Gestapo, police liaison. This police liaison confirms that I had three people, including a Gestapo man, bribed constantly. I did it also for the president of the Jewish community. I can't remember the details but somehow I helped him."

6. Mafalda was Otto's link to the July 20, 1944, plot to kill Hitler and is discussed in detail later in the chapter.

7. Klettendorf was near Wroclaw.

8. The Organization Todt in Prague was under the control of the Ministry of Armament for the protectorate of Bohemia-Moravia. It controlled labor in Silesia and exploited non-nationals for the illusory military objectives of the Nazi regime. These included prison inmates, such as Otto, and Jews. It is estimated that forced labor (also referred to as slave labor) in Bohemia under the Organization Todt (OT) numbered 70,000. Otto's daughter believes the OT in this instance also was translated as "death organization" since so many of the laborers were put on forced marches designed to kill them during the last days of the war, to ensure no survivors could give evidence against their captors.

9. Benesov is some 38 kilometers south-southeast of Prague.

10. Otto: "You know, I am an engineer. We had many good mechanics and engineers in the camp. Of course, hardware and such things were not available, but I had learned hand forging so we forged by hand whatever was needed for the camp. One of the SS men who was friendly and whom I knew already before and had bribed, he came to ask me if I would now move SS property into our large cellars, into the basements. They needed to lock it so I had to make the keys. But I made duplicate keys for us.

Soon all kinds of things came. The inmates of Theresienstadt were busy baking 'zwiebacks'—that means white bread, buttered and baked the second time, like toast—and they sent truckloads and truckloads of toasts in preparation of the flight of SS troops. Tinned meat, very good, high-class things arrived. When we unloaded it, there were bushes right and left, and we threw some tins into the bushes. When we got out, we collected them. We even stole a complete ham, in the sauce. A ham that was being cured. We stole it half cured and then we stole a big casket of wine. The SS couldn't load the wine, so we drained the wine into one- and two-gallon bottles. And, then, of course, we got terribly drunk when the liberation came. These were the last days in the camp."

11. The name is also spelled Braganca. I adopt Otto's spelling here, as throughout the transcript, since the same word may be spelled differently in German, Czech, and Portuguese.

12. The O stands for Ostriche, the German spelling for Austria.

13. Maria Adelaide, now Frau Nicolas van Uden, neé Infanta of Portugal in 1912, was the sister to Duarte Nuno, Infante of Portugal. Both were children of Miguel, Infante of Portugal and Duke of Braganza (also spelled Braganca) and Therese, Princess of Lowenstein-Wertheim-Rosenberg. One of Maria Adelaide's sisters was Maria Ana, who, when married, became Princess Karl August of Thurn und Taxis. I believe Otto traced Mafalda through the Thurn und Taxis family. Since the Thurn und Taxis family is a prominent Austrian family, it is possible Mafalda became involved in the July 20 plot through her sister's contacts. But this is speculation on my part. According to my research, Duarte Nuno was born in 1907 and died in 1976. He succeeded as head of the house of Braganza and claimant to the Portuguese throne in 1932, when his cousin—King Manuel of Portugal—died. He was also a potential claimant to the throne of Spain, after the 1936 death of his uncle, Infante Alfonso Carlos I of Spain. The current head of the house of Braganza is Dom Duarte III Pio, who succeeded Duarte Nuno, Mafalda's brother, on December 24, 1976.

14. Otto: "Through organizations in Austria, I tried to get the date of her

arrest because I knew that she would be under the secrecy of the British. Since she was arrested in Vienna, I figured the Gestapo there must have some papers. Unfortunately, this organization of Resistance fighters replied to me that the German arrest lists of that time, they were kept only until the thirtieth of June 1944. The newer ones were burned by the Gestapo. So we had no proof even that Mafalda was arrested. I have to find her and I think I will by means of the Institute for Contemporary History, who seem to be very interested and have completely different possibilities than I have. But before this is clear, I don't want to be accused of an exaggeration or something which I cannot prove, because the thing I am telling you is of historical significance."

15. Otto told me Mafalda's address but Otto's daughter and I thought it best to withhold it, in case Mafalda is still alive.

16. Carl Goerdeler (1884–1945) was mayor of Leipzig from 1930 to 1937. He resigned his post as mayor in protest over the removal of a statue of Felix Mendelssohn, a Jew. Goerdeler then spent his time working to overthrow Hilter and made numerous trips abroad to enlist Anglo-American support for the German Resistance. Stauffenberg warned Goerdeler on July 16, 1944, that the Gestapo had issued a warrant for his arrest. Goerdeler went into hiding but was caught in August. He stood trial before the People's Court and was sentenced to death. He was hanged in January 1945.

17. Otto showed me extensive documentation supporting his claims. This material is available to interested scholars, who can contact Princeton University Press. I have no way of assessing the accuracy of such claims myself.

18. Otto: "I will now do what I had done with the CIA. My CIA adventures are completely documented, because I corresponded with the CIA from 1982 about certain things and agreed to make certain changes. Everybody can claim that everything is secret in this world. You can say it was so and it has to be so. So let me show you my documents. [Otto showed me a book linking Anthony Blunt, the fourth man, to Harold Gibson, and then further documents of Otto's, signed by Gibson.] Harold Gibson was my case officer. Here is his signature. This is Harold Gibson. This is my application to enter South Rhodesia. He invited me on a date which was on the tenth of March 1948. This was two days before Jan Masaryk's attempted escape and death. The plane which came to pick up Masaryk was piloted by a guy named Victor Tepal. And aboard this plane was my first cousin, Leni Hopfengärtner."

19. I believe Otto refers to the Munich Institute for Contemporary History and to the United States Holocaust Memorial Museum in Washington, D.C.

20. Donald Maclean, Kim Philby, Guy Burgess, and Anthony Blunt were prominent Britons who spied for the KGB as part of the infamous Cambridge spy ring. Maclean was in the foreign service and served as first secretary to the British embassy in Washington after 1944. As such, he served on the Combined Policy Committee, which dealt with atomic energy and the atomic bomb. He passed on whatever he learned to the Russians, including (apparently) the information from Otto. Maclean later fled to Moscow, to avoid arrest, and died there in 1983. Burgess and Philby also defected to Russia. Blunt led a secret life, spying for Russia while serving as art historian to the queen. He was not publicly exposed

until 1979, after which Blunt was stripped of his knighthood. He died in disgrace in 1983.

21. Reinhard Heydrich (1904–1942), one of the Nazis responsible for official and secret police and security departments in Germany, chaired the Wannsee conference of January 20, 1942, where the "Final Solution" was discussed. In May 1942, Heydrich was shot by Czech fighters. He died within days from these injuries. In retaliation, the SS killed all male inhabitants of Lidice and executed over 1,331 Czech men and women in Prague. These murders did much to "roll up" the Czech Resistance, as Otto notes.

22. See Boyle 1979 for an account of the spy network run by Donald Maclean, Kim Philby, and Guy Burgess.

23. Otto: "I had my office in the American Embassy and collected there all my secret papers so that nobody could get at them. In 1948, when I had to escape, I left them there and they came out automatically by diplomatic pouch. So the documents for everything I tell you about are here and cover nearly everything, including my correspondence with the CIA about these things. I even have proof of the British part of my experience."

24. Otto spelled this Yachinmof. I have not been able to locate it.

25. I believe Otto refers to Vice Admiral Roscoe Hillenkoetter (1897–1982), who was Truman's first director of the CIA.

26. Thomas Masaryk (1850–1937) was the first president of the Czech Republic. His son, Jan Masaryk (1886–1945), initially dealt with his famous father by living in the United States. He fought in the Austrian army in World War I and served as chargé d'affaires in Washington until 1922. After his father died in 1937, Jan Masaryk was a supporter of Edvard Benes, his father's successor as Czech president. When Benes went into exile during World War II, Masaryk served as a foreign minister in Benes's exile government. When the war ended, Jan Masaryk returned to Czechoslovakia and served as foreign minister in the National Front government. After the Communist coup in February 1948, Masaryk was found dead under his bathroom window on March 10, 1948. The cause of death remains undetermined, although there has been speculation that the Communists killed him. I believe Otto included this story to show that it was not safe to be politically active in Czechoslovakia during this time period.

27. Otto: "Do you know the relative figures here of how many were saved in Holland and how many Yad Vashem awards were given to Dutchmen? In Holland, there were about 5,000 rescues. It is less known, but they said in Berlin, that there were 5,000 also. And in Prague—I have only one source on that and some people doubt it—there were only 424. I think there were fewer in Prague partly because it was a smaller city. Also, there was an anti-Semitism amongst the Slav nations everywhere, Polish, Russian, Czech. I'm going into that much closer because my father-in-law was a famous railway builder and he was a Czech Jew. Even though he, like most of the educated Czech Jews, spoke also German, he was still a Czech Jew. He studied at the Czech Technical University. Now, when it came to his being named as a professor, he was voted down. He heard only as a rumor that it was because he was a Jew. So we talked about that and I said, 'It's impossible. It's not a German university. There's a lot of Nazis among the Ger-

mans, but amongst the Czechs, no!' My father-in-law said, 'The Czechs are worse. They are not anti-Semitic. They are a-Semitic.' And I had an opportunity to check that much later. Amongst the professors at the Czech university, they were about 30 percent Jews, so the Czech Jew was not quite free. There is only one way I can explain that. There was a great tradition of anti-Semitism. The Jews mostly spoke German and went to German schools and so they were persecuted as Germans. They should have gone to the Czech university. So I think they experienced the prejudice because they were German *and* because they were Jewish. All this made a difference. For instance [after the war], my wife wanted to repossess her house, the house of her parents. She could not get it because she was told she is German and must first prove that she had suffered. She never was in a camp [so they said she never suffered enough]. But automatically, *I* got this house, because I'd been in the camp. The Communist president of our National Committee—he was a Communist bricklayer—he simply said, 'Your wife is German. I cannot do anything about it, but you are coming from a concentration camp so I don't have to ask you whether you are German or Czech.' That was the reign of the good soldiers Schweik. It's all terribly ironic, isn't it?"

28. This same quote appeared in *The Heart of Altruism* (1996). All differences in copyediting are minor except one. In this version, Otto says, "You restrict his nourishment, and he loses his 'physical beauty.'" In the 1996 book, the quote refers to "physical ability." In listening to the tapes again, I cannot tell for sure which word Otto uses.

29. As best I can ascertain, Otto is correct in his estimates. Only 500,000–600,000 Germans were Jewish, although the figures vary depending on how one counts the children of mixed marriages—what the Nazis referred to as *Mischlinge*—out of the total German population of 60 million. Also, it is important to note that the majority of *German* Jews survived only because they left Germany before 1939.

NOTES TO CHAPTER 3

1. Victims were put into freezing water, with their heads pushed under water until they almost drowned, then beaten and subjected to electrode torture.

2. John's sister was arrested in a church in Paris and died in Ravensbruck.

3. The Huguenots were French Protestants who belonged to the Reformed Church, established by John Calvin in 1550. The Huguenots were persecuted throughout the sixteenth and seventeenth centuries. Many fled to Switzerland, Germany, America, South Africa, and the French-speaking part of Belgium.

4. Suzy Kraay, a member of John's Dutch-Paris group, disobeyed orders and carried a booklet of names of other members of this group. When she was captured early in 1944, the Gestapo found the book and used it, along with threats to Suzy's parents and torture, to make Suzy talk. As a result, nearly 150 members of the Dutch-Paris group were arrested and at least 40 of these died in concentration camps. Ironically, the Gestapo kept their word about releasing Suzy's father if she would speak. But they jailed him again the next day and he died in a concentration camp. For details, see Ford 1966.

5. Ford 1966. John also was the subject of a television special, contrasting him with Klaus Barbie, known as the butcher of Lyon. Interestingly, John and Barbie had similar backgrounds. John showed me the tape during one of our interviews. Historical material about John is located at the John Weidner Center at Brandeis University. I am grateful to the Weidner Center and to Naomi Weidner for furnishing photos of John and for checking this chapter for spelling errors.

6. The Count de Menthon also participated in the Nuremberg Trials.

Notes to Chapter 4

1. This quote comes from Irene's autobiography (Opdyke and Armstrong 1999: 126), written with Jennifer Armstrong.

2. Kozienice is a small village in eastern Poland.

3. Ternopol is currently in Ukraine.

4. Irene believed Major Rügemer joined the Nazi Party but only in order to advance his career in the German army. Schulz was not a member of the Nazi Party.

5. Sturmbannführer Rokita.

6. After Hitler invaded Poland in 1939, the Polish-German border moved east, thereby annexing a large part of western Poland, including Kozlowa Göra, Irene's hometown in Upper Silesia. The treatment of Poles in this newly formed General Gouvernement—a Polish state controlled by Germans under martial law—was particularly harsh, as the murder of Irene's father for refusing to step off the sidewalk for two German soldiers illustrates.

Notes to Chapter 5

1. The Danish Underground asked that all its members who participated in the rescue of Danish Jewry be listed as a group, not as individuals.

2. Since I interviewed him, Knud related his story in Loeffler 2000.

3. Knud described Best as the effective political leader of Denmark during the war and Hanneken as the military leader.

4. Estimates of the total number caught vary, up to 400. See Goldberger 1987.

5. The Danish-Swedish Refugee Service (DSRS) included Danish saboteurs, politicians, and newsmen on the German list to be arrested, as well as Danes who had escaped to Sweden before 1943. The DSRS was organized by Leif Hendil to provide everything necessary for a secret courier service between Denmark and Sweden, including finances, boats, and equipment, with Sweden providing only the gasoline. After the war, the DSRS took its remaining money—which could not be returned to donors—and Hendil, the DSRS chief, closed the office with a "Paris in Copenhagen" week that included French films, museum exhibits, and the sale of some of the boats used in the resistance to the Nazis. See Loeffler 2000.

Leif Hendil was a Danish journalist who fled Sweden before October 1943 after his anti-Nazi sentiments angered the Germans. Hendil was in charge of establishing an organization that would encompass the various resistance groups. Because of his connections, Hendil was able to secure financing for the DSRS. See Loeffler 2000 for full details of the Danish rescue operations.

6. The concentration camp Therezienstadt was mentioned by different rescuers. I have tried to adopt the spelling preferred by the rescuer whose story is being told, out of respect for each rescuer.

Terezin was a small town, 60 kilometers from Prague. Originally a military town fortress with an enclosing wall, it was constructed between 1780 and 1790. During the Nazi occupation, Terezin was used as a Jewish ghetto and as a transit—not an extermination—camp. It is estimated that 150,000 Jews were imprisoned here during World War II and that some 35,000 died there. This is also referred to as Theresienstadt or as Therezienstadt.

7. Count Folke Bernadotte (1895–1948) was a Swedish internationalist and nephew of King Gustavus V. He is believed to have conveyed a peace offer from Heinrich Himmler to the British and U.S. authorities. Active in the Swedish Red Cross, in 1945 Bernadotte arranged the evacuation of Danish and Norwegian prisoners from German concentration camps. In 1946 he became president of the Swedish Red Cross and in 1948 was appointed United Nations mediator in Palestine, where it is believed Jewish extremists assassinated him.

8. Count Folke Bernadotte was the U.N. mediator for Palestine and a strong advocate of allowing refugees to return to their homes, a position that brought him criticism from the Israelis. He was murdered, presumably by the Stern Gang, on September 17, 1948. His policies were enshrined in international law and again were discussed during the war in Kosovo in the 1990s.

9. Raoul Wallenberg (born 1912) was a Swedish diplomat and businessman. In 1944, while assigned to Sweden's legation in Budapest, he rescued Jews by issuing Swedish passports or hiding Jews in safe houses he rented or bought. Eichmann, who was in charge of transporting Hungarian Jews to concentration camps, demanded Wallenberg stop and ordered his assassination. The attempt failed and Wallenberg is credited with saving some 20,000 Jews. After the war, the Soviets arrested Wallenberg. He supposedly died in prison of a heart attack in 1947, but there are reports that he died later and that he was executed by the Soviets, possibly because he was a rich capitalist, and therefore an embarrassment to Marxists, possibly because he was working with the Americans.

10. My friend and former student, Connie Epperson, used her mother's videocamera to film the interview with Knud, whom we met while interviewing Otto. Connie was then a senior at UCI, and Otto, Knud, Connie, and I made an unusual foursome, going out to dinner together and having a great deal of fun as we listened across the generations to the stories from the war. I include several of these stories (told by Knud), at Knud's request, to convey a feel for how lively, feisty, and full of life the rescuers could be, not at all the image of dry paper saints often conjured up by the term "moral exemplar."

There was the joke about the Germans taking heavy losses and having to retreat in Africa, Russia, and Italy. Their accounting of their losses to the news media was always on the low side. The story goes that one hundred German soldiers came up to the gates of heaven and met St. Peter and asked to be let in. St. Peter told them that according to the papers, only two soldiers had been killed on this particular time, and therefore he had to send ninety-eight of them to another location.

During most of the period of the German occupation of Denmark, an outstanding journalist by the name of Borge Outze established a Resistance news bureau, almost like an Associated Press; he duplicated almost daily news of all the happenings, which would not otherwise be published. News was distributed to "Underground groups" and illegal publications in all parts of the country. A "roll-up" of this establishment, called "Information," would have hurt the anti-German resistance enormously. Consequently, Outze and the list of "Underground" addresses was high on the Gestapo working orders. Several times the mailing list was in danger of being discovered. On a particular raid by the Gestapo on a suspected "partisan" group, the list was right under their noses. When the lady of the house heard the Gestapo smash the door, she hid the list between two blankets in their large dog's basket. Since the dog was trained to dislike intruders, especially German ones, the list was safe between the blankets, as the dog was ordered to "stay." It was my pleasure to send Outze to Sweden on a fishing boat in December 1944. He escaped from the Gestapo after some intrigues, although he for some time figured as one of the underground leaders that they most wanted to arrest.

The world-renowned physicist, Professor Niels Bohr, who was a Nobel Prize winner and often called the father of theoretical nuclear physics, was residing at the laboratory in Copenhagen for nuclear physics during the first two years of the German occupation of Denmark. Many nuclear scientists in the USA, England, and Russia were afraid that Bohr's theoretical knowledge would be used by the Germans in the development of an atomic bomb. The Allies wanted him on their side. Finally, early in 1943 Bohr thought it was time to emigrate. Besides being sure that the Allies could use some of his knowledge, he also wanted to be sure that in the expected event of a purge of the Danish Jews, Jews would be welcome for safety in Sweden.

Many stories of his "Underground" departure have been told, but this one is supposed to be the true version. With some of his close friends and a fishing skipper, Bohr left Denmark, departing from what at the time was the "dump" for Copenhagen's debris. The resistance organization to which I belonged later used this dump for many a departure. Strangely enough, a few hundred meters from the dump was a large hill where the Germans had barracks and observation posts. However, we were friendly with the superintendent of the dump, and before we arrived at nighttime, he would burn quite a bit of the debris and at the same time add enough wetness, so that the whole area, including the barracks, would be completely covered in smoke.

When the Bohr fishing boat was only a short distance from the Danish coast, the old motor conked out, and everyone had to row until they were picked up by a Swedish patrol vessel. On his arrival in Sweden, Bohr contacted the Swedish foreign minister to find out about their policy, in case there would be an exodus of the Danish Jews into Sweden. Bohr was not convinced by the answers of the minister, and therefore requested an audience with the Swedish majesty, King Gustav. The king gave him the promise he expected and so Bohr made ready for his departure to England and the USA. At an airport outside of Stockholm he was picked up by the British in a fairly small bomber with a non-pressurized hold. His oxygen mask was too small for his rather large head, and it was supposedly a very tired and almost breathless scientist that arrived at one of the many British military airports.

I cannot guarantee that the above story is absolutely correct, but my source is quite dependable.

There are funny stories, too. A man was sitting with his fishing gear at the end of a pier on a very foggy morning, when an open auto with four German officers, who had been drinking, lost their way and drove their car right over the pier and into deep water. The officers saved themselves, and when one of them climbed back up on the pier, he blamed the fisherman for not warning them. The fisherman said, "Why should I stop you? I thought you were on your way to England."

That's just a joke. But this story I know is true. There was a large motor cruiser, a Danish yacht "acquired" by the German officer Günther Pancke from the Gestapo headquarters. He thought that he was fortunate because the yacht's captain, a Dane, had agreed to be hired with the boat that he knew so well. On Pancke's very first cruise for lunch at a Danish Harbor Inn about twenty sea miles north of Copenhagen, he invited some high-ranked Gestapo and army people. They docked at the small harbor, and at the inn they ordered a fine luncheon. After lunch they returned in fine mood until they came back to the harbor and found that the Danish captain had departed with the yacht for Sweden and he didn't return till after the war. The Danish-Swedish Refugee Service made good use of the yacht in countless pick-ups of refugees and news material from occupied Denmark, meeting fishing boats at the territorial borders on the sound between Denmark and Sweden. I can't quote you the comments of Pancke when he saw his yacht missing!

11. The invitation to visit Israel was initiated and paid for by Harvey Sarner of Palm Springs, California.

NOTES TO CHAPTER 6

1. Rittener and Myers 1986.

2. Perhaps the single most important philosophical treatise on ethics is Kant's categorical imperative, which argues that we should always act in such a manner that we could generalize our behavior—or more precisely, that we should act only according to those maxims that can consistently be willed as a universal law—and we should never treat others as only means to an end.

3. I do not know enough about non-Western philosophy or literature to know if this tendency exists in other cultural traditions.

4. Both Utilitarian and Kantian ethics, for example, are designed at least in part to help people deal with agonistic choices.

5. By cognitive, I refer to the thoughts, feelings, beliefs, and pieces of knowledge and the mental process by which these are assembled.

6. I will use *character* and *identity* interchangeably throughout my discussion. Although academics do make distinctions between the two, the distinctions drawn are not universally accepted within the scholarly community, and scholars in one discipline frequently adopt different conceptual distinctions than do those in other disciplines. Furthermore, these conceptual distinctions are not widespread in the general public, nor is there rigorous scientific data supporting the use of one conceptual distinction above the others. These issues are discussed more fully in chapter 7.

7. The analysis in this chapter and in chapter 7 draws primarily on the transcripts presented in chapters 1–5. I have occasionally supplemented my analysis, however, with quotes from other rescuers. And in drawing on rescuers' interviews, I have often combined rescuers' comments on a particular topic so that occasional quotes from one part of the transcript are joined with the rescuer's responses to similar questions posed at a different time in the interview. For example, a rescuer might tell about family relations or her feelings about her mother at many different times throughout our conversations. In my analysis, I might join these different comments into one long quote. In such cases, I have noted these breaks in the conversation with ellipses. Similarly, a rescuer's response to a question might contain extraneous matter not directly relevant to the question. In my analysis, such extraneous matter would be deleted and such deletions would also be noted by ellipses.

8. Throughout my discussions of religious influences, I try to adopt the tone of the speaker, capitalizing *God* when I believe the speaker believes in a supreme deity and not capitalizing it when my sense is that the speaker did not believe in such a deity.

9. Students of altruism have noted the importance of having been saved or helped as a contributing factor in later altruism. I have discussed this and other explanations for altruism itself in *The Heart of Altruism* (1996) and do not repeat these arguments here.

10. Originating with Shaftesbury (1714/1977) and transmitted to both Hume (1740/1978) and Smith (1759/1853) via Hutcheson (1755/1971), moral sense theory argues that human beings resemble other animals in having an inborn sense of morality, much as they have an instinct for survival. Modern political scientists largely ignore moral sense theory and we find it surfacing most prominently in the contemporary literature in the work of developmental psychologists interested in morality. These psychologists build on Piaget (1928, 1948) but again turn to reason by tying the idea of an innate moral sense to developmental reasoning. This is evident in the most important cognitive-developmental models (Kohlberg 1981a, 1981b; Kegan 1982, 1988), which ask how people progress through different stages of moral reasoning and, later, ask how factors such as gender (Gilligan 1971/1981) influence a general developmental process that exists innately in all humans. (For example, Carol Gilligan [1982/1988] reworked Kohlberg's analysis to argue that gender differences are significant, with women

emphasizing caring and compassion rather than justice.) Darwin (1859/1936) also embraced the concept of a moral sense. But since relatively few evolutionary biologists focus on morality among human beings, evolutionary biological analyses of a moral sense seldom are found in contemporary political science. (Wilson's 1993 analysis of moral sense theory reveals the intellectual paucity of the contemporary political science work in moral sense theory.)

For the most part, then, the Western philosophical tradition has rejected Hume's view of an innate sense locating morality in sentiment and feeling, preferring theories that link morality to reason. Reason is said to provide the foundation for moral duty, to help us discover what morality is, and to constitute the tool by which we reach agreement when we disagree over or are torn by the particulars of moral choice. Recent work in animal behavior (see DeWaal 1996 or Barkow, Cosmides, and Tooby 1992 for an overview) suggests animals may exhibit behavior consistent with an innate moral sense. Insofar as humans are a subset of this animal grouping, then presumably this evidence lends new support for the old theory. In a similar vein, I find intriguing support for an innate moral sense in cross-cultural studies of child development that find evidence of moral behaviors—sharing, cooperating, concern with others—at such an early age that these behaviors cannot be said to be culturally taught. See Arnhart 1987 or Kagan 1998.

11. One classic illustration of a phenotype is hair color, which may lighten with exposure to sun, depending on genetic predispositions. A man with dark black hair will not have such a genetic predisposition, and hence no exposure to the sun will lighten his hair. Another man may have naturally platinum hair, which will be light regardless of whether or not he is exposed to the sun. Still a third man may have dishwater blond hair, which lightens a great deal once exposed to the sun. The same analogy is made for people's innate moral sense.

12. Corrie ten Boom was a deeply religious Dutch woman from Haarlem who hid Jews and members of the Resistance in the house she shared with her family. Betrayed in 1944, the ten Boom family was arrested on February 28, 1944. The Gestapo watched the house all day and arrested everyone seen going into the house that day, some twenty people, including most of Corrie's family. Despite a thorough search lasting two days, however, the Gestapo did not find the four Jews and two Resistance members hidden in the house. After two days, the Resistance liberated these six people, taking the four Jews to a new safe house. Three of the Jews survived the war. Corrie's father, Casper ten Boom (then eighty-four), died after only ten days in Scheveningen Prison. Corrie and her sister Betsie (fifty-nine) spent ten months in three different prisons. Betsie died in Ravensbruck but Corrie survived. Corrie's nephew Christiaan (twenty-four) died in Bergen Belsen and her brother Willem (sixty) contracted spinal tuberculosis while in prison and died shortly after the war. Corrie described her experiences in a series of writings, the best known being *The Hiding Place*, a book frequently used to teach young children about the Holocaust. She died on her ninety-first birthday, April 15, 1983.

13. Deontic refers to obligations and permission, and deontological ethics emphasize duties to follow certain ethical principles or rules. Without going into intricate philosophical discussions here (and with apologies to philosophers for oversimplification), we can think of a deontological theory as one that denies that

the good (or what we value in some ethical sense) always takes priority over the right or duty. The most frequently cited example of a deontological ethics is Kant's prohibition to avoid lying, even if telling a lie will result in a good outcome (such as saving human life) or will prevent twenty additional lies.

14. See note 16 and the next chapter for a fuller discussion of virtue ethics.

15. Oliner and Oliner 1988.

16. Also called virtue-based ethics and agent-based ethics, virtue ethics refers to the ethics that predominated in Western philosophy before the Renaissance, especially in Aristotle, and which focused on developing moral character rather than on discrete behavior or acts. For virtue ethicists, ethical rules are justified only insofar as the conduct they endorse would be in character for a virtuous person. See chapter 7 for a fuller discussion.

17. Indeed, many discussions of ethical dilemmas focus on precisely the agonistic quality of moral action that I found missing among the rescuers' explanations for their moral motivation. Consider the logic underlying what might arguably be the main philosophical explanation for moral choice: reason. Works stressing reason argue that we discover what morality is via some kind of reasoning processes—such as Kantian, contractarian, or utilitarian deliberation—or that reason helps us achieve morality by dominating the baser passions (Smith 1759/1853). This approach is illustrated in what is perhaps the single most important moral document of the modern age, Kant's *Metaphysics of Morals* (1785). Kant disagreed with the theory that located the drive for morality in the emotions and effectively closed philosophical discussion of works that accord emotions a significant role in ethical decision making, such as that found in Hume or among the moral sense theorists.

18. Many rescuers would begin talking immediately, before I could turn on the tape recorder.

19. Samuel and Pearl Oliner wrote one of the best books on altruism, *The Altruistic Personality* (1988), based on interviews with over 400 rescuers, some 126 non-rescuers, and 150 rescued survivors.

20. Margot refers to the United States Holocaust Memorial Museum in Washington, D.C.

21. See Oliner and Oliner 1988, Oliner et al. 1992, or Tec 1986 for further illustrations of this phenomenon.

22. Rittener and Myers 1986, Oliner and Oliner 1988, Tec 1986, Oliner et al. 1992 inter alia.

23. Rational choice theory assumes people's behavior is a product of a rational calculus of cost and benefits. See Monroe 1991a or Green and Shapiro 1994 for an overview and critique.

24. These findings are not an artifact of this particular sample; it is reflected in similar findings by Oliner and Oliner (1988), Monroe (1996), Rittener and Myers (1986), and Tec (1986).

NOTES TO CHAPTER 7

1. See Freud 1953/1974; Erikson 1968; and Festinger 1957, 1954.

2. There are many different discussions of the nature and structure of the self

in both psychology and philosophy. In 1997, for example, Ashmore and Jussim found over 31,000 publications in the last two decades in psychology alone (Baumeister 1991: 1). An overview of the most important scholarly literature in this area is presented in Monroe, Hanken and VanVechten 2000. with apologies for the many interesting works that had to be omitted. I also restrict my discussion of identity to adults and further exclude from discussion individuals who cannot communicate symbolically or who cannot understand and conceptualize themselves as objects of attention. While there is much important moral and legal theory on the rights of such individuals, such as babies or people who are severely brain damaged, such individuals are not included in the dominant theorizing about conceptualizations of identity and self, and I do not address such individuals or the issues they raise for us.

3. Catarina is a completely fictitious person, along with her Social Security number and car. Her name was suggested by my son as our cat walked through the room.

4. Self-awareness refers to a reflexive consciousness or knowledge about the self (Baumeister 1998). Reflexivity refers to the fact that individuals monitor their acts and the environment and adjust their behavior accordingly (Cote and Levine 1988, James 1892 and Mead 1934).

5. The concept of agency means Catarina (to continue our example) exercises control and makes choices based on her ability to be self-aware; to act toward herself, to perceive, to define, and to evaluate herself as she does others (Gurin and Markus 1989). As an agent, Catarina is able to anticipate the future, adjust and regulate her actions, and influence the physical and social environment to obtain her personal goals (Caprara and Cervona 2000).

6. Both philosophers (C. Taylor 1989) and psychologists (Baumeister 1986a, 1986b) have provided elaborate historical discussions for the development of the modern concept of self. Beginning in the early modern period (1500–1800), the self moved from being equated with visible manifestations and actions to being seen as vastly more complex, with an inner life that could be plumbed only with great skill and expertise. At the same time, Western society saw important shifts in the view of human potential and fulfillment. Life became viewed as more than just a preamble to an afterlife of eternal damnation or salvation, and Western society began to think more about fulfilling individual potential. Hence modern psychology's concern with self-actualization. Shifts in the individual's relationship to others also occurred during this period, and we now speak of self-definition as involving a changing and often uncertain mixture of choices.

7. Psychologists used to speak of "the self-concept" to refer to what people knew and believed about themselves (Baumeister 1998). This seems to imply that self-knowledge is integrated into a single concept, however, a view now considered simplistic by most psychologists, who argue that self-knowledge is imperfect, contains gaps, contradictions, and inconsistencies, and is often loosely organized. In preference to the self-concept, some psychologists now speak of the self-schema, the individual bits of information or specific beliefs about the self (Markus 1977). People have more than one self-schema and may regard themselves quite differently in different situations or points in time depending on the self-schema that becomes activated (Fazio, Effrein, and Falender 1981).

8. In political science *identity* often is used to refer to group politics, and writers often fail to understand or specify the psychology underlying the group dynamic.

9. Philosophers since Plato have attempted to define what a person is and any overview lies beyond the scope of the present volume. (See C. Taylor 1989 for an extensive overview.) But, in general, analysts typically follow one of two approaches. The first is illustrated by the Aristotelian view of human beings as biological organisms or animals. The second conceptualization builds on the Lockean view of a person as a psychological entity, distinct from the biological organism and, at least potentially, separable from it. Elements of each approach are evident in the literature on identity.

10. We find this approach in political theory (e.g., Aristotle) and in psychology (e.g., Maslow 1968/1982). See Monroe, Hankin, and VanVechten 2000 for a review.

11. Perry 1975: 12.

12. James 1890.

13. While postmoderns emphasize the fluid, unstable aspect of identity, the consensus among most social and personality psychologists is that there must be some stability and consistency among our multiple selves or, more accurately, among the varying facets of a multifaceted identity if we are to have a stable self-representation.

14. Freud 1953/1974.

15. Mead 1934.

16. Elster 1986.

17. It is worth noting the extent to which contemporary concepts of identity contain both a cognitive and an emotional component (see Nussbaum 2001). The self is not merely a mental construct located inside one's head. Identity also contains a sense of the self as a social being with the ability to engage in symbolic communication and self-awareness. Since social beings do not develop in isolation but rather in a social context, this conceptualization allows for the influence of socialization and critical others—including culture and society—in constructing a sense of self. It also rejects the idea of the self as a thing apart from the physical person and assumes we do not possess the self so much as become a self through a complex process of socialization and maturation.

18. Lakoff and Johnson 1999.

19. Research on inherited personality traits is controversial, both because of fears that it may condemn us to our genetic makeup and because the traits identified so far seem quite general (extroversion, risk taking) and based on empirical work that is less than ideal from the standpoint of scientific methodology. Bearing in mind these caveats, researchers are asking whether human beings have an inherited universal structure shaped by the demands made on the species for survival, and how culture and individual variation work on this universal structure. Researchers are asking not just how genes influence personality directly through biological makeup of the personality but also how genes influence personality indirectly through the way an individual selects, modifies, and creates the environment around her. Twin studies are providing rich, new areas for research since the siblings share a home environment and have the same genetic makeup if twins

are identical (monozygotic) but different genetic material if they are fraternal (dizygotic). The recent increase in multiple births, due to advances in fertility procedures, also has spurred work on this topic. Some studies comparing behavioral traits in identical and fraternal twins find that genetic differences can account for 40–50 percent of the differences in personality traits, while environmental influences account for about 30 percent of differences in personality traits. See Plomin 1990, Tooby, Cosmidos, and Barkow 1992, or Pinker 2002 for an overview accessible to the layperson.

20. This is the nature-nurture dichotomy, with the nurture aspect, or what we might think of as the socially constructed aspect of identity formation, serving to guide individuals in helping them function in their particular society.

21. Cognition and emotions used to be juxtaposed, although recent work suggets emotions influence the process of thinking and beliefs (see Nussbaum 2001 for an excellent review).

22. Harré 1987.

23. These social needs are ends in themselves and go beyond merely seeking to assuage a need or release tension.

24. Although I focus on individual identity, an individual's identity is made up of a variety of different components or attributes, some of which might properly be understood to be group or social identity in nature. It is worth noting the important distinction between individual and social identity. Broadly defined, social identity refers to the social categories, attributes, or components of the self-concept that are shared with others and therefore define individuals as being similar to others. In contrast, personal identity is made up of those attributes that mark an individual as different from others. For more detailed discussions of this distinction, see Reid and Deaux 1996; Turner et al. 1994; and Weigert, Teitge, and Teitge 1986.

25. Brewer 1991; Tajfel 1981.

26. One of the best depictions of this process is Lessing 1973.

27. Erikson 1959/1980.

28. See Hoover (2004) on Erikson and identity.

29. One point emerges clearly from the extensive literature about identity: scholars uniformly emphasize the importance of interactions between people and the desire for cognitive consistency. Social psychologists, in particular, discuss how behavior is influenced by others, by our perceptions of others, and by our beliefs about how others see us. The self-image seems critical to happiness and well-being; indeed, we will do a great deal to maintain a consistent sense of who we are and find it disturbing when our actions deviate from our sense of who we are (Festinger 1957). Finally, our consciousness about identity is incomplete and our self-concepts (our basic sense of who we are) are subject to continual, if subtle, changes in response to external stimuli.

30. See Baumeister 1998 or Bernichon, Cook, and Brown 2003.

31. This need for a consistent and coherent interpretation of ourselves and the world around us lies at the heart of much cognitive theory. As originally proposed (Festinger 1954), the theory of cognitive dissonance argues that we feel discomfort when there is tension between our attitudes and our actions. The sensation of dissonance will lead us to try to reduce dissonance, just as hunger leads us to eat.

Festinger's (1957) work on cognitive dissonance theory sparked a lively debate, still ongoing, over the relationship among cognition, behavior, and affect, with recent work focusing on culture's effect on needs for consistency. The universality of cognitive dissonance has been challenged by cultural theorists (Heine and Lehman 1997; Kashima et al. 1992) who argue that individuals in certain cultures will sacrifice cognitive consistency for the sake of interpersonal accommodation. Works on consonance between behavior and internal standards as a source of happiness frequently argue that there are critical differences between East and West. Consonance between behavior and internal standards is said to be the source of happiness in the Western model; but in the Far Eastern cultures, the consonance with external standards apparently plays a primary role. (See work by Markus and Kitayama 1991 on the independent self.) This work in turn has been criticized (1) for positing a "Western" culture and an "Eastern" culture when, in fact, culture is a highly concept phenomenon and (2) for ignoring the tremendous individual variation.

See any standard text (e.g., Taylor, Peplau, and Sears 1997) for discussions of cognitive dissonance, self-perception theory, and expectancy-value theory. See Ozyurt 2003 for a review of the literature on cognitive balance theory, asymmetry theory, cognitive dissonance theory, the theory of incongruence, self-consistency theory, and self-affirmation theory.

32. I am not an expert on virtue ethics so the following description is presented with apologies to experts for ignoring many intricacies of the body of literature. My thanks to Kay Mathiesen and Martin Young for their comments on this section.

33. Frequently cited virtues are courage, justice, prudence, truthfulness, temperance, and liberality, but some virtue theorists discuss as many as one hundred specific traits that make us good people.

34. In discussing virtue ethics, I draw heavily on two excellent survey articles: Pence 1984 and Trianosky 1990. Another crucial book for those interested in virtue ethics is MacIntyre 1981.

The Greek origins of virtue ethics can be found in many places, e.g., Plato's discussion of the unity of the virtue in the *Protagoras* and Aristotle's discussion in *The Nichomachean Ethics* (book 2), which focuses on the nature of moral virtue and of specific virtues. Aristotle's work on the golden mean argues that moral virtue consists of finding a mean between more extreme character traits. For example, the absence of fear is not foolhardiness or rashness, it is courage. The idea of a golden mean is found in works by other important Greek writers, who echo Aristotle in arguing that is not easy to live a virtuous life primarily because it is difficult to find the mean between two extremes and to live there. We also find this theme in works by Greek epic poets and in playwrights such as Homer and Sophocles, who talk about their heroes and anti-heroes in terms of their respective virtues or vices.

The Stoics were useful in revising the Greek approach to virtues. By the late Middle Ages, however, Aristotle's virtue theory was the definitive account of morality since it was endorsed by the medieval philosopher Thomas Aquinas. The Middle Ages discussed these virtues as the cardinal virtues, and medieval ethicists added the Christian ideas of faith, hope, and charity to the list of virtues.

With the Renaissance, the Age of Science, and the Enlightenment, Aristotle's virtue ethics declined in importance and most students of philosophy in the next centuries largely ignored discussions of virtues. See Schneewind (1990b) for a discussion of how virtues ethics were critiqued, revised, but eventually abandoned in favor of newer accounts of moral obligations. For Schneewind, virtue ethics met its biggest challenge with the rise of natural law theory, as developed by the seventeenth-century Dutch lawyer Hugo Grotius, who argued that morality involved conforming one's actions to moral laws that are fixed in nature and which even God cannot change. Grotius rejects the role of virtue developed by Aristotle for three reasons: (1) Aristotle's golden mean fails to explain basic moral concepts such as truthfulness and justice. (2) In the case of justice, the agent's particular motive does not matter. All that is important is following proper reason with respect to the rights of others. (3) Aristotle is wrong; the moral agent does not have special moral insight simply because he is virtuous. Instead, morality is fixed in natural laws that can be rationally perceived and deduced by all.

By the nineteenth century, the rule emphasis of moral theories such as utilitarianism had supplanted the idea of character found in virtue theory. Not till the 1950s do we see much contemporary interest in virtue ethics.

35. A major work in the construction of virtue ethics was Alasdair MacIntyre's 1981 book, especially chapters 1–5, and work by Richard Taylor (1985a, b). Other virtue ethicists include Gary Watson, Gerinimos Santas, and Gregory Trianosky, with Bernard Williams and Martha Nussbaum frequently classed as virtue ethicists.

Although a major theme in virtue ethics is the attack on deontological ethics, especially its criticism of both Utilitarianism and Kantianism, as virtue ethics developed into a major philosophical approach in the late 1980s, philosophers again began to speak more about judgments based on character. For Trianosky, judgments about character are independent of judgments about the rightness or wrongness of actions. For Watson, the concept of virtue is explanatorily prior to that of right conduct.

This raises a question that is unresolved among virtue ethicists: Is virtue judged by the behavior it produces or are virtues justified by the essential well-being of the one who possesses them? The rescuers suggest that the righteous behavior may have come as a result of their need to have consonance between their behavior and their standards of right and wrong. This suggests virtue ethics is in error and that there is some standard, and that the virtue ethics idea, at least as articulated by some virtue ethicists, that the value of virtue is in increasing the actor's well-being is wrong.

Not all virtue ethicists hold this view, however, but for those who do, we are returned to a kind of trap that ensnares psychological egoism: the argument that I do good because it is good for me. This becomes an even deeper hole insofar as there is no scientific foundation for the virtue ethics claim that people simply want to feel virtuous. (At least psychological egoism attempts an explanation: doing good for others makes me feel good about myself.) But the virtue ethics claim that people want to be virtuous can come remarkably close to smugness or self-complacency, and there is scant empirical evidence to support this view. If virtue ethics is calling for harmony among the virtues then possibly it allows for more complex and multiple influences as leading to doing good. But this is not yet worked out in the literature.

Other important aspects of virtue ethics include its relation to culture. The good life is rooted in a civic culture in which emotion and action established in childhood foster the virtues and habits through training, socialization, and the kind of moral development the Greeks stressed. The kind of training any particular culture gives is obviously going to be a function of that culture (see the last chapter of MacIntyre 1981). For example, the Spartan hero is not the kind of hero we would encourage in contemporary America. The Nazi Aryan soldier is not the kind of sensitive individual encouraged in the American Iron John movement. Virtue ethics roots human beings in particular cultural traditions, not in an abstract concept of individuals governed by abstract but universal principles of obligation. Human flourishing, or what it means for a human to flourish, is closely tied to community concepts of flourishing. Or is it? This question is unanswered in virtue ethics.

Virtue ethics contains some reference to moral sense theory. Both virtue ethics and moral sense theory share a reference to nature. Virtue ethics wants good acts to flow "naturally" from good character. There is little need to fight or control emotions or the passions for virtue ethicists. Nor is there an emphasis on transcending one's own particular place or particularities. Virtue ethics is not transcendent or otherworldly. Finally, being virtuous is said to be necessary for us to fulfill our potential as human beings. This suggests a referent to human nature in its claims to fulfill human potential and, even though this may have a strong local character, does it not also evoke a universalism in its reference to a distinctly human nature?

Despite the problems with virtue ethics and the incompleteness of its thought on certain issues, virtue ethics already has contributed to our thinking in several important ways.

1. Virtue ethics addresses concerns of care ethicists by saying—as do care ethicists like Carol Gilligan, Nell Noddings, or Annette Baier—that we should focus on care and human relationships, not abstract principles. Ignoring this human relationship in favor of abstract universal principles, these care ethicists claim, leads to a moral schizophrenia. Virtue ethics corresponds closely to care ethics in its emphasis on acting out of caring rather than duties as the main moral motivation. The question then becomes: Is the need to care for others part of our human nature? Is this a solution to the problem of virtue ethics noted above?

2. Supererogatory behavior. Virtue ethics has no difficulties explaining actions, such as those of the rescuers, that are "above and beyond the call of duty" since virtue ethics is not constructed to explain behavior through reference to duties.

3. By not fitting into the commonly utilized distinction in philosophy of dividing ethics into deontological (duty-based) or teleological (consequentialist) categories, virtue ethics shows that these very distinctions are not necessary in the first place. (Indeed, Watson and Trianosky argue these distinctions are not even helpful).

4. Virtue ethicists' call for a harmony among the virtues possibly opens the door to allow for more complex and multiple influences on why we do good. The psychological work is useful here. Note Freud's theory of overdetermination, suggesting an act can have one, two, or many causes.

Although we have made some strides, Anscombe's plea for more work on moral psychology remains largely unanswered. Work on the rescuers seems ideally suited as a response to this plea. The emphasis on narrative, as a method for discerning and understanding the traits of character that constitute and lead to moral virtue, provides an important way of relating ethics to morality, a way of responding to Anscombe's challenge to have ethics ask how real people act. Abstract rules or principles are neither necessary nor sufficient for moral action when we think about ethics this way.

36. For examples of works in this field, see, e.g., Anscombe 1957/1963; Foot 1978; Kekes 1989; Kupperman 1991; MacIntyre 1981; Nussbaum 1985; Slote 1983; or Williams 1981. For the connection between virtue ethics and super-erogation, see Mellema 1991: chapter 6; Trianosky 1986; or Phybus 1982.

37. My approach is that of the empirical political theorist. I ask not about logical consistency or textual analysis but rather whether the ideas expressed by virtue ethics correspond to the empirical world under observation.

38. Kupperman 1991.

39. As Aristotle notes, "[M]en must be brought up from childhood to feel pleasure and pain at the proper things; for this is correct education" (*Nichomachean Ethics*, 1104a, 11–12).

40. "When we praise the saint or hero we do not commit ourselves to saying that we should all perform similar acts. Rather we commit ourselves to saying that we ought to aim at inculcating within ourselves the dispositions and virtues from which acts of this type are produced" (Mellema 1991: 91). See also Phybus 1982.

41. Jerome Kagan (1998) makes such consonance central to morality.

42. The relationship between acts and character is not fully developed in virtue ethics. Most analysts recognize that there is some correlation and that if a "good" person consistently engages in "bad" acts these "bad" acts will shape his character so much as to alter and turn it into something different. But the relationship between the occasional "bad" act and character is not fully developed. As important as this point is for a discussion of virtue ethics, for our purposes it is more important in highlighting the distinction between general character and individual acts.

43. See Keneally 1982 on details about Oskar Schindler. Several recent books on Pope Pius XII criticize both the Pope and the church for their wartime behavior. Kertzer 2001; Zuccotti 2000; or Goldhagen 2002.

44. This quote comes from Opdyke and Armstrong 2001.

45. The struggle of will may be most appropriately said to occur as one acquires good habits. I leave to virtue ethicists the question of resolving these developmental issues in their philosophy.

46. Aronson 1992, 1998; Baumeister 1993; Blaine and Crocker 1993; Harter 1993; Kunda 1990; Stone 1998; Thibodeau and Aronson 1992; and Tice 1993 all found that people need to maintain reasonably high self-esteem to see themselves as good, competent, and decent.

47. The psychological literature is unclear about the relative importance of self-esteem versus continuity of self-image and the integration of values. As a general rule, in learning about themselves, people seem driven by both the quest for consistency and the need to find accurate information that is diagnostic of

their own traits (good or bad). People want information that confirms what they already believe to be true, and once they have formed opinions of themselves, they tend to discard these opinions with great difficulty. Furthermore, they appear to prefer information that is favorable, which casts a good light on their sense of self (Greenwald and Ronis 1978 or S. Taylor and Brown 1988).

When there is a conflict among these three functions—self-enhancement, consistency, and appraisal—self enhancement motives are frequently the strongest. Consistency is a distant second and appraisal the least important. This suggests people's desire to think well of themselves is stronger than their desire to have their beliefs confirmed or the desire to learn the truth about themselves (See Baumeister 1998.) The relative importance of the desire for consistency versus the desire to feel good about one's self cannot be resolved with my data. This area is one rich for future research.

48. The vast literature on social identity theory, summarized in Abrams and Hogg 1990, discusses this.

49. Colby and Damon 1992, 1993.

50. "When there is perceived unity between self and morality, judgment and conduct are directly and predictably linked and action choices are made with great certainty" (Colby and Damon 1993: 150).

51. This corresponds with work in political science on loosely held values.

52. This is beautifully captured by Tolstoy in *War and Peace* when Tolstoy describes Napoleon surveying the carnage after the Battle of Borodino and—Tolstoy argues—having to decide whether to continue his actions and give up his ideals or to relinquish his desires for conquest and remain the human being he is.

53. Blasi 1980, 1988, 1993, 1995. I am deeply indebted to Blasi not only for his superb work but also for his generous comments on my own work.

54. Festinger 1954, 1957.

55. One of the best illustrations of this is *Crimes and Misdemeanors,* a film by Woody Allen.

56. Blasi's work does ask about the *nature* of the self with which moral ideals are integrated. Blasi specifies different stages of development of that self, stages that differ across individuals and within the same individual at different points in time. Where we are located in these different stages of development, Blasi argues, will have important consequences for the integration of the self and moral beliefs. Blasi tries to identify these "selves" and to understand how differences among them might account for differences in the way that the self is integrated with moral ideals. But while Blasi recognizes the contradictory dimensions of one's personality, his model fails to determine which parts will be dominant when moral choices arise. Ironically, then, Blasi risks returning us to the agonistic moral dilemmas that moral theories stressing identity might be expected to alleviate. The contradictory self problem is particularly important since different moral choices may call forth different parts of one's self, thereby resulting in different values and patterns of response. It is not clear how these problems can be addressed in any other than a time-series study, in which the same individual is analyzed at different points in his/her cognitive development.

57. Frankfurt 1988.

58. Piliavan 1981.

59. The affective aspect of this processing is a rich area for future research. It may be that perspective taking depends on the actor's cognitive development and on the complexity of the issue faced. Reykowski finds several levels of development, from the simplest level in which I can see that others' perspectives differ from mine but still like mine better, to external perspective in which there is a superordinate perspective (akin to Nagel's [1986] view from nowhere) and prudent perspectives that recognize there is more than one legitimate view. It may be that the ability to take these perspectives is not stable. We move around and shift levels in a dynamic process. How does this play out in the real world? What are the implications of different perspectives for ethical actions? What happens if the personal perspective conflicts with the perspective of the role one must play, as in a defense attorney who suspects his client may be lying? The general concept of perspective taking seems like a powerful engine without a conductor to direct it, hence my coupling it with identity and categorization theory to get to the moral perspective.

60. See Browning 1992 or Lerner 1992.

61. Developmental theories suggest certain abilities, such as language, are acquired or expand in progressive stages. Most of us crawl before we walk, for example, or recognize faces that we then put names to before we speak in complete sentences. The same argument has been made about the development of moral reasoning. Psychologists such as Kohlberg (1981a, 1981b) or Gilligan (1982) have built on Piaget's (1948) work to tie the idea of an innate moral sense to developmental reasoning. Kohlberg's is the classic cognitive-developmental model, positing a stage-theoretic route through which people progress as they develop their abilities to engage in moral reasoning.

Kohlberg's classification system specified six identifiable stages, which can be divided more generally into three levels. (1) Pre-conventional morality includes stage 1. Here people behave according to socially acceptable norms because some authority figure tells them to do so and they fear punishment if they do not comply. In stage 2, "right" behavior is defined as acting in one's own best self-interest. (2) Conventional morality—so designated because Kohlberg finds it the kind of moral thinking most frequently found in society—includes stage 3, in which people seek to do what is necessary to gain the approval of others, and stage 4, in which people respond to laws and the obligations of duty. (3) Post-conventional morality, a stage not reached by most adults, includes stage 5, in which the person demonstrates a concern for social mutuality and a true interest in the welfare of others. In stage 6, individuals are guided by respect for universal principles and demands of conscience.

Later analysts, most notably Gilligan, asked whether—and how—factors such as gender influenced any general developmental process that exists innately in all humans. Gilligan's (1982) empirical work reconstructed Kohlberg's (1981a, 1981b) empirical work but used women in addition to men in her experiments. She found that gender differences are significant, with women emphasizing caring and compassion as the final stage, rather than the kinds of abstract justice that Kohlberg found and then assumed were the end goal of moral development.

A major drawback to such a developmental approach centers on the linearity implicit in the process. Individuals are said to progress through different phases one stage at a time. They can develop their abilities only through social interaction and need to successfully resolve cognitive conflicts at their current stage before they can move on to the next stage of moral reasoning. Such a progressive model may not be appropriate when discussing adult morality. While important cognitive processes—such as language—may be acquired in such a linear fashion, there is little evidence suggesting such linearity applies when we deal with adults confronting difficult moral situations. Essentially, then, I would argue that when dealing with issues such as moral reasoning, there might be a basic developmental process but that this process may well be too crude to discriminate among the relevant criteria among most adults.

62. Although I have not utilized the term *construals*, since it is not one familiar to political scientists or most lay readers, psychologists frequently use this term to convey some of what interests me. What are construals? When people interpret the social and political world, they follow certain patterns. Some of these can be discerned through use of the narrative methodology, which reveals much about how people see the world, how they construe the world around them. Social psychologists (Ross and Nisbett 1991) thus argue that we need to look at the situation from the viewpoint of the people in it, to see how they construe the world around them.

This emphasis on construal has its roots in Gestalt psychology, a school stressing the importance of studying the subjective way in which an object appears in people's minds, rather than the objective, physical attributes of the object. (Kurt Koffka, Wolfgang Kohler, and Max Wertheimer were Gestalt psychologists.) Kurt Lewin, the founding father of modern experimental social psychology, was a German-Jewish professor who applied *Gestalt* principles to situations beyond the perception of objects. Lewin focused on social perception, asking how people perceive other people and their motives, intentions, and behaviors. Lewin was the first scientist to realize the importance of taking the perspective of the people in any social situation to see how they construe, i.e., perceive, interpret, and distort, this social environment. Social psychologists now routinely focus on the importance of considering subjective situations, i.e., how they are construed by people.

In adopting this emphasis in my own work, I am arguing that we need to determine not only the individual differences in people's personalities that influence behavior, for that can ignore what may be of equal importance: the effects of the social situation on people. To understand these effects, we must understand the fundamental laws of human nature, behavioral patterns typically common to all, which explain why we construe the social world the way we do. Social psychologists have found two motives that are of primary importance: the need to be as accurate as possible, and the need to feel good about ourselves. Sometimes these pull us in the same direction; but sometimes they pull us in opposite ones, as when accurately perceiving the world will require us to accept the fact that we have behaved foolishly or immorally in the past.

63. See Monroe, Hankin, and VanVechten 2000 for a discussion of this phenomenon in the literature on social identity.

64. Experiments on bilingual subjects suggest that the language in which the test was administered affected how the same subject matter would be interpreted.

The salience of identity—linguistic identity—was in this case triggered by language. Private correspondence with Janusz Reykowski, 2002.

65. See any introductory text to social psychology, such as Aronson, Wilson, and Akert 1999 or Taylor, Peplau, and Sears 1997.

66. The concept of perspective has been used quite effectively in international relations but has not been widely applied to issues in ethics. See Jervis 2002.

67. Latané and Darley 1980.

68. Milgram 1974; Zimbardo, Ebbesen, and Maslach 1977.

69. Adorno et al. 1950.

70. Becker 1976 or Dawkins 1976.

71. Batson 1991.

72. See Latané and Darley 1980; Monroe 1996; or Post et al. 2002 for a review.

73. See ten Boom, Sherrill, and Sherrill 1974 or Gies 1987.

74. Levi 1961; Wiesel 1960/1986.

75. Gilbert 2003 is the most recent work in this genre.

76. Hunecke 1981.

77. Klingemann and Falter 1993.

78. Fogelman 1994 or Monroe 1996 provide overviews on such correlates of altruism.

79. See *The Sorrow and the Pity*, the magnificent 1972 film by Orphüls, in which a top Resistance undercover agent suggests his acts were motivated largely because he was a homosexual and felt he needed to prove he was as brave as other men.

80. Oliner and Oliner 1988.

81. Sam Oliner himself is a survivor.

82. See also Bellah, Madsen, Sullivan, Swindler, and Tipton 1985 for a discussion of the more general phenomenon by which habits of caring affect behavior.

83. Jarymowicz 1992; Reykowski 2001.

84. Tec 1986.

85. Immanuel Tanay in *The Courage to Care*, a 1986 Academy Award–nominated documentary by Rittner and Myers. Survivors' comments are instructive since they presumably have no need to justify the rescuers' acts.

86. Fogelman 1994.

87. This phenomenon had a great impact on people plotting political resistance to the German government, and worked against indigenous resisters of Nazi political policies, as is evident in Otto's discussions and in memoirs by other German Resistance members. See *The Restless Conscience*, a 1990 film by Hava Beller.

88. This distinction corresponds with the contemporary work on the role of the crowd in group behavior. See or Graumann and Moscovici 1986, who suggest it is the group in interaction with others that is critical.

89. See Monroe, Hankin, and VanVechten 2000 for an overview of this literature.

90. Social identity theory suggests we define ourselves in distinction to others, forming groups that are "us" and "them." It argues that it is the reconceptualizing of our group boundaries that leads to shifts in perceptions of our neighbors so

that individuals we have known, worked with, and lived next to for years can suddenly become "the other" and then be discriminated against, disenfranchised, persecuted, and even subjected to genocidal violence. See Monroe 1995b for a review of the literature on genocide.

91. It appears to be a very elementary function of human nature to evaluate things. We attribute valence to both objects and categories we encounter. Positively valenced objects attract us; negatively valenced objects repel us and make us want to keep our distance from them.

92. Psychologists might refer to these as the cognitive construals (which are ongoing mechanisms) or the cognitive frameworks (which can be thought of as the underlying cognitive scaffolding around which we organize incoming information). I have avoided such terminology since it is not widely utilized in other fields of social science or in everyday discourse.

93. In this regard, we can distinguish between efficacy and the altruistic perspective. Efficacy might be defined as a general sense that I am able to change things or a feeling that I can make a difference. Efficacy is frequently thought of as a general personality characteristic. While many rescuers were people who did exhibit this characteristic, just as many did not. What rescuers did seem to exhibit was a compulsion to help that then led them to find ways to help, a sense of urgency that led them to attempt what others—and perhaps rescuers themselves, in another situation—would say was impossible. This discussion underlines the importance of the situation in triggering different aspects of an identity that is complex, since we can speak about people with high levels of efficacy and still recognize that even the bravest of us experiences moments of vulnerability and fear, just as the most timid can, on occasion, feel empowered, brave, and efficacious.

94. To convey more clearly what I believe is the critical psychological linkage among identity, perspective, and moral action, let us try to isolate the process by which moral salience is activated, making the link between merely noticing the needs of another and the feeling that these needs require *me* to take action.

To do so, consider the fictionalized moment when Oskar Schindler suddenly feels a moral imperative to help Jews. This moment occurs, in a kind of epiphany, when Schindler is riding in Krakow and looks down in the town to see the ghetto being cleared. Schindler is struck by a little Jewish girl, whose coat is bright red in an otherwise black-and-white movie world. Until that moment, Schindler had been aware of and recognized the plight of the Jews. But he had used his knowledge to profit from their situation. Something further was required to bring to the foreground that part of Schindler's personality that was moral or altruistic. It is interesting that Spielberg uses color at this point in the black and white movie since one of the most frequent illustrations of how objects are accorded salience is the use of color. A red color in an otherwise beige room makes the red object jump to our attention and hence makes us notice the colored object more clearly; the color makes the object salient.

95. We might argue that so much of the rescuers' identity was altruistic or moral that it was statistically improbable that the external environment would tap into any other part. Or we can say that the rescuers' core self was one in which they defined themselves as people closely bonded to others through a shared

humanity. It is difficult to distinguish between these two phenomena without being inside the rescuers' heads. I did not think to ask about this distinction.

96. In this regard, moral salience acts much as salience acts in other situations: it distinguishes one person from others and highlights their need, just as a concern with color makes a red vase stand out in an all-beige room or as my own child stands out for me, but not for you, in a playground filled with children.

97. See Monroe 1996 for a description of canonical expectations and how they affect altruistic behavior.

98. *The Courage to Care.*

99. The Oliners (1988) describe this as extensivity, referring to the fact that rescuers had more extensive conceptions of the moral community. A number of factors can go into the creation of this more extended interpretation of who is "we" and who is "them," some of which are discussed in chapter 6 and include duty, religion, socialization, and so on.

100. Psychologists dealing with altruism have noted the importance of these cognitive factors, finding influence from both the general cognitive frameworks by which altruists organize reality and what we might call the cognitive construals of altruism or morality that come into play in response to direct exposure to a needy person. Batson's work on empathy (1991), Reykowski's work on allocentric needs (2003), and Jarymowicz's work on exocentric needs (1992) illustrate this approach.

101. Margot's willingness to let the Resistance kill the Gestapo commander is a significant exception to this. I have no obvious explanation for this exception although it is possible that the relational aspect of perspective clicked into play here, as evidenced by Margot's suggestion that she wouldn't have done it if the Gestapo commander had acknowledged the voluntary aspect of his wrongdoing.

102. A thorough exploration of this process must await a companion volume, in which I analyze interviews with individuals along the full range of the moral continuum, including just not rescuers but also bystanders, Nazi sympathizers, and Nazis.

103. See Monroe 1994a for an initial description of part of such a work, which contrasts one rescuer with his bystander cousin and several Nazis who resemble the rescuer in critical sociodemographic characteristics. A full volume is in progress.

NOTES TO CHAPTER 8

Portions of this chapter were written with the assistance of Matthew Levy and appeared in the *American Journal of Political Science.* I am grateful to Levy and to the *American Journal of Political Science* for its permission to reprint this article.

1. The importance of stories for ethics is frequently cited. The virtue ethics approach to ethics, for example, can be said to emphasize narrative in two important regards. First, it treats a person's character as a narrative in which thinking about one's character gives a sense of continuity and a sense of self that plays an important part in moral choice. It is this examination that provides the evidence

of pattern in a person's life and helps provide meaning and sense to that life for the individual. Second, some virtue ethicists argue that thinking about ethical issues in terms of personal narratives communicates what is critical about ethics in a way that discussions of abstract concepts cannot.

2. This chapter is somewhat more technical and specialized than the rest of the book. It is not intended as a finished theory so much as the opening remarks in a theoretical dialogue I hope others will join, using my initial propositions to construct their own empirical tests about the moral psychology and political action. My intent in this chapter thus is to stimulate discussion among other scholars interested in constructing empirically grounded moral theory.

3. I believe there is scientific evidence (some of which is cited in chapter 7) to support these claims. But I recognize that other scholars might well disagree with certain aspects of each claim. Hence, I make these claims explicit and treat them as the premises underlying my theory.

4. We know too little about the genetic determinants of personality, but I am prepared to accept the limited scientific evidence on this. I expect this area will be one in which major breakthroughs occur during the next century and that one finding, of significance for political scientists, will be that there are severe limitations on self-interest as the dominant force in human nature.

5. Full discussion of what constitutes a moral perspective is complex and lies beyond the scope of the present volume. One could argue that risking one's family for strangers is less moral than following a universalistic perspective, or that people who viewed rescue activities in agonistic terms were more fully aware of the moral complexities than were the rescuers, and thus were more moral.

6. There are many instances of rescues performed for financial reasons, for example, or because the rescuers were philo-semitic. These are not the focus of my analysis. For fuller discussion of these drives behind rescuing of Jews, see Tec (1986), Fogelman (1994), Jarymowicz (1992), Oliner et al. (1992), and Oliner and Oliner (1988) for the most extensive study of rescuers during the Holocaust.

7. As a piece of moral theory, what follows is prelusive. Indeed, perhaps even attempting to construct original moral theory is an audacious act. But because it is important to think about such topics, I offer my work in the hope that it will both encourage reflection and stimulate the scholarly debate necessary to advance our collective understanding of moral action.

8. See Smith 1759/1853; Harsanyi 1976; or Sen and Nussbaum 1993.

9. See Churchill and Street (2002) for a discussion of how an analysis of altruism can lead us to this conclusion.

10. Validation—the idea that others agree with our performance or presentation of identity—establishes identity as socially recognized. Self-esteem is key in both processes and is said to provide ontological security that we know who we are. This in turn relates to the need for control and predictability. Some of the rescuers' cognitive worldviews might be explained by this need to feel they had some control over their lives. Certainly the literature on political efficacy (Renshon 1974) suggests there are strong linkages between such psychological needs and political behavior. A fuller discussion of this topic lies beyond the scope of this volume.

11. It is controversial to speak of personality traits being genetically deter-

mined, but the evidence from twin studies seems too important to be ignored. Certain circles in psychology attribute as much as 50 percent of our personality traits to genetic inheritance. See chapter 7, note 19, for details.

12. Hirschman (1977) describes how the tacit assumptions of Western European society shifted so that the basic drive for self-preservation became associated with having possessions. (More goods make us less vulnerable and therefore better protected.) This associates self-identification with one's possessions. Calvinism encouraged this process, so critical for liberal capitalism.

13. By emphasizing core identity I do not ignore the extent to which people have conflicting identities. Indeed, determining how moral action is affected by conflicts between, ambivalence concerning, and shifts among critical aspects of core identity is a critical challenge for identity theorists. See Johnston 1991 or Elster 1986. This leads us back to the question of agonistic choices, however, and lies beyond the scope of this volume.

14. My discussion focuses on adults since most of the theories of moral action are concerned with adult behavior, not that of children.

15. I might argue a closely related idea, that a core self or a master identity is not created by an agent so much as it is revealed to an actor through his or her own acts and by the realization that the actor can't do X but feels compelled to do Y.

16. Indeed, this is why the rescuers' situation intrigues me, since for most of us our core values of self-preservation or desire to protect our families would have warred with our desire to save others (sociability).

17. See Ignatieff 1984.

18. This is a complicated thought, worthy of more development than space allows here. Certain people may have such high standards that even though they may in fact be morally upright people, their own self-image may be as people who fail to meet their own standards. Even though they may do good, they may not do as much as they feel they should and thus they would not find themselves to be morally praiseworthy. This was the case for some rescuers I interviewed, one of whom refused her Yad Vashem Medal because she felt she had not done enough.

19. Fogelman 1994; Jarymowicz 1992; Oliner and Oliner 1988; Oliner et al. 1992; Reykowski 2001; Tec 1986.

20. Colby and Damon 1992; Blasi 1980, 1988, 1993, 1995.

21. Marion, The *Courage to Care*, Rittener and Myers 1986.

22. This confusion is understandable, drawing on what has been called the "dissipation of moral energy" argument of Aristotle, which suggests we love those closest to us. As our ties to people become more tenuous, a kind of distancing occurs. While this may be true for many individuals, it was not true for the rescuers. Instead, rescuers often put the needs of strangers ahead of those of their families. In several instances, the children of rescuers remain estranged from their parents because of this.

23. This relevance for the rescuer was identified in studies of rescuers conducted by Jarymowicz (1992), Reykowski (2001), and Oliner et al. (1992).

24. The best analogue for this aspect of the moral perspective may be family ties that create a sense of responsibility for people to whom we are related, even though we may not have had past histories that establish ties of affection or have much in common with the family member.

25. Smith 1759/1853, 1776/1902.

26. This exempts chance corrections of moral wrongs.

27. Work on the perpetrators suggests they were able to kill people because they had successfully distanced themselves from the victims and dehumanized the victims. Browning 1992 or Glass 1997.

28. The Keneallys were our next-door neighbors for a while in Irvine yet we spoke only once of Oskar Schindler. Keneally indicated then that Schindler had remained a bit of an enigma to him, an elusive character even though he was at the heart of the novel. My comments, then, refer to the Schindler as described by Keneally in his fictionalized book and are speculative rather than empirically based.

29. The next obvious question—What makes us sometimes see ourselves as connected to others and not at other times?—lies beyond the scope of this work. But it is clearly an area in which philosophers could benefit from contact with personality and social psychologists, who emphasize the extent to which external factors trigger different parts of our identities and influence how we see ourselves in relation to others. (I am less likely to help others if friends accompanying me do nothing or if I am alone or in potentially dangerous areas, as opposed to safe havens.) These observations are the commonplace of social psychology. For a review, see Latané and Darley 1980; Reykowski 2002; or Monroe, Hankin, and VanVechten 2000.

30. For the best work on this, see Batson 1991, 2002; Batson and Shaw 1991.

31. Hume 1740/1978.

32. Finding a middle ground between the extremes of martyrdom and doing nothing reminds us of virtue ethics' defining virtue as the balance of two extremes.

33. I am reminded of Bentham's statement about animals: it is not whether they can reason but whether they can suffer.

34. Rosenberg 1979; Tetlock 1981.

35. Aronson, Wilson, and Akert 1999; 191.

36. Festinger 1957; Festinger and Aronson 1960; Brehm and Cohen 1962; Harmon-Jones and Mills 1998.

37. Aronson 1968, 1969, 1992, 1998; Aronson, Wilson, and Akert 1999; Thibodeau and Aronson 1992; Harmon-Jones and Mills 1998. See also Festinger, Riecken, and Schachter 1956; Brehm 1956; Gilovich, Medvec, and Chen 1995; Aronson and Mills 1959; Gerard and Mathewson 1966.

38. Aronson, Wilson, and Akert 1999. To discuss self-esteem, we must differentiate between the self-concept, defined as our knowledge about who we are, and self-awareness, defined as the act of thinking about ourselves. Both aspects are critical in creating a coherent sense of identity. See Gallup 1977, 1993 and Gallup and Suarez 1986 on the experiments suggesting the extent to which other animals have a sense of self. See also Povinelli 1993, 1994 and Sedikides and Skowronski 1997.

39. An interest in such matters is not restricted to psychologists. Indeed, living a fulfilled life, and asking what it means to live such a life and how best to achieve it, forms a central part of the core of ethics as traditionally conceived since the time of the ancient Greeks.

40. I am not the first to locate the impetus for interpersonal morality from

within the individual. Both Aristotle's use of virtue and Kant's discussion of universal self-regard might be said to utilize this approach.

41. Gewirth 1998.

42. See Bertenthal and Fischer 1978; Lewis 1986; Povinelli, Landau, and Perilloux 1996.

43. See Montemayor and Eisen 1977; Hart and Damon 1986; Livesley and Bromley 1973; Erikson 1959.

44. Baumeister 1998; Cross and Madson 1997; Graziano, Jensen-Campbell, and Finch 1997; Higgins 1996; Mischel, Cantor, and Feldman 1996; and Sedikides and Skowronski 1997.

45. Campbell 1990; Higgins 1987; Markus and Nurius 1986; Pelham 1991. Higgins (1987) suggests we frequently think about our actual self (our sense of who we truly are) and compare that with our "ideal" self (who we want to be) and our "ought" self (who we think we should be). If we feel our actual self falls short of our ideal self, we become depressed. If we feel our actual self falls short of our ought self, we become agitated (Aronson, Wilson, and Akert 1999: 153).

46. Dunning and Hayes 1996; Kihlstrom and Klein 1994; Markus, Smith, and Moreland 1985; Symons and Johnson 1997.

47. See Fiske and Taylor 1991 for a rather encyclopedic review of the social cognition literature.

48. Narcissism refers most frequently to the sense of being self-centered or egotistical. See Kohut 1971 for the classic text.

49. Kohut 1971, 1977, 1985; and Winnicott 1965.

50. Kohut 1971, 1977, 1985.

51. Alford argues that this threatening of ontological security constitutes the essence of evil, and he relates this phenomenon—the transgressing of others' boundaries—to political evil and mental health (1997a, b). My analysis is restricted to discussion of "normal, healthy" adult development, a concept and a limitation that I cannot address here for reasons of space.

52. A teenage rebellion against a strong parental figure who makes the teenager feel overwhelmed, even when such rebellion hurts the teenager in obvious ways, is one familiar illustration of the need for differentiation and boundary formation.

53. At least this is theoretically the case in post-Enlightenment Western-style democracies.

54. The close association of ethnic conflict and genocide with attempts to establish one dominant community serves as brutal confirmation of this claim.

55. Chomsky 1966, 1986, or 1988. Recent work by Lakoff and Johnson (1999) challenges certain of Chomsky's claims to universality and I suspect this will be an interesting area of research for future scholars.

56. For the purposes of general theory, I omit discussion of human beings with physical disabilities that make it impossible for them to acquire language.

57. Bickerton 1975.

58. Kripke 1982.

59. Chomsky 1988; Habermas 1984/1987.

60. Work suggesting similar universals in other primates raises further questions for ethics. See DeWaal 1996 or Singer 1975/1990 for an overview of the animal rights movement.

61. Harris 1960.

62. Chomsky's *Cartesian Linguistics* (1966) addresses the Port Royale group of linguists in the 1660s, who tried to organize all known languages into a general table of grammar. Descartes's philosophy was the inspiration for the Port Royale group. See Chomsky 1966 for a discussion of how Chomsky's own theories of transformational grammar were inspired by Descartes.

63. Chomsky 1966.

64. Chomsky 1986.

65. Bickerton 1975, 1995.

66. The importance of this theory of language is that it indirectly addresses questions about the translatability of principles of rational argument across cultural lines. The cultural relativist problem that confronts modern moral theory is not new; the threat that the multiplicity of cultural traditions presents to the possibility of a unitary moral law is explicitly discussed by Descartes as a primary motivation for his radical skepticism and rationalist philosophy. The connection between language and morality has been recognized since the Enlightenment; one of the primary projects of the intellectual tradition Descartes inspired was the construction of a theory of universal grammar that could systematize and translate the syntax of the various languages of the world. It was only later, in the nineteenth century, when evidence of the vast and seemingly incommensurable differences between various human languages became overwhelming, and when Romantic fascination with the "difference" of non-Western cultures and dissatisfaction with the sociological legacy of the Enlightenment became widespread, that the Cartesian, universalistic approach to language was supplanted by a linguistic and cultural relativism that sought to identify human cultures not as local variations on a basically universal human nature but as self-contained, unique, and organic entities. It was at this point also that the eighteenth-century interest in universal and rational principles of political organization was displaced by a new nationalist fascination with the racial destiny of individual peoples and with the idiosyncratic character of their cultural traditions.

67. If we try to refer our standards to Englishness, Christianity, etc., we are always faced with the unjustifiably parochial and arbitrary quality of these master signifiers. Humanism is less arbitrary because it extends from a basic communicative capacity that is at the core of respect for rights. The flaw in this is animal rights, or even animism/paranormalism. Here is where language-based humanism breaks down. See Singer 2003 for an overview. Interestingly, rescuers often referred to the value of life, not human life, as their core value.

68. Chomsky (1988, 1966, and 1986) and Habermas (1984/1987) are helpful here. I have already noted the importance of Chomskian linguistics to the universalist issue via the question of categorization and the development of universal values. Habermas's critical sociology, which also attempts to transcend the problem of cultural relativity toward a universal theory of social democratic justice, is also relevant. Habermas stresses the importance of active communal deliberation. But his theory of deliberative democracy and discourse does not stress the psychological process of categorization and reciprocation that I make central to my own theory.

69. One of the more interesting discussions of this is Bettelheim's (1982) work on Freud.

70. I deliberately use the term *sentient being* rather than *human being* since recent work in animal ethology suggests language may not be restricted to humans. Fuller discussion of this important topic lies beyond the scope of this book.

71. The phrase is Glass's (1997). See also Gross 1997 or Staub 1989.

72. See Monroe 1995b for a review.

73. See Tajfel 1970; Turner and Hogg 1987; or Monroe, Hankin, and Van-Vechten 2000 for an overview.

NOTES TO CONCLUSION

1. Herf 1997: xi.

2. See Shermer and Grobman 2000 for an overview of the work on Holocaust denial.

3. I leave it to historians to consult Otto's extensive documentation as they assess this claim. I am happy, through Princeton University Press, to forward to Otto's daughters the names of historians interested in examining Otto's documents in detail.

4. Stories of German rescuers lend insight on a longstanding controversy concerning the extent of support for Hitler's eliminationist policies among ordinary Germans. One line of argument in this debate runs as follows. If the perpetrators of genocide were ordinary Germans, in terms of their critical sociodemographic characteristics—age, religion, occupation, education, and so on—then it is reasonable to assume that other ordinary Germans, who resembled the perpetrators in terms of these same demographic characteristics, must have shared the perpetrators' support for Hitler's genocidal policies.

The stories of the German rescuers speak directly to this claim. They show us empirically that there also were Germans—people like Margot and Otto—who *did* help Jews, and that these Germans were equally ordinary in terms of their background characteristics. But does this similarity mean we should conclude that other Germans shared the rescuers' moral values, simply because they resemble rescuers in superficial, if critical sociodemographic, characteristics? No. It would be as erroneous to make this inference about the vast majority of Germans based on a few rescuers as it is erroneous to make inferences about ordinary Germans based on knowledge of the perpetrators. Neither conclusion can be reliably drawn from the data. The stories presented here thus suggest the recent public perception of Germans as Hitler's willing executioners, encouraged by Goldhagen's controversial 1996 book, may well be overstated. The rescuers teach us that good and bad exist in all people. This is as true for Germans as it is for the rest of us. Further discussion of this debate lies beyond the scope of this book. I am, however, making a more systematic examination of the claim that Germans were particularly anti-Semitic, drawing on interview data with Jews who left the Third Reich before World War II.

5. These findings reject the kind of reflective equilibrium prevalent in contractarian approaches to morality (Rawls 1971) or in rational choice theory (Monroe 1991a).

6. Blasi's empirical work underlines the importance of integration of moral values into a sense of self. His recent theoretical work (2002) stresses the importance of perceptions.

7. As utilized by psychologists, self-consistency usually refers to some combination of both behavioral and trait consistency and the many different varieties of logical and cognitive consistency, including coherence among representations of the self. These conceptualizations underlie the basic research on cognitive dissonance (Festinger 1957), as well as the work on personality integration.

8. I would hypothesize that the relationship between consistency and self-esteem is linked to the extent to which a rescuer's commitments and values are such that he/she constructs a sense of a central or core self around them. We might think of these as the values or ideals that truly matter to a person and provide a sense of meaning in the person's life. Frankfurt argues that these core values are so much a part of one's self that betraying them constitutes the same thing as betraying one's soul. See Frankfurt 1988.

9. One of the best recent works on moral psychology is by Blasi (2002). In chapter 3, Blasi traces the development of moral character as an approach within psychology. Blasi notes that behaviorism tended to reduce personality to a conglomerate of habits; not until Piaget did the American psychological community begin to understand the importance of cognition for morality. Kohlberg's work expanded on Piaget's cognitive developmental approach in such a powerful fashion that work on moral psychology is only now understanding the limitations of the cognitive developmental approach. Blasi's most recent work reintroduces the concept of moral character, but does so in a manner that draws on both philosophical discussions, especially those of virtue ethics, and the most recent, scientifically rigorous psychological work. Blasi argues that moral character involves predispositions, which Blasi defines as relatively stable and general personality characteristics (2002: 4). Blasi then defines these personality characteristics in terms of their relation to action, an approach that differentiates his view from those of the cognitive developmentalists. Finally, Blasi assumes that intentions and motives count in speaking of moral character, and that there must be some minimal grasp of what morality is and involves.

10. I am exploring these ideas in a book manuscript in which I contrast the moral psychology of rescuers, bystanders, and Nazis.

11. See Frankfurt 1988 for a discussion of identity, moral character, and will.

12. Blasi suggests that the cognitive ability to plan for possible contingencies may be related to the moral life. We could interpret the rescuers' refusal to consider betraying their fellow man a deliberate decision to take such an option off the table, but I do not know if this is what Blasi means. Otto did say that he spoke with a friend who had been tortured and that the man had experienced religious fantasies ("apparitions") while undergoing torture. This may have been the kind of cognitive preparation Blasi refers to insofar as it reflects Otto's cognitively preparing a mental safe haven. During possible torture Otto then could retreat into this haven. Such a cognitive safety net would help Otto hold fast to the ideals that he had integrated into his sense of self. Unfortunately, I did not think to ask Otto about this scenario.

13. All of this is in line with the kinds of characteristics that Frankfurt argues

we find in the type of will in which we make a wholehearted commitment to moral values and desires. Frankfurt notes that morality is only one of many possible values that an individual may care deeply about and structure his/her will around, a point I find extremely important and which I pursue empirically in a forthcoming volume on Nazis and bystanders, as well as rescuers.

14. See Churchill and Street 2002 for a discussion of this.

15. In 1887, Ferdinand Tonniës (1957) argued for two basic forms of human association, reflecting different beliefs about the nature of the self and social relationships: Gemeinschaft and Gesellschaft worldviews. Gemeinschaft (translated as community) refers to close, holistic social relationships of family and kin groups in pre-industrial communities. Individuals cannot be taken out of the context of a society and are born with obligations, ties, and identities as part of that community. People with this worldview have a "consciousness of belonging together and the affirmation of the condition of mutual dependence" (1957: 69), and a sense of moral worth is attached to these close community ties. In contrast, we find the Gesellschaft worldview, translated as association or society and characterized as post-industrial, urban, and modern. This Gesellschaft worldview conceptualizes the self as an individual independent of others, who acts rationally, efficiently, and instrumentally to further voluntarily chosen goals. Social ties are understood to be based on a union of rational wills, with membership sustained by some instrumental goal or definite end. Barry (1978) argues that we find a similar distinction between traditional sociologists and economists. With the incursion of rational choice analysis into sociology, this distinction has broken down somewhat, but we find a similar conceptual divide in the debates between liberals and rational actor theorists versus communitarians.

16. To the degree to which we emphasize the social side of the self, we need to ask about the extent to which we are trapped within that society. What if our genetic predispositions make us unhappy in the society into which we are born? Make us gravitate toward values at odds with the basic values in our community? Will we become the moral analogues of left-handed children being forced to use our right hands?

One implication of the atomistic conception of individuals is universalism since if what makes us distinct, what makes us what we are, is our ability to reason, and if all humans have this basic ability, then we move toward universalism. And if what makes us individuals is the idea of reason, then isn't every reasoning being equal? We might think of this equivalence and equality as the good aspect of universalism. A more pernicious aspect of universalism comes if we assume every individual should think in one particular manner of abstract reasoning—such as the one Descartes admired—and we then privilege individuals and cultures that excel at this particular form.

Another implication of this dichotomy concerns human connection. If, as Aristotle suggests, every person is a social being, then people in every culture want to be bound together, not just into families but into larger social groups and even polities; hence, much of our identity becomes group identity or social identity. Indeed, our *self* will not be satisfied unless it is nested in a rich set of relations with others. This need for others is a part of our basic identity, a reflection of our need to find out and to know who we are which can be satisfied only in the reflection of others. We see ourselves reflected in the eyes of others.

But which others? What if the people around us do not see us as we wish to be seen? As we genuinely feel we are? Are we merely the social construction of others? Do we have no free will? And what happens to moral responsibility if identity is not our own creation? To all these difficult questions I have no answers.

17. I leave aside discussion of what we mean by human flourishing.

18. This help need not occur at the moment of action and can extend to our early childhood days, when our early sense of self is established through our interactions with others.

19. The tension between caring for others and the loss one experiences once they are taken from us is poignantly expressed in the writings of Holocaust survivors, such as Primo Levi (1961) and Elie Wiesel (1960/1986, 1992), the filmed testimonies with survivors (Langer 1991), and films (*Shadows* or *Sophie's Choice*).

20. Marion, *The Courage to Care* by Rittener and Myers (1986).

21. Langer's (1991) analysis of the oral testimonies of concentration camp survivors focuses on the contradictory value of forgetting painful memories. For some survivors, forgetting the past was necessary in order to survive. For others, remembering the past was a survival mechanism. I might interpret this phenomenon not necessarily as a contradiction but rather as an indicator of the power of the human mind, which does not deal with difficult issues until the person is able to do so, and then does so in a complex manner, often unfathomable to the external observer. I might further argue that it was, at least in part, the rescuers' ability to retain these ties that kept them from experiencing the psychic discontinuities that Langer finds among survivors. Indeed, some of the testimonies Langer cites suggest the importance of human attachment for camp inmates. For example, Langer relates one poignant story, from a female survivor, of a baby found by a young girl, also in transit with the story's narrator. The girl refuses to give the baby to the Gestapo and is sent off to die herself, with the baby, as a result of this refusal. Years after witnessing this event, the woman relating the story is still deeply troubled by it. She seems to envy this girl, however, because the girl appeared to have found something to love and care for, even if the attachment meant her death. Wiesel (1960/1986, 1992) and Levi (1961) also allude to this phenomenon.

22. I have found this poem attributed to various sources, from Native American tribal poetry to Mary Frye. It is unattributed and untitled in Margot's book manuscript.

23. Elie Wiesel, *The Courage to Care*, Rittener and Myers 1986.

Notes to Appendix A

Much of this appendix, written with Molly Patterson, appeared in *The Annual Review of Political Science* (Patterson and Monroe 1998). I am grateful to Molly Patterson and the *Annual Review of Political Science* for their permission to republish it, in modified form, here. All changes made are my responsibility, and do not necessarily reflect the opinion of Patterson or the *Annual Review*.

1. See Barthes 1968, 1971/1974; Greimas and Courtes 1976.

2. Ibid.

3. Robeson originally sang, "I gets weary and sick of trying, I'm tired of living and scared of dying." He modified these words in different ways at different points in time; perhaps the most significant modification was, "I keep trying instead of crying, I must keep fighting or else I'm dying."

4. These groups include a variety of individuals, from neo-fascists to legitimate historians with nationalist agendas.

5. Personal Narratives Group 1989.

6. An alternative explanation for such exclusions is provided by schema theory in psychology. Schema theory suggests that people organize information in related chunks or cognitive templates (schemas), which provide a way of taking in and organizing information and enabling it to be retrieved again. They are organized around stock cultural characters or situations. One might, for example, have a schema for schoolteachers or for how to behave in a restaurant. People are included to remember those aspects of a situation that are consistent with their schemas and forget those that are inconsistent (although details that are radically dissonant with the schema may be remembered for their peculiarity). This alternative understanding of possible silences or gaps merely highlights the need for caution when interpreting what is not said, as well as what is said.

NOTE TO APPENDIX B

1. Rescues performed primarily for money are rarely given Yad Vashem status, although rescuers who have accepted money given in support of a rescue driven by more altruistic motives have been deemed acceptable. The critical distinction is that the rescuer did not exact monetary compensation in advance and as a precondition or a required part of the choice to make the rescue.

BIBLIOGRAPHY

Abrams, Dominic, and Michael Hogg. 1990. *Social Identity Theory: Constructive and Critical Advances.* New York: Simon and Schuster.

Adorno, Theodor, Betty Aron, Maria Hertz Levinson, and William Mo. 1950. *The Authoritarian Personality.* New York: Harper and Row.

Alexander, C. Norman, and Mary Glen Wiley. 1981. "Situated Activity and Identity Formation." In *Social Psychology: Sociological Perspectives,* ed. Morris Rosenberg and Ralph H. Turner, 269–90. New York: Basic Books.

Alford, C. Fred. 1997a. *What Evil Means to Us.* Ithaca: Cornell University Press.

———. 1997b. "The Political Psychology of Evil." *Political Psychology* 18, no. 1: 1–15.

Allen, V. L., and K. Scheibe. 1982. "The Social Context of Conduct." *The Psychological Writings of T. R. Sarbin.* New York: Praeger.

Almond, Gabriel, and Sidney Verba. 1963. *The Civic Culture: Political Attitudes and Democracy in Five Nations.* Princeton: Princeton University Press.

Altmeyer, B. 1981. *Right Wing Authoritarianism.* Winnipeg: University of Manitoba Press.

———. 1988. *Enemies of Freedom: Understanding Right Wing Authoritarianism.* San Francisco: Jossey-Bass.

Ancheta, Angelo. 1998. *Race Rights and the Asian-American Experience.* New Brunswick: Rutgers University Press.

Anscombe, Elizabeth. 1957/1963. *Intention.* Ithaca: Cornell University Press.

———. 1958. "Modern Moral Philosophy." *Philosophy* 33:1–19.

Arendt, Hannah. 1969/73. *Eichmann in Jerusalem: A Report on the Banality of Evil.* New York: Viking Press.

Arnhart, L. 1987. *Political Questions.* New York: Macmillan.

Aronson, Elliot. 1968. "Dissonance Theory: Progress and Problems." In *Theories of Cognitive Consistency: A Sourcebook,* ed. R. P. Abelson, E. Aronson, W. J. McGuire, T. M. Newcomb, M. J. Rosenberg, and P. H. Tanenbaum, 5–27. Chicago: Rand McNally.

———. 1969. "The Theory of Cognitive Dissonance: A Current Perspective." In *Advances in Experimental Social Psychology,* vol. 4, ed. L. Berkowitz, 1–34. New York: Academic Press.

———. 1992. "The Return of the Repressed: Dissonance Theory Makes a Comeback." *Psychological Inquiry* 3:303–11.

———. 1998. "Dissonance, Hypocrisy, and the Self-Concept." In *Cognitive Dissonance Theory: Progress on a Pivotal Theory in Social Psychology,* ed. E. Harmon-Jones and J. S. Mills, 103–27. Washington, DC: American Psychological Association.

Aronson, Elliot, and J. Mills. 1959. "The Effect of Severity of Initiation on Liking for a Group." *Journal of Abnormal and Social Psychology* 59:177–81.

Aronson, Elliot, Timothy D. Wilson, and Robin M. Akert. 1999. *Social Psychology.* New York: Longman-Addison Wesley.

Aronson, Joshua, G. Cohen, and P. Nail. 1998. "Self-Affirmation Theory: An Update and Appraisal." In *Cognitive Dissonance Theory: Progress on a Pivotal Theory in Social Psychology*, ed. E. Harmon-Jones and J. S. Mills, 127–49. Washington, DC: American Psychological Association.

Arrow, K. J. 1951. *Social Choice and Individual Values*. New Haven: Yale University Press.

———. 1984. *Social Choice and Justice*. Oxford: Basil Blackwell.

Axelrod, R. 1984. *The Evolution of Cooperation*. New York: Basic Books.

———. 1986. "An Evolutionary Approach to Norms." *American Political Science Review* 80:1095–1111.

Badhwar, Neera Kapur. 1993. *Friendship: A Philosophical Reader*. Ithaca: Cornell University Press.

Bakhtin, M. M. 1975/1981. *The Dialogic Imagination: Four Essays*. Trans. C. Emerson and M. Holquist. Austin: University of Texas Press.

Ball, R. A. 1968. "A Poverty Case: The Analgesic Subculture of the Southern Appalachians." *American Sociological Review* 33:885–95.

Bandura, A. 1986. *Social Foundations of Thought and Action: A Social Cognitive Theory*. Englewood Cliffs, NJ: Prentice-Hall.

———. 1989. "Human Agency in Social Cognitive Theory." *American Psychologist* 44:1175–84.

———. 1990. "Selective Activation and Disengagement of Moral Control." *Journal of Social Issues* 46, no. 1: 27–67.

———. 1991. "Human Agency: The Rhetoric and the Reality." *American Psychologist* 46, no. 2: 157–63.

Barber, B. 1984. *Strong Democracy*. Berkeley: University of California Press.

———. 1992. *An Aristocracy of Everyone: The Politics of Education and the Future of America*. New York: Ballantine Books.

Barkow, L., L. Cosmides, and J. Tooby. 1992. *The Adapted Mind: Evolutionary Psychology and the Generation of Culture*. New York: Oxford University Press.

Barry, B. 1978. *Sociologist, Economist and Democracy*. Chicago: University of Chicago Press.

Barry, B., and R. Hardin. 1982. *Rational Man and Irrational Society? An Introduction and Sourcebook*. Beverly Hills: Sage.

Barthes, R. 1968. *Elements of Semiology*. New York: Hill and Wang.

———. 1971/1974. *Structural Analysis and Biblical Exegesis: Interpretational Essays*. Pittsburgh: Pickwick.

Bartlett, F. A. 1932. *Remembering*. Cambridge: Cambridge University Press.

Bates, R. 1983. *Essays in the Political Economy of Rural Africa*. New York: Cambridge University Press.

———, ed. 1988. *Toward a Political Economy of Development: A Rational Choice Perspective*. Berkeley: University of California Press.

Batson, Daniel C. 1991. *The Altruism Question: Toward a Social Psychological Answer*. Hillsdale, NJ: Erlbaum.

Batson, Daniel C., and Laura Shaw. 1991. "Evidence for Altruism: Toward a Plurality of Prosocial Motives." *Psychological Inquiry* 2(2):107–22.

Baumeister, R. F. 1986a. *Identity: Cultural Change and the Struggle for Self*. New York: Oxford University Press.

————, ed. 1986b. *Public Self and Private Self.* New York: Springer-Verlag.

————. 1991. *Meanings of Life.* New York: Guilford Press, 1991.

————. 1993. *Self-Esteem: The Puzzle of Low Self-Regard.* New York: Plenum Press.

————. 1998. "The Self." In *The Handbook of Social Psychology,* 4th ed., vol. 1, ed. D. T. Gilbert, S. T. Fiske, and G. Lindzey, 680–740. New York: McGraw-Hill.

Becker, G. S. 1976. *The Economic Approach to Human Behavior.* Chicago: University of Chicago Press.

Bellah, Robert M., Richard Madsen, W. Sullivan, A. Swindler, and S. Tipton. 1985. *Habits of the Heart: Individualism and Commitment in American Life.* Berkeley: University of California Press.

Beller, Hava. 1990. *The Restless Conscience.* Documentary.

Berger, Peter L., and Thomas Luchman. 1966. *The Social Construction of Reality.* New York: Doubleday.

Bernichon, Tiffany, Kathleen E. Cook, and Jonathan D. Brown. 2003. "Seeking Self-evaluative Feedback: The Interactive Role of Global Self-esteem and Specific Self-views." *Journal of Personality and Social Psychology* 84:194–204.

Bertenthal, B. L., and K. W. Fischer. 1978. "Development of Self-Recognition in the Infant." *Developmental Psychology* 14:44–50.

Bettelheim, Bruno. 1960. *The Informed Heart: Autonomy in a Mass Age.* New York: Free Press.

————. 1982. *Freud and Man's Soul.* New York: Knopf.

Bickerton, Derek. 1975. *Dynamics of a Creole System.* New York: Cambridge University Press.

————. 1995. *Language and Human Behavior.* Seattle: University of Washington Press.

Billig, Michael. 1987. *Arguing and Thinking: A Rhetorical Approach to Social Psychology.* Cambridge: Cambridge University Press.

Black, D. 1958. *The Theory of Committees and Elections.* New York: Cambridge University Press.

Blaine B., and J. Crocker. 1993. "Self-esteem and Self-serving Biases in Reactions to Positive and Negative Events: An Integrative Review." In *Self-esteem: The Puzzle of Low Self-regard,* ed. R. F. Baumeister, 55–81. New York: Plenum.

Blasi, A. 1980. "Bridging Moral Cognition and Moral Action: A Critical Review of the Literature." *Psychological Bulletin* 88:1–45.

————. 1988. "Identity and Development of the Self." In *Self, Ego and Identity: Integrative Approaches,* ed. D. K. Lapsley and F. C. Power, 226–243. New York: Springer-Verlaag.

————. 1993. "The Development of Identity: Some Implications for Moral Functioning." In *The Moral Self,* ed. G. G. Noam and T. E. Wren, 99–123. Cambridge, MA: MIT Press.

————. 1995. "A Moral Understanding and the Moral Personality: The Process of Moral Integration." In *Moral Development: An Introduction,* ed. W. M. Kurtines and J. L. Gewirtz, 229–55. Boston: Allyn and Bacon.

————. 2003. "Character, Moral Development, and the Self." In *Character Psychology and Character Education,* ed. D. K. Lapsley and F. C. Power, 52–82. Notre Dame: University of Notre Dame Press.

Blumer, Herbert. 1969. *Symbolic Interactionism: Perspective and Method*. Englewood Cliffs, NJ: Prentice-Hall.

Bookman, Ann, and Sandra Morgen. 1988. *Women and the Politics of Empowerment*. Philadelphia: Temple University Press.

Boom, Corrie ten., John Sherrill, and Elizabeth Sherrill. 1974. *The Hiding Place*. New York: Bantam Books.

Botwinick, Rita. 1996. *A History of the Holocaust*. Upper Saddle River, NJ: Prentice-Hall.

———. 1998. *A Holocaust Reader*. Upper Saddle River, NJ: Prentice-Hall.

Boyle, A. 1979. *The Climate of Treason: Five Who Spied for Russia*. London: Hutchinson.

Brehm, J. W. 1956. "Postdecision Changes in the Desirability of Alternatives." *Journal of Abnormal and Social Psychology* 52:384–89.

Brehm, J. W., and A. R. Cohen. 1962. *Experiments in Cognitive Dissonance*. New York: Wiley.

Brewer, M. 1991. "The Social Self: On Being the Same and Different at the Same Time." *Personality and Social Psychology Bulletin* 17:475–82.

Browning, Christopher. 1992. *Ordinary Men: Reserve Police Battalion 101 and the Final Solution in Poland*. New York: Aaron Asher/HarperCollins.

Browning, Rufus P., Dale Rogers Marshall, and David H. Tabb. 1997. *Racial Politics in American Cities*. 2nd ed. New York: Longman.

Bruner, J. 1957. *Contemporary Approaches to Cognition*. Cambridge, MA: Harvard University Press.

———. 1992. *Acts of Meaning*. Cambridge, MA: Harvard University Press.

Buchanan, J. 1984a. "Constitutional Restrictions on the Power of Government." In *The Theory of Public Choice-II*, ed. J. M. Buchanan and R. D. Tollison, 439–52. Ann Arbor: University of Michigan Press.

———. 1984b. "Politics without Romance: A Study of Positive Public Choice Theory and Its Normative Implications." In *The Theory of Public Choice-II*, ed. J. M. Buchanan and R. D. Tollison, 11–23. Ann Arbor: University of Michigan Press.

Buchanan, J. M., and G. Tullock. 1962. *The Calculus of Consent: Logical Foundations of Constitutional Democracy*. Ann Arbor: University of Michigan Press.

Buchanan, J. M., and R. E. Wagner. 1977. *Democracy in Deficit*. New York: Academic Press.

Bullock, Alan. 1962. *Hitler: A Study in Tyranny*. New York: Harper and Row.

———. 1991. *Hitler and Stalin*. London: HarperCollins.

Burr, V. 1995. *The Introduction to Social Constructivism*: London: Routledge.

Calabresi, G., and Philip Bobbitt. 1978. *Tragic Choices*. New York: Norton.

Campbell, Donald T. 1965. "Ethnocentrism and Other Altruistic Motives." *Nebraska Symposium on Motivation*, vol. 13, ed. David Levine. Lincoln: University of Nebraska Press.

———. 1990. "Self-Esteem and Clarity of the Self-Concept." *Journal of Personality and Social Psychology* 59:941–51.

Caprara, G. V., and D. Cervona. 2000. *Personality*. Cambridge: Cambridge University Press.

Cash, John D. 1989. "Ideology and Affect—The Case of Northern Ireland." *Political Psychology* 10, no. 4: 703–24.

———. 1996. *Identity, Ideology and Conflict.* New York: Cambridge University Press.

Caudill, H. M. 1962. *Night Comes to the Cumberlands.* Boston: Little, Brown.

Charny, Israel W., ed. 1994. *The Widening Circle of Genocide.* Vol. 3: A Critical Bibliographic Review. London: Transaction Publishers.

Chomsky, Noam. 1966. *Cartesian Linguistics: A Chapter in the History of Rationalist Thought.* New York: Harper and Row.

———. 1986. *Knowledge of Language: Its Nature, Origin, and Use.* New York: Praeger.

———. 1988. *Language and Problems of Knowledge: The Managua Lectures.* Cambridge, MA: MIT Press.

Churchill, Robert Paul, and Erin Street. 2002. "Is There a Paradox of Altruism?" *Critical Review of International Social Philosophy and Policy,* vol. 5, no. 4 (winter 2002), 87–105.

Colby, A., and W. Damon. 1992. *Some Do Care.* New York: Free Press.

———. 1993. "The Unity of Self and Morality in the Development of Extraordinary Moral Commitment." In *The Moral Self,* ed. G. G. Noam and T. E. Wren, 149–75. Cambridge, MA: MIT Press.

Coles, R. 1967. *Children of Crisis: A Study of Courage and Fear.* Boston: Little, Brown

———. 1971. *Migrants, Sharecroppers, Mountaineers.* Vol. 2, Children of Crisis Series. Boston: Little, Brown.

———. 1989. *The Call of Stories.* Boston: Houghton Mifflin.

Cooper, J. 1980. "Reducing Fears and Increasing Assertiveness: The Role of Dissonance Reduction." *Journal of Experimental Social Psychology* 47:738–48.

———. 1998. "Unwanted Consequences and the Self: In Search of the Motivation for Dissonance Reduction." In *Cognitive Dissonance Theory: Progress on a Pivotal Theory in Social Psychology,* ed. E. Harmon-Jones and J. S. Mills, 149–74. Washington, DC: American Psychological Association.

Cote, J., and C. Levine. 1988. "A Critical Examination of the Ego Identity Status Paradigm." *Developmental Review* 8:147–84.

Cropsey, Joseph. 1977. *Political Philosophy and the Issues of Politics.* Chicago: University of Chicago Press.

Cross, S. E., and L. Madson. 1997. "Models of the Self: Self-Construals and Gender." *Psychological Bulletin* 122:5–37.

Crotty, W., ed. 1991. *Political Science: An Assessment.* Evanston, IL: Northwestern University Press.

D'Emilio, John. 1983. *Sexual Politics, Sexual Communities: The Making of a Homosexual Minority in the U.S., 1940–1970.* Chicago: University of Chicago Press.

Damasio, A. R. 1994. *Descartes' Error: Emotion, Reason and the Human Brain.* New York: Putnam.

———. 1999. *The Feeling of What Happens: Body and Emotion in the Making of Consciousness.* New York: Harcourt Brace.

Darwin, Charles. 1859/1936. *The Origin of Species by Means of Natural Selection.* London: John Murray Publishers.

Dawkins, Richard. 1976. *The Selfish Gene*. New York: Oxford University Press.

Derrida, Jacques. 1967/1976. *Of Grammatology*. Baltimore: Johns Hopkins University Press.

———. 1972/1981. *Dissemination*. Chicago: University of Chicago Press.

DeWaal, Frans. 1996. *Good Natured: The Origins of Right and Wrong in Humans and Other Animals*. Cambridge, MA: Harvard University Press.

Dobert, Rainer, Jurgen Habermas, and Gertrud Nunner-Winkler. 1977. *The Development of the Self*. Koln: Kiepenheuer and Witsch.

Dobkowski, Michael N., and Isidor Wallimann. 1992. *Genocide in Our Time: An Annotated Bibliography with Analytical Introductions*. Ann Arbor: Pierian Press.

Doise, William. 1988. "Individual and Social Identities in Intergroup Relations." *European Journal of Social Psychology* 28:99–111.

Downs, A. 1957. *An Economic Theory of Democracy*. New York: Harper and Row.

Dunning, D., and A. F. Hayes. 1996. "Evidence of Egocentric Comparison in Social Judgment." *Journal of Personality and Social Psychology* 71:213–29.

Durkheim, Emile. 1982. *The Rules of Sociological Method*. New York: Free Press.

———. 1984. *The Division of Labor in Society*. New York: Free Press.

Eckstein, H. 1984. "Civic Inclusion and Its Discontents." *Daedalus* 113:107–46.

———. 1988. "A Culturalist Theory of Change." *American Political Science Review* 82:789–804.

———. 1992. "A Theory of Stable Democracy." *Regarding Politics*. Berkeley: University of California Press.

Elster, J. 1979. *Ulysses and the Sirens: Studies in Rationality and Irrationality*. Cambridge: Cambridge University Press.

———, ed. 1982. *Rational Choice*. Oxford: Basil Blackwell.

———, ed. 1986. *The Multiple Self*. Cambridge: Cambridge University Press.

———. 1989a. *The Cement of Society*. Cambridge: Cambridge University Press.

———. 1989b. *Solomonic Judgements: Studies in the Limits of Rationality*. Cambridge: Cambridge University Press.

Erikson, Erik. 1950/64. *Childhood and Society*. 1st ed. New York: Norton.

———. 1959/1980. *Identity and the Life Cycle*. New York: Norton.

———. 1968. *Identity, Youth and Crisis*. New York: Norton.

———. 1982. *The Life Cycle Completed: A Review*. 1st ed. New York: Norton.

———. 1987. *A Way of Looking at Things: Selected Papers from 1930 to 1980*. Ed. Stephen Schlein. 1st ed. New York: Norton.

Espiritu, Yen Le. 1992. *Asian American Panethnicity: Bridging Institutions and Identities*. Philadelphia: Temple University Press.

Evans-Pritchard, E. E. 1962. *Nuer Religion*. Oxford: Clarendon Press.

Fang, Carolyn Y., Jim Sidanius, and Felicia Pratto. 1998. "Romance across the Social Status Continuum: Interracial Marriage and the Ideological Asymmetry Effect." *Journal of Cross-Cultural Psychology* 29, no. 2: 290–306.

Fazio, R. H., E. A. Effrein, and V. J. Falender. 1981. "Self Perception Following Social Interaction." *Journal of Personality and Social Psychology* 41:232–42.

Fearon, James D., and David D. Laitin. 1996. "Explaining Interethnic Cooperation." *American Political Science Review* 90, no. 4: 715–35.

Ferejohn, J. 1974. *Pork Barrel Politics: Rivers and Harbors Legislation, 1947–1968*. Stanford: Stanford University Press.

Festinger, L. 1954. "A Theory of Social Comparison Processes." *Human Relations* 7:117–40.

———. 1957. *A Theory of Cognitive Dissonance*. Stanford: Stanford University Press.

Festinger, Leon, and E. Aronson. 1960. "The Arousal and Reduction of Dissonance in Social Contexts." In *Group Dynamics*, ed. D. Cartwright and A. Zander, 214–31. Evanston, IL: Row, Peterson.

Festinger, L., H. W. Riecken, and S. Schachter. 1956. *When Prophesy Fails*. Minneapolis: University of Minnesota Press.

Fine, Reuben. 1986. *Narcissism, the Self, and Society*. New York: Columbia University Press.

Fiorina, M. 1974. *Representatives, Roll Calls, and Constituencies*. Lexington, MA: Lexington Books/D. C. Heath.

———. 1977/1989. *Congress: Keystone of the Washington Establishment*. New Haven: Yale University Press.

———. 1981. *Retrospective Voting in American National Elections*. New Haven: Yale University Press.

Fishburn, P. C. (1973). *The Theory of Social Choice*. Princeton: Princeton University Press.

Fiske, Susan T., and Shelley E. Taylor. 1991. *Social Cognition*. 2nd ed. New York: McGraw-Hill.

Fitzgerald, Thomas. 1993. *Metaphors of Identity: A Culture Communication Dialogue*. New York: State University of New York Press.

Fodor, Jerry A., and Jerrold J. Katz. 1964. *The Structure of Language: Readings in the Philosophy of Language*. Englewood Cliffs, NJ: Prentice-Hall.

Fogelman, Eva. 1994. *Conscience and Courage*. New York: Anchor Books.

Foot, P. 1978. "Virtues and Vices." In *Vice and Virtue in Everyday Life*, ed. C. Sommers and F. Sommers, 250–66. Fort Worth: Harcourt Brace.

Ford, Herbert. 1966. *Flee the Captor*. Nashville: Southern Publishing Association.

Foucault, Michel. 1976/1980. *The History of Sexuality*. Trans. R. Hurley. New York: Vintage Books.

———. 1984. *Nietzsche, Genealogy, History*. In *The Foucault Reader*, ed. P. Rabinow. New York: Pantheon.

Frankfurt, Harry. 1988. *The Importance of What We Care About*. Cambridge: Cambridge University Press.

Frazier, E. F. 1966. *The Negro Family in the United States*. Rev. and abridged ed. 1939. Reprint, Chicago: University of Chicago Press.

Freud, Sigmund. 1953/1974. *The Standard Edition of the Complete Psychological Works of Sigmund Freud*. Trans. under the general editorship of James Strachey, in collaboration with Anna Freud. London: Hogarth Press and the Institute of Psychoanalysis.

———. 1973. *Complete Psychological Works of Sigmund Freud*. Ed. C. L. Rothgeb. New York: International Universities Press.

Friedman, M. 1953. *Essays in Positive Economics*. Chicago: University of Chicago Press.

Fromm, Erich. 1965. *Escape from Freedom*. New York: Avon Books.

Frye, N. 1957. *Anatomy of Criticism*. Princeton: Princeton University Press.

Gagnon, A., and R. Y. Bourhis. 1996. "Discrimination in the Minimal Group Paradigm—Social Identity or Self-interest." *Personality and Social Psychology Bulletin* 22, no. 12: 1289–1301.

Galambos, J., R. P. Abelson, and J. B. Black. 1986. *Knowledge Structures*. Hillsdale, NJ: Erlbaum.

Gallup, G. G. 1977. "Self-Recognition in Primates: A Comparative Approach to the Bi-directional Properties of Consciousness." *American Psychologist* 32:329–39.

———. 1993. "Mirror, Mirror on the Wall, Which Is the Most Heuristic Theory of Them All." *New Ideas in Psychology* 11:37–335.

Gallup, G. G., and S. D. Suarez. 1986. "Self-Awareness and the Emergence of Mind in Humans and Other Primates." In *Psychological Perspectives on the Self*, vol. 3, ed. J. Suls and A. G. Greenwald, 3–26. Hillsdale, NJ: Erlbaum.

Gardner, H. 1985. *The Mind's New Science*. New York. Basic Books.

Gaventa, J. 1980. *Power and Powerlessness: Quiescence and Rebellion in an Appalachian Valley*. Urbana: University of Illinois Press.

Geertz, Clifford. 1953/1973. *The Interpretation of Cultures*. New York: Basic Books.

Gerard, H. B., and G. C. Mathewson. 1966. "The Effects of Severity of Initiation on Liking for a Group: A Replication." *Journal of Experimental Social Psychology* 2:278–87.

Gergen, Kenneth J. 1989. *Texts of Identity*. London: Sage.

Gergen, Kenneth J., and Mary M. Gergen. 1983. "Narratives of the Self." In *Studies in Social Identity*, ed. Theodore R. Sarbin and Karl E. Scheibe, 254–74. New York: Praeger.

Gewirth. Alan. 1998. *Self-Fulfillment*. Princeton: Princeton University Press.

Gies, Miep. 1987. *Anne Frank Remembered: The Story of the Woman Who Helped to Hide the Frank Family*. New York: Simon and Schuster.

Gilbert, Martin. 2003. *The Righteous: The Unsung Heroes of the Holocaust*. New York: Henry Holt.

Gilens, Martin, Paul M. Sniderman, and James H. Kuklinski. 1998. "Affirmative Action and the Politics of Realignment." *British Journal of Political Science* 28, no. 2: 159–84.

Gilligan, Carol. 1982. *In a Different Voice: Psychological Theory and Women's Development*. Cambridge, MA: Harvard University Press.

———, ed. 1988. *Mapping the Moral Domain: A Contribution of Women's Thinking to Psychological Theory and Education*. Cambridge, MA: Harvard University Press.

Gilovich, T., V. H. Medvec, and S. Chen. 1995. "Commission, Omission, and Dissonance Reduction: Coping with Regret in the 'Monty Hall' Problem." *Personality and Social Psychology Bulletin* 21:182–90.

Glad, Betty. 1990. *Psychological Dimensions of War*. Newbury Park, CA: Sage.

Glass, James. 1997. *Life Unworthy of Life: Racial Phobia and Mass Murder in Hitler's Germany*. New York: Basic Books.

Goffman, Erving. 1959/1973. *The Presentation of Self in Everyday Life*. Woodstock, NY: Overlook Press.

Goldberger, Leo. 1987. *The Rescue of the Danish Jews*. New York: New York University Press.

Goldhagen, D. J. 1996. *Hitler's Willing Executioners*. New York: Knopf.

———. 2002. *A Moral Reckoning: The Role of the Catholic Church in the Holocaust and Its Unfulfilled Duty of Repair*. New York: Knopf.

Graumann, Carl, and Serge Moscovici, eds. 1986. *Changing Conceptions of Leadership*. New York: Springer-Verlag.

Graziano, W. G., L. A. Jensen-Campbell, and J. F. Finch. 1997. "The Self as a Mediator between Personality and Adjustment." *Journal of Personality and Social Psychology* 73:392–404.

Green, Donald, and Ian Shapiro. 1994. *Pathologies of Rational Choice*. New Haven: Yale University Press.

Greenstein, Fred I. 1982. *The Hidden-Hand Presidency: Eisenhower as Leader*. New York: Basic Books.

Greenwald, A. G., and D. L. Ronis. 1978. "Twenty Years of Cognitive Dissonance: Case Study of the Evolution of a Theory." *Psychological Review* 85:53–57.

Greimas, A. J., and J. Courtes. 1976. "The Cognitive Dimension of Narrative Discourse." *New Literary History* 7:433–47.

Gross, Michael L. 1997. *Ethics and Activism: The Theory and Practice of Political Morality*. New York: Cambridge University Press.

Gurin, P., and H. Markus. 1989. "Cognitive Consequences of Gender Identity." In *The Social Identity of Women*, ed. S. Skevington and D. Baker, 152–73. London: Sage.

Habermas, Jurgen. 1984/1987. *The Theory of Communicative Action*. Trans. Thomas McCarthy. Boston: Beacon Press.

Hardin, R. 1982. *Collective Action*. Baltimore: Johns Hopkins University Press.

———. 1987. "Rational Choice Theories." In *Idioms of Inquiry: Critique and Renewal in Political Science*, ed. T. Ball, 67–91. Albany: State University of New York Press.

———. 1995. *One for All: The Logic of Group Conflict*. Princeton: Princeton University Press.

Harmon-Jones, E., and J. S. Mills. 1998. *Cognitive Dissonance Theory: Revival with Revisions and Controversies*. Washington, DC: American Psychological Association.

Harré, Rom. 1987. "The Social Construction of Selves." In *Self and Identity: Psychosocial Perspectives*, ed. Krysia Yardley and Terry Honess, 41–53. New York: Wiley.

Harris, Zelig. 1960. *Structural Linguistics of Structure of Language*. Chicago: University of Chicago Press.

Harsanyi, J. 1969. "Rational Choice Models of Political Behavior vs. Functional and Conformist Theories." *World Politics* 21, no. 4: 513–48.

———. 1976. *Essays on Ethics, Social Behavior, and Scientific Explanation*. Boston: D. Reidel.

Hart, D., and W. Damon. 1986. "Developmental Trends in Self-Understanding." *Social Cognition* 4:388–407.

Harter, S. 1993. "Causes and Consequences of Low Self-esteem in Children and

Adolescents." In *Self-esteem: The Puzzle of Low Self-regard*, ed. R. F. Baumeister, 87–111. New York: Plenum.

Hechter, M. 1987. *Principles of Group Solidarity*. Berkeley: University of California Press.

Heider, F. 1958. *The Psychology of Interpersonal Relations*. New York: Wiley.

Heine, Steven J., and Darrin R. Lehman. 1997. "The Cultural Construction of Self-enhancement: An Examination of Group-Serving Biases." *Journal of Personality and Social Psychology* 72, no. 6: 1268–83.

Herf, Jeffrey. 1997. *Divided Memory: The Nazi Past in the Two Germanys*. Cambridge, MA: Harvard University Press.

Hewitt, John P. 1988. *Self and Society: A Symbolic Interactionist Social Psychology*. 4th ed. Boston: Allyn and Bacon.

Higgins, E. T. 1987. "Self-Discrepancy: A Theory Relating Self and Affect." *Psychological Review* 94:319–40.

———. 1996. "The 'Self-Digest': Self-Knowledge Serving Self Regulatory Functions." *Journal of Personality and Social Psychology* 71:1062–83.

Hilberg, Raul. 1985. *The Politics of Memory: The Journey of a Holocaust Historian*. Chicago: Ivan R. Dee.

Hirschman, A. O. 1977. *The Passions and the Interests*. Princeton: Princeton University Press.

Hochschild, J. L. 1995. *Facing Up to the American Dream: Race, Class and the Soul of the Nation*. Princeton: Princeton University Press.

Hogg, Michael A. 1992. *The Social Psychology of Group Cohesiveness: From Attraction to Social Identity*. New York: New York University Press.

Hogg, Michael A., and Dominic Abrams. 1988. *Social Identifications: A Social Psychology of Intergroup Relationships and Group Processes*. New York: Routledge.

Hogg, M. A., and J. C. Turner. 1985. "Interpersonal Attraction, Social Identification and Psychological Group Formation." *European Journal of Social Psychology* 15:51–66.

———. 1987. "Social Identity and Conformity: A Theory of Referent Informational Influence." In *Current Issues in European Social Psychology*, vol. 2, ed. W. Doise and S. Moscovici, 139–77. Cambridge: Cambridge University Press.

Hogg, Michael A., Deborah J. Terry, and Katherine M. White. 1995. *A Tale of Two Theories: A Critical Comparison of Identity Theory with Social Identity Theory* 58, no. 4: 255.

Hoover, Kenneth. 2004. *The Future of Identity*. Lanham, MD: Lexington Books.

Hume, David. 1740/1978. *Enquiries Concerning Human Understanding*. Oxford: Oxford University Press.

Hunecke, Douglas K. 1981. "A Study of Christians Who Rescued Jews during the Nazi Era." *Humboldt Journal of Social Relations* 9, no. 1: 144–49.

Hutcheson, Francis. 1755/1917. *An Essay on the Nature and Conduct of the Passions and Affections*. New York: Garland.

Ignatieff, Michael. 1984. *The Needs of Strangers*. New York: Picador USA/Metropolitan Books/Henry Holt.

Insko, C. A., J. Schopler, J. F. Kennedy, K. R. Dahl, K. A. Graetz, and S. M. Drigotas. 1992. "Individual-Group Discontinuity from the Differing Perspective of Campbell Realistic Group Conflict Theory and Tajfel and Turner Social Identity Theory." *Social Psychology Quarterly* 55, no. 3: 272–91.

James, William. 1890. *Principles of Psychology*. New York: Henry Holt.

———. 1892. *Principles of Psychology: The Briefer Course*. New York: Holt.

Janis, I. L. 1983. *Groupthink: Psychological Studies of Policy Decisions and Fiascos*. Boston: Houghton Mifflin.

Jarymowicz, Maria. 1992. "Self, We, and Other(s): Schemata, Distinctiveness and Altruism." In *Embracing the Other*, ed. P. M. Oliner, S. P. Oliner, L. Baron, L. A. Blum, D. L. Krebs, and M. Z. Smolenska, 194–213. New York: New York University Press.

Jervis, Robert. 2002. "Signaling and Perception: Drawing Inferences and Projecting Images." In *Political Psychology*, ed. K. R. Monroe, 293–315. Hillsdale, NJ: Erlbaum.

Johnston, David. 1991. "Human Agency and Rational Action." In *The Economic Approach to Politics: A Critical Reassessment of the Theory of Rational Action*, ed. K. R. Monroe, 94–112. New York: HarperCollins.

Kagan, Jerome. 1998. *Three Seductive Ideas*. Cambridge, MA: Harvard University Press.

Kahneman, Daniel, and Amos Tversky. 1972. "A Subjective Probability: A Judgment of Representativeness." *Cognitive Psychology* 3:430–54.

Kahneman, Daniel, Paul Slovic, and Amos Tversky, eds. 1982. *Judgment under Uncertainty: Heuristics and Biases*. New York: Cambridge University Press.

Kant, Immanuel. 1785. *The Metaphysics of Morals*. Trans. Lewis Beck White. New York: Macmillan.

Kashima, Yoshihisa, Michael Siegal, Kenichiro Tanaka, and Emiko Kashima. 1992. "Do People Believe Behaviours Are Consistent with Attitudes? Towards a Cultural Psychology of Attribution Processes." *British Journal of Social Psychology* 31, no. 2: 111–24.

Kegan, Robert. 1982. *The Evolving Self: Problem and Process in Human Development*. Cambridge, MA: Harvard University Press.

Kekes, J. 1989. *Moral Tradition and Individuality*. Princeton: Princeton University Press.

Kelley, Harold H. 1971. *Attribution in Social Interaction*. Morristown, NJ: General Learning Press.

Kelman, Herbert. 1989. *Crimes of Obedience: Toward a Social Psychology of Authoritarianism and Responsibility*. New Haven: Yale University Press.

———. 1992. "Acknowledging the Other's Nationhood: How to Create a Momentum for the Israeli-Palestinian Negotiations." *Journal of Palestinian Studies* 22:18–38.

Keneally, Thomas. 1982. *Schindler's List*. New York: Simon and Schuster.

Kennan, G. 1993. *Around the Cragged Hill: A Personal and Political Philosophy*. New York: W. W. Norton.

Kertzer, A. 2001. *My Mother's Voice: Children, Literature, and the Holocaust*. New York: Broadview Press.

Kessel, Neil J. 1996. *Mass Hate: The Global Rise of Genocide and Terror*. New York: Plenum.

Key, V. O. 1942. *Southern Politics in State and Nation*. New York: Knopf.

Kihlstrom, J. F., and N. Cantor. 1984. "Mental Representations of the Self." In *Advances in Experimental Social Psychology*, vol. 2, ed. L. Berkowitz, 2–48. New York: Academic Press.

Kihlstrom, J. F., and S. B. Klein. 1994. "The Self as a Knowledge Structure." In *Handbook of Social Cognition*, Vol. 1: Basic Processes, ed. R. S. Wyer and T. K. Scrull, 153–206. Hillsdale, NJ: Erlbaum.

Kinder, Donald R., and David O. Sears. 1981. "Prejudice and Politics: Symbolic Racism versus Racial Threats to the Good Life." *Journal of Personality and Social Psychology* 40, no. 3: 414–31.

Klingemann Ute, and Juergen W. Falter. 1993. "Hilfe fuer Juden waehrend des Holocaust." Rheinland-Verlag GmbH Koeln.

Koffka, K. 1935. *Principles of Gestalt Psychology*. New York: Harcourt Brace and World.

Kohlberg, L. 1981a. *Essays on Moral Development*. San Francisco: Harper and Row.

———. 1981b. *The Meaning and Measurement of Moral Development*. Worcester, MA: Clark University Press.

Kohut, Heinz. 1971. *The Analysis of the Self: A Systematic Approach to the Psychoanalytic Treatment of Narcissistic Personality Disorders*. New York: International Universities Press.

———. 1977. *The Restoration of the Self*. New York: International Universities Press.

———. 1985. *Self Psychology and the Humanities: Reflections on a New Psychoanalytic Approach*. Ed. Charles Strozier. New York: Norton.

Kolm, S. C. 1983. "Altruism and Efficiency." *Ethics* 94, no. 1: 18–65.

Kracauer, S. 1947. *A Psychological History of the German Film from Caligari to Hitler*. Princeton: Princeton University Press.

Kraft, Robert N. 2002. *Memory Perceived: Recalling the Holocaust*. New York: Praeger.

Kreidie, Lina. 1999. "Islamic Fundamentalism: A New Perspective." UCI Working paper.

———. 2000. "Deciphering the Construals of Islamic Fundamentalists." Ph.D. diss., University of California, Irvine.

Kripke, Saul. 1982. *Wittgenstein on Rules and Private Language: An Elementary Exposition*. Oxford: Blackwell.

Kunda, Z. 1990. "The Case for Motivated Reasoning." *Psychological Bulletin* 108:480–98.

Kupperman, J. 1991. *Character*. New York: Oxford University Press.

Lakoff, George, and Mark Johnson. 1999. *Philosophy in the Flesh: The Embodied Mind and Its Challenge to Western Thought*. New York: Basic Books.

Langer, Lawrence. 1991. *Holocaust Testimonies: The Ruins of Memory*. New Haven: Yale University Press.

Latané, B., and J. M. Darley. 1980. *The Unresponsive Bystander: Why Doesn't He Help?* New York: Appleton-Century-Crofts.

Le Bon, Gustave. 1913. *The Psychology of Crowds*. New York: G. P. Putnam.

Lemyre, L., and P. Smith. 1985. "Inter-group Discrimination and Self-esteem in the Minimal Group Paradigm." *Journal of Personality and Social Psychology* 49:660–70.

Lerner, Richard M. 1992. *Final Solutions: Biology, Prejudice, and Genocide.* University Park: Pennsylvania State University Press.

Lessing, Doris. 1973. *Summer before the Dark.* New York: Knopf.

Levi, Primo. 1961. *Survival in Auschwitz.* New York: Macmillan.

Levi-Strauss, C. 1967. *Structural Anthropology.* New York: Basic Books.

Levine, L. 1980. "Reactions to Opinion Deviance in Small Groups." In *Psychology of Group Influence*, ed. P. B. Paulus, 187–233. Hillsdale, NJ: Erlbaum.

Lewis, M. 1986. "Origins of Self-Knowledge and Individual Differences in Early Self-Recognition." In *Psychological Perspectives on the Self*, vol. 3, ed. J. Suls and A. G. Greenwald, 55–78. Hillsdale, NJ: Erlbaum.

Lijphardt, Arend. 1981. *Conflict and Coexistence in Belgium: The Dynamics of a Culturally Divided Society.* Berkeley: Institute of International Studies, University of California.

Linville, P. W. 1987. "Self Complexity as a Cognitive Buffer against Stress Related Depression and Illness." *Journal of Personality and Social Psychology* 52:663–76.

Livesley, W. J. and D. B. Bromley. 1973. *Person Perception in Childhood and Adolescence.* New York: Wiley.

Locke, John. 1690/2000. *An Essay Concerning Human Understanding.* London: Routledge Philosophers in Focus Series.

Loeffler, Martha. 2000. *Boats in the Night: Knud Dyby's Involvement in the Rescue of Danish Jews and Danish Resistance.* Blair, NE: Lur Publications.

London, Perry. 1970. "The Rescuers: Motivational Hypotheses about Christians Who Saved Jews from the Nazis." In *Altruism and Helping Behavior*, ed. J. Macaulay and L. Berkowitz, 21–50. New York: Academic Press.

Lyotard, J. F. 1984. *The Post-Modern Condition: A Report on Knowledge.* Trans. G. Bennington, B. Massumi. Minneapolis: University of Minnesota Press.

MacIntyre, Alistaire. 1981. *After Virtue.* London: Duckworth.

Maclean, Norman. 1976. *A River Runs Through It.* Chicago: University of Chicago Press.

Maier, N. 1961. *Frustration: The Study of Behavior without a Goal.* 1949. Reprint, Ann Arbor: University of Michigan Press.

Mansbridge, J. 1980. *Beyond Adversarial Democracy.* New York: Basic Books.

———, ed. 1990. *Beyond Self-Interest.* Chicago: University of Chicago Press.

Margolis, H. 1982. *Selfishness, Altruism and Rationality.* Cambridge: Cambridge University Press.

Markus, H. 1977. "Self-Schemata and Processing Information about the Self." *Journal of Personality and Social Psychology* 35:63–78.

Markus H. R., and S. Kitayama. 1991. "Culture and Self: Implications for Cognition, Emotion and Motivation." In *The Self in Social Psychology*, ed. R. F. Baumeister, 339–67. Philadelphia: Psychology Press.

Markus, H. R., and P. Nurius. 1986. "Possible Selves." *American Psychologist* 41:954–69.

———. 1987. "Possible Selves: The Interface between Motivation and the Self-Concept." In *Self and Identity: Psychosocial Perspectives*, ed. Krysia Yardley and Terry Honess, 157–73. New York: Wiley.

Markus, H. R., J. Smith, and L. Moreland. 1985. "Role of the Self-Concept in the Social Perceptions of Others." *Journal of Personality and Social Psychology* 49:1494–1512.

Martin, W. 1996. *Recent Theories of Narrative.* Ithaca: Cornell University Press.

Maslow, Abraham H. 1968/1982. *Toward a Psychology of Being.* New York: Van Nostrand Reinhold.

Marx, Karl, and Friedrich Engels. 1932/1978. "The German Ideology: Part I." In *The Marx-Engels Reader,* ed. Robert C. Tucker, 146–200. New York: W. W. Norton.

Mead, George Herbert. 1924. "The Genesis of the Self and Social Control." *International Journal of Ethics* 35:251–77.

———. 1934. *Mind, Self, and Society.* Chicago: University of Chicago Press.

Mellema, Gregory. 1991. *Beyond the Call of Duty: Supererogation, Obligation and Offence.* Albany: State University of New York Press.

Milgram, Stanley. 1974. *Obedience to Authority: An Experimental View.* New York: Harper and Row.

Miller, Arthur H., M. Wattenberg, and O. Malanchuk. 1986. "Schematic Assessments of Presidential Candidates." *The American Political Science Review* 80, no. 2: 521–40.

Mischel, W. 1979. "On the Interface of Cognition and Personality: Beyond the Person-Situation Debate." *American Psychologist* 97:76–79.

Mischel, W., N. Cantor, and S. Feldman. 1996. "Principles of Self-Regulation: The Nature of Willpower and Self-Control." In *Social Psychology: Handbook of Basic Principles,* ed. E. T. Higgins and A. W. Kruglnski, 329–60. New York: Guilford.

Mitchell, W. C. 1988. "Virginia, Rochester, and Bloomington: Twenty-Five Years of Public Choice and Political Science." *Public Choice* 56:101–19.

Monroe, Kristen Renwick. 1991a. *The Economic Approach to Politics: A Critical Reassessment of the Theory of Rational Action.* New York: HarperCollins.

———. 1991b. "The Theory of Rational Action: What Is It? How Useful Is It for Political Science?" In *Political Science: Looking to the Future,* ed. W. R. Crotty, 77–98. Evanston, IL: Northwestern University Press.

———. 1994a. "'But What Else Could I Do?' A Cognitive Theory of Ethical Political Behavior." *Political Psychology* 15:201–26.

———. 1994b. "John Donne's People: Explaining Differences between Rational Actors and Altruists through Cognitive Frameworks." *Journal of Politics* 53, no. 2: 394–433.

———. 1994c. "A Fat Lady in a Corset: Altruism and Social Theory." *American Journal of Political Science* 38, no. 4: 861–93.

———. 1995a. "Psychology and Rational Actor Theory." Editor's Introduction to a special issue of *Political Psychology* 16, no. 1: 1–42.

———. 1995b. "The Psychology of Genocide: A Review of the Literature." *Ethics and International Affairs* 9:215–39.

———. 1996. *The Heart of Altruism: Perceptions of a Common Humanity.* Princeton: Princeton University Press.

———. 1997. "Human Nature, Identity and the Search for a General Theory of Politics." In *Contemporary Empirical Political Theory,* ed. Kristen R. Monroe, 279–306. Berkeley: University of California Press.

————. 2003. "How Identity and Perspective Constrain Moral Choice." *International Political Science Review* 24, no. 4: 405–425.

Monroe, Kristen Renwick, and Lina H. Kreidie. 1997. "The Perspectives of Islamic Fundamentalists and the Limits of Rational Choice Theory." *Political Psychology* 9:215–39.

Monroe Kristen Renwick, James Hankin, and Renee VanVechten. 2000. "The Psychological Foundations of Identity Politics: A Review of the Literature." *Annual Review of Political Science* 3:419–47.

Montemayor, R., and M. Eisen. 1977. "The Development of Self-Conceptions from Childhood to Adolescence." *Developmental Psychology* 13:314–19.

Morgan, D. L., and M. L. Schwalbe. 1990. "Mind and Self in Society—Linking Social Structure and Social Cognition." *Social Psychology Quarterly* 53, no. 2: 148–64.

Morris, Aldon D. 1984. *The Origins of the Civil Rights Movement: Black Communities Organizing for Change.* New York: Free Press.

Moscovici, Serge. 1988. "Notes towards a Description of Social Representations." *European Journal of Social Psychology* 18:211–50.

Moynihan, D. P., and N. Glazer. 1966. *Beyond the Melting Pot.* Cambridge, MA: MIT Press and Harvard University Press.

Mueller, D. C. 1984. "Public Choice: A Survey." In *The Theory of Public Choice-II*, ed. J. M. Buchanan and R. D. Tollison, 23–71. Ann Arbor: University of Michigan Press.

Muñoz, Carlos. 1989. *Youth, Identity, Power: The Chicano Movement.* New York: Verso.

Myers, M. 1983. *The Soul of Economic Man.* Chicago: University of Chicago Press.

Nagel, Thomas. 1986. *The View from Nowhere.* New York: Oxford University Press.

Neisser, Ulric, and Robyn Fivush. 1994. *The Remembering Self: Construction and Accuracy in the Self-narrative.* New York: Cambridge University Press.

Nisbett, R. E., and E. Borgida. 1975. "Attribution and the Psychology of Prediction." *Journal of Personality and Social Psychology* 32:932–43.

Nisbett, R. E., and L. Ross. 1980. *Human Inference: Strategies and Shortcomings of Social Judgment.* Englewood Cliffs, NJ: Prentice-Hall.

Noll, R., and B. M. Owen. 1983. *The Political Economy of Deregulation: Interest Groups in the Regulatory Process.* Washington, DC: American Enterprise Institute.

Nussbaum, Martha. 1985. *The Fragility of Goodness.* New York: Cambridge University Press.

————. 2001. *Upheavals of Thought: The Intelligence of Emotions.* Cambridge: Cambridge University Press.

Oakes, P. J., and J. C. Turner. 1980. "Social Categorization and Inter-group Behavior: Does Minimal Inter-group Discrimination Make Social Identity More Positive?" *European Journal of Social Psychology* 10:295–301.

Oakes, Penelope J., S. A. Haslam, and J. C. Turner. 1994. *Stereotyping and Social Reality.* Oxford: Cambridge, MA: Blackwell.

Oliner, Pearl M., and Samuel P. Oliner. 1995. *Toward a Caring Society: Ideals into Action.* Westport, CT: Praeger.

Oliner, Pearl M., Samuel P. Oliner, L. Baron, L. A. Blum, D. L. Krebs, and M. Z.

Smolenska. 1992. *Embracing the Other: Philosophical, Psychological, and Historical Perspectives on Altruism*. New York: New York University Press.

Oliner, Samuel P. 2003. *Do Unto Others: Extraordinary Acts of Ordinary People*. Boulder, CO: Westview.

Oliner, Samuel P., and Pearl M. Oliner. 1988. *The Altruistic Personality: Rescuers of Jews in Nazi Europe*. New York: Free Press.

Olson, M., Jr. 1965. *The Logic of Collective Action*. Cambridge, MA: Harvard University Press.

———. 1982. *The Rise and Decline of Nations*. New Haven: Yale University Press.

Opdyke, Irene Gut, and Jennifer Armstrong. 2001. *In My Hands: Memories of a Holocaust Survivor*. New York: Anchor Books.

Ozyurt, Saba S. 2003. "Cognitive Determinants of Coping." UCI Working Paper.

Page, B. 1978. *Choices and Echoes in Presidential Elections*. Chicago: University of Chicago Press.

Pateman, C. 1970. *Participation and Democratic Theory*. Cambridge: Cambridge University Press.

———. 1988. *The Sexual Contract*. Stanford: Stanford University Press.

Patterson, Molly, and Kristen R. Monroe. 1998. "Narrative." *Annual Review of Political Science* 1, no. 1: 315–31.

Pelham, B. W. 1991. "On Confidence and Consequence: The Certainty and Importance of Self-Knowledge." *Journal of Personality and Social Psychology* 60:518–30.

Pence, Gregory. 1984. "Recent Work on Virtues." *American Philosophical Quarterly* 21, no. 4: 281–99.

Perry, John. 1975. "The Problem of Personal Identity." In *Personal Identity*, ed. J. Perry, 3–32. Berkeley: University of California Press.

Personal Narratives Group, ed. 1989. *Interpreting Women's Lives: Feminist Theory and Personal Narratives*. Bloomington: Indiana University Press.

Phybus, Elizabeth. 1982. "Saints and Heroes." *Philosophy* 57:193–200.

Piaget, Jean. 1928. *Judgement and Reasoning in Children*. London: Routledge.

———. 1948. *The Moral Development of the Child*. Glencoe: Free Press.

Piliavin, J. A. 1981. *Emergency Intervention*. New York: Academic Press.

Pinker, Steven. 2002. *The Blank Slate: The Modern Denial of Human Nature*. New York: Viking.

Plomin, Robert. 1990. *Nature and Nurture: An Introduction to Human Behavioral Genetics*. Pacific Grove, CA: Brooks/Cole.

Popkin, S. 1979. *The Rational Peasant*. Berkeley: University of California Press.

Portelli, A. 1994. *The Text and the Voice: Writing, Speaking, and Democracy in American Literature*. New York: Columbia University Press.

Posner, R. A. 1977. *Economic Analysis of Law*. Boston: Little, Brown.

Post, S. G., L. Underwood, J. P. Schloss, and W. B. Hurlbut. 2002. *Altruism and Altruistic Love: Science, Philosophy and Religion in Dialogue*. New York: Oxford University Press.

Povinelli, D. J. 1993. "Reconstructing the Evolution of Mind." *American Psychologist* 48:493–509.

———. 1994. "A Theory of Mind Is in the Head, Not the Heart." *Behavioral and Brain Sciences* 17:573–74.

Povinelli, D. J., K. R. Landau, and H. K. Perilloux. 1996. "Self-Recognition in Young Children Using Delayed versus Live Feedback: Evidence of a Developmental Asynchrony." *Child Development* 67:1540–54.

Pratto, Felicia, Lisa M. Stallworth, Jim Sidanius, and Bret Siers. 1997. "The Gender Gap in Occupational Role Attainment: A Social Dominance Approach." *Journal of Personality and Social Psychology* 72, no. 1: 37–53.

Propp, V. I. 1928/1968. *Morphology of the Folktale.* Trans. L. Scott. Austin: University of Texas Press.

Putnam, Robert, D. 1993. *Making Democracy Work.* Princeton: Princeton University Press.

Quattrone, G. A., and A. Tversky. 1988. "Contrasting Rational and Psychological Analyses of Political Choice." *American Political Science Review* 82:719–37.

Rabbie, J. M., J. C. Schot, and L. Visser. 1989. "Social Identity Theory—A Conceptual and Empirical Critique from the Perspective of a Behavioral Interaction Model." *European Journal of Social Psychology* 19, no. 3: 171–202.

Rawls, John. 1971. *A Theory of Justice.* Cambridge, MA: Harvard University Press.

Reid, Anne, and Kay Deaux. 1996. "Relationship between Social and Personal Identities: Segregation or Integration." *Journal of Personality and Social Psychology* 71, no. 6: 1084.

Renshon, Stanley. 1974. *Psychological Needs and Political Behavior: A Theory of Personality and Political Efficacy.* New York: Free Press.

———. 1996. *High Hopes: The Clinton Presidency and the Politics of Ambition.* New York: New York University Press.

Reykowski, Janusz. 2001. "The Justice Motive and Altruistic Helping: Rescuers of Jews in Nazi-Occupied Europe." In *The Justice Motive in Everyday Life,* ed. M. Ross and D. T. Miller, 251–71. New York: Cambridge University Press.

———. 2003. "The Political Psychology of Political Change: The Peaceful Transition from Socialism to Democracy in Poland." Chancellor's Distinguished Fellow Talk. University of California, Irvine.

Ricoeur, P. 1981. "Narrative Time." In *On Narrative,* ed. W.J.T Mitchell, 302–06. Chicago: University of Chicago Press.

Riker, W. H. 1962. *The Theory of Political Coalitions.* New Haven: Yale University Press.

———. 1986. *The Art of Political Manipulation.* New Haven: Yale University Press.

Riker, W. H., and P. C. Ordeshook. 1973. *An Introduction to Positive Political Theory.* Englewood Cliffs, NJ: Prentice-Hall.

Rittener, Carol, and Sandra Myers. 1986. *The Courage to Care.* New York: New York University Press.

Robinson, Dawn T., and Lynn Smith-Lovin. 1992. "Selective Interaction as a Strategy for Identity Maintenance: An Affect Control Model." *Social Psychology Quarterly* 55, no. 1: 12.

Rodman, H. 1971. *Lower Class Families: The Culture of Poverty in Negro Trinidad.* New York: Oxford University Press.

Rosenberg, M. J. 1979. *Conceiving the Self*. New York: Basic Books.

Rosenberg, Morris J., and Ralph H. Turner, eds. 1981. *Social Psychology: Sociological Perspectives*. New York: Basic Books.

Rosenberg, S. 1988. *Reason, Ideology and Politics*. Princeton: Princeton University Press.

Rosenwald, G. C., and R. L. Ochberg. 1992. *Storied Lives*. New Haven: Yale University Press.

Ross, Marc. 1995. "Psycho-cultural Interpretation Theory and Peacemaking in Ethnic Conflict." *Political Psychology* 16:523–44.

Ross, Lee, and Richard E. Nisbett. 1991. *The Person and the Situation: Perspectives of Social Psychology*. New York: McGraw Hill.

Rossiter, C. 1956. *The American Presidency*. New York: Harcourt Brace and World.

Rudolph, Susanne Hoeber, and I. Lloyd. 1993. "Modern Hate." *The New Republic*, 14:24–25, 28–29.

Rudolph, S. H., and L. Rudolph. 2002. *Reversing the Gaze: Amar Singh's Diary, a Colonial Subject's Narrative of Imperial India*. Boulder, CO: Westview Press.

Sachdev, I., and R. Y. Bourhis. 1985. "Social Categorization and Power Differentials in Group Relations." *European Journal of Social Psychology* 14:35–52.

Sandel, M. 1984. *Liberalism and Its Critics*. New York: New York University Press.

Sarbin, Theodore R., and Karl E. Scheibe, eds. 1983. *Studies in Social Identity*. New York: Praeger.

Scarry, Elaine. 1985. *The Body in Pain: The Making and Unmaking of the World*. New York: Oxford University Press.

Schelling, T. C. 1978a. "Altruism, Meanness, and Other Potentially Strategic Behaviors." *American Economic Review* 68:229–30.

———. 1978b. *Micromotives and Macrobehavior*. New York: Norton.

———. 1984. *Choice and Consequence*. Cambridge, MA: Harvard University Press.

Schlenker, Barry R., ed. 1985. *The Self and Social Life*. New York: McGraw-Hill.

———. 1986. "Self-Identification: Toward an Integration of the Private and Public Self." In *Public Self and Private Self*, ed. Roy F. Baumeister, 21–62. New York: Springer-Verlag.

Schneewind, J. B. 1990a. *Moral Philosophy from Montaigne to Kant: An Anthology*. New York: Cambridge University Press.

———. 1990b. "The Misfortunes of Virtue." *Ethics* 101, no. 1: 42–63.

Schofield, N. 1985. *Social Choice and Democracy*. Berlin: Springer-Verlag.

Scott, J. 1991. "The Evidence of Experience." *Critical Inquiry* 17:773–97.

Sdorow, Lester. 1990. *Psychology*. Dubuque, IA: Wm. C. Brown Publishers.

Sears, David O. 1988. "Symbolic Racism." In *Eliminating Racism: Profiles in Controversy*, ed. Phyllis A. Katz and Dalmas A. Taylor, 53–80. New York: Plenum Press.

———. 1993. "Symbolic Politics." In *Explorations in Political Psychology*, ed. Shanto Iyengar and William J. McGuire, 113–49. Durham: Duke University Press.

Sears, David O., and Carolyn L. Funk. 1999. "Evidence of Long-term Persistence of Adult's Political Predispositions." *Journal of Politics* 61, no. 1: 1–28.

Sears, David O., Colette van Laar, Mary Carrillo, and Rick Kosterman. 1997. "Is It Really Racism? The Origins of White Americans' Opposition to Race-Targeted Policies." *Public Opinion Quarterly* 61, no. 1: 16–53.

Secord, Paul. 1982. "The Origin and Maintenance of Social Roles: The Case of Sex Roles." In *Personality, Roles and Social Behavior*, ed. W. Ickes and E. S. Knowles, 33–55. New York: Springer-Verlag.

———. 1982. *Explaining Human Behavior: Consciousness, Human Action, and Social Structure*. Beverly Hills: Sage.

Sedikides, C., and J. J. Skowronski. 1997. "The Symbolic Self in Evolutionary Context." *Personality and Social Psychology Review* 1:80–102.

Sen, Amartya. 1977. "Rational Fools: A Critique of the Behavioral Foundations of Economic Theory." *Philosophy and Public Affairs* 6, no. 4: 317–44.

———. 1984. *Collective Choice and Social Welfare*. 2nd ed. New York: North-Holland, Elsevier Science Publications.

Sen, Amartya, and Martha Craven Nussbaum, eds. *The Quality of Life (Studies in Developmental Economics)*. New York: Oxford University Press.

Shaftesbury, 3rd Earl of (Anthony Ashley Cooper). 1714/1977. *An Inquiry Concerning Virtue, or Merit*. Manchester: Manchester University Press.

Sherif, Muzafer. 1962. *Intergroup Relations and Leadership: Approaches and Research in Industrial, Ethnic, Cultural, and Political Areas*. New York: Wiley.

———. 1967. *Group Conflict and Cooperation*. London: Routledge and Kegan Paul.

———. 1973. *Groups in Harmony and Tension: An Integration of Studies on Intergroup Relations*. New York: Octagon Books.

Shermer, Michael, and Alex Grobman. 2000. *Denying History: Who Says the Holocaust Never Happened and Why Do They Say It?* Berkeley: University of California Press.

Shklovsky, Victor. 1990. *Theory of Prose*. Elmwood Park, IL: Dalkey Archive Press.

Shotter, John. 1984. *Social Accountability and Selfhood*. New York: B. Blackwell.

———. 1985. "Social Accountability and Self Specification." In *The Social Construction of the Person*, ed. Kenneth J. Gergen and Kenneth E. Davis, 167–86. New York: Springer-Verlag.

Sidanius, James. 1993. "Social Dominance Theory." In *Explorations in Political Psychology*, ed. Shanto Iyengar and William J. McGuire, 183–224. Durham: Duke University Press.

Sidanius, James, Erik Devereux, and Felicia Pratto. 1992. "A Comparison of Symbolic Racism Theory and Social Dominance Theory as Explanations for Racial Policy Attitudes." *Journal of Social Psychology* 132, no. 3: 377–95.

Sidanius, James, Felicia Pratto, and M. Mitchell. 1994. "In-group Identification, Social Dominance Orientation, and Differential Intergroup Social Allocation." *Journal of Social Psychology* 134, no. 2: 151–67.

Sidanius, James, James H. Liu, John S. Shaw, and Felicia Pratto. 1994. "Social Dominance Orientation, Hierarchy Attenuators and Hierarchy Enhancers: Social Dominance Theory and the Criminal Justice System." *Journal of Applied Social Psychology* 24, no. 4: 338–67.

Simon, H. A. 1982. *Models of Bounded Rationality*. Vols. 1–2. Cambridge, MA: MIT Press.

————. 1983. *Reason in Human Affairs*. Stanford: Stanford University Press.

————. 1985. "Human Nature in Politics: The Dialogue of Psychology with Political Science." *American Political Science Review* 79:293–304.

Singer, Peter. 1975/1990. *Animal Liberation*. New York: New York Review of Books.

Slote, Michael. 1983. *Goods and Virtues*. New York: Oxford University Press.

Smiley, Marion. 1992. *Moral Responsibility and the Boundaries of Community: Power and Accountability from a Pragmatic Point of View*. Chicago: University of Chicago Press.

Smith, Adam. 1759/1853. *The Theory of Moral Sentiments*. London: Henry G. Bohn.

————. 1776/1902. *The Wealth of Nations*. New York: Modem Library.

Smith, A. G., and David G. Winter. 2002. "Right-wing Authoritarianism, Party Identification, and Attitudes toward Feminism in Student Evaluations of the Clinton-Lewinsky Story." *Political Psychology* 23:355–83.

Sniderman, Paul, and Edward Carmines. 1997. *Reaching beyond Race*. Cambridge, MA: Harvard University Press.

Sniderman, Paul, T. Piazza, P. Tetlock, and A. Kendrick. 1991. "The New Racism." *American Journal of Political Science* 35, no. 2: 423–47.

Snyder, M. 1987. *Public Appearances/Private Realities: The Psychology of Self Monitoring*. New York: Freeman.

Somers, M. R., and G. D. Gibson. 1994. "Reclaiming the Epistemological 'Other': Narrative and the Social Constitution of Identity." In *Social Theory and the Politics of Identity*, ed. C. Calhoun, 37–100. Oxford: Blackwell.

Spivak, G. C. 1988. "Subaltern Studies: Deconstructing Historiography." In *In Other Worlds*. New York: Routledge.

Staub, Ervin. 1989. *The Roots of Evil: The Origins of Genocide and Other Group Violence*. New York: Cambridge University Press.

Stone, J. 1998. "The Role of Self-Attribute Accessibility in Dissonance." In *Cognitive Dissonance Theory: Progress on a Pivotal Theory in Social Psychology*, ed. E. Harmon-Jones and J. S. Mills, 175–201. Washington, DC: American Psychological Association.

Stryker, Sheldon. 1987. "Identity Theory: Developments and Extensions." In *Self and Identity: Psychosocial Perspectives*, ed. Krysia Yardley and Terry Honess, 89–105. New York: Wiley.

Stryker, Sheldon, and Richard T. Terpe. 1982. "Commitment, Identity Salience and Role Behavior: Theory and Research Example." In *Personality, Roles and Social Behavior*, ed. W. Ickes and Eric S. Knowles, 199–216. New York: Springer-Verlag.

Suedfeld, Peter. 2001. *Light from the Ashes: Social Science Careers of Young Holocaust Refugees and Survivors*. Ann Arbor, MI: University of Michigan Press.

Sullivan, H. S. 1953. *The Interpersonal Theory of Psychiatry*. New York: Norton.

Symons, C. S., and B. T. Johnson. 1997. "The Self-Reference Effect in Memory." *Psychological Bulletin* 121:371–94.

Tajfel, Henri. 1959. "Quantitative Judgment in Social Perception." *British Journal of Psychology* 50:16–29.

————. 1970. "Experiments in Intergroup Discrimination." *Scientific American* 223:96–102.

———. 1972. "Experiments in a Vacuum." In *The Context of Social Psychology: A Critical Assessment*, ed. J. Israel and H. Tajfel, 69–122. London: Academic Press.

———. 1981. "Human Groups and Social Categories." *Studies in Social Psychology*. New York: Cambridge University Press.

Tajfel, H., and J. C. Turner. 1979. "An Integrative Theory of Intergroup Conflict." In *The Social Psychology of Intergroup Relations*, ed. W. G. Austin and S. Worchel, 7–25. Monterey: Brooks/Cole.

Taylor, A.J.P. 1962. *Origins of the Second World War*. New York: Atheneum.

Taylor, Charles. 1989. *Sources of the Self: The Making of Modern Identity*. Cambridge, MA: Harvard University Press.

Taylor, Donald M., and M. Moghaddam Fathali. *Theories of Intergroup Relations: International Social Psychological Perspectives*. Westport, CT: Praeger.

Taylor, M. 1982. *Community, Anarchy and Liberty*. Cambridge: Cambridge University Press.

———. 1987. *The Possibility of Cooperation*. Cambridge: Cambridge University Press.

Taylor, Richard. 1985a. *Ethics, Faith and Reason*. Englewood Cliffs, NJ: Prentice-Hall.

———. 1985b. *Good and Evil: A New Direction: A Forceful Attack on the Rationalistic Tradition in Ethics*. Buffalo: Prometheus Books.

Taylor, S., and J. Brown. 1988. "Illusion and Well-Being: A Social Psychological Perspective on Mental Health." *Psychological Bulletin* 103:193–210.

Taylor, Shelley E., and Susan T. Fiske. 1975. "Point-of-View and Perceptions of Causality." *Journal of Personality and Social Psychology* 32:439–45.

———. 1991. *Social Cognition*. 2nd ed. New York: McGraw Hill.

Taylor, Shelley, Letitia Peplau, and David Sears. 1997. *Social Psychology*. Upper Saddle River, NJ: Prentice-Hall.

Tec, Nechama. 1986. *When Light Pierced the Darkness: Christian Rescue of Jews in Nazi-Occupied Poland*. New York: Oxford University Press.

Tetlock, P. 1981. "The Influence of Self-Presentational Goals on Attributional Reports." *Social Psychology Quarterly* 44:300–311.

———. 1985. "Toward an Intuitive Politician Model of Attribution Processes." In *The Self and Social Life*, ed. Barry R. Schlenker, 203–35. New York: McGraw-Hill.

Thibodeau, R., and E. Aronson. 1992. "Taking a Closer Look: Reasserting the Role of the Self-Concept in Dissonance Theory." *Personality and Social Psychology Bulletin* 18:591–602.

Tice, D. M. 1993. "The Social Motivations of People with Low Self-esteem." In *Self-esteem: The Puzzle of Low Self-regard*, ed. R. F. Baumeister, 37–51. New York: Plenum.

Tönnies, Ferdinand. 1957. *Community and Association [Gemeinschaft und Gesellschaft]*. Trans. Charles P. Loomis. East Lansing: Michigan State University Press.

Tooby, J., L. Cosmidos, and J. H. Barkow. 1992. *The Adapted Mind: Evolutionary Psychology and the Generation of Culture*. New York: Oxford University Press.

Toulmin, S. 1958. *An Examination of the Place of Reason in Ethics*. New York: Cambridge University Press.

Toynbee, A. 1946. *A Study of History*. New York: Oxford University Press.

Trianosky, Gregory. 1986. "Superogation, Wrongdoing, and Vice: On Autonomy of the Ethics of Virtue," *Journal of Philosophy* 83:26–41.

———. 1990. "What Is Virtue Ethics All About?" *American Philosophical Quarterly* 24, no. 4: 335–44.

Turner, J. 1987. *The Reemergence of the Social Group: A Self Categorization Theory*. New York: Basil Blackwell.

———. 1982. "Towards a Cognitive Redefinition of the Social Group." In *Social Identity and Intergroup Relations*, ed. Henri Tajfel, 15–36. New York: Cambridge University Press.

Turner, John C., and M. A. Hogg. 1987. *Rediscovering the Social Group: A Self-Categorization Theory*. Oxford: Basil Blackwell.

Turner, J. C., P. J. Oakes, S. A. Haslam, and C. McGarty. 1994. "Self and Collective: Cognition and Social Context." *Personality and Social Psychology Bulletin* 20, no. 5: 454–64.

Turner, Marlene E., Preston Probasco, Anthony R. Pratkanis, and Craig Leve. 1992. "Threat, Cohesion, and Group Effectiveness: Testing a Social Identity Maintenance Perspective on Groupthink." *Journal of Personality and Social Psychology* 63, no. 5: 781.

Tversky, A., and D. Kahneman. 1974. "Judgment under Uncertainty: Heuristics and Biases." *Science* 185:1124–31.

Van den Berghe, Pierre. 1978. "Race and Ethnicity: A Sociobiological Perspective." *Ethnic and Racial Studies* 1, no. 4: 402–7, 409–11.

VanVechten, Renee. 1999. "The Christian Right and American Politics." Working paper, University of California, Irvine.

Wagener, U., L. Lampen, and J. Syllwasschy. 1986. "In-group Inferiority, Social Identity and Out-Group Devaluation in a Modified Minimal Group Study." *British Journal of Social Psychology* 25:15–23.

Wald, Kenneth. 1997. *Religion and Politics in the United States*. 3rd ed. New York: St. Martin's Press.

Walzer, Michael. 2003. "The Present of the Past." *The New Republic* 18:36–38.

Warren, Carol. 1974. *Identity and Community in the Gay World*. New York: Wiley.

Waugh, Evelyn. 1945/1960. *Brideshead Revisited*. London: Chapman and Hall.

Weigert, A. J., J. S. Teitge, and D. W. Teitge. 1986. *Society and Identity: Toward a Sociological Psychology*. Cambridge: Cambridge University Press.

Weiner, B., ed. 1974. *Achievement, Motivation and Attribution Theory*. Morristown, NJ: General Learning Press.

Weingartner, H. 2001. "Remembering the Holocaust: Snapshots from a Cognitive Science Perspective. In *Light from the Ashes*, ed. P. Suedfeld, 331–57. Ann Arbor: University of Michigan Press.

White, H. 1981. "The Value of Narrativity." In *On Narrative*, ed. W.J.T. Mitchell, 1–23. Chicago: University of Chicago Press.

Widdicombe, Sue. 1988. "Dimensions of Adolescent Identity." *European Journal of Social Psychology* 18:471–83.

Wiesel, Elie. 1960/1986. *Night*. New York: Bantam.

———. 1992. *The Forgotten*. New York: Summit Books.

Wiley, Mary G., and C. Norman Alexander. 1987. "From Situated Activity to Self-Attribution: The Impact of Social Structural Schemata." In *Self and Identity: Psychosocial Perspectives*, ed. Krysia Yardley and Terry Honess, 105–19. New York: Wiley.

Williams, Bernard. 1981. *Moral Luck*. New York: Cambridge University Press.

Wilson, James Q. 1993. *The Moral Sense*. New York: Free Press.

Winnicott, David W. 1965. *The Maturational Processes and the Facilitating Environment: Studies in the Theory of Emotional Development*. Madison, CT: International Universities Press.

Wurf, E., and H. Markus. 1983. "Cognitive Consequences of the Negative Self." Paper presented at the annual meeting of the American Psychological Association, Anaheim, CA.

Zimbardo, Philip, E. B. Ebbesen, and C. Maslach. 1977. *Influencing Attitudes and Changing Behavior: An Introduction to Method, Theory, and Applications of Social Control and Personal Power*. New York: Random House.

Zuccotti, Susan. 2000. *Under His Very Windows: The Vatican and the Holocaust in Italy*. New Haven: Yale University Press.

INDEX

Adler, Alfred, 58
agency, 213; and character, ix
agents, adults as, 241
agonistic choice(s), 188, 201, 259
Alfred, 2, 6, 21, 22, 24, 25, 35, 53, 54
altruism, ix, xv, xvi, 95, 209, 241, 249,
    256; literature on, 229; reflexive, 249;
    of rescuers, 228; studies on, 227
altruistic, 97, 188; personality(ies), x, 199,
    211, 217, 229; perspective, 225, 250,
    319n.93
Anscombe, G.E.M., 215, 314n.36
Anti-Defamation League, 161
Aquinas, Thomas, 215, 311n.34
Arbeitsdienst, 66
Aristotle, 199, 245, 307n.16, 312n.34,
    314n.39, 324n.40, 328n.16
Auschwitz, 67, 189, 207
Austrian Resistance Organization, 72, 75, 76

Baier, A., 313n.35
Bakhtin, M., 271
Bandura, A., 291n.3
Barber, B., 277
Barry, B., 328n.15
Batson, D. C., 228, 320n.100, 323n.30
Baumeister, R. F., 308nn. 4, 6, 7
Becker, G., 318n.70
Becker, Hans von, 72, 77, 98, 208
Benes, Edvard, 299n.26
Bernadotte, Count Folke, 181, 302nn. 9, 10
Best, Werner, 170
Bettelheim, B., 325n.69
Blasi, A., 223, 315n.56, 327nn. 6, 9
Blunt, Anthony, 76, 77, 298n.20
Bohr, Niels, 303–4n.10
Boom, Corrie ten, 112, 197, 306n.12
Boyle, 299n.22
Brewer, M., 310n.25
British Intelligence Service, 70, 82
British Secret Service, 71, 72
Browning, C., 314n.60, 323n.27
Bruner, J., 273, 274, 277, 278
Buddha, 244
Buddhist, 42, 43

Bumbala, Dr. Raul, 70, 72, 73, 74, 77
Burgess, Guy, 298n.20

calculation of risks, costs, and benefits, 261
calculus of reason, 259
Camp Gräditz, 67, 68
Camp Klettendorf, 66
Caprara, G. V., and D. Cervona, 308n.5
care ethics, 313n.35
categorical imperative, 90, 92, 187, 190,
    244, 261, 304n.2
categorization, 230, 233, 239; framework
    for, 234; how people construct cate-
    gories, 234; and language, 252; of
    others, xi; and reciprocation, 255; res-
    cuers' schema for, 235; self-esteem
    and, 251
categorize: innate drive to, 255; ourselves
    in relation to others, 233
category(-ies): common, 235; constructed,
    234; morally salient, 234
Chomsky, N., 252, 253, 254, 255,
    324n.55, 325n.62, 325nn. 62, 68
Christ, 244
Churchill, R., and E. Street, 321n.9
Churchill, Winston, 71, 74, 75, 258
CIA, 81, 82, 85
CIC, the American Counter Intelligence
    Corps of the Army, 83
cognition, 291n.1, n.3
cognitive: construals, xi, xiii, 238, 317n.62,
    309n.92; consistency, 239, 240, 241;
    dissonance, 222, 250; factors, x;
    frameworks, 225, 238, 319n.92; fram-
    ing, 240; maps, 269; processing, 224,
    317n. 61
Colby, A., and W. Damon, 222, 223,
    315n.50
Coles, R., 273, 274
collaborators, 70, 125, 181; Danish, 181
Collonges, 103
Commission for Selecting of Soldiers, 166
communitarianism, 243
concentration camp(s), 30, 57, 63, 64, 66,
    68, 80, 113, 123, 125, 135, 175,

concentration camp(s) (*cont.*)
    176, 181, 199; Auschwitz, 67, 189,
    207; Buchenwald, 176; Gross Rosen,
    67; Neuengamme, 176, 181;
    Therezienstadt, 181, 297n.10,
    302n.8
Congressional Medal, 109
constructing a moral life, 199
construction of moral theory, 241
cost and benefit calculus, 112, 206
Cote, J., and C. Levine, 308n.4
Count of Menthon, 122, 136, 301n.6
Count Thurn and Taxis, 75
Count von Stauffenberg. *See* Stauffenberg,
    Graf
Courage to Care, The, 320n. 98, 322n.
    21, 320nn. 20, 23
Creole languages, 254
cultural and gender differences in self rec-
    ognition, 251
cultural relativism, 253, 325n. 66, 68
culture, 214, 241; how it shapes people,
    35, 36

Danish rescuers, 166
Danish-Swedish Refugee Service, 173, 177,
    301n.5
Dante, 19
Darwin, C., 306n.10
Darwinian world, 265
Dawkins, R., 318n.70
D-Day, 104
deconstruction, 272
De Gaulle, C., 104, 107, 108, 122
dehumanization, 88, 233
deity, supreme, 253
deontic, 306n.13
Derrida, J., 254, 271, 272
Descartes, R., 325nn. 62, 66, 328n.16
developmental reasoning, 316n.61
DeWaal, F., 306n.10, 324n.60
Dewey, General, 181
dispositions, 216; genetic, 231
Duckwitz, Georg, 171
Dutch Reformed Church, 104
duty, 49, 92, 111, 117, 118, 259; feeling
    of, 202

efficacy, 319n.93
Eisenhower, General, 104
Elster, J., 309n.16, 322n.13

empathy, 49, 242; cognitive aspect of, 249;
    and perspective, 248–50
entrepreneurs, 292n.4
Epperson, C. 302n.12
Erikson, E., 214, 307n.1, 310n.27
ethical: beliefs, 42, 198; decision-making
    process, 204; duty, 254; political be-
    havior, 241
ethics, xvi, 130, 195; core of, 238; and
    identity, 216; and morality, 259, 260;
    rule-based, 197
ethnic violence, 256
evolutionary biology, xv
experiments in social psychology, 227

fate, 41, 206
Fazio, R. H., E. A. Effrein, and V. J. Fa-
    lender, 308n.7
fellow feeling, 245–46
Festinger, L., 223, 307n.1, 310n.29,
    311n.31, 327n.7
Fogelman, E., 229, 230, 292n.11,
    318n.78, 321n.6
folktales, 274
Foreign Broadcast Information Service, 84,
    86
Foucault, M., 254, 272
Frank, Anne, 59
Frankfurt, H., 315n.57, 327nn. 8, 11, 13
free will, 122
French Revolution, 230
Freud, S., 213, 307n.1, 309n.14, 313n.35,
    325n.69

Gallup, G. G., 323n.38
Gandhi, 244
Gemeinschaft und Gesellschaft, 93,
    328n.15
genetic propensities, 241
genocidalists, 256
genocide, 231, 256, 265
George Bernard Shaw, 40, 41
Gestalt psychologists, 317n.62
Gestapo, xii, 15, 29, 31, 32, 60, 61, 63,
    73, 75, 102, 103, 104, 106, 108,
    126, 144, 154, 166, 171, 173, 175,
    176, 178, 179, 181, 220; French,
    105, 106, 108; German, 105, 106,
    107, 108, 112, 197; Prague, 64
Gewirth, A., 324n.41
Gibson, H., 298n.18

Gilbert, M., 318n.75
Gilligan, C., 282, 304n.10, 313n.35, 316n.61
Glass, J., 323n.27
Goerdeler, C. 74, 298n.16
Golden Rule, 188, 261
Goldhagen, D., 314n.43, 326n.4
Graumann, C., and S. Moscovici, 318n.88
Greenwald, A. G., and D. L. Ronis, 315n.47
Grotius, Hugo, 312n.34
Guard Service, 168; for the Castles, 168
Gypsy(ies), 140, 219

Habermas, J., 325n.68
habits, 216; virtuous, 222
Hacha, Emil, 295n.2
Hanneken, General von, 170, 175
Harré, R. 310n.22
Harris, Z., 254
The Heart of Altruism, ix, xv, 236, 292n.4, 300n.28, 305n.9
Hedtoft, Hans, 171, 185
Heidegger, M., 254
Hendil, Leif, 301n.6
Herf, J., 258, 326n. 1
heroes, 292n.4
Heydrich, Reinhard, 77, 299n.21
Higgins, E. T., 324n.45
Hillenkoetter, Admiral, 82, 299n.25
Himmler, H., 170, 181
Hirshman, A. O., 275, 322n.12
Hochschild, J. L., 277
Holocaust, ix, xii, 4, 7, 87, 88, 108, 113, 123, 135, 191, 194, 227, 228, 231, 256, 258, 277
Holocaust museum(s), xvi, 22, 50, 76, 183, 204
Holocaust Testimonies, 3, 294n.2
Holubrov, 56
Hoover, K., 310n.28
Hopfengärtner, Leni, 298n.18
Huguenots, 119, 300n.3
human communication, 162
human connection, 264, 265, 328n.16
humanitarian: desires, 180, 234; instincts, 209
human nature, xv, 35, 133
human need to classify and simplify, 189
Hume, D., 244, 249, 250, 306n.10
Hutcheson, F., 304n.10

identity, x, xii, 2, 93, 131, 201, 208, 210, 212, 218, 226, 259, 262, 269, 291n.1, 309n.8; basic, 328n.16; and categorization, 256; or character, xiii, 242, 305n.6; cognitive aspect of, 214; cognitive and emotional component of, 309n.17; and consistency, 250; as constrains action, 262; as constrains choice, 222, 223, 225, 242; construction of, 213, 214; and ethics, 216; group's, 232; how perspective affects, 225; maintenance of, 250; master, 242; as multifaceted and complex, 213, 226, 232, 237, 260; multiple aspects of, 213; and morality, 224; and perceptions, 263; and perspective, xiii, 239, 250; political psychology of, 210; power of, 261; rescuers' complex, 188; and self, 212–15, 241; short-circuit choice, 210
Ignatieff, M., 322n.17
impulsive helping, 224
individuation, need for, 252
in-group members, favor, 226
instincts, 231
Institute for Contemporary History, 76
intelligence service of the Danish navy, 178
intersubjective communication, 239
intrapersonal emotions and attitudes, 213
Israeli government, 287

James, W., 213, 308n.4
Jarymowicz, M., 320n.100, 321n.6, 322n.23
Jewish Historical Committee in Krakow, 157
Jewish problem, 296n.4; final solution to the, 62
Johnston, D., 322n.13
judgment, 114, 121; the Judgment Day, 128
July 20 Plot, 71, 258, 296n.4

Kagan, J., 314n.41
Kant, I., or Kantian, 93, 187, 244, 250, 254, 261, 304n.2, 307n.17, 324n.40
Katek, 85
Kegan, R., 305n.10
Keneally, T., 243, 248, 323n.28
King Christian X, 167, 170
Klingemann, U., 288, 318n.77

Knorringa, Werner and Eileen, 292n.4
Kohlberg, L., 282, 305n.10, 316n.61, 327n.9
Kraay, Suzy, 125–126, 300n.4
Kracauer, S., 275
Krakow, 156, 157
Kristallnacht, 13, 59, 296n.4
Kupperman, J., 314n.38

Lakoff, G., and M. Johnson, 309n.18, 324n.55
Langer, L., 3, 4, 7, 329n.21
language acquisition, 254
Latané, B., and J. M. Darley, 227, 318n.71, 323n.29
law of God, 121
Le Bon, G., 230
Lerner, R., 316n.60
Lessing, D., 310n.26
Levi, P., 329n.19, 21
Levi-Strauss, C., 271
Lewin, K., 317n.62
Library of Congress, 6, 52
Lord Burleigh. See William of Burleigh
Lyotard, J. F., 271, 279

MacIntyre, A., 312n.35
Maclean, Donald, 76, 77, 79, 81, 82, 298n.20
Mafalda, 64, 71, 73–75, 296n.6, 297n.13. See also Princess Maria Adelaide de Braganza
Maria Adelaide de Braganza. See Mafalda; Princess Maria Adelaide de Braganza
Markus, H., and S. Kitayama, 308n.7, 311n.31
Masaryk, Thomas and Jan, 82, 84, 299n.26
Mathiesen, K., 311n.32
Mayer, Kari, 96
Mayor of Liepzig, 74
Mead, G. H., 213, 308n.4, 309n.15
Medal of Honor, 159
Mein Kampf, 46, 159
Mellema, G., 314n.40
mental categories, 225
Methon, Count de, 122
Milgram, S., 227
Milgram's experiments, 227
Mischel, W., 291n.3
mixed-marriage violations, 64

Monroe, K. R., 279, 281, 307n.24, 318n.78, 319n.90, 320n.97, 320n.103, 326n.5
Monroe, K. R., J. Hankin, and R. Van-Vechten, 308n.3, 309n.10, 317n.63
moral: absolutes, 237; action, xiii, 188, 189, 190, 210, 220–26, 235, 237, 240–46, 259, 322n.14; beliefs, 223, 224; character, 198, 259; choice(s), ix, xi, xiii, 2, 26,98, 131, 195, 208, 211; dilemmas, 188, 242; education, 215, 220; during the Holocaust, 263; identity, 240, 246; imperative, 225, 236, 261; life, complexity of, 187; maxims, 189; perspective, 242, 243, 322n.24; psychology, xi, xii, xiii, 3, 188, 211, 225, 238–240, 241, 242, 247, 250, 256, 260–61; questions, 234; reasoning, 282; relativism, 237; and religious systems, 226; salience, 230, 234, 236, 240, 242, 245–48, 261; sense, innate, 187, 194–98, 217, 259; sensitivity, 216, 245–47; situations, 240; systems, 4; theory, ix, 4, 239, 242, 250, 305n.10; values, 211; values, how identity shapes, 241
morality, phenotypic quality of, 195; forces driving, 259; foundation of, 215
Mother Teresa, 112, 136
Munich Institute, 76

narcissism, 252, 324n.48; inborn, 252
narrative(s), 191, 201, 217, 230, 241, 267–85; conceptual, 280; cultural contestation, 275; and feminists, 281; and interpretation, 274, 281; kinds of, 279; meta-, 280; ontological, 279; and ordinary discourse, 273; and postmodernism, 272; public, 280; selective appropriation, 284; shared, and national history, 277; universals in, 271; use of in political and social science, 270
nature, our inheritance from, 184
Netherlands Security Service, 101
Nichomachean Ethics, 245, 311n.34, 314n39
Noddings, N., 313n.35
Nuremberg laws, 95
Nussbaum, M., 309n.17, 310n.20, 314n.36, 321n.8

Oliner, S., and P. Oliner, 50, 203, 229, 292n.11, 296n.8, 307n.19, 320n.99, 321n.6, 322n.23
oral culture, 272
Organization Todt, 67, 69, 297n.8
Orphuls, M., 318n.79
out-group members, discrimination against, 226
Ozyurt, S., 311n.31

pantheist, 94, 192
patriotism, 180, 234
Patterson, M., 329
Pearl Harbor, 33
Peplau, L., 311n.31
perpetrators: behavior of, 231; wartime activities of, 231
Perry, J., 309n.11
personality, 231; traits, 309n.19
perspective, 211, 225, 249–54, 260; and empathy, 248–50; and identity, 250; importance of, 210, 237; and moral salience, 246
Pétain, General, 124
philanthropists, 292n.4
Philby, Harold "Kim," 76, 77, 298n.20
Philby Conspiracy, 76, 78
Piaget, J., 316n.61, 327n.9
Pinker, S., 310n.19
Plato, 215
Plomin, R., 310n.19
Pope Pius XII, 220, 314n.43
post-structuralists, 271, 272
post-traumatic shock syndrome, 99
predispositions, 225; genetic, 231
Princess Maria Adelaide de Braganza, 72, 74, 297n.13
Propp, S., 271
psychology of crowd, 231

Queen Elizabeth I, 295n.1
Quislings, 170, 181

Radom, Poland, 140, 142
Raschke, Herman, 44
rational: action, xv; actor theory, 293n.3, 307n.23; calculus, 205
rational-choice theory, 201
Rawls, J., 326n.5
reason, 2, 306n.10
Red Army, 155

reflexive consciousness, 212
Reid, A., and K. Deaux, 310n.24
reincarnation, 43
religion, 2, 42, 43, 109, 117, 187, 190–94, 259; and beliefs, 184; and institutions, 190; people of, 129; and rescuer(s), 191, 192; and zealots, 180
rescue activities, 127, 131
rescuers' cognitive processing, 224; and lack of choice, 223; and memories, 249; and motivations, 229
Resistance, 2, 15, 16, 18, 26, 30, 31, 42, 70, 95, 101, 171, 179, 181, 209, 320n.101; Austrian, xii, 60, 95, 74, 77, 208; Czech, 77; French, 33; German, 71, 72, 74, 258; organizations, 183
Reykowski, J., 316n.59, 318n.64, 320n.100, 322n.23
Ricoeur, P., 279
Rittener, C., and S. Myers, 205, 307n.24, 322n.21, 320n.23
Rokita, Sturmbannführer, 144, 301n.5
role model(ing), 94, 129, 198, 199, 201, 259; critical, 200
Rosh Hashanah, 171
Ross, L., and R. E. Nisbett, 317n.62
Rügemer, Major, 301n.4
Russian Intelligence Service, 79

Salvation Army, 112, 115, 136
Sarner, Harvey, 304n.13
Scharff, Hans, 45
schemas, 252, 330n.6
schema theory, 330n.6
Schindler, O., 220, 243, 248, 314n.43, 319n.94
Schneewind, J. B., 312n.34
Schulz, Sergeant, 162
Scott, J., 282, 283
scripts, 249
Sears, D., 311n.31
self, 212–15, 328n.16; complex, 227; nature of, 315n.56; and need to protect and nurture, 239, 240, 241; and other(s), 226, 248
self-awareness, 212, 308n.4, 323n.38
self-categorization, 256
self-concept, xi, 211, 224, 236, 242–43, 249, 260, 291n.1, 308n.7, 323n.38; and rescuers' sense of self, 238, 261; shift in, 270

self (*cont.*)
  self-consistency, 214, 223, 225
  self-enhancement, 214
  self-esteem, 211, 212, 222, 240, 260,
    262, 314n.47; and categorization,
    251–52; desire for, 237, 251; need
    for, 251
  self-image, 241, 251, 314n.47; continu-
    ity of, 237; rescuers', 236
  self-interest, xv, 92, 114, 130, 239, 241,
    262, 292n.4; perceived, 205
  self-perceptions, 242, 243
  self-recognition, 251
  self-respect, 97, 189
  self-schema, 249
Sen, A., 321n.8
sense of compassion, 22, 26, 194
sense of duty, 189
sense of individuality, 229
sense of right and wrong, 194,
sense of self, xi, 188, 201–10, 211, 214,
    223, 224, 229, 238, 240, 243,
    327n.12; in relation to other people,
    260; values integrated into one's, 223;
    worth of, 263
Seven-day Adventist(s), 109, 118, 129,
    134, 136, 220; college, 102, German,
    110; pastor, 102
Shaftesbury, 305n.10
Shermer, M., and A. Grobman, 325n.2
Shlovsky, V., 271
Sicherheitsdienst, 62
Singer, P., 324n.60
situation, power of, 230; importance of,
    231; in shaping human behavior, 232
situational/contextual factors, 241
situational factors, 240
Smiley, M., 252, 255
Smith, A., 244, 245, 249, 250, 305n.10,
    321n.8
sociability, 241, 264, 322n.16
social identity theory, 233, 256, 318n.90
socialization processes, 199
socialization, 187, 196–98, 201, 259; and
    integration of values, 224
social responsibility, 118
Somers, M. R., and G. D. Gibson, 278,
    279, 280, 284
Spinoza, 94
Spivak, G. C., 277
Stanford Prison experiments, 227, 228

star of David, 65, 169, 170
Stauffenberg, Graf, 71, 73–74
Stern Gang, 182
Stoics, 215, 311n.34
Suedfeld, P., 294n.3
superordinate moral status, 235
systems of ethical rules and prescriptions,
    189

Tajfel, H., 310n.25, 326n.73
Tanay, Immanuel, 187, 318n.85
Taylor, C., 308n.6, 309n.9
Taylor, S., 311n.31, 315n.47
Tec, N., 229, 292n.11, 307n.24,
    321n.6
Ternopol, 144, 301n.3
theory of consciousness, 277
theory of moral perspective, 240
Third Reich, xi, 229, 326n.4
Thurn und Taxis, 75, 297n.13
Todesgesetz, 63
Tolstoy, L. 315n.52
Tonniës, Ferdinand, 328n.15
Tooby, J., L. Cosmidos, and J. H. Barkow,
    310n.19
Trianosky, G., 311n.34, 312n.35
Turner, J., 310n.24

Underground, 23, 94, 110, 118, 169, 181,
    182; Danish, 168, 169, 183
United Nations, 157
universal grammar, 254
universal morality, 237, 251; problem of,
    255
universals of human language, 253
universal standards of fairness and justice,
    254

Van Uden, 75
vegetarian, 127
veil of ignorance, 245
Vichy, 124
virtue ethics, 199, 215–22, 230, 246, 247,
    259, 307n.16, 311–13
Von Moldt, Alexander, 72

Waldheim, Kurt, 68
Wallenberg, Raul, 182, 302n.11
Wall of Honor, 287
Watson, G., 312n.35
White, H., 275, 278

Wiesel, E., 329n.21
Wiesenthal, Simon, 137
William of Burleigh, 10, 295n.1
Wittgenstein, L., 255
World War II, x, xvi, 11, 101, 103, 139,
    220, 235, 256, 261, 263, 270,
    295n.4, 326n.4

Yachinmof, 80, 299n.24
Yad Vashem, xi, 3, 18, 50, 88, 159, 166,
    182, 185, 196, 203, 287–88,
    293n.17, 299n.27, 322n.18, 330n.1
Young, M., 311n.32

Zimbardo, P., 227, 228